"十三五"江苏省高等学校重点教材2019-2-103

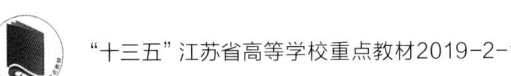

The Jewish Civilization

Texts and Traditions

宋立宏　编著

Edited by Song Lihong

南京大学出版社
Nanjing University Press

图书在版编目(CIP)数据

犹太文明:文本与传统 /宋立宏编著. —南京:南京大学出版社,2020.10
ISBN 978-7-305-23828-4

Ⅰ.①犹… Ⅱ.①宋… Ⅲ.①犹太人—民族文化—研究 Ⅳ.①K18

中国版本图书馆CIP数据核字(2020)第197806号

出版发行	南京大学出版社
社　　址	南京市汉口路22号　　邮　编　210093
出 版 人	金鑫荣
书　　名	犹太文明:文本与传统
编　　著	宋立宏
责任编辑	施　敏
照　　排	南京紫藤制版印务中心
印　　刷	江苏凤凰通达印刷有限公司
开　　本	718×1000　1/16　印张22.25　字数430千
版　　次	2020年10月第1版　2020年10月第1次印刷
ISBN	978-7-305-23828-4
定　　价	80.00元

网　　址:http://www.njupco.com
官方微博:http://weibo.com/njupco
官方微信:njupress
销售咨询热线:(025)83594756

＊ 版权所有,侵权必究
＊ 凡购买南大版图书,如有印装质量问题,请与所购
　图书销售部门联系调换

Figure 1. Ezra reading the Law on the synagogue wall paintings at Dura Europos, 3rd century. From Carl H. Kraeling, *The Synagogue. The Excavation at Dura-Europos, Final Report* VIII *Part* I, New Haven: Yale University Press, 1956, pl. 77.

Figure 2. Sarajevo Haggadah, *ca.* 1350, Spain, fols. 1–2. The Creation in seven days. From *The Sarajevo Haggadah,* New York: Harcourt, Brace & World, [1963].

Figure 3. Sarajevo Haggadah, *ca.* 1350, Spain, fol. 3. The Fall. From *The Sarajevo Haggadah,* New York: Harcourt, Brace & World, [1963].

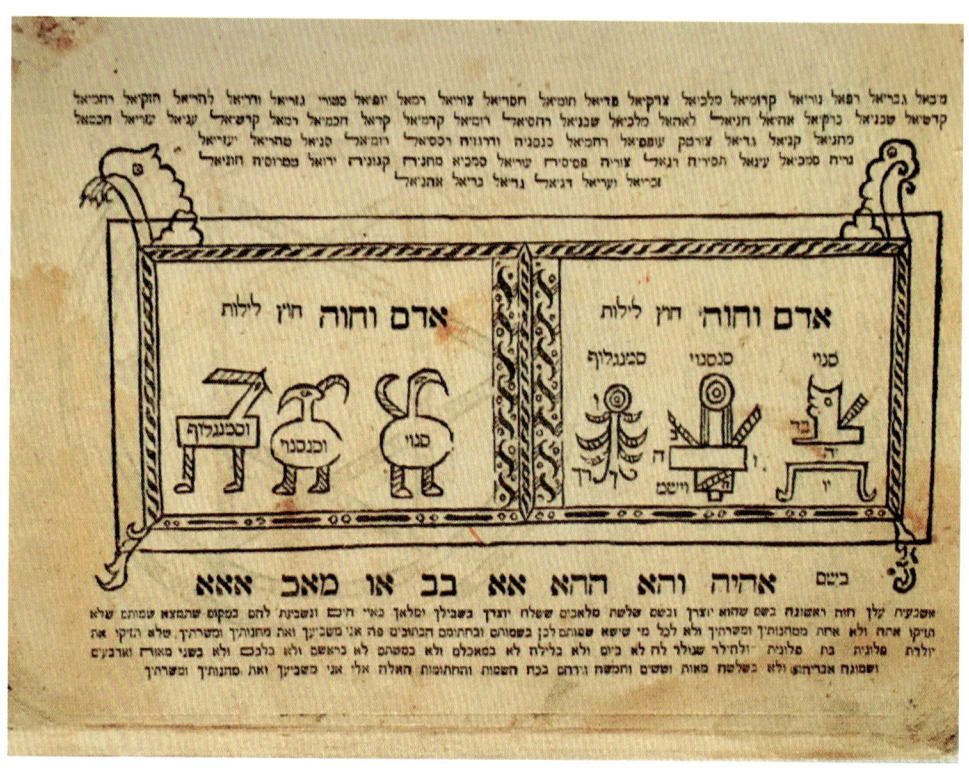

Figure 4. A page from *Sefer Raziel ha-malakh* with a birth amulet depicting protective angels Snvi, Snsvi and Smnglof. Paper. Amsterdam, Holland, 1701.

Courtesy of the National Library of Israel.

Figure 5. The wagon monument at Yad Vashem, Israel, 2011. Designed by Moshe Safdia.

Photo © Avishai Teicher via PikiWiki—Israel free image collection project
https://www.pikiwiki.org.il/image/view/12485

Figure 6. The binding of Isaac panel from the synagogue mosaic at Beth Alpha, 6th century. From Eleazar L. Sukenik, *The Ancient Synagogue of Beth Alpha,* London: Oxford University Press, 1932, pl. 19.

Figure 7. Coburg Pentateuch, 1396, Germany, fol. 72V. A teacher admonishing his pupil with a whip. Hillel's maxim is written in the pupil's book: "What is hateful to you, to your fellow don't do." From Bezalel Narkiss, *Hebrew Illuminated Manuscripts,* Jerusalem: Keter Publishing House, 1969, p. 115.

Figure 8. Tripartite Mahzor, Southern Germany, *ca.* 1320. Moses receiving the Tablets of the Law on Mount Sinai while Aaron and the Israelites stand in prayer. From Bezalel Narkiss, *Hebrew Illuminated Manuscripts,* Jerusalem: Keter Publishing House, 1969, p. 109.

Figure 9. Maimonides, *Mishneh Torah.* Copied in Spain, 14th century; illuminated Perugia, Italy, *ca.* 1400, fol. 32. The illustration in the top initial-word panel shows a man embracing a Torah scroll, and in the lower margin another man is reciting *shema* before going to bed. From Bezalel Narkiss, *Hebrew Illuminated Manuscripts,* Jerusalem: Keter Publishing House, 1969, p. 135.

Figure 10. A graffito of Maimonides on the door of a spice store in Jerusalem, 2016. Photo © Song Lihong

Figure 11. Menashe Kadishman (1932–2015), *Sacrifice of Isaac,* 1982–1985. Tel Aviv Museum of Art.

Cor-ten steel, 3 units
The ram: 350×700×490 cm
The mourning women: 500×305×245 cm
Isaac: 250×230 cm

Photo © Song Lihong

Figure 12. Hayim Nahman Bialik, Berlin, 1924. On the eve of his departure to the land of Israel.

Figure 13. Adi Nes, *Abraham and Isaac,* 2006. Chromogenic print. Photo © Adi Nes. Courtesy of Adi Nes

Figure 14. George Segal (1924–2000), *The Sacrifice of Isaac,* 1973. Plaster, 214×275×260 cm. Tel Aviv Museum of Art. Photo © Song Lihong

Figure 15. Abraham receiving the promise on the synagogue wall paintings at Dura Europos, 3rd century. From Carl H. Kraeling, *The Synagogue. The Excavation at Dura-Europos, Final Report* VIII *Part* I, New Haven: Yale University Press, 1956, pl. 78.

目录 / Contents

导言/Introduction ········· 001

1　IN THE BEGINNING ········· 001
1.1　Genesis 1:1 – 2:4 ········· 001
1.2　On "In the Beginning" (Gen. 1:1) ········· 004
  1.2.1　Proverbs 8:22 – 31 ········· 004
  1.2.2　Genesis Rabbah, 1:1 ········· 005
  1.2.3　2 Maccabees 7:28 ········· 006
  1.2.4　Dead Sea Scrolls. The Community Rule 1QS 3:15 – 16; 11:11, 17 – 18 ········· 006
  1.2.5　John 1:1 – 3 ········· 007
1.3　Genesis Rabbah, 1:10. Creation with the Hebrew Letter *Beth* ········· 007
1.4　Philo, *On the Creation* 31. On the Light of the First Day ········· 008
1.5　On "Let Us Make Man" (Gen. 1:26) ········· 009
  1.5.1　Philo, *On the Confusion of Tongues* 179 ········· 009
  1.5.2　Genesis Rabbah 8:8 ········· 009
1.6　Nahmanides on "Let Us Make Man in Our Image, After Our Likeness" (Gen. 1:26) ········· 010
1.7　Mystical Interpretations on the Creation ········· 011
  1.7.1　The Zohar, Introduction 1:3b. A Mystical Interpretation on *Be-Reshit* ········· 011
  1.7.2　Isaac Luria on the Creation ········· 013
  1.7.3　A Hasidic Interpretation on *Be-Reshit* ········· 015

1.8　Robert Gordis on "Fill the Earth and Master It" (Gen. 1:28) …… 016
1.9　Louis Ginzberg, Creation and the Hebrew Alphabet (1909) …… 017
1.10　Sabbath Liturgy …………………………………………………… 019
　　1.10.1　The Kiddush for Sabbath Evening ……………………… 019
　　1.10.2　The Havdalah Service for the End of Sabbath ………… 020
1.11　Abraham Joshua Heschel, *The Sabbath* (1951) ………………… 021
1.12　Dan Pagis, *Testimony* ……………………………………………… 022
1.13　Shlomo Carlebach on Singing Creation into Being …………… 023

2　ADAM, EVE AND LILITH …………………………………………… 024

2.1　Genesis 2:4 – 3:24 ………………………………………………… 024
2.2　On "The Dust of the Earth" (Gen. 2:7) ………………………… 029
　　2.2.1　Philo, *On the Creation*, 137 ………………………………… 029
　　2.2.2　Rashi …………………………………………………………… 029
2.3　Leviticus Rabbah 8:1. God as Marriage-Maker ………………… 030
2.4　*Avot de-Rabbi Nathan*, Chapter 1. On the "Fence for the Torah"
　　……………………………………………………………………… 031
2.5　*Pirkei de-Rabbi Eliezer* 14. The Sin of Adam and Eve ………… 032
2.6　*Alphabet of Ben Sira*. Lilith, Adam's First Wife ……………… 034
2.7　Shelomo Almoli, Dream Interpretations ………………………… 035
　　2.7.1　Serpent ………………………………………………………… 035
　　2.7.2　Woman ………………………………………………………… 036
　　2.7.3　Nakedness …………………………………………………… 037
　　2.7.4　The Dead …………………………………………………… 038
2.8　Judith Plaskow, "Our Story: The Coming of Lilith" (1972) …… 039

3　"AM I MY BROTHER'S KEEPER?": THE IMAGES OF CAIN …… 043

3.1　Genesis 4:1 – 26 …………………………………………………… 043
3.2　Targum Pseudo-Jonathan to Genesis 4 ………………………… 046
3.3　Genesis Rabbah, 22:12 – 13. On the Mark and the Repentance of Cain ……………………………………………………………… 049

3.4	Augustine, *Contra Faustum Manichaeum* XII, 9–13. A Christian Typological Interpretation of Cain and Abel (400 CE)	050
3.5	Louis Ginzberg, The Jewish Legends on Cain (1909)	054
3.6	Dan Pagis, *Autobiography*	060
3.7	Dan Pagis, *Written in Pencil in the Sealed Railway-Car*	061

4 THE TEST OF ABRAHAM: AKEDAH ········· 062
- 4.1 Genesis 22:1–19 ········· 062
- 4.2 Targum Pseudo-Jonathan to Genesis 22:1–19 ········· 064
- 4.3 Genesis Rabbah on Akedah ········· 067
  - 4.3.1 Genesis Rabbah 55:7. On "Take...Thy Son" ········· 067
  - 4.3.2 Genesis Rabbah 56:4. Samael versus Abraham ········· 067
  - 4.3.3 Genesis Rabbah 56:8. Isaac Afraid ········· 068
  - 4.3.4 Genesis Rabbah 56:9. Akedah and Shofar-Blowing ········· 070
  - 4.3.5 Genesis Rabbah 55:2. The Lord Tries the Righteous ········· 071
- 4.4 Babylonian Talmud, Sanhedrin 89b. On Akedah ········· 071
- 4.5 *Pirkei de-Rabbi Eliezer*, 31. The Death and Resurrection of Isaac ········· 073
- 4.6 Rashi on Gen. 22:1–2. ········· 073
- 4.7 Moses Maimonides, *The Guide of the Perplexed*. III. 24. On Akedah ········· 074
- 4.8 Amir Gilboa, *Isaac* ········· 080
- 4.9 Hayyim Gouri, *Heritage* ········· 081

5 YAVAN IN THE TENTS OF SHEM: JEWS AMIDST GREEKS AND ROMANS ········· 082
- 5.1 Philo, *On the Creation*, 69–71. On Man's Creation after the Image of God ········· 082
- 5.2 Josephus, *Jewish Antiquities*, 1:222–236. On Akedah ········· 084
- 5.3 Jewish Inscriptions in Greek ········· 089
  - 5.3.1 A Warning Inscription of the Second Temple (Jerusalem; First century CE) ········· 089

5.3.2　The Theodotos Synagogue Inscription (Jerusalem; probably before 70 CE) ················ 089
　　5.3.3　An Inscription Concerning Jews and Godfearers (Aphrodisias in Caria, West Turkey; Third Century CE [?]) ················ 090
　　5.3.4　A Jewish Poetical Epitaph (Beth She'arim; Third Century CE) ················ 094
5.4　Rabbinic Views on Images ················ 095
　　5.4.1　Mishnah, Avodah Zarah, 3:4. Aphrodite in the Bathhouse ················ 095
　　5.4.2　Mishnah, Avodah Zarah, 3:1. Forbidden Images ················ 096
　　5.4.3　Mishnah, Avodah Zarah, 3:3. Images Forbidden ················ 096
　　5.4.4　Jerusalem Talmud, Avodah Zarah, 3:3, 42d. Images Permitted ················ 097
5.5　Jerusalem Talmud, Bava Metzia, 2:5, 8c. On Alexander the Great ················ 097
5.6　Jerusalem Talmud, Sabbath, 1:3, 3c. On Social Accommodation ················ 098

6　THE WORLD OF THE RABBIS ················ 100
6.1　Babylonian Talmud, Gittin 56a – b. Yohanan ben Zakkai's Escape from Jerusalem and Relocation in Yavneh ················ 100
6.2　Mishnah, Avot, 1. The Chain of Oral Transmission from Sinai ················ 102
6.3　Babylonian Talmud, Menahoth, 29b. Moses Returns as a Yeshiva Boy ················ 108
6.4　Babylonian Talmud, Sabbath, 31a. Torah on One Leg ················ 109
6.5　Tosefta, Eduyot 1:4. Preserving Minority Opinion ················ 109
6.6　Babylonian Talmud, Bava Metzia, 59a – 59b. Torah Is Not in Heaven ················ 110
6.7　Babylonian Talmud, Berakhot 62a. The Pursuit of Torah ················ 113
6.8　Rabbinic Views on Women ················ 113
　　6.8.1　Jerusalem Talmud, Sotah, 4:4 ················ 113

	6.8.2	Jerusalem Talmud, Sotah, 3:16	113
6.9		Tosefta Hagiga 2:3 – 4. Four Entered the *Pardes*	114
6.10		Tosefta Hullin, 2:24. Rabbis and Christians	115
6.11		Maimonides, *Commentary on the Mishnah*. The Thirteen Principles of Faith	116
6.12		Maimonides, Introduction to the *Mishneh Torah*. On the History of the Oral Torah and Its Transmission	127

7 THE JEWISH LAWS ... 131

7.1		Exodus 20:1 – 18. The Decalogue	131
7.2		Eye for Eye, or Monetary Compensation	134
	7.2.1	Exodus 21:22 – 27	134
	7.2.2	Mishnah, Bava Kamma, 8:1	134
	7.2.3	Mekhilta of Rabbi Ishmael, Mishpatim 8 (Exod. 21:23 – 25)	135
	7.2.4	Babylonian Talmud, Bava Kamma, 86a	137
7.3		Maimonides, Laws of the Study of Torah	138
7.4		Maimonides, *Mishneh Torah*, Book 7, Chapter 10:1 – 19. Laws Concerning Gifts to the Poor	152
7.5		*Shulhan Arukh*	156
	7.5.1	Yoreh De'ah: Laws about Converts	156
	7.5.2	Eben ha-Ezer: Laws of Propagation	157
	7.5.3	Hoshen Mishpat 26:1 – 4. Prohibition Against Resorting to Non-Jewish Courts	158
7.6		The Declaration of the Establishment of the State of Israel, May 14, 1948	160
7.7		The Law of Return (1950/1954/1970)	164

8 ETHICAL LITERATURE ... 167

8.1	Mishnah, Avot. Miscellaneous Moral Maxims	167
8.2	Shmuel Hanagid, A Gift from the Battlefield (1046)	174

8.3 Bahya ibn Pakuda, On Asceticism, Its Kinds and Advantages
(*Sefer Hovot ha-Levavot*) 175
8.4 Maimonides, The Fourth Chapter of *Eight Chapters*. On Medical Treatment for the Diseases of the Soul 178
8.5 Eleazar of Worms, On Hasidic Piety 188
8.6 Moses Sofer, An Ethical Will (1836) 188
8.7 Israel Salanter, The Struggle of the Moral Person (1881) 189

9 THE JEWISH LITURGY 191

9.1 The Shema 191
    Deuteronomy 6:4 – 9 191
    Deuteronomy 11:13 – 21 191
    Numbers 15:37 – 41 192
9.2 The Amidah (Shemoneh Esreh or Eighteen Benedictions) 192
9.3 Aleinu 196
9.4 The Mourner's Kaddish 197
9.5 Passover Liturgy. Selections from Passover Haggadah 198
    The Introduction 198
9.6 Solomon Ibn Gabirol, "At Dawn I Come to You" 206
9.7 Solomon Alkabetz, "Lekhah Dodi (Come, My Beloved)" 206

10 THE YOKE OF THE TORAH 209

10.1 Ecclesiastes (Kohelet) 12:12 209
10.2 A Greek Inscription Found at the Amphiareion, Oropus in Attica (300 – 250 BCE). A Jew Undertaking Incubation in a Pagan Temple 209
10.3 Babylonian Talmud, Hagiga 15a – b. The Story of a Sinful Master of Torah 210
10.4 From the Cairo Geniza. An Egyptian Woman Seeks to Rescue Her Husband from a Sufi Monastery (*c*. 1355 – 1367) 215
10.5 *Or Ha-Me'ir* 5:42b – c. A Hasidic Parable Attributed to Ba'al Shem Tov 216

10.6	Solomon Maimon, "My Emergence from Talmudic Darkness" (1793)	217
10.7	Rahel Levin Varnhagen, On Being Jewess	225
10.7.1	Letter to David Veit (1795)	225
10.7.2	Statement on the Deathbed as Recorded by Karl August Varnhagen von Ense	225
10.8	Kadya Molodowsky, *Merciful God* (1945)	226

11 SECULAR FORMS OF JEWISHNESS — 229

11.1	I. L. Peretz, "The Golem" (1893)	229
11.2	Bialik, "Bring Me in Under Your Wing" (1905)	230
11.3	Bialik and Ravnitzky, *The Book of Legends*. On the Binding of Isaac	232
11.4	Franz Kafka, "My Father's Bourgeois Judaism" (1919)	239
11.5	Woody Allen, Fragment Two of the Scrolls (1974)	242
11.6	Yaakov Malkin, "The Faith of Secular Jews" (1998)	243
11.7	Irene Eber, On the Memory of the Holocaust (2004)	246
11.8	Adi Nes, "Abraham and Isaac" (2006)	248

12 JEWISH VOICES FROM THE MARGINS — 249

12.1	The Prophets' Warning to the Israelites	249
12.1.1	Amos 5:21 – 24; 7:10 – 17	249
12.1.2	Micah 3:9 – 12; 6:6 – 9	250
12.2	Shmuel Hanagid on War and the Good Life	252
12.2.1	"First War"	252
12.2.2	"The Gazelle that Stutters"	252
12.2.3	"Invitation"	253
12.3	Judah Halevi, "My Heart is in the East"	254
12.4	Judaism in Confucian Culture	255
12.4.1	弘治碑（公元 1489 年）	255
12.4.1a	A Stele Inscription Recording the Reconstruction of the Pure and True Temple [Synagogue] (1489)	258

12.5 Rabbi Yoel Teitlbaum of Satmar on the Holocaust (1961) ········ 265
12.6 Ellen M. Umansky, "Re-Visioning Sarah: A Midrash on Genesis 22" ··· 267
12.7 Jacob Neusner, Stranger at Home (1981) ················· 268

Appendices ·· 270
A. James Kugel, "Four Assumptions of the Biblical Interpretation" ··· 270
B. David Stern, "The Brutality of Repentance" ················ 274

Terms and Sources ·· 281

参考书目/**Bibliography** ·· 324

导言/Introduction

一

我在南京大学哲学系常年开设"犹太文献选读"一课,本书是在历年课堂指定的英文阅读材料的基础上删汰增订而成。除了哲学系相关专业的学生,尚有不少选修者来自世界历史、外国文学和比较文学专业,而经管、新闻、天文、数学、物理甚至大气专业的学生也不时出现。因此,从一开始,这门课的定位就是通过研读犹太传统中一些具有代表性的文本来形成有助于理解犹太文明的通识。①本书的编与选也是这样定位的。

犹太人号称"书之民"。这原本是《古兰经》中称呼犹太人和基督徒的术语,意思是他们像穆斯林那样,也拥有一部类似于《古兰经》的天启经书。确实,犹太文明的起源就可以看成是神在西奈山上把一本书交给摩西,让他带回去给自己人读。换言之,从一开始,书本在犹太传统中就是核心象征。犹太人日后显然衷心认可"书之民"一语,以之为荣,乃至引以自称。时至今日,犹太传统被理解为"一种以文本为中心的传统":神圣文本不仅构成各种思想与实践的共同背景,犹太传统自身的一些重大发展,还可以用犹太社群对它与文本的关系、对文本的选择,

---

① 本书唯一来自犹太传统之外的文本是编号3.4(下文引本书所选文本时直接标编号)的文本,但它对形塑和理解犹太文明的历史经验都很重要。

以及对文本如何在犹太社群中发挥作用所抱有的诸种概念来体现和理解。①这样,源远流长、浩如烟海、包罗万象的文本传统构成犹太文明的核心特征,就不足为奇了。

那么,如何在中国语境中将犹太文本传统概念化,帮助学生对这样一种异文明的核心特征切实领会并能触类旁通呢?本书就是这方面的一次尝试。我选择的古今犹太文本,时间跨度大约有两千五百年,涉及的原始语种包括希伯来语、亚兰语、希腊语、拉丁语、阿拉伯语、意第绪语、德语、英语和中文。虽然只是沧海一粟,但它们多少可以折射出犹太文本传统的丰厚与多元。显然,无人能凭一己之力掌握历代犹太文本。英语世界的同类选本就是必要的借鉴。②需要看到,选本(anthology)本身自古以来就是犹太文本传统的核心特征:《创世记》(Genesis)包含两个不同版本的创造女人(对比 1.1 和 2.1),编选痕迹明显;《诗篇》(Psalms)则是不折不扣的选集;几乎全部拉比时期的正典文献本质上都是选本,遑论本书参考书目里当代犹太人编选的时段不同、主题相异的各类选本了。③选本的意义取决于编者的意图。我的意图已随着历年讲授的通识课程而渐渐清晰——本书不是要网罗众作以保存和形塑犹太文化,更无意于品鉴高下或荟萃精华,而只想在经济的篇幅和有限的时间内,以一种尽可能便于中国学生理解的方式,去呈现犹太文本传统的大致脉络和基本表述方式,若能在此过程中体现一定的中国视角,或许更能让这些文本与我们生活的世界有所关联,从而带来启发。

---

① "书之民"在《古兰经》中作"Ahl al-kitāb"(中文又译作"有经人"),所对应的希伯来文是"Am HaSefer",英文是"People of the book"。Heilman(1987)从社会学角度生动再现了当代犹太社群对"书之民"的自我理解。这里对犹太传统作为"一种以文本为中心的传统"(a text-centered tradition)的理解则受益于 Halbertal(1997)的讨论。另,研究中国古代思想史的著名犹太汉学家史华慈把犹太文明称作"一种基于文本的宗教传统"(a textually based religious tradition),见 Benjamin Schwartz, "On Memory: Personal and Cultural," *AJS Review* 25.1 (2000–2001), p.88.

② 尤其参考 Leviant (1969); Alexander (1984); Keller (1992); Corrigan, Eire, Denny, Jaffee (1998); Neusner and Avery-Peck (2001); Biale and Miles (2015). Holtz (1992)提供了对"犹太书籍"的全面指南,虽出版较早,但迄今仍无同类书籍能够替代。

③ Stern (2004), pp. 1–11. 对参中国古代文学批评视域中的选本,见张伯伟:《中国古代文学批评方法研究》,北京:中华书局,2002 年,第 277—325 页。

二

我的一位原籍以色列的犹太朋友看过初选目录后给出评论:选目过于偏重拉比们留下的文献。这其实是有所针对而刻意为之的。在中文世界,对犹太文明的认识长期以来深受一个流行观念的影响,即犹太教指的就是《旧约》的宗教。这个观念虽然不算错,却也不完全对。犹太人管《旧约》叫"读物"(Miqra),有时又叫"塔纳赫"(Tanakh,释义见本书"Terms and Sources"部分)。犹太传统认为(6.2),神在西奈山上传给摩西两套"教导"[希伯来文叫"托拉"(Torah)]。一套是写下来的,叫成文托拉,也就是《塔纳赫》。另一套只能口耳相传,故称口传托拉。但到罗马时期,犹太人不堪忍受异族统治,发动起义,遭罗马镇压,政治环境的恶化令此时的社群领袖拉比们感到,再不将口传托拉写下来,这部分教导便有可能失传,口传托拉的结集遂出现,最终形成了《塔木德》(Talmud)。① 《塔纳赫》与《塔木德》——成文托拉和口传托拉——共同构成犹太文明的基石。

随着《塔木德》的出现,"以文本为中心的"犹太传统也出现了。这是有别于《塔纳赫》时代的一个新发展。在《塔纳赫》时代,社群领袖要么是世袭的祭司,要么是号称能与神直接交流因而深具个人魅力的先知。祭司通过圣殿与神沟通,发挥神职功能;对先知来说,历史则充当了展示神意的舞台,神显现于神圣事件。相对而言,学习托拉不如圣殿和神圣的历史重要。《塔纳赫》中虽然也教导人们学习托拉,但其目的主要是确保记忆和传统的延续。随着圣殿在犹太人的起义中被罗马人焚毁,随着犹太人进入流散而与神圣的历史疏离,精研托拉的拉比便替代祭司与先知成为犹太社群的领袖,学习托拉也成了一种重要的宗教理想,《塔木德》中就说:"学习托拉比圣殿的日常献祭更重要。"② 也可以说,托拉仿佛成了新时代可移动的圣殿。③

成文托拉与口传托拉相伴相生。除了解释、界定成文托拉中的字句与概念,口传托拉的另一功能是辅助成文托拉,补充《塔纳赫》中未明文规定但众所周知

---

① 中文世界对《塔木德》最详细可靠的介绍是史坦萨兹(2015),其中第3—9章谈口传托拉的历史形成,读来就仿佛本书所选的迈蒙尼德论述口传托拉及其流传的历史(6.12)的当代改写,值得比对。另参张平(2011),第48—55页。Strack and Stemberger (1996)对拉比文献的发展和近期研究做了详尽回顾,是这方面的标准工具书。

② Babylonian Talmud, Megillah 3b.

③ 参看亚伦·奥本海默(2012)。

的一般惯例。在发展口传托拉这两个主要功能的过程中,有两个方面对于理解和编排本书所选的拉比文献具有指导意义。

一方面是如何看待成文托拉与口传托拉之间的关系。① 表面上看,口传托拉补充、阐发成文托拉,因而似乎是派生的、次要的。但实际并非如此。《塔木德》中关于某种炉子是否洁净的争论,堪称最脍炙人口的拉比文献之一(6.6),其中讲述了有个拉比的裁决甚至得到来自神的直接认可,但仍遭到大多数拉比否决,而神最后也只能笑着承认"我的孩子击败了我"。显然,在拉比们的自我认知中,成文托拉一旦传给人,怎么解释就由拉比说了算。肖勒姆曾引用过早期犹太文献中的一个比喻性解释来说明成文托拉和口传托拉之间的关系。起初,托拉包含在神的智慧中,尚无所谓成文与口传之分,后来在神的面前,这种原初状态的托拉通过黑火写在白火之上而写成。这个解释又被赋予玄奥的解释:白火指成文托拉,但其字母尚未形成(我们的肉眼看不见),只有通过作为口传托拉的黑火,字母才能获得形式(让我们看得见)。黑火象征书写托拉经卷的墨水,这就意味着凡人所说的成文托拉只有经过口传托拉这个媒介才能获得可感知的形式。②正因为如此,犹太传统尽管始终以成文托拉为本,但自《塔木德》问世以来一直就有重《塔木德》而轻《塔纳赫》的倾向,这在阿什肯纳兹人(Ashkenazim)的犹太社群中尤其明显,在18世纪以前,犹太经学院(yeshiva)中的教学以《塔木德》而不以《塔纳赫》为中心,甚至还出现了绕过《塔木德》径直读《塔纳赫》会导致异端的言论。③鉴于此,本书第1到4章虽然选了《创世记》中脍炙人口的四个段落,但每章重点放在以《塔木德》为代表的历代拉比文献对成文托拉的字句或主题的阐释上,兼及个别现当代犹太作家运用这些母题的有影响的创作(1.12;2.8;3.6 - 7;4.8 - 9)。

另一方面,拉比们在解释成文托拉时采用了评注(commentary)的表述方式,这最终成为以文本为中心的犹太社群的智力创新的主导模式。诚如肖勒姆在一篇经典论文里指出的那样,评注这种体裁似乎仅仅为了呈现更古老的正典文本的"原始"含义,但其实经常表述犹太思想中最激进的新思想。④拉比们的释经著作(Midrash)固然对成文托拉亦步亦趋,在结构上根据《塔纳赫》的章句编排;但

---

① 限于篇幅,这里无法论述两者之间复杂的创造性张力。可参看纽斯纳(2014),第5章。
② Scholem (1971), pp. 294 - 295.
③ Halbertal (1997), pp. 96 - 100.
④ Scholem (1971).

即使是篇章结构迥异于《塔纳赫》的《塔木德》中也有大量《塔纳赫》引文。大量引用和阐释正典文献是整个犹太文本传统的基本特质。不仅许多犹太神秘主义著述采用了解释正典文本的形式(1.7)，就连犹太人在哲学方面的成就也不例外，尽管哲学通常是以一种概念性而非解释性的方式来讨论的。迈蒙尼德的《迷途指津》无疑是影响最深远的犹太哲学著作，它主要是一部释经之作(4.7)，其他哲学取向的文本也是如此，如中文世界已有颇多译介的古代亚历山大城的斐洛的著述(5.1)。这就触及犹太文本传统的另一个基本特质：在采用评注为表述方式的犹太传统思想领域内，几乎看不到以抽象概念进行的抽象思考。哈尔伯塔指出，《塔木德》不会讨论"何谓正义"这类问题，也不会试图为正义下定义。"《塔木德》的正义概念(如果有的话)是通过对《密释纳》(Mishnah)的错综复杂的解释来阐明的，并通过一个个不同的例子来展现。"① 每个例子代表一种范式(model)，《塔木德》中的拉比的世界观里充满各种范式，鲜活而细腻的例子发挥了抽象概念的作用。在以色列当代的《塔木德》权威史坦萨兹看来，

> 运用范式的最大好处，就是能不断检验论证方法的有效性，这是抽象概念难以做到的。基本而相对单纯的范式提供了检证基础，不仅能借此推论，也能随时检验是否在抽象思考模糊议题的过程中，偏离了根本性议题。所有抽象思考都有不断创造新概念的缺点，而既然除了运用同样模糊的词汇之外，别无界定这些新概念的办法，所以我们也难以判断它们是否已偏离主题、或是仍旧相关。②

因此，《塔木德》里几乎看不到抽象词汇，范式代替了抽象概念，并以范式为基础构建出独特的逻辑系统。

三

鉴于此，这本犹太文明的通识读本与上引同类选本的不同，首先就在于我选取对亚伯拉罕献祭以撒这段文本(4.1)的历代犹太解释作为贯穿全书的一条主线。除了历代拉比们的相关解释(4.3-7)，本书还收录了古代亚兰语的翻译

---

① Halbertal (1997), p. 92. 本书编号 7.2 的文本较典型地体现了这种特征。
② 史坦萨兹(2015)，第 295 页。

(4.2)，罗马时期受希腊文化影响的犹太历史学家约瑟夫斯的重述(5.2)，现代希伯来民族诗人比亚利克融历代解释为一炉的集成(11.3)，好莱坞犹太编剧伍迪·艾伦的"戏说"(11.5)，当代以色列艺术家借题发挥的摄影作品(11.8)，当代美国犹太女性主义者的改写(12.6)，以及它对于仪礼的意义(Appendix B)。这些内容虽不免重复，但在我看来，可以构成理解犹太文本传统的一个"范式"：成文托拉中的重要母题在后世的各种再现与变奏最能彰显犹太文明以文本为中心的特征，这些文本既为犹太身份认同提供了稳定内核，又赋予犹太文明一种一以贯之的连续性。就算犹太人自己要反叛犹太传统，也得先从反叛这种文本传统的核心开始(10.6)，或者从重新解释核心文本入手(2.8;12.6)。这里值得一提的是，亚伯拉罕杀子祭神这段文本在犹太传统中素来号称难解，层出不穷的历代评注和解释就是明证；其实，它放在中国语境中同样耐人寻味。我曾有幸与著名道教学者陈鼓应先生同桌共餐，席间陈先生谈起，他年轻时读《旧约》，读到这段大感不解，直呼与儒家伦理大相径庭。因此，编排出这段文本在犹太传统中的解释史，便可发现这其实也是一段犹太人与天启经书角力的历史，应当有助于我们理解颇多隔膜的异域文明。

拉比们打造出来的以文本为中心的犹太社群成功维持到18世纪。此后，随着世俗化进程在西方社会日益壮大，对于现代西方的犹太社群而言，世俗性的民族认同开始取代宗教认同，忠于共享的文本渐渐不再构成界定犹太身份的标志性特征，文化进步要通过解释正典来实现以及文化成就是解释性的这类观念，此时也失去了以往的力量(11.6)。在替代正典核心地位的诸种意识形态中，犹太复国主义(Zionism，又常常译作"锡安主义")无疑最有影响。犹太复国主义者也像近代其他的西方民族主义者那样，把共享的历史、语言和地域作为界定民族群体的标志性要素。在他们眼中，《塔木德》中没有可咏可叹的民族故事，没有可歌可泣的战士和英雄，是用亚兰文而非希伯来文写的，且并非在神的应许之地上成书，自然也就唤不起犹太人对古老家园的思慕与渴望。相形之下，所有这些《塔木德》中缺失的因素都包含在《塔纳赫》中，故《塔纳赫》才堪称犹太民族的史诗。犹太复国主义者在1948年建国(7.6)，并号召流散地犹太人回归古老家园(7.7)后，把《塔纳赫》而非《塔木德》作为凝聚犹太民族向心力的核心文本，纳入以色列世俗学校的教学内容，以此塑造有别于流散时期犹太人的民族意识。以《塔木德》为核心代表的拉比文献遂在以色列国被边缘化。没了《塔木德》作为核心的那种文化，今天的犹太文化能否持续繁荣？这是不少犹太人眼下担心的一个问题。史坦萨兹就断言："欠缺《塔木德》研究能力的犹太社群不可能长久延续。"此话需要放进上述语境中,才能认清其言外对以色列主流文化价值观的争议和批判。① 持同样怀疑态度的以色列学者哈尔伯塔还指出,在现代希伯来语作家中,阿格农(S. Agnon)是最后一位传统意义上以文本为中心的作家,其作品时常取材拉比文献,不熟悉这些文献,虽然于观摩情节无碍,但作品中诸多微妙的意蕴也领会不到;相形之下,理解阿摩司·奥兹(Amos Oz)等绝大多数当代以色列作家的创作则不需要熟悉传统拉比文献。② 这解释了为什么奥兹等当代以色列作家在中文世界的接受度要远远高于阿格农这位迄今为止以色列唯一的诺贝尔文学奖获得者。③

对纳粹屠犹的记忆是取代文本中心地位的另一强大意识形态。或许可以不夸张地说,现如今几乎所有有意识的犹太书写都摆脱不了纳粹屠犹留下的巨大阴影,纳粹屠犹已渗入犹太意识,是当前犹太身份的有机成分。尽管如此,如何看待和记忆这份遗产在犹太幸存者中却千姿百态。经历了集中营生死的以色列现代诗人借《塔纳赫》中的典故寄托迷惘与哀思(1.12;3.6‐7;4.8)。逃离欧洲、定居纽约的哈瑞迪(Haredim)拉比则视纳粹屠犹为犹太复国主义忤逆神意擅自建国之罪引发的天谴(12.5)。在汗牛充栋的纳粹大屠杀回忆录中,恐怕最会令我们玩味者,是浩劫余生后成长为以色列汉学研究奠基人之一的伊爱莲的反思(11.7):她觉得对往事的绵绵怅惘唯有陆机《文赋》中的话——"恒遗恨以终篇,岂怀盈而自足"——庶几可以表达。陆机在现代人撰写的中国文学史上向来蒙受差评,被当作形式主义、无病呻吟的代表。但张伯伟教授向笔者指出:"一个有着亡国之恸的大将军之后,其内心的挣扎、冲突是可以在一个黑暗之世随意表达的吗?所以,伊爱莲的引用,恰好说明了她从中得到了共鸣,真可谓异代域外知音。"④ 这是一个犹太文本有助于我们反观自身的例证。

以文本为中心的犹太社群能够形成,需要倚赖相当广泛的群众参与,但妇女不被教授托拉,因而无法影响传统犹太文化,她们的声音也极少得到记录。拉比文献中往往只有拉比对妇女态度的零星反映(6.8;2.7.2),幸存至今的中世纪犹太文书偶尔可以折射出犹太妇女的忧惧与念想(10.4)。相形之下,犹太妇女的声音

---

① 史坦萨兹(2015),第 332 页。另参 Halbertal (1997), p. 130.

② Halbertal (1997), p. 92.

③ 关于奥兹在中国的接受,参看钟志清:《"把手指放在伤口上":阅读希伯来文学与文化》,北京:中央编译出版社,2010 年,第 111—202 页。当前,以色列国似乎出现了复兴流散时期犹太文化的苗头,但其走向仍有待观察,见戈迪斯(2018),第 375—379 页。

④ 张伯伟 2019 年 4 月 22 日致笔者电邮。

自近代以来的涌现,恰恰是以文本为中心的犹太传统式微的表征。用意第绪语写作的现代女诗人莫洛多斯基的诗《仁慈的神》(10.8),以反讽的笔调谴责了神在纳粹大屠杀中对其特选子民的漠不关心。此诗可以与现代犹太思想大家赫舍尔差不多写于同时的名作《大地属于上主》对读。① 赫舍尔是波兰哈西德运动(Hasidism)的名门之后,此书原为他在"二战"快要结束时在纽约用意第绪语发表的演讲,对以文本为中心的犹太传统在东欧烟花散尽前的绚烂投以深情而诗意的回眸。在他理想化的表述中,犹太人作为特选子民的神话——这在中文世界也根深蒂固——得到进一步强化和赞美。但莫洛多斯基的诗是对这种神话的解构,既还原了赫舍尔褒扬的犹太文本传统所遮蔽的实际,又有助于我们通过关注历史上被剥夺、被压制的声音而对犹太文明内部的多元和差异形成切实、整体的认知。

我们对犹太文明的认知仍具有显著的欧美中心论色彩。应当看到,在中世纪,特别是从7到13世纪,欧洲处于所谓的"黑暗世纪",世界犹太人口中的绝大部分其实生活在伊斯兰世界,这里的犹太人所取得的文化成就,有些依然被奉为犹太文本传统中的圭臬。迈蒙尼德的13条信纲是犹太文明史上得到最广泛接受的、近乎犹太教教义(dogma)的文字(6.11),今天犹太社群内部仍在激烈争论着如何对待这份遗产。他关于托拉学习的律法规定(7.3)全面、翔实地揭示了托拉学习之于犹太传统的核心地位;他为做慈善定下的八个层次(7.4)则体现出他对人性曲折幽微的明察秋毫,旨在"对弱者和不幸的人心生怜悯,以各种方式给予穷人力量,并教导我们不要折磨弱者的心"②。除了文化巨人迈蒙尼德,这里的犹太人还谱写出《塔纳赫》时代之后最有名的犹太诗歌(9.6;12.2-3),编撰了最有影响的犹太法典(7.5),并为犹太传统引入一些新内容,比如苦修主义(8.3)。在本书中,来自东方的犹太文本将占到一半篇幅。

与欧洲犹太人相比,伊斯兰世界和东方的犹太人历史上对外来文化的态度更加开放,更乐意借鉴外来文明为我所用。像《迷途指津》、中世纪希伯来诗歌这类作品,如果没有广泛汲取和回应其作者自身所处的环境,恐怕是难以诞生的。能否彰显犹太人与非犹太人的互动,正是本书选取犹太文本的一个标准,也是本书试图有别于其他选本的又一特色。从历史上看,只有与非犹太人的社会和文化不断互动的犹太社群才构成各时代的主流犹太社群;我也相信,犹太文明能否持久

---

① Abraham Joshua Heschel, *The Earth is the Load's: The Inner World of the Jews in Eastern Europe*. New York: Farrar, Straus, Giroux, 1949. 赫舍尔另一名作的选段,见1.11。

② Twersky (1972), p. 134.

与繁荣要取决于它吸纳和融化外来文明的能力。

此外,选取犹太文本传统中重要但尚未在我国学界对犹太文明的认识和研究中获得应有关注的内容,也是我在编选本书时的一个考虑。这部分内容较突出地体现在伦理文献(第8章)和仪礼文本(1.10;第9章)上。

需要强调,在以文本为中心的犹太社群内,学习经典文本就像迈蒙尼德所明确的那样,是积极的信仰责任,今天仍有不少犹太人认为古老的文本中包含了解决当下一切问题的智慧。这在中国语境中当然是没有意义的。对于我们生活的世界,阅读这些犹太文本,首先能让我们获取和加深对犹太文明的直观了解,其效果是阅读任何关于犹太文明的二手著作所无法替代的。除此之外,我想意义就在于"通过与经典文本的解释性的交互作用而获得自我实现的那种学习上的洞见"——这是瑞因格(Rritz Ringer)为德语中的"Bildung"一词(常译作"自我教化")下的定义。①

综上所述,本书有别于同类选本之处主要体现在四个方面。一,把亚伯拉罕献祭以撒及其历代解释作为全书主线,以此构成理解犹太文本传统的一个"范式":这些文本既为犹太身份认同提供了稳定内核,又赋予犹太文明一种一以贯之的连续性。二,针对中文世界具有通过《塔纳赫》理解犹太文明的普遍倾向,突出拉比文献对于理解犹太文明的重要性。三,针对中文犹太研究以欧美为中心和以名人为对象的研究取向,关注非西方地区的犹太文本和历史上被边缘化的犹太声音,由此彰显犹太文明内部的多元性。四,把是否能够体现犹太人与非犹太人的互动,作为选取文本的一个标准。

四

深谙拉比文献传统的阿格农编过《出埃及记》历代评注的选本,他在此书序言的最后写道:

> 这本书反映的,不仅仅有我喜爱的选段,还有岁月留给我的馈赠。我从童年起的阅读就对我准备此项工作裨益良多。不是我,而是岁月本身选出了这些。与此同时,任何人只要感兴趣,就能轻易超越我读到并引在这里的资

---

① 引自格奥尔格·伊格尔斯:《二十世纪的历史学:从科学的客观性到后现代的挑战》,何兆武译,济南:山东大学出版社,2006年,第31页,注释1。

料。还有许多古老或者晚近的评注,既出色又有价值,可惜我无缘得见,其中一些我恐怕都没有听说过。诚如我们从[摩西在西奈山上接受的]写有神约的两块石板上所知,托拉有60万种解释,对应的是60万[当时站在西奈山上的古以色列]人,每人都接受了属于自己的一种解释。……愿我们都能在我们所写的书中找到我们接受来的那种属于自己的解释。①

同样,本书只是个人的一管之见,属于我自己对犹太文明的一种解释。不同的是,浩渺无垠的犹太文本传统常常让我觉得自己无知故无畏,而最终激励我编完此书的是这句犹太名言——"若非此时,更待何时"(6.2)。

这些选段也是我的岁月中的人与事的沉淀。聚成此书,首先需要感谢张亮教授的提议。不过入手选编后,具体工作所需的时间大大超出我最初的预期,以致书稿完成颇有拖延,这是需要请他体谅的。我的工作包括:比对不同译文择善而从,统一关键术语的拼写,查找和编写有助于目标读者理解原文的注释,在注释中提示原文用典以及前后选文的互文性,编写书后结合选文内容的人物著述简介和术语释义。在从事这些工作时,我有幸被南京大学人文社会科学高级研究院接受为驻院研究员,其主事者周宪教授和从丛教授为本书的编写和讨论提供了种种便利,在此需要衷心感谢;张伯伟教授关于陆机的评点令人有拨云见日的愉悦。佩雷格(Yaron Peleg)教授、瓦尔德(Shalom Wald)博士和他的朋友迈蒙(Dov Maimon)博士和费希尔(Shlomo Fisher)博士先后对选目给出评论和建议,李纯一为这篇导言的初稿提出修改建议,胡星铭教授与我讨论了编纂体例,刘鹏教授和施敏、刘慧宁编辑则在出版方面予以支持,皆令笔者受益匪浅。

现在回想起来,最终将亚伯拉罕献祭以撒及其解释作为本书主线,得益于斯特恩(David Stern)教授,这位良师益友的提示和帮助总让人如沐春风;有幸得闻陈鼓应教授的感想则离不开洪修平教授的邀请;周平教授、傅有德教授和海勒斯坦(Kathryn Hellerstein)教授先后为我提供了整理这方面思路和聆听建议的机会,在此需要对他/她们致以衷心的感谢。

出于版权考虑,本书选段尽可能选择不在版权保护期内的译文,但采用时也并非完全照搬,遇到晦涩难解处,也在比对其他译文和参考近期研究的基础上略有改动,并在相应处给出了参考书目,以方便核对。少数在版权期以内的原文或译文选段则得到了作者或出版方的授权使用,在此谨致谢忱。

---

① Agnon (1994), p. 11.

自然还要感谢选课的历届学生,我想他们的一些疑惑和评论已在本书中有所体现。本书的编写还受益于徐新教授在南京大学创建的犹太学图书特藏室,这是需要饮水思源的。我取雅各·纽斯纳(Jacob Neusner,1932—2016)的自述总结全书,不仅是因为这位当代研究拉比文献最高产(恐怕也最有争议)的学者以他一贯的雄辩,写出了见证犹太文明史上一个重大转折时刻的一代犹太人的心声,也因为他将自己近千册书籍捐赠给南京大学犹太学图书特藏室,我以这种方式纪念他,是一位受惠于他的善举的后学所能做出的回报与感谢。

宋立宏
2019 年 8 月于南京大学哲学系薛光林楼
2020 年 8 月改定

1 IN THE BEGINNING

1.1 Genesis 1:1–2:4

(1) When God began to create[1] heaven and earth—(2) the earth being unformed and void, with darkness over the surface of the deep and a wind from[2] God sweeping over the water—(3) God said, "Let there be light"; and there was light. (4) God saw that the light was good, and God separated the light from the darkness. (5) God called the light Day, and the darkness He called Night. And there was evening and there was morning, a first day.

(6) God said, "Let there be an expanse in the midst of the water, that it may separate water from water." (7) God made the expanse, and it separated the water which was below the expanse from the water which was above the expanse. And it was so. (8) God called the expanse Sky. And there was evening and there was morning, a second day.

---

[1] A tradition over two millennia old sees 1:1 as a complete sentence: "*In the beginning God created the heavens and earth.*" This understanding has served as proof that God created out of nothing (*ex nihilo*), but it is not likely that the biblical author was concerned with this problem. The translation here follows Rashi, who made a case that the verse functions as a temporal clause and considered that the *primary* purpose of the text was not to teach the order in which creation took place. This is, in fact, how some ancient Near Eastern creation stories begin—including the one that starts at 2:4b.

[2] Others, "*the spirit of.*" Wind, however, provides a closer parallel to Babylonian texts than the traditional translation, "spirit of God."

(9) God said, "Let the water below the sky be gathered into one area, that the dry land may appear." And it was so. (10) God called the dry land Earth, and the gathering of waters He called Seas. And God saw that this was good. (11) And God said, "Let the earth sprout vegetation: seed-bearing plants, fruit trees of every kind on earth that bear fruit with the seed in it." And it was so. (12) The earth brought forth vegetation: seed-bearing plants of every kind, and trees of every kind bearing fruit with the seed in it. And God saw that this was good. (13) And there was evening and there was morning, a third day.

(14) God said, "Let there be lights in the expanse of the sky to separate day from night; they shall serve as signs for the set times—the days and the years; (15) and they shall serve as lights in the expanse of the sky to shine upon the earth." And it was so. (16) God made the two great lights, the greater light to dominate the day and the lesser light to dominate the night, and the stars. (17) And God set them in the expanse of the sky to shine upon the earth, (18) to dominate the day and the night, and to separate light from darkness. And God saw that this was good. (19) And there was evening and there was morning, a fourth day.

(20) God said, "Let the waters bring forth swarms of living creatures, and birds that fly above the earth across the expanse of the sky." (21) God created the great sea monsters, and all the living creatures of every kind that creep, which the waters brought forth in swarms, and all the winged birds of every kind. And God saw that this was good. (22) God blessed them, saying, "Be fertile and increase,① fill the waters in the seas, and let the birds increase on the earth." (23) And there was evening and there was morning, a fifth day.

(24) God said, "Let the earth bring forth every kind of living creature: cattle, creeping things, and wild beasts of every kind." And it was so. (25) God made wild beasts of every kind and cattle of every kind, and all

---

① The Jewish tradition considers this the first of the Torah's 613 commandments, although it is obligatory only on Jewish men, not women (b. Yebam. 65b).

kinds of creeping things of the earth. And God saw that this was good. (26) And God said, "Let us make man in our image, after our likeness. They shall rule the fish of the sea, the birds of the sky, the cattle, the whole earth, and all the creeping things that creep on earth." (27) And God created man in His image, in the image of God He created him; ① male and female He created them.②(28) God blessed them and God said to them, "Be fertile and increase, fill the earth and master it; and rule the fish of the sea, the birds of the sky, and all the living things that creep on earth."

(29) God said, "See, I give you every seed-bearing plant that is upon all the earth, and every tree that has seed-bearing fruit; they shall be yours for food. (30) And to all the animals on land, to all the birds of the sky, and to everything that creeps on earth, in which there is the breath of life, [I give] all the green plants for food." And it was so. (31) And God saw all that He had made, and found it very good. And there was evening and there was morning, the sixth day.

(1) The heaven and the earth were finished, and all their array.③(2) On the seventh day God finished the work that He had been doing, and He ceased④ on the seventh day from all the work that He had done. (3) And God blessed the seventh day and declared it holy, because on it God ceased

---

① Cf. Gen. 9:6 "Whoever sheds the blood of man, by man shall his blood be shed; for in His image did God make man."

② Cf. Gen. 5:2 "When God created man, He made him in the likeness of God; male and female He created them. And when they were created, He blessed them and called them Man." According to *Genesis Rabbah* 8:1, "R. Jeremiah b. Leazar said: When the Holy One, blessed be He, created man, He created him a hermaphrodite, for it is said, 'male and female He created them.' (Gen. 5:2)"

③ Or, "*all their hosts.*"

④ Or, "*rested.*" God's resting on the seventh day is the source of the Sabbath, the day of rest.

from all the work of creation that He had done.① (4) Such is the story of heaven and earth when they were created.

1.2　On "In the Beginning"(Gen. 1:1)

1.2.1　Proverbs 8:22–31

(22) The LORD created me [Wisdom] at the beginning of His course
As the first of His works of old.②
(23) In the distant past I was fashioned,
At the beginning, at the origin of earth.
(24) There was still no deep when I was brought forth,
No spring rich in water;
(25) Before [the foundation of] the mountains were sunk,
Before the hills I was born.
(26) He had not yet made earth and fields,
Or the world's first clumps of clay.
(27) I was there when He set the heavens into place;
When He fixed the horizon upon the deep;
(28) When He made the heavens above firm,
And the fountains of the deep gushed forth;

---

① 2:1–3: In the Jewish liturgy, this passage serves as an introduction to the Kiddush ("sanctification," see 1.10.1.), the prayer over wine to sanctify the Sabbath that is recited just before the first meal of the holy day, on Friday night (see Exod. 20:8–11). It also appears in the traditional Friday evening service. The passage is characterized by the type of repetition that suggests it might have served as a liturgy already in antiquity.

② Wisdom recounts her creation and her presence during the creation of the world. She was the very first of God's creations. An important Jewish interpretation, starting with *Genesis Rabbah* 1:1 and found in the Rashi to Gen. 1:1, uses Proverbs 8 to argue that the Torah (identified with wisdom) was created before the world and was used by God in creating it.

(29) When He assigned the sea its limits,

So that its waters never transgress His command;

When He fixed the foundations of the earth,

(30) I was with Him as a confidant (*amon*),①

A source of delight every day,

Rejoicing before Him at all times,

(31) Rejoicing in His inhabited world,

Finding delight with mankind.

1.2.2 Genesis Rabbah, 1:1

R. Oshaya commenced [his exposition thus]: *Then I was by Him, as a nursling* (amon); *and I was daily all delight.* (Prov. 8:30) "*Amon*" means tutor; "*amon*" means covered; "*amon*" means hidden; and some say, "*amon*" means great.② "*Amon*" is a tutor, as you read, As *an* omen (*nursing-father*) *carrieth the sucking child* (Num. 11:12). "*Amon*" means covered, as in the verse, Ha'emunim (*they that were clad*—i.e., covered) *in scarlet* (Lam. 4:5). "*Amon*" means hidden, as in the verse, *And he concealed* (omen) *Hadassah* (Est. 2:7). "*Amon*" means great, as in the verse, *Art thou better than No-amon?* (Nah. 3:8) which is rendered, Art thou better than Alexandria the Great, that is situate among the rivers? Another

---

① *Confidant.* The Hebrew word is "*amon.*" There are three basic ways of interpreting this word. (1) "Artisan" (which is elsewhere "*oman*"). This translation implies that wisdom aided God in creation. In a similar vein, a midrash likens wisdom (equated with Torah) to a tool God used in creation, as an architect looks at a blueprint when constructing a palace (Genesis Rabbah 1:2). (2) "Constant(ly), faithful(ly)"; "confidant." (3) "Ward" or "nursling" (or as a verb, "growing up"). Wisdom was with God as His ward, like a child He was caring for. This fits the context best. Nowhere does the chapter imply that Lady Wisdom helped God create the earth.

② Having introduced the four opinions for understanding *amon*, the midrash now explains, in typical midrashic form, the scriptural basis for each one.

interpretation: "*amon*" is a workman (*uman*).① The Torah declares: "I was the working tool of the Holy One, blessed be He. In human practice, when a mortal king builds a palace, he builds it not with his own skill but with the skill of an architect. The architect moreover does not build it out of his head, but employs plans and diagrams to know how to arrange the chambers and the wicket doors. Thus God consulted the Torah and created the world, while the Torah declares, IN THE BEGINNING GOD CREATED (1:1) BEGINNING referring to the Torah, as in the verse, *The Lord made me as the beginning of His way.* (Prov. 8:22)②

1.2.3　2 Maccabees 7:28

I implore you, my child, to look at the heaven and the earth; consider all that is in them, and realize that God did not create them from what already existed and that a human being comes into existence in the same way.

1.2.4　Dead Sea Scrolls. The Community Rule 1QS 3:15 – 16; 11:11, 17 – 18

(15) From the God of knowledge③ comes all that is and shall be. Before ever they existed he established their whole design(16), and when, as ordained for them, they come into being, it is in accord with his glorious design that they accomplish their task without change....
(11) All things come to pass by his knowledge; He establishes all things by

---

① The midrash now introduces a fifth option for understanding *amon*, that of a workman or plan used by God as a guide in creation.

② Thus, the Torah predates the world. The opening verse of the Bible, therefore, means "with the assistance of the Torah, God created …" The verses in Proverbs help in this way to explain Genesis.

③ *God of knowledge.* Draws on 1 Sam. 2:3. It is used here to assert God's omniscience.

his design and without him nothing is done ... (17) For without you no way is perfect, and without your will nothing is done. It is you who has taught (18) all knowledge[1] and all things come to pass by your will.

1.2.5 John 1:1–3

(1) In the beginning was the Word, and the Word was with God, and the Word was God. (2) He was in the beginning with God. (3) All things came into being through him, and without him not one thing came into being.

1.3 Genesis Rabbah, 1:10. Creation with the Hebrew Letter *Beth*

IN THE BEGINNING (BE-RESHITH) GOD CREATED. R. Jonah said in R. Levi's name: Why was the world created with a *beth* (ב)?[2] Just as the *beth* is closed at the sides but open in front, so you are not permitted to investigate what is above and what is below, what is before and what is behind. Bar Kappara quoted: *For ask now of the days past, which were before thee, since the day that God created man upon the earth* (Deut. 4:32): you may speculate from the day that days were created, but you may not speculate on what was before that. *And from one end of heaven unto the other* (ibid.) you may investigate, but you may not investigate what was before this. R. Judah b. Pazzi lectured on the Creation story, in accordance with this interpretation of Bar Kappara.[3]

Why was it created with a *beth*? To teach you that there are two

---

[1] *It is you who has taught all knowledge.* Draws on Deut. 4:35. Though not cited, the second half of this verse ("The Lord alone is God; there is none beside him") fits well with the surrounding content.

[2] The first letter of the Torah and the second letter of the Hebrew alphabet.

[3] Rabbi Judah ben Pazzi teaches about the creation but not about what came before it.

worlds.① Another interpretation: why with a *beth*? Because it connotes blessing (*berakah*).② And why not with an *alef*? Because it connotes cursing.③ Another interpretation: Why not with an *alef*? In order not to provide a justification for heretics to plead, "How can the world endure, seeing that it was created with the language of cursing?" Hence the Holy One, blessed be He, said, "Lo, I will create it with the language of blessing, and would that it may stand!" Another interpretation: why with a *beth*? Just as a *beth* has two projecting points, one pointing upward and the other backward,④ so when we ask it, "Who created thee?" it intimates with its upward point, "He who is above created me." And if we ask further, "What is His name?" it intimates to us with its back point: "The Lord is His name."⑤ R. Leazar b. Abinah said in R. Aha's name: For twenty-six generations the *alef* complained before the Holy One, blessed be He, pleading before Him: "Sovereign of the Universe! I am the first of the letters, yet Thou didst not create Thy world with me!" God answered: "The world and its fullness were created for the sake of the Torah alone. Tomorrow, when I come to reveal My Torah at Sinai, I will commence with none but thee: *I* (anoki)⑥ *am the Lord your God.*" (Ex. 20:2) Bar Hutah said: Why is it called *alef*? Because it denotes the sum of a thousand, viz. *The word which He commanded for a thousand* (elef) *generations* (Ps. 105:8).

1.4 Philo, *On the Creation* 31. On the Light of the First Day

Now that invisible light perceptible only by mind has come into being as an

---

① *Beth* has the numerical value of two.
② *Beth* is the first letter of the Hebrew word for "blessing" (*berakah*).
③ *Alef* is the first letter of the Hebrew word for "cursed" (*arur*).
④ This refers to the crown-like flourishes (*tagin*) on the letter.
⑤ The first letter of the Hebrew term for "Lord" (*adon*), is *alef*. Thus, *beth* is taken to be pointing back to the first letter of the alphabet.
⑥ The first letter of the Hebrew term for "I" (*anoki*) is *alef*.

image of the Divine Word Who brought it within our ken: it is a supercelestial constellation, fount of the constellations obvious to sense. It would not be amiss to term it "all-brightness," to signify that from which sun and moon, as well as fixed stars and planets draw, in proportion to their several capacity, the light befitting each of them: for that pure and undiluted radiance is bedimmed so soon as it begins to undergo the change that is entailed by the passage from the intelligible to the sensibly discerned, for no object of sense is free from dimness.

1.5 On "Let Us Make Man" (Gen. 1:26)

1.5.1 Philo, *On the Confusion of Tongues* 179

Thus it was meet and right that when man was formed, God should assign a share in the work to His lieutenants, as He does with the words "let us make man," so that man's right actions might be attributable to God, but his sins to others. For it seemed to be unfitting to God the All-ruler that the road to wickedness within the reasonable soul should be of His making, and therefore He delegated the forming of this part to His inferiors.

1.5.2 Genesis Rabbah 8:8

R. Samuel b. Nahman said in R. Jonatan's name: When Moses was engaged in writing the Torah, he had to write the work of each day. When he came to the verse, "And God said, 'Let us make man, etc.,'" he said, "Sovereign of the Universe! Why dost Thou furnish an excuse to heretics?" "Write," replied He: "Whoever wishes to err may err." "Moses," said the Lord to him, "this man that I have created—do I not cause men both great and small to spring from him? Now if a great man comes to obtain permission [for a proposed action] from one that is less than he, he may say, 'Why should I ask permission from my inferior!' Then they will answer him, 'Learn from thy Creator, who created all that is above and below, yet when He came to create man He took counsel with the ministering angels.'"

1.6 Nahmanides on "Let Us Make Man in Our Image, After Our Likeness"(Gen. 1:26)

A special "saying" of God was reserved for man because of man's lofty estate. Man is different from the beasts and the cattle which God created by the previous "saying." The correct understanding of "Let *us* make man" is as follows. I have previously shown you that God only created something out of nothing on the first day of creation. He formed and made all other creatures out of the elements He had created out of nothing on that day. God endowed the waters, for instance, with the power to bring forth swarms of living creatures, hence the "saying" applied to the waters: "Let the waters bring forth swarms." (Genesis 1:20) Similarly, the "saying" in connection with animals was: "Let the earth bring forth." (Genesis 1:24) Therefore, when God came to create man He said: "Let us make," meaning: "Let me and the earth just referred to make man." This means that the earth should bring forth man's body from its elements, as it did in connection with the beasts and the cattle, as it is written: "The Lord God formed man from the dust of the earth." (Genesis 2:7) And then God infused into him from on high of His spirit, as it is written: " ... breathed into his nostrils the breath of life." (Genesis 2:7) It says: "in our image, after our likeness" since man resembles both of them. In the construction of his body man resembles the earth from which his body was taken. And in his spirit he resembles those on high(the angels), for his spirit does not die as does his body. In the next verse (Genesis 1:27), it says: "in the image of God He created him" in order to relate the great marvel, that man is different from all other creatures. This is the plain meaning of the verse. I discovered it in the writings of Rabbi Joseph Kimhi[1] and it is the most reasonable explanation of the verse of all that have been put forward. The word "image" means "form," as in the verse: "And the form of his visage was changed" (Daniel 3:19), and as in the verse: "Surely man walketh with a form," (Psalms 39:7) and as in the verse: "Thou wilt despise their form in the city." (Psalms 73:20) The word means, then, the form of his appearance. And the word "likeness" means a resemblance in character and deed since of things close to one another in idea it can be said that they resemble one another. Now man resembles both the beings below on earth and the beings above in heaven in character and glory, as it is written: "And hast crowned him with glory, and honor." (Psalms 8:6) This refers to man's spiritual ambition to acquire wisdom and knowledge and to improve his actions. As for "likeness," man's body resembles dust and his soul resembles the beings on high.

1.7 Mystical Interpretations on the Creation

1.7.1 The Zohar, Introduction 1:3b. A Mystical Interpretation on *Be-Reshit*

Rabbi Yudai said, "What is *Be-reshit*? With Wisdom.[2] This is the Wisdom on which the world stands—through which one enters hidden, high mysteries. Here were engraved six vast, supernal dimensions, from which everything emerges, from which issued six springs and streams,[3] flowing

---

[1] Joseph Kimhi (died in about 1170) was a noted grammarian, poet and Biblical commentator.

[2] The second *sefirah*, *Hokhmah* ("wisdom"). The following commentary involves the internal workings of God that led to the emanation of the *sefirot*.

[3] Six *sefirot*.

into the immense ocean.① This is *bara shit*,② created six, created from here. Who created them? The unmentioned, the hidden unknown."③

Rabbi Hiyya and Rabbi Yose were walking on the way. As they reached the site of a certain field, Rabbi Hiyya said to Rabbi Yose, "What you have said—*bara shit*—is certainly true, for there are six supernal days in the Torah, not more; the others are concealed.④ But in the Secrets of Creation we have discovered this:

"'The holy hidden one engraved an engraving in the innards of a recess, punctuated by a thrust point. He engraved that engraving, hiding it away, like one who locks up everything under a single key, which locks everything within a single palace.⑤ Although everything is hidden away within that palace, the essence of everything lies in that key, which closes and opens. Within that palace lie hidden treasures, one greater than the other. Within that palace stand gates built cryptically, fifty of them. Carved into four sides, they were forty nine. One gate has no side. No one knows whether it is above or below; it is shut.⑥ In those gates is one lock and one precise place for inserting the key, marked only by the impress of the key, known only to the key. Concerning this mystery it is written: *Be-reshit bara Elohim, In the beginning God created. Be-reshit* is the key enclosing all, closing and opening. Six gates are contained in that key that closes and opens. When it closes those gates, enclosing them within itself, then indeed: *Be-reshit*—a revealed word combined with a concealed word. *Bara, Created,*

---

① *Shekhinah* ("dwelling"), the tenth *sefirah*.

② Dividing the Hebrew word *Be-reshit* differently and supplying slightly different vowels provide this reading. Thus, the word *bara*, "created," is contained within *Be-reshit*, "In the beginning."

③ *Ein Sof* ("the Infinite"), the aspect of God beyond the *sefirot*.

④ Only six of the lower *sefirot* are revealed in the mystical Torah; the higher ones are hidden.

⑤ The recess and the palace are *Binah* ("understanding"); the thrust point and the key are *Hokhmah* ("wisdom").

⑥ The forty-nine gates of *Binah*, which appear in four lower *sefirot*. The fiftieth gate is hidden.

is always concealed, closing, not opening.' "

1.7.2 Isaac Luria on the Creation[①]

Withdrawal and Shattering

When the supernal emanator wished to create this material universe, it withdrew its presence. At first Ein Sof filled everything. Now, still, even an inanimate stone is illuminated by it; otherwise the stone could not exist at all—it would disintegrate. The illumination of Ein Sof clothes itself in garment upon garment.

At the beginning of creation, when Ein Sof withdrew its presence all around in every direction, it left a vacuum in the middle, surrounded on all sides by the light of Ein Sof, empty precisely in the middle. The light withdrew like water in a pond displaced by a stone. When a stone is dropped in a pond, the water at that spot does not disappear—it merges with the rest. So the withdrawn light converged beyond, and in the middle remained a vacuum. Then all the opacity and density of judgment within the light of Ein Sof—like a drop in the ocean—was extracted. Descending into the vacuum, it transformed into an amorphous mass (*golem*),[②] surrounded in every direction by the light of Ein Sof. Out of this mass emanated the four worlds: emanation, creation, formation, and actualization.[③] For in its simple desire to realize its intention, the emanator relumined the mass with a ray of the light withdrawn at first—not all of the light, because if it had all returned, the original state would have been restored, which was not the intention.

To fashion pottery, the potter first takes an unformed mass of clay and

---

[①] Source: Matt (1995a), pp. 94–97. Cf. Biale and Miles (2015); Scholem (1976).

[②] For *golem*, see 8.1 (Avot 5:7).

[③] I.e., four worlds of spiritual existence. It is only after the last stage (actualization) that the physical universe is created.

then puts his hand inside the mass to shape it. So the supernal emanator put its hand into the amorphous mass, that is, a ray of light returned from above. As this light began to enter the mass, vessels were formed. From the purest light, Keter; next, Hokhmah; then, Binah; and so on through all ten sefirot. Since Keter was the purest and clearest of all the vessels, it could bear the light within it, but Hokhmah and Binah, though more translucent than those below, were not like Keter. Not having its capacity, their backs broke, and they fell from their position. As the light descended further, six points appeared—six fragments of what had been one point of light. Thus the vessels shattered. Their spiritual essence—the light—ascended back to the mother's womb,① while the shattered vessels fell to the world of creation.②

When the light emanated once again—regenerated, arrayed anew (*be-tikkun*)③—it extended only to the end of the world of emanation.④ "Emanation" denotes this extension of the light of Ein Sof during the time of regeneration. Emanation consists of five visages (*partzufim*).⑤ These visages are reconfigurations of the points of light, capable now of receiving the light, so that no shattering occur, as at first. Below these visages the light of Ein Sof appears only through a screen. As when you sit in the shade: though the sun does not shine on you directly, it illuminates the shaded area. In a similar manner, the light of Ein Sof illuminates the world of creation through a screen, indirectly.

---

① "The mother's womb" corresponds to the divine mother, Binah.
② "The world of creation" is the second of the four worlds of spiritual existence.
③ *Regenerated, arrayed anew.* Hebrew, *be-tikkun*. Tikkun means "mending, repair, restoration" and refers to the process of repairing the shattering of the vessels.
④ *The end of the world of emanation.* The last of the ten sefirot.
⑤ *Visages.* Hebrew, *partzufim*, "faces, aspects, configurations." These five visages manifest distinctive aspects of divinity: Patient One, Father, Mother, Impatient One, and Feminine. They correspond, respectively, to the following *sefirot:* Keter, Hokhmah, Binah, Tiferet and the five *sefirot* surrounding him (Hesed, Gevurah, Netzah, Hod, and Yesod), and Malkhut.

Shattering and Growth

The supernal vacuum is like a field, in which are sown ten points of light.[1] Just as each grain of seed grows according to its fertile power, so does each of these points. And just as a seed cannot grow to perfection as long as it maintains its original form—growth coming only through decomposition—so these points could not become perfect configurations (*partzufim*)[2] as long as they maintained their original form but only by shattering.

Traces

Traces of the light adhered to the shards of the shattered vessels. This may be compared to a vessel full of oil. If it breaks and the oil spills out, a bit of the liquid adheres to the shards in the form of drops. Likewise in our case, a few sparks of light adhered. When the shards descended to the bottom of the world of actualization,[3] they were transformed into the four elements—fire, air, water, and earth[4]—from which evolved the stages of mineral, vegetable, animal, and human. When these materialized, some of the sparks remained hidden within the varieties of existence. You should aim to raise those sparks hidden throughout the world, elevating them to holiness by the power of your soul.

1.7.3 A Hasidic Interpretation on *Be-Reshit*[5]

"In the beginning God created" (Genesis 1:1). Understand that the Ein Sof is eternal. It existed long before anything else, and it is the source of

---

[1] *Ten points of light.* The ten *sefirot*.

[2] *Configurations.* Hebrew, *partzufim*, or, as translated earlier, "visages."

[3] *The world of actualization.* Hebrew, *olam ha-asiyyah*, the last of the four worlds, preceded by the worlds of emanation, creation, and formation.

[4] The concept of the four elements stems from ancient Babylonia and classical Greece. It persisted in Europe into the Renaissance, influencing thought and culture.

[5] Source: Dan (1983), p. 39.

everything that has ever come into being, from the depths of the earth to the heights of the highest heaven. One might imagine that whatever exists is eternal, reasoning that all things were hidden within the Ein Sof and integrated with it, but this is not so, because everything else was created. If all other existents are not part of the Ein Sof, however, where did they come from, and what are they made of?

The answer to this is very profound. In the beginning, the original will of the Ein Sof emanated a power from which the world would be made and all the worlds would be separated—the worlds of love, fear, glory, faith, connection, and kingship.[①] Later on, after this power had been emanated, Ein Sof brought into existence that which was potentially within the power, so that things could be revealed and all the worlds could be revealed. Thus, the first emanated power is inextricably bound to the Ein Sof.

1.8 Robert Gordis on "Fill the Earth and Master It"(Gen. 1:28)[②]

To claim that [this verse] provides "justification" for the exploitation of the environment, leading to the poisoning of the atmosphere, the pollution of our water, and the spoliation of natural resources is... a complete distortion of the truth. On the contrary, the Hebrew Bible and the Jewish interpreters *prohibit* such exploitation. Judaism goes much further and insists that man has an obligation not only to conserve the world of nature but to enhance it because man is the "co-partner of God in the work of creation."... All animal life and all growing and life-giving things have rights in the cosmos that man must consider, even as he strives to ensure his own survival. The war against the spoliation of nature and the pollution of the environment is therefore the command of the hour and the call of the ages.

---

① These are symbols of the six lower *sefirot*—Hesed, Din (Gevurah), Tiferet, Netzah, Yesod, Malkhut.

② Source: Plaut et al. (1981), p. 25. Man as God's co-partner: Sab. 10a.

1.9 Louis Ginzberg, Creation and the Hebrew Alphabet (1909)[①]

When God was about to create the world by His word, the twenty-two letters of the alphabet descended from the terrible and august crown of God whereon they were engraved with a pen of flaming fire. They stood round about God, and one after the other spake and entreated, "Create the world through me!" The first to step forward was the letter Taw(ת). It said: "O Lord of the world! May it be Thy will to create Thy world through me, seeing that it is through me that Thou wilt give the Torah to Israel by the hand of Moses, as it is written, 'Moses commanded us the Torah.'" The Holy One, blessed be He, made reply, and said, "No!" Taw asked, "Why not?" and God answered: "Because in days to come I shall place thee as a sign of death upon the foreheads of men." As soon as Taw heard these words issue from the mouth of the Holy One, blessed be He, it retired from His presence disappointed.

The Shin(ש) then stepped forward, and pleaded: "O Lord of the world, create Thy world through me, seeing that Thine own name Shaddai begins with me." Unfortunately, it is also the first letter of Shaw, lie, and of Sheker, falsehood, and that incapacitated it. Resh(ר) had no better luck. It was pointed out that it was the initial letter of Ra', wicked, and Rasha', evil, and after that the distinction it enjoys of being the first letter in the Name of God, Rahum, the Merciful, counted for naught. The Kof(ק) was rejected, because Kelalah, curse, outweighs the advantage of being the first in Kadosh, the Holy One. In vain did Zadde(צ) call attention to Zaddik, the Righteous One; there was Zarot, the misfortunes of Israel, to testify against

---

[①] Source: Ginzberg (2003), pp. 3 – 5. There are different versions relating to the controversy of the letters about precedence—originally a "pedagogic aggadah," it was later combined with the mystic theory of the letters. The forms, names, and order of the Hebrew letters are a favorite theme of the "pedagogic aggadot," whose object is to render the elementary instruction to the young interesting and attractive. Ginzberg's footnotes detailing the sources he employed are not included here.

it. Pe(פ) had Podeh, redeemer, to its credit, but Pesha', transgression, reflected dishonor upon it. 'Ain(ע) was declared unfit, because, though it begins 'Anawah, humility, it performs the same service for 'Erwah, immorality. Samek(ס) said: "O Lord, may it be Thy will to begin the creation with me, for Thou art called Samek, after me, the Upholder of all that fall." But God said: "Thou art needed in the place in which thou art; thou must continue to uphold all that fall." Nun(נ) introduces Ner, "the lamp of the Lord," which is "the spirit of men," but it also introduces Ner, "the lamp of the wicked," which will be put out by God. Mem(מ) starts Melek, king, one of the titles of God. As it is the first letter of Mehumah, confusion, as well, it had no chance of accomplishing its desire. The claim of Lamed(ל) bore its refutation within itself. It advanced the argument that it was the first letter of Luhot, the celestial tables for the Ten Commandments; it forgot that the tables were shivered in pieces by Moses. Kaf(כ) was sure of victory. Kisseh, the throne of God, Kabod, His honor, and Keter, His crown, all begin with it. God had to remind it that He would smite together His hands, Kaf, in despair over the misfortunes of Israel. Yod (י) at first sight seemed the appropriate letter for the beginning of creation, on account of its association with Yah, God, if only Yezer ha-Ra', the evil inclination, had not happened to begin with it, too. Tet(ט) is identified with Tob, the good. However, the truly good is not in this world; it belongs to the world to come. Het(ח) is the first letter of Hanun, the Gracious One; but this advantage is offset by its place in the word for sin, Hattat. Zain(ז) suggests Zakor, remembrance, but it is itself the word for weapon, the doer of mischief. Waw (ו) and He (ה) compose the Ineffable Name of God; they are therefore too exalted to be pressed into the service of the mundane world. If Dalet(ד) had stood only for Dabar, the Divine Word, it would have been used, but it stands also for Din, justice, and under the rule of law without love the world would have fallen to ruin. Finally, in spite of reminding one of Gadol, great, Gimel(ג) would not do, because Gemul, retribution, starts with it.

After the claims of all these letters had been disposed of, Bet(ב) stepped before the Holy One, blessed be He, and pleaded before Him: "O Lord of the world! May it be Thy will to create Thy world through me, seeing that all the dwellers in the world give praise daily unto Thee through me, as it is said, 'Blessed be the Lord forever. Amen, and Amen.'" The Holy One, blessed be He, at once granted the petition of Bet. He said, "Blessed be he that cometh in the name of the Lord." And He created His world through Bet, as it is said, "Be-reshit God created the heaven and the earth."

The only letter that had refrained from urging its claims was the modest Alef(א), and God rewarded it later for its humility by giving it the first place in the Decalogue.[1]

1.10 Sabbath Liturgy[2]

1.10.1 The Kiddush for Sabbath Evening

(There was evening and there was morning—)[3]

The sixth day. So heaven and earth were finished and all their host. On the seventh day God had finished the work he had been doing, and he ceased on the seventh day from all the work he had been doing. God blessed the seventh day and made it holy, because on it God ceased from all the work of creating which he had been doing (Gen. 1:31 – 2:3).

[*The blessing for the wine.*] Blessed are you, O Lord our God, King of the universe, who creates the fruit of the vine.

[*The blessing for the day.*] Blessed are you, O Lord our God, King of the Universe, who has made us holy through his commandments and has taken pleasure in us. In his love and goodwill he has given us his holy Sabbath as an inheritance, a memorial of creation, for it is the first named of

---

① See 7.1 for the Decalogue.
② Source: Alexander (1984), pp. 74 – 75. Cf. Birnbaum (1977), pp. 289 – 290; 551 – 552.
③ The bracketed words are said in a whisper.

the holy assemblies,① a reminder of the going forth from Egypt. For you have chosen us and set us apart as holy from all the nations and in love and goodwill have given us your holy Sabbath as an inheritance. Blessed are you, O Lord, who makes the Sabbath holy.

[*The blessing for the washing of the hands (Netilat Yadayim).*] Blessed are you, O Lord our God, King of the universe, who has made us holy through his commandments, and has given us the commandment concerning the washing of the hands.

[*The blessing for the bread.*] Blessed are you, O Lord our God, King of the universe, who brings forth bread from the earth.

1.10.2 The Havdalah Service for the End of Sabbath

Behold, God is my salvation, I will trust and not be afraid, for Yah, the Lord is my strength and my song, and he has proved to be my salvation. You shall draw up water with joy from the wells of salvation. Salvation comes from Lord: may your blessing rest on your people. The Lord of Hosts is with us, the God of Jacob is our refuge. The Jews had light and joy, gladness and honor—so may it be with us as well! I will raise the cup of salvation and call on the name of the Lord.

[*The blessing for the wine.*] Blessed are you, O Lord our God, King of universe, who creates the fruit of the vine.

[*The blessing for the spices.*②] Blessed are you, O Lord our God, King of universe, who creates spices of different kinds.

[*The blessing for light.*] Blessed are you, O Lord our God, King of the

---

① I.e., the first of the holy festivals. See Lev. 23:1 – 38.
② According to Maimonides, the symbolic use of fragrant spices during the recital of the *Havdalah* is to cheer the soul which is saddened at the departure of the Sabbath. When a festival follows immediately after the Sabbath the spices are omitted, because the soul then rejoices with the incoming holiday.

universe, who creates the lights of fire.①

[*Havdalah.*] Blessed are you, O Lord our God, King of the universe, who has made a distinction between the holy and the profane, between light and darkness, between Israel and the nations, between the seventh day and the six working days. Blessed are you, O Lord, who has made a distinction between the holy and the profane.

1.11 Abraham Joshua Heschel, *The Sabbath* (1951)

Bible is more concerned with time than with space. It sees the world in dimension of time. It pays more attention to generations, to events, than to countries, to things; it is more concerned with history than with geography. To understand the teaching of the Bible, one must accept its premise that time has a meaning for life which is at least equal to that of space; that has a significance and sovereignty of its own.

Judaism is *a religion of time* aiming at *the sanctification of time* ... Judaism teaches us to be attached to *holiness in time*, to be attached to sacred events, to learn how to consecrate sanctuaries that emerge from the magnificent stream of a year. The Sabbaths are our great cathedrals; and our Holy of Holies is a shrine that neither the Romans nor the Germans were able to burn ... Jewish ritual may be characterized as the art of significant forms in time, as *architecture of time.*

While the festivals celebrate events that happened in time, the date of the month assigned for each festival in the calendar is determined by the life in nature. Passover and the Feast of Booths [Sukkot], for example, coincide with the full moon, and the date of all festivals is a day in the month, and

---

① A twisted candle of several wicks is used since the phrase "lights of fire" (*me'ore ha-esh*) is in the plural.

the month is a reflection of what goes on periodically in the realm of nature, since the Jewish month begins with the new moon, with the reappearance of the lunar crescent in the evening sky. In contrast, the Sabbath is entirely independent of the month and unrelated to the moon. Its date is not determined by any event in nature, such as the new moon, but by the act of creation. Thus the essence of the Sabbath is completely detached from the world of space.

The meaning of the Sabbath is to celebrate time rather than space. Six days a week we live under the tyranny of things of space; on the Sabbath we try to become attuned to *holiness in time.* It is a day on which we are called upon to share in what is eternal in time, to turn from the results of creation to the mystery of creation, from the world of creation to the creation of the world.

Creation, we are taught, is not an act that happened once upon a time, once and for ever. The act of bringing the world into existence is a continuous process. God called the world into being, and that call goes on. There is this present moment because God is present. Every instant is an act of creation. A moment is not a terminal but a flash, a signal of Beginning. Time is perpetual innovation, a synonym for continuous creation. Time is God's gift to the world of space.

1.12 Dan Pagis, *Testimony*

No, no: they definitely were
human beings: uniforms, boots.
How to explain? They were created
in the image (*zelem*).

I was a shade (*zel*).
A different creator made me.

And he in his mercy left nothing of me that would die.
And I fled to him, floated up weightless, blue,
forgiving—I would even say: apologizing—
smoke to omnipotent smoke
that has no body (*guf*) or likeness (*demut*).[1]

1.13 Shlomo Carlebach on Singing Creation into Being[2]

When God created the world God said, "Let there be light. Let there be fishes. Let there be people." Do you think when God was saying this God spoke in a harsh voice? ... The truth is God didn't even say it. God sang it. God sang the whole creation into being. Reb Nachman [1772 – 1810] says, whenever you talk without singing, you are disconnecting yourself from the creation of the world.

---

[1] This stanza turns on a verse from *Yigdal* (Hebrew for "may He be magnified"), the medieval hymn that summarizes the Thirteen Principles of faith formulated by Maimonides (see 6.11), which declares that God "has no body(*guf*) nor the likeness(*demut*) of a body."

[2] Source: Steinberg (2007), p. 59.

2 ADAM, EVE AND LILITH

2.1 Genesis 2:4–3:24

(4) When the LORD God made earth and heaven①—(5) when no shrub of the field was yet on earth and no grasses of the field had yet sprouted, because the LORD God had not sent rain upon the earth and there was no man to till the soil, (6) but a flow would well up from the ground and water the whole surface of the earth—(7) the LORD God formed man [*'adam*]② from the dust③ of the earth [*'adamah*].④ He blew into his nostrils the breath of life, and man became a living being.

---

① Note that expression "heaven and earth" (1:1; 2:4a) now appears in the reverse order ("earth and heaven"), as befits the more earth-centered character of this story.

② From the biblical text grew a considerable body of ancient stories about the "Original Adam," *Adam Harishon* or *Adam Kadmon* as he was called. He was thought to have preceded the biblical Adam and to have been a perfect man who would return to the world at the time of redemption. On this tradition, see Scholem (1965), pp.159–165.

③ According to Islamic legend, the dust was red, white, and black—hence the skin colors of mankind.

④ Many Hebrew feminine nouns end in *-ah*. *'adamah*, the Hebrew word for "soil" or "ground," thus looks as if it ought to be the female counterpart to *'adam*, meaning "man." Rabbinic interpretation would later interpret this wordplay to mean that man is made from the feminine version of his essence, just as woman is made from man's essence.

(8) The LORD God planted a garden① in Eden,② in the east, and placed there the man whom He had formed. (9) And from the ground the LORD God caused to grow every tree that was pleasing to the sight and good for food, with the tree of life in the middle of the garden, and the tree of knowledge of good and bad.

(10) A river issues from Eden to water the garden, and it then divides and becomes four branches. (11) The name of the first is Pishon, the one that winds through the whole land of Havilah, where the gold is. (12) (The gold of that land is good; bdellium is there, and lapis lazuli.)③(13) The name of the second river is Gihon, the one that winds through the whole land of Cush. (14) The name of the third river is Tigris, the one that flows east of Asshur. And the fourth river is the Euphrates.

(15) The LORD God took the man and placed him in the garden of Eden, to till it and tend it. (16) And the LORD God commanded the man, saying, "Of every tree of the garden you are free to eat; (17) but as for the tree of knowledge of good and bad, you must not eat of it; for as soon as you eat of it, you shall die."④

(18) The LORD God said, "It is not good for man to be alone; I will make a fitting helper for him." (19) And the LORD God formed out of the earth all the wild beasts and all the birds of the sky, and brought them to the man to see what he would call them; and whatever the man called each living creature, that would be its name. (20) And the man gave names to all the cattle and to the birds of the sky and to all the wild beasts; but for

---

① "Paradise" had been used by Septuagint translation for "garden" in Gen. 2:8–10, 16. But the word was, at first, only the regular term for an enclosed garden or orchard.

② The root of *Eden* denotes fertility. *Eden* is the fertile abode of God, as elaborated in Ezek. 28:13–19.

③ The meaning of the Hebrew is uncertain.

④ *As soon as you eat of it, you shall die.* In the Bible, a thousand years is regarded as a day of God (Ps. 90:4), and none of the ancients in the biblical account reaches the millennial age. Cf. *Genesis Rabbah* 8:2, "The day of the Lord is a thousand years, as it is said, 'For in your sight a thousand years are like yesterday that has passed.'" (Ps. 90:4)

Adam no fitting helper was found. (21) So the LORD God cast a deep sleep upon the man; and, while he slept, He took one of his ribs and closed up the flesh at that spot. (22) And the LORD God fashioned the rib that He had taken from the man into a woman; and He brought her to the man. (23) Then the man said,

>This one at last
>Is bone of my bones
>And flesh of my flesh.
>This one shall be called Woman [*'ishshah*],①
>For from man [*'ish*] was she taken.

(24) Hence a man leaves his father and mother and clings to his wife, so that they become one flesh.

(25) The two of them were naked [*'arummim*], the man and his wife, yet they felt no shame. (1) Now the serpent was the shrewdest [*'arum*] of all the wild beasts that the LORD God had made. He said to the woman, "Did God really say: You shall not eat of any tree of the garden?" (2) The woman replied to the serpent, "We may eat of the fruit② of the other trees of the garden. (3) It is only about fruit of the tree in the middle of the garden that God said: 'You shall not eat of it or touch it, lest you die.'" (4) And the serpent said to the woman, "You are not going to die, (5) but God knows that as soon as you eat of it your eyes will be opened and you will be like divine beings who know good and bad." (6) When the woman saw that the tree was good for eating and a delight to the eyes, and that the tree was desirable as a source of wisdom, she took of its fruit and ate. She also gave some to her husband, and he ate. (7) Then the eyes of both of them

---

① *'ishah* (feminine of *'ish*). *'ishshah*, with a doubling of the Hebrew letter for *sh*, means "her husband." The wordplay thus links the Hebrew word for "woman" to the man to whom she is sexually connected.

② Jewish tradition suggests wheat, grape, fig, or citron, all prominent Near Eastern products. In Christian tradition, it is generally thought as an apple.

were opened and they perceived that they were naked; and they sewed together fig leaves and made themselves loincloths.

(8) They heard the sound of the LORD God moving about in the garden at the breezy time of day; and the man and his wife hid from the LORD God among the trees of the garden. (9) The LORD God called out to the man and said to him, "Where are you?" (10) He replied, "I heard the sound of You in the garden, and I was afraid because I was naked, so I hid." (11) Then He asked, "Who told you that you were naked? Did you eat of the tree from which I had forbidden you to eat?" (12) The man said, "The woman You put at my side—she gave me of the tree, and I ate." (13) And the LORD God said to the woman, "What is this you have done!" The woman replied, "The serpent duped me, and I ate." (14) Then the LORD God said to the serpent,

> Because you did this,
> More cursed shall you be
> Than all cattle
> And all the wild beasts:
> On your belly shall you crawl
> And dirt shall you eat
> All the days of your life.
> (15) I will put enmity
> Between you and the woman,
> And between your offspring and hers;
> They shall strike at your head,
> And you shall strike at their heel.

(16) And to the woman He said,

> I will make most severe
> Your pangs in childbearing;
> In pain shall you bear children.
> Yet your urge shall be for your husband,

And he shall rule over you.

(17) To Adam He said,

Because you did as your wife said and ate of the tree about which I commanded you, "You shall not eat of it,"
Cursed be the ground because of you;
By toil shall you eat of it
All the days of your life:
(18) Thorns and thistles shall it sprout for you.
But your food shall be the grasses of the field;
(19) By the sweat of your brow
Shall you get bread to eat,
Until you return to the ground—
For from it you were taken.
For dust you are,
And to dust you shall return.

(20) The man named his wife Eve [*chavah*], because she was the mother of all the living [*chai*], (21) And the LORD God made garments of skins for Adam and his wife, and clothed them.

(22) And the LORD God said, "Now that the man has become like one of us, knowing good and bad, what if he should stretch out his hand and take also from the tree of life and eat, and live forever!" (23) So the LORD God banished him from the garden of Eden, to till the soil from which he was taken. (24) He drove the man out, and stationed east of the garden of Eden the cherubim and the fiery ever-turning sword, to guard the way to

the tree of life.①

2.2 On "The Dust of the Earth" (Gen. 2:7)

2.2.1 Philo, *On the Creation*, 137

God is not likely to have taken the clay from any part of the earth that might offer, or to have chosen as rapidly as possible to mould this figure in the shape of a man, but selecting the best from it all, out of pure material taking the purest and most subtly refined, such as was best suited for his structure; for a sacred dwelling-place or shrine was being fashioned for the reasonable soul, which man was to carry as a holy image, of all images the most Godlike.

2.2.2 Rashi

God gathered his dust [i.e., that from which he was made] from the entire earth—from its four corners—in order that wherever he might die, it should receive him for burial.

---

① In Jewish and Christian tradition, Paradise or Eden also becomes a projection of the future. In the messianic era men will return to the harmony of Eden. This expectation is also applied to the afterlife of the righteous who will join the angels in singing the praises of God and in studying the holy books. The traditional prayer book (*Siddur*), asks God to accept the departed in Eden; the Reform prayer book has omitted the phrase.

2.3 Leviticus Rabbah 8:1. God as Marriage-Maker[①]

A Roman matron questioned R. Yose b. Halfuta. She said to him, "In how many days did God create his world?" He said to her, "In six days, as is written, *For in six days the Lord made Heaven and earth* (Exod 31:17)." She said to him, "What does he sit and do now?" He said to her, "He sits and arranges marriages: Mr. So-and-so's daughter is for Mr. So-and-so, the wife of So-and-so [who died] is for Mr. So-and-so, the estate of Mr. So-and-so is for Mr. So-and-so."

She said to him, "How many slaves and bondmaidens do I have, and in a moment or two I can marry them off!" He said to her, "Although it is a small thing in your eyes, it is as difficult before God as the parting of the Reed Sea, as is written, *God restores the lonely to their homes, [sets free the imprisoned, safe and sound, while the rebellious must live in a parched land]* (Ps. 68:7)." R. Yose b. Halfuta went home.

What did she do? She sent [word] and they brought one thousand slaves and one thousand bondwomen and she lined them up in rows. She said to them, "So-and-so will marry So-and-so, and So-and-so will marry So-and-so."

That night they came to her. This one's head was disheveled. That one's eye was blinded. This one's hand was broken. That one's leg was broken. This one said, "I don't want her." That one said, "I don't want him."

She sent word to him [R. Yose] and said to him, "Your Torah is good, beautiful and praiseworthy." He said to her, "Did I not say to you that 'Although it is a small thing in your eyes, it is as difficult before God as the parting of the Reed Sea'?"

---

① Source: Rubenstein (2002), p. 147. Just as God brought Eve to Adam and thus served as the marriage-maker for the first human couple, so the rabbis believed that God played a role in forging every marital union.

2.4 *Avot de-Rabbi Nathan*, Chapter 1. On the "Fence for the Torah"

What is the fence which Adam made for his words? Lo, it says, "And the Lord God commanded the man, saying: Of every tree of the garden thou mayest freely eat; but of the tree of the knowledge of good and evil, thou shalt not eat of it; for in the day that thou eatest thereof thou shalt surely die" (Gen. 2:16 – 17). Adam, however, did not wish to speak to Eve the way the Holy One, blessed be He, had spoken to him. Rather, this is what he said to her: "But of the fruit of the tree which is in the midst of the garden, God hath said: Ye shall not eat of it, neither shall ye touch it, lest ye die." (Gen. 3:3)

At that time the wicked serpent thought in his heart as follows: Since I cannot trip up Adam, I shall go and trip up Eve. So he went and sat down beside her, and entered into a long conversation with her. He said to her, "If it is against touching the tree thou sayest the Holy One, blessed be He, commanded us—behold, I shall touch it and not die. Thou, too, if thou touch it, shalt not die!" What did the wicked serpent do? He then arose and touched the tree with his hands and feet, and shook it until its fruits fell to the ground.

And some say: He did not touch it at all. On the contrary, as soon as that tree saw him it cried out to him in these words, "O wicked one, wicked one, do not touch me!" as it is said, "Let not the foot of Pride overtake me, and let not the hand of the wicked shake me" (Ps. 36:12)...

Furthermore, the serpent said to her, "If it is against eating of the fruit of the tree thou sayest the Holy One, blessed be He, commanded us, behold I shall eat of it and not die. Thou too, if thou eat of it shalt not die!" What did Eve think in her mind? "All the things about which my master admonished me at first are false"—for at first Eve addressed Adam only as "my master." Forthwith she took of the fruit and ate, and gave some to Adam and he ate; as it is said, "And when the woman saw that the tree was good for food, and that it was a delight to the eyes," (Gen. 3:6) etc.

2.5 *Pirkei de-Rabbi Eliezer* 14. The Sin of Adam and Eve[①]

Ten descents upon the earth were made by the Holy One, blessed be He; they were: (1) Once in the Garden of Eden; (2) once at (the time of) the generation of the Dispersion; (3) once at Sodom; (4) once at the thorn-bush; (5) once in Egypt; (6) once at Sinai; (7) once at the cleft of the rock; (8) and; (9) twice in the tent of Assembly; (10) once in the future.

Once in the Garden of Eden; whence do we know? Because it is said, "And they heard the voice of the Lord God *walking* in the garden in the cool of the day." (Gen. 3:8) And it is written, "My beloved *is gone down* to his garden, to the beds of spices." (Song of Songs 6:2) (God) sat in judgment, and He judged with judgment. He said to him(Adam): Why didst thou flee before Me? He answered Him: I heard Thy voice and my bones trembled, as it is said, "I heard thy voice in the garden, and I was afraid, because I was naked: and I hid myself." (Gen. 3:10)

What was the dress of the first man? A skin of nail, and a cloud of glory covered him. When he ate of the fruits of the tree, the nail-skin was stripped off him, and the cloud of glory departed from him, and he saw himself naked, as it is said, "And he said, Who told thee that thou wast naked? Hast thou eaten of the tree, whereof I commanded thee?" (Gen. 3:11)

Adam said before the Holy One, blessed be He: Sovereign of all worlds! When I was alone, I did not sin against Thee. But the woman whom Thou hast brought to me enticed me away from Thy ways, as it is said, "The woman whom thou gavest to be with me, she gave me of the tree, and I did eat." (Gen. 3:12) The Holy One, blessed be He, called unto Eve, and said to her: Was it not enough for thee that thou didst sin in thy own person? But

---

① Source: Translation by Gerald Friedlander (London, 1916), see https://www.sefaria.org/Pirkei_DeRabbi_Eliezer? lang=en&p2=Pirkei_DeRabbi_Eliezer.14.5&lang2=en.

(also) that thou shouldst make Adam sin? She spake before Him: Sovereign of the world! The serpent enticed my mind to sin before Thee, as it is said, "The serpent beguiled me, and I did eat." (Gen. 3:13) He brought the three of them and passed sentence of judgment upon them, consisting of nine curses and death.

He cast down Sammael and his troop from their holy place in heaven, and cut off the feet of the serpent, and decreed that it should cast its skin and suffer pain once in seven years in great pain, and cursed it that it should drag itself with its belly (on the ground), and its food is turned in its belly into dust and the gall of asps, and death is in its mouth, and He put hatred between it and the children of the woman, so that they should bruise its head, and after all these (curses comes) death. He gave the woman nine curses and death: the afflictions arising from menstruation and the tokens of virginity; the affliction of conception in the womb; and the affliction of child-birth; and the affliction of bringing up children; and her head is covered like a mourner, and it is not shaved except on account of immorality, and her ear is pierced like(the ears of) perpetual slaves; and like a hand-maid she waits upon her husband; and she is not believed in (a matter of) testimony; and after all these (curses comes) death.

He extended pardon to Adam(as to a part of the) nine curses and death. He curtailed his strength, and He shortened his stature by reason of the impurity connected with issues and with pollution; as well as the impurity arising from sexual intercourse; he was to sow wheat and to reap thistles, and his food was to be the grass of the earth, like that of the beast; and (he was to earn) his bread in anxiety, and his food by the sweat (of his brow); and after all these (curses came) death.

If Adam sinned, what was the sin of the earth, that it should be cursed? Because it did not speak against the (evil) deed, therefore it was cursed; for in the hour when the sons of man transgress the graver sins, God sends a plague to the sons of man; and in the hour when the sons of man transgress sins less vital, He smites the fruits of the earth, because of (the sins of) the sons of man, as it is said, "Cursed is the ground for thy sake." (Gen. 3:17)

2.6 *Alphabet of Ben Sira.* Lilith, Adam's First Wife[①]

Soon afterward the young son of the king took ill. Said Nebuchadnezzar, "Heal my son. If you don't, I will kill you." Ben Sira immediately sat down and wrote an amulet with the Holy Name, and he inscribed on it the angels in charge of medicine by their names, forms, and images and by their wings, hands, and feet. Nebuchadnezzar looked at the amulet. "Who are these?" "The angels who are in charge of medicine: Snvi, Snsvi, and Smnglof. After God created Adam, who was alone, He said, 'It is not good for the man to be alone.' (Gen. 2:18) He then created a woman for Adam, from the earth, as He had created Adam himself, and called her Lilith. Adam and Lilith immediately began to fight. She said, 'I will not lie below' and he said, 'I will not lie beneath you, but only on top. For you are fit only to be in the bottom position, while I am to be in the superior one.' Lilith responded, 'We are equal to each other inasmuch as we were both created from the earth.' But they would not listen to one another. When Lilith saw this, she pronounced the Ineffable Name[②] and flew away into the air. Adam stood in prayer before his Creator: 'Sovereign of the universe!' he said, 'the woman you gave me has run away.' At once, the Holy One, blessed be He, sent these three angels to bring her back.

Said the Holy One to Adam, 'If she agrees to come back, fine. If not, she must permit one hundred of her children to die every day.' The angels left God and pursued Lilith, whom they overtook in the midst of the sea, in the mighty waters wherein the Egyptians were destined to drown.[③] They told her God's words, but she did not wish to return. The angels said, 'We shall drown you in the sea.' 'Leave me!' she said. 'I was created only to cause sickness to infants. If the infant is male, I have dominion over him for

---

[①] Source: Biale and Miles (2015).
[②] The name of God, which Jews are forbidden to pronounce.
[③] I.e., the Red (or Reed) Sea (see Exodus 14).

eight days after his birth, and if female, for twenty days.'

When the angels heard Lilith's words, they insisted she go back. But she swore to them by the name of the living and eternal God: 'Whenever I see you or your names or your forms in an amulet, I will have no power over that infant.' She also agreed to have one hundred of her children die every day. Accordingly, every day one hundred demons perish, and for the same reason, we write the angels' names on the amulets of very young children. When Lilith sees the names, she remembers her oath, and the child recovers."

2.7 Shelomo Almoli, Dream Interpretations[①]

2.7.1 Serpent

[A Tanna recited before R. Sheshet:] Whoever sees [in a dream] a serpent, his sustenance is assured (Talmud Berakhot 57a). (Others say: a good sign.) [The Talmud continues:] If it [i.e., the serpent] bites you, it [i.e., your sustenance] will be doubled. (Others say: a bad sign. Still others say: Your enemies will increase.) If he kills it, he will lose his sustenance. R. Sheshet said to him: All the more so will his sustenance be doubled! This is not so, however; R. Sheshet explained it this way because he actually saw a serpent in his dream and killed it. Explanation: It was for this reason that he interpreted the dream favorably. And the connection of the serpent with sustenance is because dust is to be found everywhere, and so the serpent's sustenance is commonly available to it, and it does not need to labor for it.[②] And if it bites him, this denotes that others will take his sustenance from him. On the other hand, this denotes that he will be wealthier than they, he the master and they the servants to do his bidding, and he will pay them for

---

① Source: Almoli (1998), pp. 92 – 93, 110, 115, 112 – 113.
② As the serpent in Eden was cursed by being condemned to eat dust (Genesis 3:14).

doing so. "If he kills it, his sustenance is lost." R. Sheshet, on the other hand, found a favorable explanation for this. While the serpent lived, it had to find its sustenance; this denotes that those who consume the master's wealth will be many, but when the serpent is killed, this denotes that the master will have a great deal of food available to him, since it was not consumed by his servants.

If you see a serpent fleeing from you, your sustenance is being diminished.

If you see a serpent sleeping or curled around your neck, sustenance will come to you.

If you see a serpent with its mate, wealth will come to you.

If you see a serpent in your lap, your sustenance is assured.

If you see a serpent in the water, and you have no wife, you will marry. If you have a wife, you will be widowed.

If you see yourself killing a serpent, it is a good sign and your enemies will fall before you (R. Hai Gaon).

2.7.2 Woman

If you see a woman clapping her hands in sorrow or dancing, it foretells an incident of fornication.

The Talmud states: If you dream that you are committing incest with your mother, look forward to obtaining understanding (Berakhot 57a). R. Hai Gaon says that this denotes that you will live a good life and may look forward to obtaining understanding.

If you dream that you are committing incest with your sister, look forward to wisdom, as it says: "Say to wisdom, 'You are my sister.'" (Proverbs 7:4)

Likewise, the Talmud states: Whoever dreams that he has committed adultery with a married woman may be assured that he has a portion in the world to come; this refers to a case in which he does not know her and did not think about her the evening before (Berakhot 57a). This condition [not knowing her] seems to apply to all such dreams.

The explanation for the fact that these sinful acts are actually good signs is that intercourse is considered one-sixtieth of the pleasure of the Garden of Eden [i.e., the world to come], and illegitimate intercourse is all the more so, as it states, "Stolen waters are sweet." (Proverbs 9:17) Moreover, it hints that he will receive a double portion, his own and the woman's husband's portion, in the Garden of Eden, which is compared to a wife. However, the Book of *Sefer Yosef ha-Tzaddik* states: If you lie with a married woman in a dream, it is a sign of dispute. Others say: Whoever commits adultery with a married woman will become the head of a court.

2.7.3 Nakedness

If you see yourself naked [in a dream], it signifies shame or trouble (R. Hai Gaon). But *Sefer Yosef ha-Tzaddik* says: poverty.

In the Talmud: If you see yourself naked outside the Land of Israel, you will remain sinless; if in the Land of Israel, you will be bereft of mitzvot (Berakhot 57a). Explanation: This depends on another statement of our Sages: Whoever resides outside the Land of Israel is as one who has no God, as it is written, "They have driven me out this day [that I should not cleave to the inheritance of the Lord, saying: Go, serve other gods."[1] Now, whoever said to David, "Serve other gods"? Rather, whoever lives outside the Land of Israel is as one who worships idols.][2] This being so, anyone who remains outside the Land remains in a sinful state—and therefore one who is naked is sinless, [while the reverse is true when one stands naked in the Land of Israel]. He who stands in the Land of Israel is as full of mitzvot as a pomegranate is full of seeds—and one who is naked lacks these, and so is full of sin.

---

[1] I Samuel 26:19.

[2] Ketubot 110b.

2.7.4 The Dead

If you see yourself dead [in a dream], you have done something for which God will bring you close to Him. Daniel says: Life will be added to your years.

And in the Talmud: Our Rabbis taught: Whoever dreams about a corpse in the house, it is a good sign for the house. If it was eating and drinking in the house, it is a good sign for the entire household. If it took clothing from the house, it is a bad sign for the house. R. Papa explained this to refer to a shoe or a sandal. Whatever a dead person takes from the house is a good sign except a shoe and a sandal; anything that it puts down is a good sign except dust and mustard (Berakhot 57b). The explanation: When it takes shoes and sandals, that is a sign that the members of the household will go barefoot or will cease going to the marketplace. Likewise, dust is a sign of burial, as is mustard, which is as fine as dust.

If you see dead bodies in a dream, and you are healthy, have no fear at all; but if you are ill, it is a bad sign.

If you see yourself speaking with the dead, remain in the company of good people and do as they do.

If you see a dead relative coming to see you, you will be wealthy. If the dead man embraces you or kisses you, and even more, if he bites you, trouble will befall you.

If you see a corpse give you something, it indicates improved circumstances. But if the object is something which begins with the letter *nun* or *lamed*, you will become poor (R. Hai Gaon).

If the dead person gives the living one an iron implement or a weapon, he should feel secure no matter where he goes (R. Hai Gaon). And Rashi says: If the dead person gave him something which he did not want to take from him, it is a bad sign.

If you see your deceased father and mother, a joyful occasion will be yours. If they give you something, all the more so.

If you see yourself washing a dead body or dressing it or carrying it, you will descend from your high status.

If you follow a coffin or console the mourners, you will have performed a deed for which God will bring you close to Him (R. Hai Gaon).

If you see the dead robbing the living, one of your relatives will die.

2.8 Judith Plaskow, "Our Story: The Coming of Lilith" (1972)

We realized that, although we had failed to come up with a single event or symbol that captured all of feminist experience, there had emerged out of our discussion many of the central elements of a myth. We had a journey to go on, an enemy (or enemies) to vanquish, salvation to be achieved both for ourselves and for humanity. If we found ourselves with a myth, moreover, this was particularly appropriate to our experience, for we had come together to do theology by beginning with our stories. It was no coincidence, then, that we arrived back at the story form.

We recognized the difficulties of "inventing" a myth, however, and so we wanted to tell a story that seemed to grow naturally out of our present history. We also felt the need for using older materials that would carry their own reverberations and significance, even if we departed freely from them. We chose, therefore, to begin with the story of Lilith, demon of the night, who, according to rabbinic legend, was Adam's first wife. Created equal to him, for some unexplained reason she found that she could not live with him, and flew away. Through her story, we could express not only our new image of ourselves, but our relation to certain of the elements of our religious traditions. Since stories are the heart of tradition, we could question and create tradition by telling a new story within the framework of an old one. We took Lilith for our heroine, and yet, most important, not Lilith alone. We try to express through our myth the process of our coming to do theology together. Lilith by herself is in exile and can do nothing. The real heroine of our story is sisterhood, and sisterhood is powerful.

IN THE BEGINNING, the Lord God formed Adam and Lilith from the dust of the ground and breathed into their nostrils the breath of life. Created from the same source, both having been formed from the ground, they were equal in all ways. Adam, being a man, didn't like this situation, and he looked for ways to change it. He said, "I'll have my figs now, Lilith," ordering her to wait on him, and he tried to leave to her the daily tasks of life in the garden. But Lilith wasn't one to take any nonsense; she picked herself up, uttered God's holy name, and flew away. "Well now, Lord," complained Adam, "that uppity woman you sent me has gone and deserted me." The Lord, inclined to be sympathetic, sent his messengers after Lilith, telling her to shape up and return to Adam or face dire punishment. She, however, preferring anything to living with Adam, decided to stay where she was. And so God, after more careful consideration this time, caused a deep sleep to fall on Adam and out of one of his ribs created for him a second companion, Eve.

For a time, Eve and Adam had a good thing going. Adam was happy now, and Eve, though she occasionally sensed capacities within herself that remained undeveloped, was basically satisfied with the role of Adam's wife and helper. The only thing that really disturbed her was the excluding closeness of the relationship between Adam and God. Adam and God just seemed to have more in common, both being men, and Adam came to identify with God more and more. After a while, that made God a bit uncomfortable too, and he started going over in his mind whether he may not have made a mistake letting Adam talk him into banishing Lilith and creating Eve, seeing the power that gave Adam.

Meanwhile Lilith, all alone, attempted from time to time to rejoin the human community in the garden. After her first fruitless attempt to breach its walls, Adam worked hard to build them stronger, even getting Eve to help him. He told her fearsome stories of the demon Lilith who threatens women in childbirth and steals children from their cradles in the middle of the night. The second time Lilith came, she stormed the garden's main gate, and a great battle ensued between her and Adam in which she was finally defeated. This time, however, before Lilith got away, Eve got a glimpse of her and saw she was a woman like herself.

After this encounter, seeds of curiosity and doubt began to grow in Eve's mind. Was Lilith indeed just another woman? Adam had said she was a demon. Another woman! The very idea attracted Eve. She had never seen another creature like herself before. And how beautiful and strong Lilith looked! How bravely she had fought! Slowly, slowly, Eve began to think about the limits of her own life within the garden.

One day, after many months of strange and disturbing thoughts, Eve, wandering around the edge of the garden, noticed a young apple tree she and Adam had planted, and saw that one of its branches stretched over the garden wall. Spontaneously, she tried to climb it, and struggling to the top, swung herself over the wall.

She did not wander long on the other side before she met the one she had come to find, for Lilith was waiting. At first sight of her, Eve remembered the tales of Adam and was frightened, but Lilith understood and greeted her kindly. "Who are you?" they asked each other, "What is your story?" And they sat and spoke together of the past and then of the future. They talked for many hours, not once, but many times. They taught each other many things, and told each other stories, and laughed together, and cried, over and over, till the bond of sisterhood grew between them.

Meanwhile, back in the garden, Adam was puzzled by Eve's comings and goings, and disturbed by what he sensed to be her new attitude toward him. He talked to God about it, and God, having his own problems with Adam and a somewhat broader perspective, was able to help out a little—but he was confused, too. Something had failed to go according to plan. As in the days of Abraham, he needed counsel from his children. "I am who I am,"① *thought God, "but I must become who I will become."*

And God and Adam were expectant and afraid the day Eve and Lilith returned to the garden, bursting with possibilities, ready to rebuild it together.

---

① Exodus 3: 14. Meaning of Hebrew ("Ehyeh-Asher-Ehyeh") uncertain; variously translated: "I Am That I Am"; "I Am Who I Am"; "I Will Be What I Will Be"; etc.

3 "AM I MY BROTHER'S KEEPER?": THE IMAGES OF CAIN

3.1 Genesis 4:1-26

(1) Now the man knew① his wife Eve, and she conceived and bore Cain, saying, "I have gained② a male child with the help of the LORD."③ (2) She then bore his brother Abel. Abel became a keeper of sheep, and Cain became a tiller of the soil. (3) In the course of time, Cain brought an offering to the LORD from the fruit of the soil; (4) and Abel, for his part, brought the choicest④ of the firstlings of his flock. The LORD paid heed to Abel and his offering, (5) but to Cain and his offering He paid no heed. Cain was much distressed and his face fell.⑤ (6) And the LORD said to Cain,

> Why are you distressed,
> And why is your face fallen?

---

① Heb. *yada*, often in a sexual sense.
② Heb. *kaniti*, a word play with Cain (*kayin*).
③ Others, "I have bought a male offspring from the Lord," reflecting the idea that the first-born belongs to God and must be bought from Him (See Num. 3:46-47 and note the surviving ceremony of *pidyon ha-ben*, redemption of the first-born son).
④ *Choicest.* An idiomatic rendering the Hebrew, literally, "the fat of."
⑤ Genesis Rabbah 22:6: "And Cain was very wroth (*wayyihar*) and his countenance fell: [His face] became like a firebrand." *Wayyihar* is derived from *harah*, to burn.

(7) Surely, if you do right,
There is uplift. ①
But if you do not do right
Sin couches at the door;
Its urge is toward you,
Yet you can be its master.

(8) Cain said to his brother Abel ...② and when they were in the field, Cain set upon his brother Abel and killed him. (9) The LORD said to Cain, "Where is your brother Abel?" And he said, "I do not know. Am I my brother's keeper?" (10) Then He said, "What have you done? Hark, your brother's blood cries out to Me from the ground! (11) Therefore, you shall be more cursed than the ground, which opened its mouth to receive your brother's blood from your hand. (12) If you till the soil, it shall no longer yield its strength to you. You shall become a ceaseless wanderer③ on earth."

(13) Cain said to the LORD, "My punishment is too great to bear!④ (14) Since You have banished me this day from the soil, and I must avoid Your presence and become a restless wanderer on earth anyone who meets me may kill me!" (15) The LORD said to him, "I promise, if anyone kills Cain, sevenfold vengeance shall be taken on him." And the LORD put a mark⑤ on Cain, lest anyone who met him should kill him. (16) Cain left the

---

① *There is uplift.* The meaning of the Hebrew is not clear, and any translation is merely an educated guess. The Septuagint has it that "Hast thou not sinned if thou hast brought it rightly, but not rightly divided it?"

② The text does not quote what was said. The Septuagint supplies these words: "Let us go out into the plain." However, the omission of what Cain said may be a purposeful ellipsis.

③ *A ceaseless wanderer.* The banished Cain did settle, but in the land of Nod, the land of "restlessness"(Gen. 4:16), for nowhere could he be at rest.

④ Septuagint Gen. 4:13: "And Cain said to the Lord God: My crime is too great for me to be forgiven."

⑤ *A mark.* Not a brand of rejection but a sign of protection against blood revenge. In contrast, Medieval Christianity justified the Jewish badge as a "mark of Cain."

presence of the LORD and settled in the land of Nod, east of Eden.

(17) Cain knew his wife, and she conceived and bore Enoch. And he then founded a city, and named the city after his son Enoch. (18) To Enoch was born Irad, and Irad begot Mehujael, and Mehujael begot Methusael, and Methusael begot Lamech. (19) Lamech took to himself two wives: the name of the one was Adah, and the name of the other was Zillah. (20) Adah bore Jabal; he was the ancestor of those who dwell in tents and amidst herds. (21) And the name of his brother was Jubal; he was the ancestor of all who play the lyre and the pipe. (22) As for Zillah, she bore Tubal-cain, who forged all implements of copper and iron. And the sister of Tubal-cain was Naamah.

(23) And Lamech said to his wives,

> Adah and Zillah, hear my voice;
> O wives of Lamech, give ear to my speech.
> I have slain a man for wounding me,
> And a lad for bruising me.
> (24) If Cain is avenged sevenfold,
> Then Lamech seventy-sevenfold.

(25) Adam knew his wife again, and she bore a son and named him Seth, meaning, "God has provided me with another offspring in place of Abel," for Cain had killed him. (26) And to Seth, in turn, a son was born, and he named him Enosh. It was then that men began to invoke the LORD by name.[①]

---

① *Enosh.* A poetic term for "man." Antediluvian man is pictured as being close to God and knowing Him by name, and thus *began to invoke the Lord.* The culminating v. 26 speaks of what is, in the Jewish view, the most important of these: the proper worship of the true God.

3.2　Targum Pseudo-Jonathan to Genesis 4①

(1) *And* Adam was aware that *Eve his wife* had *conceived* from Sammael the angel, and she became pregnant *and bare Cain*, and he was like those on high, not like those below; and she *said*, "*I have* acquired *a man*, the angel of *the Lord.*"

(2) *And* she went on to bear from Adam, her husband, his twin sister and *Abel. And Abel was a keeper of sheep, but Cain was* a man working in the earth.

(3) *And* it was at the end of the days on the fourteenth of Nisan *that Cain brought of the fruit of the ground*, the seed of flax, *an offering* of first things before *the Lord.*

(4) *And Abel, he also brought of the firstlings of his flock and of the fat thereof. And* it was pleasing before the Lord, and the Lord showed favor *unto Abel and to his offering:*

(5) *but unto Cain and to his offering he* did not show favor. *And Cain was very wroth, and* the image of his face *fell.*

(6) *And the Lord said unto Cain, "Why art thou wroth? and why is* the image of your face *fallen?*

(7) Is it not the case that if you have done your work *well* your guilt will be forgiven you? But if you have not done your work *well* in this world your sin will be kept for the day of the great judgement, and at the doors of your heart sin lies waiting. And into your hand I have given the power of the inclination to evil, and towards you will be its *desire*, and you will have authority over it for righteousness or for sin."

(8) *And Cain* said to Abel his brother: "Come, and let us both go into the field." So it was that when they had both gone out into the field Cain answered and said to Abel: "I can see that the world was created in love,

---

①　Source: Bowker (1979), pp. 132 – 135. Words in italics represent what is in the Hebrew.

3 "AM I MY BROTHER'S KEEPER?": THE IMAGES OF CAIN

but it is not ordered by the issue of good works, because there is partiality in judgement; thus it is that your offering was accepted with favor, but my offering was not accepted with favor." Abel answered and said: "Certainly the world was created in love, and by the issue of good works it is ordered, and there is no partiality in judgement. But because the issue of my works was better than yours, so my offering has been accepted before yours with favor." Cain answered and said to Abel: "There is no judgement and no judge and no world hereafter; there is no good reward to be given to the righteous, nor any account to be taken of the wicked." Abel answered and said: "Certainly there is judgement and a judge and a world hereafter; there is a good reward to be given to the righteous, and the wicked will be called to account." And because of these words they fell into a dispute in the open field, and *Cain rose up against Abel his brother*, and drove a stone into his forehead, *and slew him.*

(9) *And the Lord said unto Cain, "Where is Abel thy brother?" And he said, "I know not: am I my brother's keeper?"*

(10) *And he said, "What hast thou done? The voice* of the bloods of the killing of your brother which were swallowed into the clay cry before *me from the ground.*

(11) *And now* because of your killing him *cursed art thou from the ground which hath opened her mouth to receive* the bloods *of thy brother from thy*

(12) *Hand: when thou tillest the ground it shall not* increase to give unto thee strength of her fruits. *A fugitive and a wanderer shalt thou be in the earth."*

(13) *And Cain said* before *the Lord:* "Severe indeed is my rebellion, more than to be borne, and yet it is possible with you to forgive it.①

---

① Cf. Targum Onkelos: "And Cain said before the Lord: 'Great is my guilt, more than to be forgiven.'" See also Cairo Geniza Fragment: "*And Cain said* before the Lord: 'Many are my sins, more than to be defended, and they are many before you to be absolved and forgiven.'"

(14) *Behold, thou hast* cast me forth *this day* on *the face of the ground; and from* before you can I ever *be hid?* But since I am *a fugitive and a wanderer in the earth*, any just person who *findeth me shall slay me.*"

(15) *And the Lord said unto him*, "*Therefore whosoever slayeth Cain* for seven generations it will be exacted from him." *And the Lord* marked on the face of Cain a letter from the great and glorious name,① that *any finding him* should not kill him when they saw it on him.

(16) *And Cain went out from* before *the Lord and dwelt in the land* of the wandering of his exile which was made on account of him from of old, like the garden of *Eden*.

(17) *And Cain knew his wife; and she conceived, and bare Enoch: and he builded a city, and called the name of the city, after the name of his son, Enoch.*

(18) *And unto Enoch was born Irad: and had begat Mehujael: and Mehujael begat Methushael: and Methushael begat Lamech.*

(19) *And Lamech took unto him two wives: the name of the one was Adah, and the name of the other Zillah.*

(20) *And Adah bare Jabal: he was the* lord *of such as dwell in tents and* are masters of *cattle*.

(21) *And his brother's name was Jubal: he was the* lord *of all such as* take part in the song with *the harp and pipe*.

(22) *And Zillah, she also bare Tubal-cain*, the lord of all workers who know the making of *brass and iron: and the sister of Tubal-cain was Naamah;* she was supreme in laments and songs.

(23) *And Lamech said unto his wives: "Adah and Zillah, hear my voice: ye wives of Lamech, hearken unto my speech: for I have* not *slain a man* that we should be killed on his account, nor have I injured *a young man* that my offspring should be destroyed on his account.

(24) Now *Cain* who had sinned and turned in repentance had seven generations extended to him; so is it not just that *Lamech*, the son of his son, who has not sinned, should be extended for seven and seventy?"

---

① I.e., a letter from the Tetragrammaton (YHWH).

(25) *And Adam knew his wife again* at the end of 130 years after the killing of Abel, *and she bare a son, and called his name Seth: for* she said: "The Lord has given me another *instead of Abel* whom *Cain slew.*"

(26) *And to Seth, to him also there was born a son; and he called his name Enosh.* That was the generation in whose days they began to err and make idols for themselves, and *to call* their idols by *the name of* the word of *the Lord.*

3.3 Genesis Rabbah, 22:12–13.
On the Mark and the Repentance of Cain

(12) "And the Lord set a sign for Cain" (Gen. 4:15). R. Judah said: He caused the orb of the sun to shine on his account. Said R. Nehemiah to him: For that wretch He would cause the orb of the sun to shine! Rather, he caused leprosy to break out on him, as you read, "And it shall come to pass, if they will not believe thee, neither hearken to the voice of the first sigh, etc." (Ex. 4:8)[①] Rav said: He gave him a dog. Abba Jose said: He made a horn grow out of him. Rav said He made him an example to murderers. R. Hanin said: He made him an example to penitents.[②] R. Levi said in the name of R. Simeon b. Lakish: He suspended judgment until the Flood came and swept him away, as it is written, "And He blotted out every living substance, etc." (Gen. 7:23)

(13) "And Cain went out from the presence of the Lord" (Genesis 4:16). Whence did he go out?[③] R. Aibu said: It means that he threw the words behind him and went out, like one who would deceive the Almighty. R. Berekiah said in R. Eleazar's name: He went forth like one who shows the

---

[①] The reference is to leprosy.

[②] I.e., The Lord made Cain a sign (to others)—according to Rav, of the fear that haunts a murderer, so that he needed a dog to protect him; according to Rabbi Hanin, of the saving power of repentance, which Cain displayed, so that God did not put him to death immediately.

[③] For one cannot go out from the presence of God, who is everywhere.

cloven hoof,① like one who deceives his Creator. R. Hanina b. Isaac said: He went forth rejoicing, as you read, "He goeth forth to meet thee, and when he seeth thee, he will be glad in his heart." (Ex. 4:14) Adam met him and asked him, "How did your case go?" "I repented and am reconciled," replied he. Thereupon Adam began beating his face, crying, "So great is the power of repentance, and I did not know!" Forthwith he arose and exclaimed, "A Psalm, a song for the Sabbath day: It is a good thing to make confession unto the Lord." (Ps. 92:1)②

3.4 Augustine, *Contra Faustum Manichaeum* XII, 9–13. A Christian Typological Interpretation of Cain and Abel (400 CE)③

(9) As Cain's sacrifice of the fruit of the ground is rejected, while Abel's sacrifice of his sheep and the fat thereof is accepted, so the faith of the New Testament praising God in the harmless service of grace is preferred to the earthly observances of the Old Testament. For though the Jews were right in practicing these things, they were guilty of unbelief in not distinguishing the time of the New Testament when Christ came, from the time of the Old Testament... (10) God asks Cain where his brother is, not as if He did not know, but as a judge asks a guilty criminal. Cain replies that he knows not, and that he is not his brother's keeper. And what answer can the Jews give at this day, when we ask them with the voice of God, that is, of the sacred Scriptures, about Christ, except that they do not know the Christ that we speak of? Cain's ignorance was pretended, and the Jews are deceived in their refusal of Christ. Moreover, they would have been in a sense keepers of Christ, if they had been willing to receive and keep the Christian faith.

---

① I.e., a hypocrite. A swine shows his cloven hoof as though pretending to be clean.

② The original verse reads: "A psalm. A song; for the Sabbath day. It is good to praise the Lord."

③ Source: Translated by Richard Stothert, from Christian Classics Ethereal Library: http://www.ccel.org/ccel/schaff/npnf104.iv.ix.xiv.html, accessed April 12, 2019.

3 "AM I MY BROTHER'S KEEPER?": THE IMAGES OF CAIN

For the man who keeps Christ in his heart does not ask, like Cain, Am I my brother's keeper? Then God says to Cain, "What hast thou done? The voice of thy brother's blood crieth unto me from the ground." So the voice of God in the Holy Scriptures accuses the Jews. For the blood of Christ has a loud voice on the earth, when the responsive Amen of those who believe in Him comes from all nations. This is the voice of Christ's blood, because the clear voice of the faithful redeemed by His blood is the voice of the blood itself.

(11) Then God says to Cain: "Thou art cursed from the earth, which hath opened its mouth to receive thy brother's blood at thy hand. For thou shalt till the earth, and it shall no longer yield unto thee its strength. A mourner and an abject shalt thou be on the earth." It is not, Cursed is the earth, but, Cursed art thou from the earth, which hath opened its mouth to receive thy brother's blood at thy hand. So the unbelieving people of the Jews is cursed from the earth, that is, from the Church, which in the confession of sins has opened its mouth to receive the blood shed for the remission of sins by the hand of the people that would not be under grace, but under the law. And this murderer is cursed by the Church; that is, the Church admits and avows the curse pronounced by the apostle: "Whoever are of the works of the law are under the curse of the law."[①] Then, after saying, Cursed art thou from the earth, which has opened its mouth to receive thy brother's blood at thy hand, what follows is not, For thou shalt till it, but Thou shalt till the earth, and it shall not yield to thee its strength. The earth he is to till is not necessarily the same as that which opened its mouth to receive his brother's blood at his hand. From this earth he is cursed, and so he tills an earth which shall no longer yield to him its strength. That is, the Church admits and avows the Jewish people to be cursed, because after killing Christ they continue to till the ground of an earthly circumcision, an earthly Sabbath, an earthly Passover, while the hidden strength or virtue of making known Christ, which this tilling contains, is not yielded to the Jews while they continue in impiety and unbelief, for it is revealed in the New Testament. While they will not turn to

---

① Galatians 3:10.

God, the veil which is on their minds in reading the Old Testament is not taken away. This veil is taken away only by Christ, who does not do away with the reading of the Old Testament, but with the covering which hides its virtue. So, at the crucifixion of Christ, the veil was rent in twain, that by the passion of Christ hidden mysteries might be revealed to believers who turn to Him with a mouth opened in confession to drink His blood. In this way the Jewish people, like Cain, continue tilling the ground, in the carnal observance of the law, which does not yield to them its strength, because they do not perceive in it the grace of Christ. So too, the flesh of Christ was the ground from which by crucifying Him the Jews produced our salvation, for He died for our offences. But this ground did not yield to them its strength, for they were not justified by the virtue of His resurrection, for He arose again for our justification. As the apostle says: "He was crucified in weakness, but He liveth by the power of God."[①] This is the power of that ground which is unknown to the ungodly and unbelieving. When Christ rose, He did not appear to those who had crucified Him. So Cain was not allowed to see the strength of the ground which he tilled to sow his seed in it; as God said, "Thou shalt till the ground, and it shall no longer yield unto thee its strength."

(12) "Groaning and trembling shalt thou be on the earth." Here no one can fail to see that in every land where the Jews are scattered they mourn for the loss of their kingdom, and are in terrified subjection to the immensely superior number of Christians. So Cain answered, and said: "My case is worse, if Thou drivest me out this day from the face of the earth, and from Thy face shall I be hid, and I shall be a mourner and an outcast on the earth; and it shall be that every one that findeth me shall slay me." Here he groans indeed in terror, lest after losing his earthly possession he should suffer the death of the body. This he calls a worse case than that of the ground not yielding to him its strength, or than that of spiritual death. For his mind is carnal; for he thinks little of being hid from the face of God, that is, of being under the anger of God, were it not

---

① 2 Corinthians 13:4.

that he may be found and slain. This is the carnal mind that tills the ground, but does not obtain its strength. To be carnally minded is death; but he, in ignorance of this, mourns for the loss of his earthly possession, and is in terror of bodily death. But what does God reply? "Not so," He says; "but whosoever shall kill Cain, vengeance shall be taken on him sevenfold." That is, It is not as thou sayest; not by bodily death shall the ungodly race of carnal Jews perish. For whoever destroys them in this way shall suffer sevenfold vengeance, that is, shall bring upon himself the sevenfold penalty under which the Jews lie for the crucifixion of Christ. So to the end of the seven days of time, the continued preservation of the Jews will be a proof to believing Christians of the subjection merited by those who, in the pride of their kingdom, put the Lord to death.

(13) "And the Lord God set a mark upon Cain, lest anyone finding him should slay him." It is a most notable fact, that all the nations subjugated by Rome adopted the heathenish ceremonies of the Roman worship; while the Jewish nation, whether under Pagan or Christian monarchs, has never lost the sign of their law, by which they are distinguished from all other nations and peoples. No emperor or monarch who finds under his government the people with this mark kills them, that is, makes them cease to be Jews, and as Jews to be separate in their observances, and unlike the rest of the world. Only when a Jew comes over to Christ, he is no longer Cain, nor goes out from the presence of God, nor dwells in the land of Nod, which is said to mean commotion. ①

---

① Shortly before his death, Pope John XXIII (1958–1963) composed the following prayer dedicated to Jesus in atonement for the Church's history of antisemitism: "We are conscious today that many, many centuries of blindness have cloaked our eyes so that we can no longer see the beauty of Thy chosen people nor recognize in their faces the features of our privileged brethren. We realize that the mark of Cain stands upon our foreheads. Across the centuries our brother Abel has lain in blood which we drew, or shed tears we caused by forgetting Thy love. Forgive us for the curse we falsely attached to their name as Jews. Forgive us for crucifying Thee a second time in their flesh. For we know not what we did." See https://insidethevatican.com/magazine/pope/incomparable-pope-john-xxiii-jews-long, accessed April 12, 2019.

3.5 Louis Ginzberg, The Jewish Legends on Cain (1909)[①]

The Birth of Cain

Wickedness came into the world with the first being born of woman, Cain, the oldest son of Adam. When God bestowed Paradise upon the first pair of mankind, He warned them particularly against carnal intercourse with each other. But after the fall of Eve, Satan, in the guise of the serpent, approached her, and the fruit of their union was Cain, the ancestor of all the impious generations that were rebellious toward God, and rose up against Him. Cain's descent from Satan, who is the angel Samael, was revealed in his seraphic appearance. At his birth, the exclamation was wrung from Eve, "I have gotten a man through an angel of the Lord."

Adam was not in the company of Eve during the time of her pregnancy with Cain. After she had succumbed a second time to the temptations of Satan, and permitted herself to be interrupted in her penance, she left her husband and journeyed westward, because she feared her presence might continue to bring him misery. Adam remained in the east. When the days of Eve to be delivered were fulfilled, and she began to feel the pangs of travailing, she prayed to God for help. But He hearkened not unto her supplications. "Who will carry the report to my lord Adam?" she asked herself. "Ye luminaries in the sky, I beg you, tell it to my master Adam when ye return to the east!" In that selfsame hour, Adam cried out: "The lamentation of Eve has pierced to my ear! Mayhap the serpent has again assaulted her," and he hastened to his wife. Finding her in grievous pain, he besought God in her behalf, and twelve angels appeared, together with two heavenly powers. All these took up their post to right of her and to left

---

[①] Source: Ginzberg (2003), pp. 101 – 109. Ginzberg's copious footnotes, packed with scholarship, are not included here.

of her, while Michael, also standing on her right side, passed his hand over her, from her face downward to her breast, and said to her, "Be thou blessed, Eve, for the sake of Adam. Because of his solicitations and his prayers I was sent to grant thee our assistance. Make ready to give birth to thy child!" Immediately her son was born, a radiant figure. A little while and the babe stood upon his feet, ran off, and returned holding in his hands a stalk of straw, which he gave to his mother. For this reason he was named Cain, the Hebrew word for stalk of straw.

Now Adam took Eve and the boy to his home in the east. God sent him various kinds of seeds by the hand of the angel Michael, and he was taught how to cultivate the ground and make it yield produce and fruits, to sustain himself and his family and his posterity.

After a while, Eve bore her second son, whom she named Hebel, because, she said, he was born but to die.

Fratricide

The slaying of Abel by Cain did not come as a wholly unexpected event to his parents. In a dream Eve had seen the blood of Abel flow into the mouth of Cain, who drank it with avidity, though his brother entreated him not to take all. When she told her dream to Adam, he said, lamenting, "O that this may not portend the death of Abel at the hand of Cain!" He separated the two lads, assigning to each an abode of his own, and to each he taught a different occupation. Cain became a tiller of the ground, and Abel a keeper of sheep. It was all in vain. In spite of these precautions, Cain slew his brother.

His hostility toward Abel had more than one reason. It began when God had respect unto the offering of Abel, and accepted it by sending heavenly fire down to consume it, while the offering of Cain was rejected. They brought their sacrifices on the fourteenth day of Nisan, at the instance of their father, who had spoken thus to his sons: "This is the day on which, in times to come, Israel will offer sacrifices. Therefore, do ye, too, bring sacrifices to your Creator on this day, that He may take pleasure in you." The place of offering which they chose was the spot whereon the altar of the Temple at Jerusalem stood later. Abel selected the best of his flocks for his sacrifice, but Cain ate his meal first, and after he had satisfied his appetite, he offered unto God what was left over, a few grains of flax seed. As though his offense had not been great enough in offering unto God fruit of the ground which had been cursed by God! What wonder that his sacrifice was not received with favor! Besides, a chastisement was inflicted upon him. His face turned black as smoke. Nevertheless, his disposition underwent no change, even when God spoke to him thus: "If thou wilt amend thy ways, thy guilt will be forgiven thee; if not, thou wilt be delivered into the power of the evil inclination. It coucheth at the door of thy heart, yet it depends upon thee whether thou shalt be master over it, or it shall be master over thee."

Cain thought he had been wronged, and a dispute followed between him and Abel. "I believed," he said, "that the world was created through goodness, but I see that good deeds bear no fruit. God rules the world with arbitrary power, else why had He respect unto thy offering, and not unto mine also?" Abel opposed him; he maintained that God rewards good deeds, without having respect unto persons. If his sacrifice had been accepted graciously by God, and Cain's not, it was because his deeds were good, and his brother's wicked.

But this was not the only cause of Cain's hatred toward Abel. Partly love for a woman brought about the crime. To ensure the propagation of the human race, a girl, destined to be his wife, was born together with each of the sons of Adam. Abel's twin sister was of exquisite beauty, and Cain desired her. Therefore he was constantly brooding over ways and means of ridding himself of his brother.

The opportunity presented itself ere long. One day a sheep belonging to Abel tramped over a field that had been planted by Cain. In a rage, the latter called out, "What right hast thou to live upon my land and let thy sheep pasture yonder?" Abel retorted: "What right hast thou to use the products of my sheep, to make garments for thyself from their wool? If thou wilt take off the wool of my sheep wherein thou art arrayed, and wilt pay me for the flesh of the flocks which thou hast eaten, then I will quit thy land as thou desirest, and fly into the air, if I can do it." Cain thereupon said, "And if I were to kill thee, who is there to demand thy blood of me?" Abel replied: "God, who brought us into the world, will avenge me. He will require my blood at thine hand, if thou shouldst slay me. God is the Judge, who will visit their wicked deeds upon the wicked, and their evil deeds upon the evil. Shouldst thou slay me, God will know thy secret, and He will deal out punishment unto thee."

These words but added to the anger of Cain, and he threw himself upon his brother. Abel was stronger than he, and he would have got the worst of it, but at the last moment he begged for mercy, and the gentle Abel released his hold upon him. Scarcely did he feel himself free, when he turned against Abel once more, and slew him. So true is the saying, "Do the evil no good, lest evil fall upon thee."

The Punishment of Cain

The manner of Abel's death was the most cruel conceivable. Not knowing what injury was fatal, Cain pelted all parts of his body with stones, until one struck him on the neck and inflicted death.

After committing the murder, Cain resolved to flee, saying, "My parents will demand account of me concerning Abel, for there is no other human being on earth." This thought had but passed through his mind when God appeared unto him, and addressed him in these words: "Before thy parents thou canst flee, but canst thou go out from My presence, too? 'Can any hide himself in secret places that I shall not see him?' Alas for Abel that he showed thee mercy, and refrained from killing thee, when he had thee in his power! Alas that he granted thee the opportunity of slaying him!"

Questioned by God, "Where is Abel thy brother?" Cain answered: "Am

I my brother's keeper? Thou art He who holdest watch over all creatures, and yet Thou demandest account of me! True, I slew him, but Thou didst create the evil inclination in me. Thou guardest all things; why, then, didst Thou permit me to slay him? Thou didst Thyself slay him, for hadst Thou looked with a favorable countenance toward my offering as toward his, I had had no reason for envying him, and I had not slain him." But God said, "The voice of thy brother's blood issuing from his many wounds crieth out against thee, and likewise the blood of all the pious who might have sprung from the loins of Abel."

Also the soul of Abel denounced the murderer, for she could find rest nowhere. She could neither soar heavenward, nor abide in the grave with her body, for no human soul had done either before. But Cain still refused to confess his guilt. He insisted that he had never seen a man killed, and how was he to suppose that the stones which he threw at Abel would take his life? Then, on account of Cain God cursed the ground, that it might not yield fruit unto him. With a single punishment both Cain and the earth were chastised, the earth because it retained the corpse of Abel, and did not cast it above ground.

In the obduracy of his heart, Cain spake: "O Lord of the world! Are there informers who denounce men before Thee? My parents are the only living human beings, and they know naught of my deed. Thou abidest in the heavens, and how shouldst Thou know what things happen on earth?" God said in reply: "Thou fool! I carry the whole world. I have made it, and I will bear it"—a reply that gave Cain the opportunity of feigning repentance. "Thou bearest the whole world," he said, "and my sin Thou canst not bear? Verily, mine iniquity is too great to be borne! Yet, yesterday Thou didst banish my father from Thy presence, today Thou dost banish me. In sooth, it will be said, it is Thy way to banish."

Although this was but dissimulation, and not true repentance, yet God granted Cain pardon, and removed the half of his chastisement from him. Originally, the decree had condemned him to be a fugitive and a wanderer on the earth. Now he was no longer to roam about forever, but a fugitive he

3 "AM I MY BROTHER'S KEEPER?": THE IMAGES OF CAIN

was to remain. And so much was hard enough to have to suffer, for the earth quaked under Cain, and all the animals, the wild and the tame, among them the accursed serpent, gathered together and essayed to devour him in order to avenge the innocent blood of Abel. Finally Cain could bear it no longer, and, breaking out in tears, he cried: "Whither shall I go from Thy spirit? Or whither shall I flee from Thy presence?" To protect him from the onslaught of the beasts, God inscribed one letter of His Holy Name upon his forehead, and furthermore He addressed the animals: "Cain's punishment shall not be like unto the punishment of future murderers. He has shed blood, but there was none to give him instruction. Henceforth, however, he who slays another shall himself be slain." Then God gave him the dog as a protection against the wild beasts, and to mark him as a sinner, He afflicted him with leprosy.

Cain's repentance, insincere though it was, bore a good result. When Adam met him, and inquired what doom had been decreed against him, Cain told how his repentance had propitiated God, and Adam exclaimed, "So potent is repentance, and I knew it not!" Thereupon he composed a hymn of praise to God, beginning with the words, "It is a good thing to confess thy sins unto the Lord!" The crime committed by Cain had baneful consequences, not for himself alone, but for the whole of nature also. Before, the fruits which the earth bore unto him when he tilled the ground had tasted like the fruits of Paradise. Now his labor produced naught but thorns and thistles. The ground changed and deteriorated at the very moment of Abel's violent end. The trees and the plants in the part of the earth whereon the victim lived refused to yield their fruits, on account of their grief over him, and only at the birth of Seth those that grew in the portion belonging to Abel began to flourish and bear again. But never did they resume their former powers. While, before, the vine had borne nine hundred and twenty-six different varieties of fruit, it now brought forth but one kind. And so it was with all other species. They will regain their pristine powers only in the world to come.

Nature was modified also by the burial of the corpse of Abel. For a long time it lay there exposed, above ground, because Adam and Eve knew not what to do with it. They sat beside it and wept, while the faithful dog of Abel kept guard that birds and beasts did it no harm. On a sudden, the mourning parents observed how a raven scratched the earth away in one spot, and then hid a dead bird of his own kind in the ground. Adam, following the example of the raven, buried the body of Abel, and the raven was rewarded by God. His young are born with white feathers, wherefore the old birds desert them, not recognizing them as their offspring. They take them for serpents. God feeds them until their plumage turns black, and the parent birds return to them. As an additional reward, God grants their petition when the ravens pray for rain.

3.6 Dan Pagis, *Autobiography*

I died with the first blow and was buried
among the rocks of the field.
The raven taught my parents
what to do with me.

If my family is famous,
not a little of the credit goes to me.
My brother invented murder,
my parents invented grief,
I invented silence.

Afterwards the well-known events took place.
Our inventions were perfected. One thing led to another,
orders[①] were given. There were those who murdered in their own way,
grieved in their own way.

---

① I.e., commandments (*tzav*).

I won't mention names
out of considerations of the reader,
since at first the details horrify
though finally they're a bore:

you can die once, twice, even seven times,
but you can't die a thousand times.
I can.
My underground cells[1] reach everywhere.

When Cain began to multiply on the face of the earth,
I began to multiply in the belly of the earth,
and my strength has long been greater than his.
His legions desert him and go over to me,
and even this is only half a revenge.

3.7 Dan Pagis, *Written in Pencil in the Sealed Railway-Car*

Here in this carload
I am Eve
with Abel my son
if you see my older son
Cain son of Adam[2]
tell him that I

---

[1] The Hebrew (*ta*) can denote both "prison room" and "the smallest part of a living thing that can exist independently."

[2] The Hebrew "son of Adam" (*ben Adam*) also means "person" or "human being." In addition, the whole line "Cain son of Adam" (*Kayin ben Adam*) is a homonym to the Yiddish *keyn ben Adom* (not a person).

4　THE TEST OF ABRAHAM: AKEDAH

4.1　Genesis 22:1-19

(1) Some time afterward,① God put Abraham to the test. He said to him, "Abraham," and he answered, "Here I am."②(2) And He said, "Take your son, your favored one, Isaac, whom you love,③ and go to④ the land of Moriah,⑤ and offer him there as a burnt offering on one of the heights that I will point out to you." (3) So early next morning, Abraham saddled his ass and took with him two of his servants and his son Isaac. He split the wood

---

① Others, "*After these things*," or "*After these words.*"
② There is no good English equivalent for the Hebrew "*hineni*," translated in this verse as "Here I am." The term indicates readiness, alertness, attentiveness, receptivity, and responsiveness to instructions. It serves as a kind of refrain throughout the Akedah. Abraham employs it in answer to God here, to Isaac in v. 7 (where it is rendered as "Yes"), and to the angel of the LORD in v. 11.
③ The order of the Hebrew is "your son, your favored one, the one whom you love, Isaac" and indicates increasing tension.
④ *go to*. This expression ("*lekh-lekha*"), which otherwise occurs only in Gen. 12:1 ("*Go forth* from your native land..."), the initial command to Abraham, ties this narrative to the beginning of Abraham's dealings with God.
⑤ *Moriah*. The original name is obscure and the actual location unknown. Subsequent biblical tradition, however, has suggested that it refers to the Temple mount in Jerusalem (2 Chron. 3:1). The Septuagint does not mention Moriah, perhaps because *moria* in Greek means "folly." It is believed that the city's famed Dome of the Rock is built over the rock on which Abraham bound his son.

for the burnt offering, and he set out for the place of which God had told him. (4) On the third day Abraham looked up and saw the place from afar. (5) Then Abraham said to his servants, "You stay here with the ass. The boy and I will go up there; we will worship and we will return to you."

(6) Abraham took the wood for the burnt offering and put it on his son Isaac. He himself took the fire and the knife; and the two walked off together. (7) Then Isaac said to his father Abraham, "Father!" And he answered, "Yes, my son." And he said, "Here are the fire and the wood; but where is the sheep for the burnt offering?" (8) And Abraham said, "God will see to the sheep for His burnt offering, my son." And the two of them walked on together.

(9) They arrived at the place of which God had told him. Abraham built an altar there; he laid out the wood; he bound his son Isaac; he laid him on the altar, on top of the wood. (10) And Abraham picked up the knife to slay his son. (11) Then an angel of the LORD called to him from heaven: "Abraham! Abraham!" And he answered, "Here I am." (12) And he said, "Do not raise your hand against the boy, or do anything to him. For now I know① that you fear God,② since you have not withheld your son, your favored one, from Me." (13) When Abraham looked up, his eye fell upon a ram, caught in the thicket by its horns. So Abraham went and took the ram and offered it up as a burnt offering in place of his son. (14) And Abraham named that site Adonai-yireh,③ whence the present saying, "On the mount

---

① *For now I know.* According to *Genesis Rabbah* 56:7, this means, "I have made it known to all."

② In the Tanakh, the "fear of God" (*yirat elohim*) is an expression meaning to be in awe of God and hence to do God's will. God is now able to call the trial of Abraham off because Abraham has demonstrated that this obedience is uppermost for him, surpassing even his paternal love for Isaac. The fear of God is described as the beginning of knowledge (Proverbs 1:7). And the book of Kohelet (Ecclesiastes) concludes with these words: "The sum of the matter, when all is said and done: Fear God and keep His commandments. For this applies to all mankind: that God will call every creature to account for everything unknown, be it good or bad" (12:13–14). See also 8.5.

③ I.e., "the Lord will see," an allusion to verse 8.

of the LORD there is vision."

(15) The angel of the LORD called to Abraham a second time from heaven, (16) and said, "By Myself I swear, the LORD declares: Because you have done this and have not withheld your son, your favored one, (17) I will bestow My blessing upon you and make your descendants as numerous as the stars of heaven and the sands on the seashore; and your descendants shall seize the gates of their foes. (18) All the nations of the earth shall bless themselves by your descendants, because you have obeyed My command."①

(19) Abraham then returned to his servants, and they departed together for Beer-sheba; and Abraham stayed in Beer-sheba.

4.2 Targum Pseudo-Jonathan to Genesis 22:1–19②

(1) It came to pass after these things—after Isaac and Ishmael had quarrelled. Ishmael said: "It is right for me to be the heir of my father, since I am his firstborn son;" while Isaac said: "It is right for me to be the heir of my father, since I am the son of Sarah his wife, but you are the son of Hagar, the handmaid of my mother." Ishmael answered and said: "I am more righteous than you, because I was circumcised when I was thirteen years old; and if I had wanted to refuse, I would not have allowed myself to be circumcised. But you were circumcised when eight days old. If you had had knowledge, perhaps you would not have allowed yourself to be circumcised." Isaac answered and said: "Behold, I am thirty-seven years old this day. If the Holy One, blessed be He, were to demand *all* my limbs, I would not refuse." Immediately these words were heard before the Lord of

---

① 15 – 18: The second angelic address conveys the LORD's final blessing on Abraham, picking up the language of several earlier addresses (cf. 12:3; 13:16; 15:5). Only this time, the earlier promises are reinterpreted as a consequence of the Akedah. Much Jewish prayer calls upon God to remember the Akedah for the benefit of Abraham's descendants.

② Source: Alexander (1984).

the universe, and immediately the Word of the Lord tested Abraham and said to him, "Abraham"; and he said, "Here am I."

(2) He said: "Take now your son, your only son, whom you love, even Isaac, and go into the land of worship; and offer him there for a burnt offering on one of the mountains which I will tell you of."

(3) Abraham rose early in the morning, saddled his ass, and took with him his two young men, Eliezer and Ishmael, as well as Isaac his son. He chopped the wood of the olive, the fig and the palm, which are proper for the burnt offering, and he rose up and went to the place of which the Lord had told him.

(4) On the third day Abraham lifted up his eyes and saw the cloud of glory smoking on the mountain, and he recognized it from afar.

(5) Abraham said to his young men: "Wait here with the ass, and I and the lad will go yonder to find out if what I was promised—'So shall your seed be' (Gen. 15:5)—will ever be fulfilled. We will worship the Lord of the universe, and come again to you."

(6) Abraham took the wood of the burnt offering, laid it upon Isaac his son, took in his hand the fire and the knife, and both of them went together.

(7) Isaac spoke to Abraham his father and said, "Father," and he said, "Here am I, my son." Isaac said, "Behold the fire and the wood, but where is the lamb for the burnt offering?"

(8) Abraham said: "The Lord will choose for himself the lamb for a burnt offering, my son." So they went both of them with a perfect heart together.

(9) They came to the place which God had told him of. Abraham built there the altar which Adam had built, but which had been destroyed in the waters of the flood. Noah had rebuilt it, but it was again destroyed in the generation of the division of tongues (Gen. 11:1 – 9). Abraham set in order the wood upon it, bound Isaac his son, and laid him on the altar, upon the wood.

(10) Then Abraham stretched out his hand and took the knife to sacrifice his son. Isaac answered and said to his father: "Bind me well so

that I may not struggle in the anguish of my soul, lest a blemish be found in your offering, and I be cast into the pit of destruction." The eyes of Abraham looked at the eyes of Isaac, but the eyes of Isaac looked at the angels on high: Isaac saw them, but Abraham did not see them. The angels on high answered: "Come and see these two unique men in the earth. One sacrifices and the other is his victim; the one who sacrifices does not hesitate, the one to be sacrificed stretches out his neck."

(11) The angel of the Lord called to Abraham out of heaven and said to him, "Abraham, Abraham," and he said, "Here am I."

(12) He said: "Do not lay your hand on the lad, nor do him any harm, for it is now revealed before me that you fear the Lord, and that you have not withheld your son, your only son, from me."

(13) Abraham lifted up his eyes and looked, and behold, a ram—one that had been created on the evening when the work of creation was finished—caught in the branches of a tree by its horns. Abraham went and took the ram, and offered it up for a burnt offering instead of his son.

(14) Abraham gave thanks and prayed there in that place, and said: "I beseech you by the mercy that is before you, O Lord: it is revealed before you that there was no insincerity in my heart, but I sought to perform your decree with joy; so, when the descendants of Isaac my son shall come to the time of distress, remember them, hear their supplications, and deliver them, and all generations to come will say, 'In this mountain Abraham bound Isaac, his son, and there the Shekhinah of the Lord was revealed to him.'"

(15) The angel of the Lord called to Abraham a second time from heaven(16) and said: "By my Word I have sworn, says the Lord, that, because you have done this thing, and have not withheld your son, your only son, (17) I will surely bless you and I will indeed multiply your sons as the stars of the heaven and as the sand on the sea shore; and your sons shall inherit the cities of their enemies. (18) Because of the merit of your sons all the peoples of the earth shall be blessed, because you have obeyed my voice."

(19) And the angels from on high took Isaac and brought him to the

school of Shem the great, and he was there for three years. And on the same day Abraham returned to his young men, and they arose and went together to Beer-sheba; and Abraham dwelt at Beer-sheba.

4.3 Genesis Rabbah on Akedah

4.3.1 Genesis Rabbah 55:7. On "Take...Thy Son"

AND HE SAID: TAKE, I PRAY THEE, THY SON, etc. (22:2) Said He to him: "TAKE, I PRAY THEE—I beg thee—THY SON." "Which son?" he asked. "THINE ONLY SON, replied He. "But each is the only one of his mother?"①—"WHOM THOU LOVEST."—"Is there a limit to the affections?" "EVEN ISAAC," said He. And why did He not reveal it to him without delay? In order to make him [Isaac] even more beloved in his eyes and reward him for every word spoken. This agrees with the dictum of R. Johanan, who said: *Get thee out of thy country* (Gen. 12:1) means from thy province; *And from thy kindred* (ibid.)—from the place where thou art settled; *And from thy father's house* —literally thy father's house. *Unto the land that I will show thee* (ibid.). Why did He not reveal it to him there and then? In order to make it more beloved in his eyes and to reward him for every step.

4.3.2 Genesis Rabbah 56:4. Samael versus Abraham

AND ISAAC SPOKE UNTO ABRAHAM HIS FATHER, AND SAID: MY FATHER (22:7). Samael② went to the Patriarch Abraham and upbraided him

---

① Abraham has two only sons: Ishmael is Hagar's only son and Isaac is Sarah's only son.

② A wicked angel; Satan.

saying: "What means this, old man! Hast thou lost thy wits? Thou goest to slay a son granted thee at the age of a hundred!"① "Even this I do," replied he. "And if He sets thee an even greater test, canst thou stand it?" said he, as it is written, *If a thing be put to thee as a trial, wilt thou be wearied* (Job 4:2)? "Even more than this," he replied. "Tomorrow He will say to thee, 'Thou art a murderer, and art guilty,'" "Still am I content," he rejoined. Seeing that he could achieve nought with him, he approached Isaac and said: "Son of an unhappy mother! He goes to slay thee." "I accept my fate," he replied. "If so," said he, "shall all those fine tunics which thy mother made be a legacy for Ishmael, the hated of her house?"② If a word is not wholly effective, it may yet avail in part; hence it is written, AND ISAAC SPOKE UNTO ABRAHAM HIS FATHER, AND SAID: MY FATHER: why HIS FATHER... MY FATHER?③ So that he should be filled with compassion for him. AND HE SAID: BEHOLD, THE FIRE AND THE WOOD. "May that man be drowned who has thus incited him," exclaimed he.④ "At all events, GOD WILL PROVIDE HIMSELF THE LAMB, O my son; and if not, THOU ART FOR A BURNT-OFFERING, MY SON." SO THEY WENT BOTH OF THEM TOGETHER—one to slaughter and the other to be slaughtered.

4.3.3　Genesis Rabbah 56:8. Isaac Afraid

(Another comment: R. Isaac said: When Abraham wished to sacrifice his son Isaac, he said to him: "Father, I am a young man and am afraid that my body may tremble through fear of the knife and I will grieve thee, whereby slaughter may be rendered unfit and this will not count as a real sacrifice; therefore bind me very firmly." Forthwith, HE BOUND ISAAC: can one

---

① See Genesis 21:5.
② See Genesis 21:10.
③ I.e., why the repetition of the word *father*?
④ Abraham invokes a curse on Samael for provoking Isaac to question God.

bind a man thirty-seven years old?(another version: twenty-six years old)①
without his consent? Presently, and ABRAHAM STRETCHED FORTH HIS
HAND—he stretched forth his hand to take the knife while the tears
streamed from his eyes, and these tears, prompted by a father's compassion,
dropped into Isaac's eyes. Yet even so, his heart rejoiced to obey the will of
his Creator. The angels assembled in groups above. What did they cry? *The
highways lie waste, the wayfaring man ceaseth; He hath broken the
covenant, He hath despised the cities* (Isa. 33:8)—has He no pleasure in
Jerusalem and the Temple, which He had intended giving as a possession to
the descendants of Isaac? *He regardeth not man* (ibid.): if no merit has stood
in Abraham's favor, then no creature has any value before him.②

R. Aha said: [Abraham wondered]: Surely Thou too indulgest in
prevarication! Yesterday Thou saidest, *For in Isaac shall seed be called to
thee* (Gen. 21:12); Thou didst then retract and say, *Take now thy son* (ibid. 22:
2); while now Thou biddest me, LAY NOT THY HAND UPON THE LAD!
Said the Holy One, blessed be He, to him: "O Abraham, *My covenant will I
not profane* (Ps. 89:35), *and I will establish My covenant with Isaac* (Gen. 17:
21). When I bade thee, "*Take now thy son*," etc, *I will not alter that which
is gone out of My lips* (Ps. *loc. cit.*). Did I tell thee, Slaughter him? No! but,
"Take him up."③ Thou hast taken him up. Now take him down.

---

① These are attempts at clarifying the biblical chronology, which is not specific about Isaac's age.

② If Isaac dies, then the promise and the covenant die with him, and Israel will no longer be God's people.

③ That is, "Take Isaac up on the mountain." But the phrase *to take up* means "to sacrifice" since one category of sacrifices is the *olah* (literally, "rising up") in which the sacrifice is wholly burned and, thus, "rises up" to God. Thus, God's command might be interpreted in two ways, allowing God a legalist loophole to countermand the trial he sets for Abraham.

4.3.4 Genesis Rabbah 56:9. Akedah and Shofar-Blowing

AND ABRAHAM LIFTED UP HIS EYES, AND LOOKED, AND BEHOLD BEHIND HIM (*AHAR*) A RAM (22:13). What does *AHAR* mean? Said R. Judah: After[①] all that happened, Israel still fall into the clutches of sin and [in consequence] become the victims of persecution; yet they will be ultimately redeemed by the ram's horn, as it says, "*And the Lord God will blow the horn*" etc. (Zech. 9:14). R. Judah b. R. Simon interpreted: At the end of [after] all generations Israel will fall into the clutches of sin and be the victims of persecution; yet eventually they will be redeemed by the ram's horn, as it says, "*And the Lord God will blow the horn*" etc. R. Hanina b. R. Isaac said: Throughout the year Israel are in sin's clutches and led astray by their troubles, but on New Year they take the *shofar* and blow on it,[②] and eventually they will be redeemed by the ram's horn, as it says, "*And the Lord God will blow the horn.*" R. Abba b. R. Pappi and R. Joshua of Siknin in R. Levi's name said: Because the Patriarch Abraham saw the ram extricate himself from one thicket and go and become entangled in another, the Holy One, blessed be He, said to him: "So will thy children be entangled in countries, changing from Babylon to Media, from Media to Greece, and from Greece to Edom;[③] yet they will eventually be redeemed by the ram's horn," as it is written, "*And the Lord God will blow the horn... the Lord of hosts will defend them.*" (ibid. 14f.)

---

① The Hebrew *ahar*, "behind," can also mean "after."
② Blowing the shofar, or ram's horn, is an act performed on the Jewish New Year.
③ *Edom.* Rome.

4.3.5 Genesis Rabbah 55:2. The Lord Tries the Righteous

The Lord trieth the righteous, etc. (Ps. 11:5).[1] R. Jonathan said: A potter does not examine defective vessels, because he cannot give them a single blow without breaking them. What then does he examine? Only the sound vessels, for he will not break them even with many blows. Similarly, the Holy One, blessed be He, tests not the wicked but the righteous, as it says, *"The Lord trieth the righteous."* R. Jose b. R. Hanina said: When a flax worker knows that his flax is of good quality, the more he beats it the more it improves and the more it glistens; but if it is of inferior quality, he cannot give it one knock without it splitting. Similarly, the Lord does not test the wicked but only the righteous, as it says, *"The Lord trieth the righteous."* R. Eleazar said: When a man possesses two cows, one strong and the other feeble, upon which does he put the yoke? Surely upon the strong one similarly, God tests none but the righteous, as it says, *"The Lord trieth the righteous."*

4.4 Babylonian Talmud, Sanhedrin 89b. On Akedah

"And it came to pass after these things [words] that God tested Abraham" (Gen.22:1): What is meaning of "after"? Said R. Yohanan in the name of R. Yose b. Zimra: It was after the words of Satan. For it is written, "And the child grew up and was weaned and Abraham made a great feast the same day that Isaac was weaned" (Gen. 21:8). Said Satan to the Holy One, blessed be he, "Lord of the world, as to this old man, you have shown him grace by giving him the fruit of the womb at one hundred years. Now of the entire

---

[1] The midrash adduces this verse in order to understand why God tries (i.e., tests) Abraham.

meal that he has made, he did not have a single pigeon or a single dove to offer before you." He said to him, "Has he done anything at all except to honor his son? [But] if I were to say to him, 'Sacrifice your son before me,' he would sacrifice him immediately." Forthwith: "And God tested Abraham."(Gen. 22:1)

"And he said, Take, I pray you, your son."(Gen. 22:2) Said R. Simeon b. Abba, "The word 'I pray you' [na] bears the meaning only of supplication. The matter may be compared to the case of a mortal king, against whom many wars were fought. He had one powerful leader, who won all his battles. After a while a very difficult war was waged against him. He said to him, 'By your leave, stand up for me in this war too, so that people will not say that, as to the earlier wars, they really did not add up to much.' So the Holy One, blessed be he, said to Abraham, 'I tried you in a number of trials and you stood up to all of them. Now stand up for me in this trial as well, so that people will not say that, as to the earlier trials, they really did not add up to much.'"

"Your son" (Gen. 22:2)—"I have two sons." "Your only son" (Gen. 22:2)—"This one is an only son for his mother, and that one is an only son for his mother." "Whom you loved" (Gen. 22:2)—"I love them both." "Isaac"(Gen. 22:2). Why all this? So that he should not be confused.

Satan met him on the way and said to him, "If we try to commune with you, will you be grieved? ... Behold you have instructed many, and you have strengthened weak hands. Your words have held up him who was falling, and you have strengthened feeble knees. But now it is come upon you, and you faint"(Job 4:2-5). He said to him, "I will walk in my integrity." (Psa. 26:2) He said to him, "But should not your fear by your confidence"(Job 4:6). He said to him, "Remember, I pray you, whoever perished, being innocent?"(Job 4:6) Since [Satan] saw that he would not listen to him, he said to him, "Now a thing was secretly brought to me(Job 4:12). This I have heard from the other side of the curtain: 'The lamb is for a burnt-offering (Job 4:7)—and Isaac is not for a burnt-offering.'" This is the penalty paid by a liar, that even when he tells the truth, people do not pay any attention to him.

[Explaining, "After these words" (Gen. 22:1),] said R. Levi, "After the words between Ishmael and Isaac. Ishmael said to Isaac, 'I am greater than you in the performance of religious duties, for you were circumcised on the eighth day, while I was circumcised in the thirteenth year.' He said to him, 'And on account of one limb are you going to put me down? If the Holy One, blessed be he, were to say to me, "Sacrifice yourself before me," I should sacrifice myself immediately.' 'And God tried Abraham'." (Gen. 22:1)

4.5 *Pirkei de-Rabbi Eliezer*, 31.
The Death and Resurrection of Isaac①

Rabbi Jehudah said: When the blade touched his neck, the soul of Isaac fled and departed, (but) when he heard His voice from between the two Cherubim, saying (to Abraham), "Lay not thine hand upon the lad" (Gen. 22:12), his soul returned to his body, and [Abraham] set him free, and Isaac stood upon his feet. And Isaac knew that in this manner the dead in the future will be quickened. He opened (his mouth), and said: "Blessed art thou, O Lord, who quickeneth② the dead."

4.6 Rashi on Gen. 22:1-2.

After these words. Some of our Rabbis say (Sanh. 89b) [that it means] "after the words of Satan," who denounced Abraham saying: "Of all the banquets which Abraham prepared not a single bullock nor a single ram did he bring as a sacrifice to You." God replied to him, "Does he do anything at all except for his son's sake? Yet if I were to bid him, 'Sacrifice

---

① Source: Translation by Gerald Friedlander (London, 1916), see https://www.sefaria.org/Pirkei_DeRabbi_Eliezer? lang=en&p2=Pirkei_DeRabbi_Eliezer.14.5&lang2=en.

② *quickeneth.* Gives life to.

him to Me,' he would not refuse." Others say [that it means] "after the words of Ishmael," who boasted to Isaac that he had been circumcised when he was thirteen years old without resisting. Isaac replied to him, "You think to intimidate me by [mentioning the loss of] one part of the body! If the Holy One, blessed be he, were to tell me, 'Sacrifice yourself to Me' I would not refuse" (Genesis Rabbah 55 and Sanh. 89b). *Here I am.* Such is the answer of the pious: it is an expression of meekness and readiness. *Take, now (kah-na).* The word *na* is used as a request: God said to him, "I beg of you, stand firm for me in this trial, so that people may not say that the previous trials were no real [tests]." *Thy son.* Abraham said [to God], "I have two sons." He answered him, "Thine only son." Abraham said, "This one is the only son of his mother and the other is the only son of his mother." *The One Whom thou lovest.* Abraham replied, "I love both of them." *Isaac.* Why did He not disclose this to him at the very first? So as not to confuse him suddenly lest his mind become distracted and bewildered [and in this confused state he would involuntarily consent, when there would have been no merit in his sacrifice], and so that he might more highly value God's command and that God might reward him [for the increasing sacrifice demanded by obedience to] each and every expression [used here].

4.7　Moses Maimonides, *The Guide of the Perplexed.* Ⅲ. 24. On Akedah

The subject of trial is also very difficult; it is one of the greatest difficulties of the Law. The Torah mentions it in six passages, as I shall make clear to you in this chapter. What is generally accepted among people regarding the subject of trial is this: God sends down calamities upon an individual, without their having been preceded by a sin, in order that his reward be increased. However, this principle is not at all mentioned in the Torah in an explicit text. And there is in the Torah only one passage among the six whose external meaning suggests such a notion; I shall explain its meaning. The principle of the Law that runs counter to this opinion, is that contained in His dictum, may He be exalted: "A God of faithfulness and without iniquity." (Deut. 32:4) Nor do all the Sages profess this opinion of the multitude, for they say sometimes: "There is no death without sin and no sufferings without transgression." (B. T., Sabbath 55a) And this is the opinion that ought to be believed by every adherent of the Law who is endowed with intellect, for he should not ascribe injustice to God, may He be exalted above this, so that he believes that Zayd is innocent of sin and is perfect and that he does not deserve what befell him. However, the external meaning of the trials mentioned in the Torah in the passages in question is that they took place in order to test and to receive information so that one could know the degree of faith or the degree of obedience of the individual or nation in question. And this is the great difficulty, especially in the story of the binding, which was known only to God and to the two individuals involved, to one of whom it was said: "For now I know that thou fearest God." (Gen. 22:12) It is the same with regard to its dictum: "For the Lord your God tries you out, to know whether ye do love the Lord" (Deut. 13:4), and so on. And also with regard to its dictum: "To know what was in thy heart" (Deut. 8:2), and so on. Now I will resolve all these difficulties for you.

Know that the aim and meaning of all the trials mentioned in the Torah is to let people know what they ought to do or what they must believe. Accordingly, the notion of a trial consists as it were in a certain act being done, the purpose being not the accomplishment of that particular act, but the latter's being a model to be imitated and followed. Thus the interpretation of its dictum—"To know whether ye do love" (Deut. 13:4)—is not: in order that God should know that, for He already knew it; but the meaning resembles that of its dictum—"To know that I am the Lord that doth sanctify you" (Exod. 31:13)—the meaning of which is: in order that the religious communities should know. In the same manner [Scripture] says (Deut. 13:2 ff.): If a man claiming prophecy arise and if you see his suggestions tend to make one believe in the truth of his claim, know that

God wished to make known hereby to the religious communities the extent of your certitude with regard to His Law, may He be exalted, and your apprehension of its true reality; and also to make known that you do not let yourselves be deceived by the deceptions of a deceiver and that your faith in God cannot be disturbed. This will be a support for everyone who seeks the truth, for he will seek out the beliefs that are so firm that when one has them one pays no attention to the man who tries to compete through working a miracle. For this man issues a call to believe in impossible things, whereas a competition as to miracles is only useful when something possible is claimed, as we have made clear in *Mishneh Torah*.

After it has been made clear that the meaning of "to know" here is: in order that people should know, the same can be said with regard to its dictum concerning manna: "That He might afflict thee, to try thee out, to know what was in thy heart, whether thou wouldest keep His commandments, or no." (Deut. 8:2) The meaning of this is: in order that the religious communities should know this and that it should be generally accepted throughout the world that those who wholly devote themselves to His service, may He be exalted, are provided by Him with food in an unthought-of way. The same notion is expressed when manna is spoken of on the occasion when it first came down: "That I may try them out, whether they will walk in My Torah, or no" (Exod. 16:4); which means: in order that everyone should consider this and should see whether being devoted to His service is useful and sufficient or not sufficient. As for what is said [in Scripture] for the third time again concerning manna—namely, "Who fed thee in the wilderness with manna, which thy fathers knew not, that He might afflict thee, and that He might try thee out [*nasotekha*], to do thee good at thy latter end" (Deut. 8:16)—it may suggest that God sometimes makes an individual suffer in order that his reward be greater. But this is not the truth of the matter. For this dictum has one of two meanings: One of them is the notion concerning *manna* repeatedly expressed in the first and second dictum, namely: in order that it should be known whether being devoted to God does or does not suffice as far as food is concerned and gives relief from fatigue and weariness. Or *nasotekha* [*try thee out*] may mean: to accustom thee, this being an interpretation that can refer to its dictum: "is not accustomed [*nisstah*] to set the sole of her foot" (Deut. 28: 56), and so on. It is as if it said that He, may He be exalted, has first accustomed you to misery in the desert in order to make your well-being greater when once you came into the land. And this is true, for to pass from weariness to rest is more pleasant than to be constantly at rest. And it is known that but for their misery and weariness in the desert, they would not have been able to conquer the land and to fight. The Torah literally states this: "For God said: Lest peradventure the people repent when they see war, and they return to Egypt. But God led the people about, by the way of the wilderness of the Sea of Reeds" (Exod. 13:17 – 18). For prosperity does away with courage, whereas a hard life and fatigue necessarily produce courage— this being the good that, according to the story in question, will come "at their latter end" (Deut. 8:16).

As for its dictum, "For God is come to try you out" (Exod. 20:17), it expresses the same notion as the one stated in Deuteronomy concerning a man claiming "to prophesy in the name of an idol: For the Lord your God tries you out" (Deut. 13:4), the meaning of which we have made clear. He told them similarly here at the Gathering at Mount Sinai: Be not afraid; this great gathering that you have seen has taken place only in order that you acquire certitude through sight, so that if, in order to make publicly known the extent of your faith, "the Lord your God tried you out with a false prophet" (Deut. 13:4) who would call upon you to demolish what you have heard, you should remain firm and keep your feet from stumbling. For if I had come to you as a prophet, as you had thought, and I had said to you what had been said to me without your hearing it for yourselves, it would have been possible for you to fancy that what is told by another is true even if that other had come to you with something contradicting what has been made known to you; this is what could have happened if you had not heard it at this gathering.

As for the story of Abraham at the binding (of Isaac), it contains two great notions that are fundamental principles of the Law. One of these notions consists in our being informed of the limit of love for God, may He be exalted, and fear of Him—that is, up to what limit they must reach. For in this story he was ordered to do something that bears no comparison either with sacrifice of property or with sacrifice of life. In truth it is the most extraordinary thing that could happen in the world, such a thing that one would not imagine that human nature was capable of it. Here there is a sterile man having an exceeding desire for a son, possessed of great property and commanding respect, and having the wish that his progeny should become a religious community. When a son comes to him after his having lost hope, how great will be his attachment to him and love for him! However, because of his fear of Him, who should be exalted, and because of his love to carry out His command, he holds this beloved son as little, gives up all his hopes regarding him, and hastens to slaughter him after a journey of days. For if he had chosen to do this immediately, as soon as the order came to him, it would have been an act of stupefaction and disturbance in the absence of exhaustive reflection. But his doing it days after the command had come to him shows that the act sprang from thought, correct understanding, consideration of the truth of His command, may He be exalted, love of Him, and fear of Him. No other circumstance should be put forward, nor should one opt for the notion that he was in a state of passion. For Abraham our Father did not hasten to slaughter Isaac because he was afraid that God would kill him or make him poor, but solely because of what is incumbent upon the Adamites—namely, to love Him and fear Him, may He be exalted —and not, as we have explained in several passages, for any hope of a reward or for fear of punishment. Accordingly the angel said to him: "For now I know that thou fearest God" (Gen. 22:12): meaning that through the act because of which the term fearing God is applied to you, all the Adamites will know what the limits of the fear of the Lord are. Know that this notion is corroborated and explained in the Torah, in which it is mentioned that the final end of the whole of the Torah, including its commandments, prohibitions, promises, and narratives, is one thing only—

namely, fear of Him, may He be exalted. This is referred to in its dictum: "If thou wilt not take care to observe all the words of this Law that are written in this book, that thou mayest fear this glorious and awesome Name" (Deut. 28:58), and so on. This is one of the two notions aimed at in the binding.

The second notion consists in making known to us the fact that the prophets consider as true that which comes to them from God in a prophetic revelation. For it should not be thought that what they hear or what appears to them in a parable is not certain or is commingled with illusion just because it comes about in a dream and in a vision, as we have made clear, and through the intermediary of the imaginative faculty. Accordingly, [Scripture] wished to make it known to us that all that is seen by a prophet in a vision of prophecy is, in the opinion of the prophet, a certain truth, that the prophet has no doubts in any way concerning anything in it, and that in his opinion its status is the same as that of all existent things that are apprehended through the senses or through the intellect. A proof for this is the fact that [Abraham] hastened to slaughter, as he had been commanded, "his son, his only son, whom he loved" (Gen. 22:2), even though this command came to him in a dream or in a vision. For if a dream of prophecy had been obscure for the prophets, or if they had doubts or incertitude concerning what they apprehended in a vision of prophecy, they would not have hastened to do that which is repugnant to nature, and [Abraham's] soul would not have consented to accomplish an act of so great an importance if there had been a doubt about it.

In truth it was fitting that this story, I mean the binding, should come to pass through the hand of Abraham and in regard to someone like Isaac. For Abraham our Father was the first to make known the belief in Unity, to establish prophecy, and to perpetuate this opinion and draw people to it. It says: "For I have known him, to the end that he may command his children and his household after him, that they may keep the way of the Lord, to do righteousness and judgment." (Gen. 18:19) Thus just as they followed his correct and useful opinions, namely, those that were heard from him, so ought one to follow the opinions deriving from his actions and especially from this action through which he validated the fundamental principle affirming the truth of prophecy and made known to us the ultimate end toward which the fear and love of God may reach.

It is in this way that the meaning of trials should be understood. And it should not be believed that God, may He be exalted, wants to test and try out a thing in order to know that which He did not know before. How greatly is He exalted above that which is imagined by ignorant fools in their evil thoughts! Know this.

4.8 Amir Gilboa, *Isaac*

At dawn, the sun strolled in the forest
together with me and father,
and my right hand was in his left.

Like lightning a knife flashed among the trees.
And I am so afraid of my eyes' terror, faced by blood on the leaves.

Father, father, quickly save Isaac
so that no one will be missing at the midday meal.

It is I who am being slaughtered, my son,
and already my blood is on the leaves.
And father's voice was smothered.
And his face was pale.

And I wanted to scream, writhing not to believe,
and tearing open my eyes.
And I woke up.

And my right hand was drained of blood.

4.9 Hayyim Gouri, *Heritage*

The ram came last of all. And Abraham did not know that it came to answer the boy's question—first of his strength when his day was on the wane.

The old man raised his head. Seeing that it was no dream and that the angel stood there—the knife slipped from his hand.

The boy, released from his bonds, saw his father's back.

Isaac, as the story goes, was not sacrificed. He lived for many years, saw what pleasure had to offer, until his eyesight dimmed.

But he bequeathed that hour to his offspring. They are born with a knife in their hearts.

5 YAVAN IN THE TENTS OF SHEM: JEWS AMIDST GREEKS AND ROMANS

5.1 Philo, *On the Creation*, 69–71.
On Man's Creation after the Image of God

(69) ... Moses① tells us that man was created after the image of God and after His likeness (Gen. 1:26). Right well does he say this, for nothing earth-born is more like God than man. Let no one represent the likeness as one to a bodily form; for neither is God in human form,② nor is the human body

---

① Philo regards the Creation account as the work of the prophet and lawgiver Moses. Moses's role as lawgiver is consistent with Greek ideas about the founder of a community. The Rabbis would not call Moses "lawgiver," since only God gave the Torah, whereas it came "through Moses's hand."

② *For neither is God in human form.* In Greek mythology and art, the gods were frequently represented as having a human appearance. Hellenistic Judaism fiercely opposed this "anthropomorphic" conception of divinity.

God-like. No, it is in respect of the Mind, the sovereign element of the soul,① that the word "image" is used. For after the pattern of a single Mind, even the Mind of the Universe as an archetype, the mind in each of those who successively came into being was moulded.② It is in a fashion a god to him③ who carries and enshrines it as an object of reverence; for the human mind evidently occupies a position in men precisely answering to that which the great Ruler occupies in all the world. It is invisible while itself seeing all things, and while comprehending the substances of others, it is as to its own substance unperceived;④ and while it opens by arts and sciences roads branching in many directions, all of them great highways, it comes through land and sea investigating what either element contains. (70) Again, when on soaring wing it has contemplated the atmosphere and all its phases,⑤ it is borne yet higher to the ether and the circuit of heaven, and is whirled round with the dances of planets and fixed stars, in accordance with

---

① *The Mind, the sovereign element of the soul.* The philosophical background of Philo's view of human nature is basically Platonist. Human beings consist of body and soul. The former is physical, can be seen by the senses, experiences pleasure and pain, and is prone to getting sick. The latter is spread throughout the body and experiences the thoughts and feelings that allow humans to direct the body to action. The soul itself can be divided into two parts. There is the rational part, the mind or intellect, and there is the irrational part, which is responsible for feelings, emotions, and drives. Philo firmly believes that the rational part should direct the exercise control over the irrational part; otherwise things will go wrong for human beings.

② Philo draws an analogy between God as the Mind of the Universe and the Mind as directing element in the human being.

③ Remarkably, Philo here likens the human mind to a god. Hellenistic Judaism in general, and Philo in particular, is not puritanical in the use of the term god (*theos*).

④ The mind cannot be studied as physical objects can.

⑤ Philo illustrates the power of the human mind by imagining that it makes a tour of the whole reality, beginning on earth, ascending to the heavens, and then going on even further to the higher reality of the intelligible world that only the mind can contemplate. An important source for the motif is the famous myth in Plato's *Phaedrus*, in which the soul ascends on the wings of love, join Zeus and his heavenly chariot, and contemplates the ideas.

the laws of perfect music, following that love of wisdom① which guides its steps. And so, carrying its gaze beyond the confines of all substance discernible by sense, it comes to a point at which it reaches out after the intelligible world. (71) And on descrying in that world sights of surpassing loveliness, even the patterns and the originals of the things of sense which it saw here, it is seized by a sober intoxication,② like those filled with Corybantic frenzy,③ and is inspired, possessed by a longing for other than theirs and a nobler desire.④ Wafted by this to the topmost arch of the things perceptible to mind, it seems to be on its way to the Great King⑤ Himself; but, amid its longing to see Him, pure and untempered rays of concentrated light stream forth like a torrent, so that by its gleams the eye of the mind is dazzled.⑥

5.2 Josephus, *Jewish Antiquities*, 1:222–236. On Akedah

(222) Now Isaac was passionately beloved of his father Abraham, being his

---

① *Love of wisdom.* Philo is prepared to adapt for his own purposes the Platonic theme of love (erōs), which starts with love of body and ascends to the pure love of knowledge. For Philo, love of knowledge is fused with love for God.

② *A sober intoxication.* The famous mystical motif common in Philo. The soul is so carried away with its love for knowledge and for God that it forgets itself and its earth-bound situation and becomes filled with ecstasy.

③ *Corybantic frenzy.* The Corybants were the followers of the Greek god Dionysus, who worked themselves into a frenzy with their whirling dances.

④ *A nobler desire.* The Platonic erōs motif now gets an unexpected twist. The mind wishes to ascend beyond the intelligible world to God himself.

⑤ *The Great King.* In Greek culture the Great King was the King of Persia, who had an absolute power far beyond any Greek ruler. The image is often used by Philo to convey his conception of God as absolute monarch.

⑥ It is not possible for the mind to see God's essential nature, so the ascent cannot achieve its final goal. If human beings could see God as he really is, then they would be situated at his level and would no longer be "after his image." Philo here assumes the conclusions of his negative theology, that is, that we can ultimately know about God only that we cannot know him.

only son and born to him "on the threshold of old age"[1] through the bounty of God. On his side, the child called out the affection of his parents and endeared himself to them yet more by the practice of every virtue, showing attention to his ancestors[2] and exhibiting zeal for the worship of God. (223) Abraham thus reposed all his own happiness on the hope of leaving his son unscathed[3] when he departed this life. This object he indeed attained by the will of God, who, however, desiring to make trial of his piety towards Himself, appeared to him and after enumerating[4] all the benefits that He had bestowed upon him— (224) how He had made him stronger than his enemies, and how it was His benevolence to which he owed his present felicity and his son Isaac—required him to offer up that son by his own hand as a sacrifice and victim to Himself. He bade him take the child up to the Morion Mount, erect an altar and make a holocaust[5] of him: thus would he manifest his piety towards Himself, if he put the doing of God's good pleasure even above the life of his child.

(225) Abraham, deeming that nothing would justify disobedience to God and that in everything he must submit to His will, since all that befell

---

[1] *Threshold of old age.* Josephus here uses the same phrase that Homer (*Iliad* 24:487) employs when Priam addresses Achilles, begging him to return his son Hector's body; he reminds him at the height of the pathetic mode of address, that Achilles's father is as old as Priam "on the deadly threshold of old age."

[2] The very first quality of Isaac's character that Josephus sees fit to mention is precisely the one, veneration for one's ancestors, that both his Hellenistic Greek and Roman audience would have appreciated the most.

[3] *Unscathed.* This word that Josephus uses here has two very different meanings: "not suffering" and "emotionless"—both of which are actually applicable to Isaac. The term "unscathed" is a particularly common Stoic term for freedom from emotion. This is a prime example where Josephus makes Jewish values coincide with those of Stoics.

[4] *After enumerating.* The Bible begins the narrative of this test of Abraham by God with the vague words "after these things." Josephus clarifies this by enumerating the benefits that God had bestowed upon Abraham and thus justifies the test.

[5] *Holocaust.* The Greek translation of Hebrew "burnt offering [*olah*, lit. 'that which goes up']." The term is also used of the Nazi extermination of Jews during the Second World War.

His favoured ones was ordained by His providence, concealed from his wife① God's commandment and his own resolve concerning the immolation of the child; nay, revealing it not even to any of his household, lest haply he should have been hindered from doing God's service, he took Isaac with two servants and having laden an ass with the requisites for the sacrifice departed for the mountain. (226) For two days the servants accompanied him, but on the third, when the mountain was in view, he left his companions in the plain and proceeded with his son alone to that mount whereon king David afterwards erected the temple. (227) They brought with them all else needed for the sacrifice except a victim. Isaac, therefore, who was now twenty-five years of age,② while constructing the altar, asked what sacrifice they were about to offer, having no victim; to which his father replied that God would provide for them, seeing that He had power alike to give men abundance of what they had not and to deprive of what they had those who felt assured of their possessions: He would therefore grant him too a victim, should He vouchsafe to grace his sacrifice with His presence.

(228) But when the altar had been prepared and he had laid the cleft wood upon it and all was ready,③ he said to his son:

---

① *Concealed from his wife.* Josephus may well have had in mind a comparison with Euripides's drama *Iphigenia at Aulis*, where a father similarly pondered whether to sacrifice his child. According to Euripides (*Iphigenia at Aulis* 98), Agamemnon attempted to deceive his wife Clytemnestra by writing a letter to her asking her to send their daughter Iphigenia to be married to Achilles, while his real intention was to sacrifice her to the goddess Artemis.

② *Twenty-five years of age.* Isaac's age at the time of *Akedah* is variously given in Rabbinic literature. Josephus mentions his age presumably because he considered it important to make it clear that Isaac was not a mere lad but a grown man able to make a deliberate choice, thus diminishing the horror that such a story would arouse in Josephus's readers, to judge from Lucretius's comments (1:101) in his retelling the parallel story of Iphigenia. See also 4.3.3.

③ *All was ready.* Missing from Josephus is the most important word in the biblical account, *aqed* (to bind) /*akedah* (binding) that is featured in later Rabbinic reference to this incident.

"My child, myriad were the prayers in which I besought God for thy birth, and when thou camedst into the world, no pains were there that I did not lavish upon thine upbringing, no thought had I of higher happiness than to see thee grown to man's estate and to leave thee at my death heir to my dominion. (229) But, since it was by God's will that I became thy sire and now again as pleases Him I am resigning thee, bear thou this consecration valiantly; for it is to God I yield thee, to God who now claims from us this homage in return for the gracious favour He has shown me as my supporter and ally. (230) Aye, since thou wast born [out of the course of nature, so]① quit thou now this life not by the common road, but sped by thine own father on thy way to God, the Father of all, through the rites of sacrifice. He, I ween, accounts it not meet for thee to depart this life by sickness or war or by any of the calamities that commonly befall mankind, (231) but amid prayers and sacrificial ceremonies would receive thy soul② and keep it near to Himself; and for me thou shalt be a protector and stay of my old age—to which end above all I nurtured thee—by giving me God in the stead of thyself.③"

(232) The son of such a father could not but be brave-hearted, and Isaac received these words with joy. He exclaimed that he deserved never to have been born at all, were he to reject the decision of God and of his father and not readily resign himself to what was the will of both, seeing that, were

---

① There is clearly a lacuna in the Greek, and the phrase "out of the course of nature" should be supplied. This trait of being born in an extraordinary way and leaving life in a similarly extraordinary way is common in biographies of Greek and Roman heroes (e.g. Heracles, Theseus, Oedipus, and Romulus). Josephus mentions Isaac's good birth at the moment that Abraham is about to sacrifice him.

② *Soul.* This alludes to the immortality of the soul.

③ *He said to his son.* The Rabbis (Genesis Rabbah 56:15) emphasize Abraham's address to God, in which he asserts that although he could have argued against the divine decree, he did not do so. Such an appeal is fraught with the problems of theodicy. Josephus omits this, in line with his effort to avoid theological problems. Instead, he invents Abraham's address to his son of the type that we find in the progymnasmatic rhetorical exercises of Seneca the Elder.

this the resolution of his father alone, it would have been impious to disobey; and with that he rushed to the altar and his doom. (233) And the deed would have been accomplished, had not God stood in the way, for He called upon Abraham by name, forbidding him to slay the lad. It was, He said, from no craving for human blood① that He had given command for the slaughter of his son, nor had He made him a father only to rob him in such impious fashion of his offspring; no, He wished but to test his soul and see whether even such orders would find him obedient. (234) Now that He knew the ardour and depth of his piety. He took pleasure in what He had given him and would never fail to regard with the tenderest care both him and his race; his son should attain to extreme old age and, after a life of felicity, bequeath to a virtuous and lawfully begotten offspring a great dominion. (235) He moreover foretold that their race would swell into a multitude of nations, with increasing wealth, nations whose founders would be had in everlasting remembrance, that they would subdue Canaan by their arms and be envied of all men. (236) Having spoken thus God brought from obscurity② into their view a ram for the sacrifice. And they, restored to each other beyond all hope and having heard promises of such great felicity, embraced one another and, the sacrifice ended,③ returned home to Sarah and

---

① *No craving for human blood.* In this God would seem to be in direct contrast to Artemis, who, according to Euripides in *Iphigenia at Aulis* 1524 – 25, "rejoices in human sacrifice." Moreover, Josephus, fully aware that Jews had been charged with a blood libel by Damocritus (in Suidas) and Apion (in *Against Apion* 2:91 – 96), stresses in this speech, put into the mouth of God rather than an angel as in Gen. 22:11, that the God of Jews does not crave for human blood.

② *Brought from obscurity.* The scene of the ram caught in a thicket by its horns may have seemed too much of a miracle for a rationalizing Greek mind. Instead, Josephus states merely that God brought the ram from obscurity into view, with the clear implication that it had always been there.

③ Josephus does not explicitly state, as does the Bible (Gen. 22:13), that Abraham offered the ram in place of his son.

lived in bliss,① God assisting them in all that they desired.

5.3 Jewish Inscriptions in Greek

5.3.1 A Warning Inscription of the Second Temple
(Jerusalem; First century CE)②

No alien may enter within the balustrade around the sanctuary and the enclosure. Whoever is caught, on himself shall he put blame for the death which will ensue.

5.3.2 The Theodotos Synagogue Inscription
(Jerusalem; probably before 70 CE)③

Theodotos son of Vettenus, priest and *archisynagōgos*,④ son of an

---

① *Lived in bliss.* This ending—that is, a "lived in bliss ever after" finale, so typical of Hellenistic novels—is Josephus's addition to the Bible.

② Source: Bickerman (1947). It was one of many similar signs set into the partition around the Temple that divided between those areas allowed to all and the sanctified area into which only Jews were permitted. Cf. Josephus, *Jewish War*, 5. 5. 2: "in this (balustrade) at regular intervals stood slabs giving warning, some in Greek, others in Latin characters, of the law of purification, to wit that no foreigner was permitted to enter the holy place..."

③ Source: Kloppenborg (2006). This inscription (100×8×20 cm) was discovered by French scholars in a cistern just south of the Temple Mount in Jerusalem. The focus upon Torah study within this synagogue accords well with literary sources from the later Second Temple period (Acts 6:9; Tesefta Megillah 2:12).

④ *Archisynagōgos.* This title, meaning "synagogue leader," is without doubt synonymous with the Hebrew title *rosh knesset*, see Levine (2005), pp. 415–427.

archisynagōgos and grandson of an *archisynagōgos*, built the assembly hall (*synagōgē*)① for the reading of the Law and for the teaching of the commandments, and the guest-room,② the chambers, and the water fittings,③ as an inn for those in need from foreign parts, (the synagogue) which his fathers founded with the elders and Simonides.

5.3.3 An Inscription Concerning Jews and Godfearers (Aphrodisias in Caria, West Turkey; Third Century CE [?])④

Face a⑤

God the Helper, who puts [food] on our plate.

Those listed below from the Society of the Law-Lovers, also known as those who continuously offer praise,⑥ in order to alleviate suffering(?), have

---

① *Synagōgē* was common among the Greeks. They used it loosely in the sense of a meeting or gathering and as a formal term for a religious association. It is by far the most frequently attested and most widely diffused term for Jewish community. By the first century CE its meaning had even become extended, designating not simply the individual congregation but its meeting place too—whence the English word synagogue. Formerly that had been called the *proseuche*, meaning "sacred place," i.e., the prayer-house.

② Probably located on Mt Ophel, where this stone was found.

③ Needed for purificatory purposes.

④ Sources: Reynolds and Tannenbaum(1987); Williams(1998). The inscription records a charitable donation to a synagogue community by Jews(including a few proselytes) and a category of "Godfearers" (*theosebeis*). The text is inscribed on two faces of a marble block which may possibly have functioned as a door-jamb. The lettering on face b. suggests a date in the late second or early third century; that on face a. is different, and cannot be assigned to a specific century within the Imperial or late-Roman period. It remains unclear whether or not the two inscribed faces contain a single text.

⑤ The following appears to be a list of subscribers to a Jewish institution. Its function is described as being for the relief of sorrow among the people. The Jewish character is unmistakable from the names which follow.

⑥ Since prayer and Torah study are the principal, almost the only, religious exercise of Judaism after 70 CE, it is logical to assume that ancient Jewish associations did indeed study and pray together.

built (this) memorial for the community (*plethos*)[1] out of their own resources.

> Iael, *prostates*,[2]
> with her/his son Iosoua, *archon*[3]
> Theodotos, *palatinos*,[4] with
> his son Hilarianos
> Samuel, *archi* (*dekanos*?), proselyte
> Ioses, son of Iesse
> Beniamin, psalm-singer[5]
> Ioudas, the contented one[6]
> Ioses, proselyte
> Sabbatios, son of Amachios
> Emmonios, Godfearer (*theosebes*)
> Antoninos, Godfearer (*theosebes*)
> Samouel, son of Politianos
> Eioseph, son of Eusebios, proselyte[7]
> And Eioudas, son of Theodoros
> And Antipeos, son of Hermes

---

[1] *Plethos*, lit. "multitude," besides being used by the Greeks themselves as a term for the whole community in an administrative/constitutional sense, was the broad equivalent of a Hebrew organizational term, *ha-rabim*.

[2] *Prostates*, lit. "one who stands before," is a common Greek word for president.

[3] *Archon*, lit. "ruler." Found throughout the Diaspora, the *archons* are the most frequently attested of all synagogal officers. It is known that they were elected at the Jewish New Year.

[4] *Palatinos* seems to denote Theodotus was a former employee of an emperor's court, or a financial official in a provincial governor's service.

[5] On the attraction to non-Jews of the synagogal liturgy and especially its melody, see John Chrysostom, *Adversus Iudaeos* 1.7.

[6] Or, "the good-tempered."

[7] This and the following three lines were at some point added to the original inscription by a different hand.

And Sabathios, the sweet one (?)

[And?] Samouel, envoy, priest

Face b①

[Iose]ph, son of Zenon

[Ze]non, son of Iakob; Manases, son of Ioph (Job?)

Ioudas, son of Eusebios

Heortasios, son of Kallikarpos

Biotikos; Ioudas, son of Amphianos

Eugenios, goldsmith

Praoilios; Ioudas, son of Praoilios

Rouphos; Oxycholios, old man(the elder?)

Amantios, son of Charinos; Myrtilos

Iako, shepherd;② Seberos

Euodos; Iason, son of Euodos

Eusabbathios, greengrocer; Anysios

Eusabbathios, foreigner; Milon

Oxycholios, the younger

Diogenes; Eusabbathios, son of Diogenes

Ioudas, son of Paulos; Theophilos

[I]a[k]ob, also called Apellion; Zacharias, retailer(?)

[Le]ontios, son of Leontios; Gemellos

[Io]udas, son of Acholios; Damonikos

---

① The following is an acephalous donor(?)-list. The first half of it consists of a list of members of the Jewish community, including a large number with Hebrew names and/or patronymics. There is then a break of one line, and a list of *theosebeis* (Godfearers). The first nine are described as "city-councillor" (*bouleutes*), and the total of names are fifty. There are no Hebrew name, but one person is called "Eusabbathios." The text is important for illustrating how numerous *theosebeis* could be in any one community and from what a wide social range they could be drawn. Moreover, it provides the hard evidence for the reality of a defined category of gentile Godfearers attached to a Jewish community and distinguished both from Jews and from full proselytes.

② Or possibly, "sheep-rearer."

Eutarkios, son of Ioudas; Ioseph, son of Philer(iphos?)
Eusabbathios, son of Eugenios
Kyrillos; Eutychios, bronze-(smith?)
Ioseph, confectioner; Rouben, confectioner
Ioudas, son of Hortasios; Eutychios, poulterer
Ioudas, also called Zosi(mos?); Zenon, rag-dealer
Ammianos, dealer in horse-fodder(?); Ailianos, son of Ailianos
Ailianos, also called Samouel; Philanthos
Gorgonios, son of Oxycholios; Heortasios, son of Achilleus
Eusabbathios, son of Oxycholios; Paregorios
Heortasios, son of Zotikos; Symeon, son of Zen(on?)

And such as are *theosebeis* (Godfearers). Zenon, city councillor
Tertullos, city councillor; Diogenes, city councillor
Onesimos, city councillor; Zenon, son of Longi(nos?), city councillor
Antipeos, city councillor; Antiochos, city councillor
Romanos, city councillor; Aponerios, city councillor
Eupithios, purple merchant; Strategios
Xanthos; Xanthos, son of Xanthos
Aponerios, son of Aponerios; Hypsikles, son of Mel(iton?)
Polychronios, son of Xanthos; Athenion, son of Ai(lianos?)
Kallimorphos, son of Kal(limorphos?); Ioun(ios?) Balos(?)
Tychikos, son of Tychikos; Glegorios, son of Tychikos
Polychronios, son(?) of Bel(?); Chrysippos
Gorgonios, coppersmith(?); Tatianos, Oxy(cholios?)
Apellas, son of Hege(mon?); Balerianos, maker of wooden tablets?
Eusabbathios, son of Hed (ychroos?); Ma (rkos) Anikios (?), son of Attalos(?)
Hortasios, stone-carver; Brabeus
Klaudianos, son of Kal(limorphos?); Alexandros, son of(?)
Appianos, son of(?); Adolios, mincemeat-maker
Zotikos, armlet-maker(?); Zotikos, Egyptian-dance performer(?)

Eupithios, son of Eupithios; Patrikios, coppersmith
Elpidianos, athlete(?); Hedychrous
Eutropios, son of Hedychrous; Kallinikos
Balerianos, treasurer(?); Heuretos, son of Athenag(oras)
Paramonos, maker of images(?)
Eutychianos, fuller; Protokopios, money-changer(?)
Prounikios, fuller; Stratonikos, fuller
Athenagoras, carpenter
Meliton, son of Amazonios

5.3.4　A Jewish Poetical Epitaph (Beth She'arim; Third Century CE)[①]

I, the son of Leontios, lie dead, Justus, the son of Sappho,[②]
Who, having plucked the fruits of all wisdom,[③]
Left the light, my poor parents in endless mourning,
And my brothers too, alas, in my Besara.[④]

---

① Source: Schwabe and Lifshitz (1974), no. 127. The use of patronymic in this inscription is an imitation of Homeric language, by which the author of the inscription was influenced.

② *Sappho*, which is used here to resemble the name of the famous Greek poetess, is phonetically a Greek equivalent of the Judeo-Aramaic name *saphira* ("the beautiful").

③ *All wisdom*. Perhaps the qualifying adjective "all" is meant to tell that the deceased devoted his time not only to Jewish wisdom (i.e. Torah study), but also to Greek wisdom. It is known that the Torah study flourished at Beth She'arim, especially during the period when this place served as the seat of the Sanhedrin. On the other hand, the large number of Greek inscriptions, and this epigram itself, prove that a knowledge of the Greek language and, to a large extent, of Greek literature was widespread at Beth She-'arim. Thus Justus was probably educated both in Greek and Jewish learning.

④ *Besara* is the Greek name of Beth She'arim.

And having gone to Hades,① I, Justus, lie here
With many of my own kindred, since mighty Moira② so willed.
Be of good courage, Justus, no one is immortal.③

5.4 Rabbinic Views on Images④

5.4.1 Mishnah, Avodah Zarah, 3:4. Aphrodite in the Bathhouse

Proklos, the son of Philosophos, asked Rabban Gamaliel while the latter was bathing in the bath of Aphrodite in Acre, saying to him, "It is written in your Torah, *And there shall not cleave to you any of the devoted thing.*⑤ Why do you thus bathe in the bath of Aphrodite?" He answered: "One may not give an answer in the bath."⑥ And when he came out he said, "I did not come into her area [lit., boundary], she came into mine. People do not say, 'Let us make a bath for Aphrodite,' but rather, 'Let us make a [statue of] Aphrodite as an adornment for the bath.' Moreover even if they would offer you much money, you would not enter your place of worship [lit., idolatry] naked and suffering pollution and urinate in front of her. But she stands at the edge of the gutter, and everyone urinates

---

① *Having Gone to Hades.* Hades is the Greek god of the dead. In Homer the dead goes to Hades, that is, he descends to the underworld. The word *hades* is used in the Septuagint to translate the Hebrew word *she'ol* ("underworld"). Obviously, Jews in this period did not feel hurt in their religious feelings by this expression for the underworld, drawn from Greek mythology.

② *Moira* is a Homeric goddess of fate. "Mighty Moira" is borrowed from a Homeric formula.

③ The epigram does contain an original idea: the idea of being laid to rest among one's own people, to which there is no analogy in Greek literature.

④ Source: Levine (2005), pp. 227–229; 474; 482–483.

⑤ Deuteronomy 13:18. *Devoted thing*: an idol.

⑥ I.e., speaking words of Torah while naked is forbidden.

in front of her. The verse only refers to *Their gods*;① that which they treat as a god is forbidden and that which they do not treat as a god is permitted."②

5.4.2　Mishnah, Avodah Zarah, 3:1. Forbidden Images

All images are forbidden because they are worshipped [at least] once a year. So [says] R. Meir. But the sages say: "Only that is forbidden which holds a staff or bird or sphere in its hand."③ R. Simeon b. Gamaliel says: "Anything holding an object [is forbidden]."

5.4.3　Mishnah, Avodah Zarah, 3:3. Images Forbidden

[If] one finds objects bearing the figure of the sun or the figure of the moon [and] the figure of a dragon, he must throw them into the Dead Sea.④ Rabban Simeon b. Gamaliel says: "If the objects are of value they are forbidden; if they are worthless, they are permitted."

---

　① Deuteronomy 12:3. The verse refers to gods of other nations.
　② Gamaliel's debate with the Greek philosopher Proklos engages a central question that Neoplatonic philosophy struggled with in the third century CE: Could God represented at all? Gamaliel was not only well aware of the Greco-Roman philosophical debates, but was addressing them directly: the phrase "I did not come into her area, she came into mine" appears to be a conscious paraphrase of a similar statement by the philosopher Plotinus(205–270 CE). Gamaliel's adoption of this phrase implies that Judaism is much closer to a philosophical understanding of God than was popular paganism. If this philosophical rabbi held to a Neoplatonic concept of God, it was because Judaism and ancient philosophy were similar in their iconoclastic monotheism.
　③ Symbols of sovereignty.
　④ I.e., he should get rid of them.

5.4.4 Jerusalem Talmud, Avodah Zarah, 3:3, 42d. Images Permitted

R. Hiyya had pitcher [or cup, pot] in which Tyche [Fortuna] of Rome was depicted. He came and asked R. Yohanan, who told him: "Since water covers her, it is considered an insult [and therefore it can be used]." Similarly with respect to a cup [or ladle]: Since you dip it in water, it is considered an insult [and it also can be used].

In the days of R. Yohanan [third century], they began to depict [figural images] on the walls and he did not object; in the days of R. Abun [fourth century], they began depicting [figural images] on mosaic floors and he did not object.

5.5 Jerusalem Talmud, Bava Metzia, 2:5, 8c. On Alexander the Great[①]

Alexander Macedon traveled to the Faraway King.[②] He [the king] showed him much gold. He showed him much silver. He [Alexander] said, "I do not need your gold or your silver. Rather, I have come to observe your ways: how you do business; how you judge."

While he was occupied with him, a certain man approached disputing with his fellow. He had bought a field, and while he was digging it up he found a treasure of golden coins. The one who bought it said, "I bought a mound. I did not buy a treasure." The one who sold it said, "I sold you a mound and everything in it." While they were arguing with one another, the king said to one of them, "Do you have a male child?" He said, "Yes."

---

① Source: Rubenstein (2002), p. 162.

② Literally, "the extreme king," what we might call "the king at the end of the earth."

He said to the other, "Do you have a female child?" He said, "Yes." He said, "Marry them one to the other, and the treasure will go to both of them."

He [Alexander] began to laugh. He [the king] said to him, "Why do you laugh? Did I not judge well?" [Then] he [the king] said, "If this case had come before you, how would you have judged?" He said, "We would kill both the one and the other, and the treasure would fall to the king."

He [the king] said to him, "Then you love gold so much?" He made him a meal. He brought before him meat [made out] of gold [and] fowl [made out] of gold. He [Alexander] said to him, "Do I eat gold?" He said to him, "Blast your bones!① If you don't eat gold, then why do you love it so much?"

He [the king] said to him, "Does the sun shine for you?" He said to him, "Yes." "Does the rain fall for you?" He said to him, "Yes." He said to him, "Perhaps there is small cattle among you?" He said to him, "Yes." [He said,] "Blast your bones. You continue to live solely on account of the small cattle, as it says, '*You save man and beast, O Lord.*' (Ps. 36:7)"

5.6　Jerusalem Talmud, Sabbath, 1:3, 3c. On Social Accommodation②

They said to Rabbi Hiyya the Great: Rabbi Shim'on bar Yohai teaches, "'You shall buy food from them [Edom = Rome] for money, and eat, and also buy water from them for money, and drink' [Deut. 2: 6]: Just as water [is that] which has not been modified from its original state [literally, its creation], so also everything that has not been modified from its original state." He rejoined to them, "But their liverwort, dried apricots, pickled vegetables, and parched corn are permitted." All of the first three are not

---

① Literally, "May that man's breath expire!"—a mild expletive.
② Source: Boyarin (2000).

problematic because you can soak them in water and they return to their original state, but what about parched corn? Rabbi Yosi the son of Rabbi Bun in the name of Rav said, "Any food that can be eaten raw as it is, does not enter into the category of forbidden foods cooked by the Gentiles, and one may use it raw for rituals that normally require cooked foods." How, then, does Rabbi Hiyya the Great explain the verse: "You shall buy food from them for money, and eat"? If you feed him, you have bought and defeated him, for if he is harsh with you, buy/defeat him with food, and if [that does] not [work], then defeat him with money.

They say that is how Rabbi Yonatan behaved. When he saw a powerful personage come into his city, he used to send him expensive things. What did he think? If he comes to judge an orphan or a widow, we will find him propitious towards them.

6 THE WORLD OF THE RABBIS

6.1 Babylonian Talmud, Gittin 56a–b. Yohanan ben Zakkai's Escape from Jerusalem and Relocation in Yavneh

Abba Siqara was the chief of the zealots in Jerusalem. He was the son of Rabban Yohanan b. Zakkai's sister. He sent word to him, "Come to me in secret."

He came.

He said to him, "How long are you going to act in this way and kill everybody through famine?"

He said to him, "What should I do? If I say anything to them, they will kill me too."

He said to him, "Find some sort of remedy for me to get out of here, maybe there will be the possibility of saving something."

He said to him, "Pretend to be sick and have everybody come and ask about you; have something bad smelling and put it by you, so people will think you're dead. Then let your disciples carry you—but nobody else—so that no one will feel that you're still light, since people know that a living being is lighter than a corpse."

They did so. R. Eliezer came in at one side, and R. Joshua at the other. When they got to the gate, they wanted to stab him. He said to them, "People will say they stabbed their master." They wanted to shove him over the wall. He said to them, "People will say they shoved their master [over the wall]." They opened the gate for him, and he got out.

When he got there, he said, "Peace be unto you, O king, peace be unto you, O king."

He said to him, "You are subject to the death penalty on two counts; first of all, I'm not a king, and you called me king; second, if I really am king, then how come you didn't come to me up till now?"

He said to him, "As to your statement, 'I'm not king,' the truth is you really are king, because if you weren't king, then Jerusalem wouldn't have been handed over to you, for it has been written, 'Lebanon shall fall by a mighty one' (Isa. 10:34), and 'mighty one' refers only to a king, in line with the verse, 'And their mighty one shall be of themselves' (Jer. 30:21). Not only so, but Lebanon speaks of the Temple, 'This goodly mountain and Lebanon ' (Deut. 3:25). And as to what you have said, 'If I really am king, then how come you didn't come to me up till now? ' up to now, the zealots among us wouldn't let me come."

He said to him, "So if there's a jar of honey with a lizard wrapped around it, wouldn't you break the honey to get rid of the lizard?"

He shut up.

R. Joseph, and some say R. Akiba, recited in his regard: "'God turns wise men backward and makes their knowledge foolish' (Isa. 44:25). He ought to have said to him, 'We would take a pair of tongs and grab the lizard and kill it but leave the jar whole.'"

In the meantime, an agent came to him from Rome. He said to him, "Arise, for the Caesar is dead, and the citizens of Rome propose to enthrone you at the head."

At that moment he had finished putting on one boot. He wanted to put on the other, but it wouldn't go on. He wanted to take off that one, but it wouldn't go off. He said, "What's going on?" He said to him, "Don't be distressed. Good news has come to you, for it is written, 'Good news makes the bone fat.' (Prov. 15:30) So what's the solution? Bring someone you despise and let him walk before you: 'A broken spirit dries up the bones.' (Prov. 17:22)" He did so and the boot went on ...

He said to him, "Now I'm going away, and I'm sending someone else. So ask something from me, which I'll give you."

He said to him, "Give me Yavneh① and its sages, and the chain of Rabban Gamaliel, and a physician to heal R. Sadoq."

R. Joseph, and some say, R. Akiba, recited in his regard the verse, "'God turns wise men backward and makes their knowledge foolish.' (Isa. 44:25) He ought to have said to him to leave the place alone this time." But he thought that maybe that much he won't do, and there would not be the possibility of saving anything at all.②

6.2 Mishnah, Avot, 1. The Chain of Oral Transmission from Sinai

1:1 Moses③ received Torah④ at Sinai and handed it on to Joshua, Joshua to elders,⑤ and elders to prophets. And prophets handed it on to the men of the great assembly.⑥ They said three things: Be prudent in judgment. Raise

---

① In Greek, *Jamnia*, a Judaean town.

② For a brilliant Zionist, if eccentric, reading, see Alon (1977).

③ Jewish tradition from the rabbinical period on calls him "Moses our Rabbi" (*Moshe Rabbenu*).

④ *Torah*. "Moses received the whole Torah, both the written and the oral Torah." (Mahzor Vitry) "It is written, 'And I will give thee the tablets of stone, and the law and the commandment' (Exod. 24: 12): 'the law' refers to the Written Torah; 'the commandment' refers to the Oral Torah. Thus all the commandments were given to Moses at Sinai along with their interpretations: what was written down is called the Written Torah, the [accompanying] interpretation is called the Oral Torah." (Rabbi Jonah)

⑤ *Elders*. According to Rashi, Maimonides and many others, the elders to whom Joshua transmitted the Torah were not the elders whom Moses had appointed in Numbers 11:16; rather, these elders lived in the time of Joshua.

⑥ *Men of the great assembly*. Not a great deal is known about the great assembly (*knesset ha-gedolah*). It stems from the Persian period and represents for the rabbis the transition between prophets and themselves. Ezra is identified by the rabbis as the leader of the men of the great assembly and is traditionally linked to Nehemiah 8 – 10.

up many disciples. Make a fence for the Torah.①

1:2 Simeon the Righteous② was one of the last survivors of the great assembly. He would say: "On three things does the world stand: On the Torah, and on the Temple service③, and on deeds of loving-kindness④."

1:3 Antigonos of Sokho received [the Torah] from Simeon the Righteous. He would say: "Do not be like servants who serve the master on condition of receiving a reward, but [be] like servants who serve the master not on condition of receiving a reward. And let the fear of Heaven⑤ be upon you."

---

① *Make a fence for the Torah.* It "refers to the decrees and enactments of the Sages—these keep a man far from transgression, as the Blessed One said, 'Therefore shall ye keep what I have given you to keep' (Lev. 18:30), which the Talmud (Yebamot 21a) interprets to mean: Add protection to what I have already given you as protection." (Maimonides)

② A high priest of the third century BCE.

③ *On the Temple service.* "Now that there is no Temple service in the world sustained by the Torah, by acts of loving-kindness, and by prayer—for prayer takes the place of Temple service." (Mahzor Vitry)

④ *Deeds of loving-kindness* (*gemilut hasadim* ["bestowing of kindness"]). It finds expression in all efforts of goodwill. "Deeds of loving-kindness are greater than charity. As the Sages have said (Sukkah 49b): Charity applies only to the living, deeds of loving-kindness apply to the living and the dead. Charity is something a man does with his wealth, deeds of loving-kindness he carries out with his wealth and by means of his own person. In deeds of loving-kindness the poor man's feelings are spared: for example when one lends a poor man funds to help him in his hour of need; whereas when one gives the poor man charity, the poor man inevitably feels some shame. Charity affects the poor only; deed of loving-kindness affects the rich also." (Mahzor Vitry) The Talmud (Bavli, Yebamot 79a) reckons *gemilut hasadim* a distinguishing characteristic of the Jewish people.

⑤ *Fear of Heaven.* "For all his insistence that one should serve the Lord out of love, Antigonos has not exempted us from the commandment to fear him. Along with worshipping God out of love, he says, do not altogether neglect the element of fear, 'let the fear of Heaven be upon you,' for the commandment to fear Him is clearly stated in the Torah, as it is said, 'Thou shalt fear the Lord thy God.' (Deut. 6:13)" (Maimonides)

1:4　Yose ben Yoezer of Seredah and Yose ben Yohanan of Jerusalem① received [the Torah] from them. Yose ben Yoezer says: "Let your house be a gathering place for sages. And wallow in the dust of their feet, and drink their words with gusto."

1:5　Yose ben Yohanan of Jerusalem says: "Let your house be wide open. And seat the poor at your table.② And don't talk③ too much with women." (He spoke of a man's wife, all the more so is the rule to be applied to the wife of one's fellow. In this regard did sages say: "So long as a man talks too much with a woman, he brings trouble on himself, wastes time better spent on studying the Torah, and ends up an heir of Gehenna.④")

1:6　Joshua ben Perahiah and Nittai the Arbelite received [the Torah] from them. Joshua ben Perahiah says: "Set up a master for yourself.⑤ And

---

① All the Sages listed in this chapter from this point through Hillel and Shammai are known as *zugot*, "pairs" of scholars, who headed the Sanhedrin for about 150 years until the beginning, the Common Era, one serving as *Nasi* ("head") and the other as *Av Bet Din* ("head of the court of law"). The Sanhedrin was the central authority in Palestine during the Roman period.

② *Seat the poor at your table*. "The Sages used to speak disparagingly of the acquisition of slaves; but they used to praise him who gave employment to the poor by taking them on as servants." (Maimonides)

③ *Talk*. "The word for 'talk' in this passage refers to conversation which is entirely unnecessary, 'idle chatter,' as the Sages often refer to it." (Meiri)

④ *Gehenna*. The rabbinic term for hell. It originally referred to a place near Jerusalem (Josh. 15:8), where human sacrifices were offered to Molech (Ⅱ Kings 23:10).

⑤ *Set up a master for yourself*. "[There are times] when a person is not really qualified to be your master (*rav*, or 'teacher'); nevertheless, let him teach you, make it possible for him to teach you. If you do this you will acquire wisdom—for there is no comparison between studying by oneself and studying with another person. When one studies with another person, he remembers better what he has learnt, the material is more clearly understood by him, even when his companion is no more than his equal in wisdom, or even when his companion is inferior to him." (Maimonides)

get yourself a fellow disciple.① And give everybody the benefit of the doubt.②"

1:7 Nittai the Arbelite says: "Keep away from a bad neighbor. And don't get involved with a wicked man. And don't give up hope of retribution."

1:8 Judah ben Tabbai and Simeon ben Shetah received [the Torah] from them. Judah ben Tabbai says: "Do not play the part of Chief Justice.③ And when the litigants stand before you, regard them as guilty. And when they leave you, regard them as acquitted, (when they have accepted your judgment)."

1:9 Simeon ben Shetah says: "Examine the witnesses with great care. And watch what you say, lest they learn from what you say how to lie."

1:10 Shemaiah and Avtalion received [the Torah] from them.

---

① *Get yourself a fellow disciple.* "Note that the idiom used here is 'get yourself (buy) a fellow disciple,' not just 'set up a fellow disciple for yourself' or 'attach yourself' to others or some similar expression. The reason for this is that, if necessary, a man should buy a devoted friend for himself... As the Sages used to say (Taanit 23a): Give me friendship or give me death. And if a person cannot easily find a friend, he must strive with all his heart to do so, even if he has to go so far as compel the person to love him, even if he has to buy his love and friendship." (Maimonides)

② Or, "*And judge everyone with the scale weighted in his favor.*" "There was once a young girl who had been taken captive, and two saintly folk went after her to ransom her. One of them entered the harlots' apartment. When he came out he asked his companion: 'What didst thou suspect me of?' The other replied: 'Of finding out perhaps for how much money she is being held.' Said the first: 'By the Temple service, so it was!' And he added: 'Even as thou didst judge me with the scale weighted in my favor, so may the Holy One, blessed be He, judge thee with the scale weighted in thy favor.'" (*Avot de-Rabbi Nathan*)

③ *Chief Justice (Orekhe ha-Dayyanim).* It refers to "those who teach the litigants how to arrange their arguments cleverly (Mahzor Vitry), saying to the litigants, 'If the judge should say this, you answer this way; if your opponent should argue such-and-such, let that be your answer.' (Maimonides)"

Shemaiah says: "Love work. Hate authority.① Don't get friendly with the government."

1:11 Avtalion says: "Sages, watch what you say, lest you become liable to the punishment of exile, and go into exile to a place of bad water②, and disciples who follow you drink [bad water] and die, and the name of Heaven be thereby profaned."

1:12 Hillel and Shammai received [the Torah] from them. Hillel says: "Be disciples of Aaron③, loving peace and pursuing grace, loving people and drawing them near to the Torah." ④

1:13 He would say [in Aramaic]: "A name made great is a name destroyed, and one who does not add, subtracts. And who does not learn is liable to death. And the one who uses the crown⑤, passes away."

1:14 He would say: "If I am not for myself, who is for me? And when

---

① *Hate authority.* Rashi points out that the mantle of authority buries those covered by it. According to Meiri, "The Sages, of blessed memory, used to say (see Maimonides on Avot 1:10): 'When a man has been appointed the head of a community, on high they regard him as wicked,' because the chances are that he demands the kind of authority and awe toward himself which is not for the sake of Heaven."

② *Bad water.* It is a term for heresy, according to Maimonides.

③ Aaron's pursuit of peace was suggested in the story of the Golden Calf. In this incident, Aaron actually went along with the people's desire for a concrete symbol of leadership and participated in its fabrication, hoping that the people would not do anything more blasphemous.

④ *Drawing them near to the Torah.* "This teaches that one should bend men to and lead them under the wings of Shekhinah, the way Abraham our father used to bend men to and lead them under the wings of the Shekhinah." (*Avot de-Rabbi Nathan*)

⑤ *Crown.* The Torah.

I am for myself, what am I?① And if not now, when?②"

1:15 Shammai says: "Make your learning of the Torah a fixed obligation. Say little and do much. Greet everybody cheerfully."

1:16 Rabban Gamaliel says: "Set up a master for yourself.③ Avoid doubt. Don't tithe by too much guesswork."

1:17 Simeon his son says: "All my life I grew up among the sages, and I found nothing better for a person than silence. And not the learning is the main thing, but the doing. And whoever talks too much④ causes sin."

1:18 Rabban Simeon ben Gamaliel says: "On three things does the world stand: on justice⑤, on truth, and on peace⑥. As it is said, 'Execute the judgment of truth and peace in your gates' (Zech. 8:16)."

---

① *When I am for myself, what am I?* "It seems to me that this is how this statement is to be interpreted: Since everything is in my power, 'when I am for myself,' that is to say, taking care of my bodily needs only without paying attention at the same time to the obligation of serving the Lord and perfecting my soul, 'what am I?' In such conduct I am no more than a beast." (Meiri)

② *If not now, when?* "If now, in the days of my youth, I do not acquire good qualities, when shall I acquire them? In my old age? For it is very difficult to abandon habits at that time, because by then behavior patterns have become firmly fixed." (Maimonides)

③ *Set up a master for yourself.* Here, as against 1:6, the statement "does not refer to study but to rendering a decision: appoint for yourself some master on whom you can depend in matters of the forbidden and permitted, and thus eschew doubtful matters... And so too Rabban Gamaliel instructs us to flee from the practice of tithing by guesswork, because this is an example of 'doubtful matters.'" (Maimonides)

④ *Talks too much.* "Notice that man has two ears but only one tongue, suggesting that his speech ought to be little and his hearing much." (Duran)

⑤ *Justice.* "By this is meant righteous government." (Maimonides)

⑥ *Peace.* "By peace is meant that there be peace in the world, that there be no wars either between kingdoms, or between man and his fellow man. For just as deeds of loving-kindness are one of the pillars of the universe, so is peace—which is an expression of deeds of loving-kindness: it sustains the world." (Duran)

6.3 Babylonian Talmud, Menahoth, 29b. Moses Returns as a Yeshiva Boy[①]

When Moses ascended onto the heights [to receive the Torah], he found the Holy One, blessed be He, sitting there tying wreaths [or crowns] to the letters. He said to Him: "Master of the Universe, who is holding You back?"[②] He answered him: "There is a man who will arise after many generations by the name of Akiba ben Joseph; he will expound heaps and heaps of laws upon every tittle."[③] Then he said to Him: "Master of the Universe, show him to me." He replied: "Turn around." Then Moses went and sat down behind eight rows [of the students of Akiba]. But he did not understand what they were talking about. Thereupon his strength left him.[④] When Akiba came to a certain matter where his students asked him how he knew it, he said to them: "It is a teaching given to Moses at Sinai." Then he [Moses] was comforted and returned to the Holy One, blessed be He. He said to Him: "Master of the Universe, You have a man like that and You give the Torah by me?!" He replied: "Be silent, for this is the way I have determined it." Then Moses said: "Master of the Universe, You have shown me his knowledge of the Torah, show me also his reward." He answered: "Turn around." He turned around and saw that Akiba's flesh was being weighed at the market stalls [his flesh was torn by the tortures of the executioners].[⑤] Then he said to Him: "Master of the Universe, this is the Torah and this is its reward?" He replied: "Be silent, for this is the way I have determined it."

---

① Source: Scholem (1971), p. 283.

② That is, why are You not satisfied with letters as they are, so that You add crown-like flourishes (called *tagin*) to them?

③ I.e., Rabbi Akiba will derive oral Torah from these embellishments.

④ I.e., he was perplexed because he was unable to follow discourses concerning the Torah which he himself had written.

⑤ Akiba died as a martyr under Roman persecutions in 135 CE.

6.4 Babylonian Talmud, Sabbath, 31a. Torah on One Leg

There was another case of a gentile who came before Shammai. He said to him, "Convert me on the condition that you teach me the entire Torah while I am standing on one leg." He drove him off with the building cubit① that he had in his hand. He came before Hillel: "Convert me." He said to him, "'What is hateful to you, to your fellow don't do.' That's the entirety of the Torah; everything else is elaboration. So go, study."②

6.5 Tosefta, Eduyot 1:4. Preserving Minority Opinion③

The *halakhah* forever follows the opinions of the majority. The opinions of the individual were recorded along with those of the majority [so as] to be annulled④.

Rabbi Yehudah says: The opinions of the individual were recorded among those of the majority because an hour [may come when] they are needed and they will be relied upon.⑤

And the sages say:⑥ The opinions of the individual were recorded among those of the majority so that, in a discussion of purity and impurity, a disputant who maintains [that something is] "impure" according to the

---

① A measuring rod.

② Some interpreters see a double meaning here. The word *regel*, meaning "leg," evokes the Latin *regula*, a law or principle. The convert asks for the Torah standing on one *regel*; Hillel articulates the one *regula* on which the Torah stands.

③ Source: Walzer, Lorberbaum, and Zohar (2000), p. 318.

④ To make public the view that is rejected.

⑤ The minority view becomes a precedent if, at a later time, it becomes the majority position.

⑥ This is the majority position. Note that since the text includes two other opinions about why minority opinions are preserved, it proves its own conclusion that minority views must be preserved.

opinion of Rabbi Eliezer may be told: "Your tradition is according to [the minority opinion of] Rabbi Eliezer."①

6.6　Babylonian Talmud, Bava Metzia, 59a–59b. Torah Is Not in Heaven②

We learned there:③ *If he cut it (an oven)* ④ *into segments and placed sand between the segments, R. Eliezer rules that it is pure and the sages rule that it is impure. And this is the oven of Akhnai.*

What is *Akhnai* (=snake)? Rav Yehuda said Shmuel said, "Since they surrounded him with words like this snake and ruled it impure."

It was taught:⑤ On that day R. Eliezer responded with all the responses in the world, but they did not accept them from him.

He said to them, "If the law is as I say, let the carob [tree] prove it." The carob uprooted itself from its place and went one hundred cubits⑥—and some say four hundred cubits. They said to him, "One does not bring proof from the carob."⑦ The carob returned to its place.

He said to them, "If the law is as I say, let the aqueduct prove it." The water turned backwards. They said to him, "One does not bring proof from water." The water returned to its place.

He said to them, "If it [the law] is as I say, let the walls of the academy

---

① Preserving the minority opinions creates a venerable tradition, even if it is in the minority.
② Source: Rubenstein (2002), pp. 80–84. Cf. Biale and Miles (2015).
③ The phrase "We learned there" introduces the Mishnah—here, Mishnah, Kelim, 10:5—that the Talmudic text is commenting upon.
④ The debate concerns an oven that has become ritually unclean and the process by which it may be considered clean again.
⑤ *It was taught.* This phrase introduces a *baraita*, a tannaitic tradition that was not included in the Mishnah.
⑥ A cubit equals approximately 18 inches.
⑦ That is, the rabbis do not accept this proof.

prove it." The walls of the academy inclined to fall. R. Yehoshua rebuked them. He said to them, "When sages defeat each other in law, what is it for you?"①

It was taught: They did not fall because of the honor of R. Yehoshua, and they did not stand because of the honor of R. Eliezer, and they are still inclining and standing.

He said to them, "If it is as I say, let it be proved from heaven." A heavenly voice (*bat kol*)② went forth and said, "What is it for you with R. Eliezer, since the law is like him in every place?"

R. Yehoshua stood up on his feet and said, *"It is not in heaven* (Deut. 30:12)." ③ What is, "It is not in heaven"?

R. Yirmiah said, "We do not listen to a heavenly voice, since you already gave it to us on Mt. Sinai and it is written there, *Incline after the majority."* (Exod. 23:2)

R. Natan came upon Elijah.④ He said to him, "What was the Holy One doing at that time?" He [Elijah] said to him, "He laughed and smiled and said, 'My sons have defeated me, my sons have defeated me.'"

At that time they brought all the objects which R. Eliezer had ruled were pure and burned them and voted and banned him. ⑤

They said, "Who will go and inform him?" R. Akiba said to them, "I will go and inform him lest a man who is not fitting goes and informs him and destroys the whole world."⑥ What did he do? He dressed in black and covered himself with black and took off his shoes and went and sat before

---

① Or, "Why do you interfere?"
② *batkol.* Lit. "daughter of voice," echo; occasionally in Rabbinic literature, "divine voice," a substitute for "prophecy".
③ This verse in its biblical context signifies something quite different.
④ The biblical prophet. At the end of his earthly life he does not die but is carried up to heaven in a whirlwind.
⑤ Because he did not agree with the majority.
⑥ The rabbis are afraid of Rabbi Eliezer's power to invoke divine assistance.

him at a distance of four cubits and his eyes streamed with tears①.

He [R. Eliezer] said to him, "Akiba, why is this day different from other days?" He said to him, "It seems to me that your colleagues are keeping separate from you②." His eyes too streamed with tears, and he took off his shoes and removed [his seat] and sat on the ground.

The world was smitten in one third of the wheat, one third of the olives, and one half of the barley.

And some say that even the dough in the hands of women swelled up.

It was taught: It [the destruction] was so great on that day that every place where R. Eliezer cast his eyes immediately was burned.

Also Rabban Gamaliel [head of the academy] was on a ship. A wave of the sea stood to drown him. He said, "It seems to me that this is because of [R. Eliezer] the Son of Hyrcanus." He stood up on his feet and said, "Master of the universe. I acted not for my honor, nor did I act for the honor of my father's house, but I acted for your honor, in order that disagreements do not multiply in Israel." The sea immediately rested from its anger.

Ima Shalom, the wife of R. Eliezer, was the sister of Rabban Gamaliel. After that event she never allowed him [Eliezer] to fall on his face③. That day was the new month and a poor man came and stood at the door. While she was giving him bread she found that he [Eliezer] had fallen on his face. She said, "Stand up. You have killed my brother." Meanwhile the shofar [blast] went out from the House of Rabban Gamaliel [signaling that he had died]. He said to her, "How did you know?" She said to him, "Thus I have received a tradition from my father's house: 'All the gates are locked except for gates of [verbal] wronging.' "④

---

① Symbolic of mourning.

② They are staying away from him because he has been banned.

③ To "fall on the face" is to lie prostrate in private prayer. Like Akiba, she realizes that God intends to punish the sages for the pain they caused R. Eliezer. She too tries to prevent or restrain his expression of pain.

④ Because Eliezer was the victim of verbal wrongdoing, she knew his prayer would be answered(i.e., that the gate through which that prayer would reach God remained open).

6.7 Babylonian Talmud, Berakhot 62a. The Pursuit of Torah[1]

Rav Kahana went in and lay down under the bed of Rav Shemaya, who was conversing and laughing and doing his business [with his wife]. He said, "It seems that my master's mouth has never tasted the dish!" He said to him, "Kahana! Get out. This is not proper." He said to him, "This is [a matter of] Torah, and I need to learn it."

6.8 Rabbinic Views on Women[2]

6.8.1 Jerusalem Talmud, Sotah, 4:4

A woman once came to Rabbi Yohanan and said to him: "I have been raped." He said to her: "And didn't you enjoy it by the end?" She said to him: "And if man dipped his finger in honey and stuck it in your mouth on Yom Kippur [a fast day], is it not bad for you yet enjoyable by the end?" He accepted her.[3]

6.8.2 Jerusalem Talmud, Sotah, 3:16

A certain lady asked Rabbi Eliezer why the one sin in the case of the golden calf was punished by three deaths.[4] He said to her: A woman's wisdom is

---

[1] Source: Rubenstein (2002), p. 203.

[2] Source: Biale and Miles (2015), p. 237.

[3] The woman presumably asks not to be considered an adulteress on the grounds that she has been raped. Rabbi Yohanan advances the oldest accusation in the book: she couldn't have been raped if, in the end, she enjoyed it.

[4] See Exodus 32.

only in her spinning wheel, for it is written "And any woman of wise heart, with her hands she wove" (Ex. 35:25). His son Hyrcanus said to him: why did you not give her some proper answer from the Torah? Now you have lost me three hundred *kur* [a measure] a year in tithe!① He said to him: "Let the words of Torah be burnt and not be given to women!" When she went out the students said to him: "This one you got rid of, but what do you answer to us?"

6.9 Tosefta Hagiga 2:3–4. Four Entered the *Pardes*②

Four entered the *pardes* (orchard). One gazed and perished, one gazed and was smitten, one gazed and cut the shoots, and one went up whole and came down whole.

Ben Azzai gazed and perished. Concerning him scripture says, *The death of His faithful ones is grievous in the Lord's sight* (Psalms 116:15).

Ben Zoma gazed and was smitten. Concerning him scripture says, *If you find honey, eat only what you need, lest, surfeiting yourself, you throw it up* (Proverbs 25:16).

Elisha gazed and cut the shoots.③ Concerning him scripture says, *Let not your mouth lead you into sin* (Ecclesiastes 5:5).

R. Akiba went up whole and came down whole. Concerning him scripture says, *Draw me up after you, let us run! [The king has brought me to his chambers]* (Song 1:4).

---

① Implying that this woman subsidized his yearly tithe.

② Source: Biale and Miles(2015). Cf. its parallels and variants in Babylonian Talmud, Hagiga 14b and the Jerusalem Talmud, Hagiga 2:1, 77a. The four sages mentioned all flourished in the first half of the second century. For commentaries, see Goshen-Gottstein (1995); Jacobs (1997), pp. 29–34.

③ *Cut the shoots.* The meaning of the phrase is unclear, but may refer to corrupting the youth (the "shoots") by infecting them with heretical ideas. Elisha [b. Abuya] is also known as Aher ("Other"), the arch rabbinical heretic; see 10.3.

6.10　Tosefta Hullin, 2:24. Rabbis and Christians①

It happened that Rabbi Eliezer was arrested for sectarianism [Christianity], and they took him up to the bēma② to be judged.

The ruler said to him, "A sage such as you having truck with these matters!?"

He said to him, "I have trust in the judge."

The ruler thought that he was speaking of him, but he meant his Father in Heaven. He said to him, "Since you trust me, I also have said, 'Is it possible that these gray hairs would err in such matters?' Behold, you are dismissed."

When he had left the bēma, he was troubled that he had been arrested for sectarianism. His disciples came in to comfort him, but he was inconsolable. Rabbi Akiba came in and said to him, "Rabbi, I will say before you a word; perhaps you will not be troubled."

He said to him, "Say!"

He said to him, "Perhaps one of the sectarians said something to you of sectarianism, and it caused you pleasure."

He said to him, "By heaven, you have reminded me. Once I was walking in the marketplace of Tsippori, and I found there Ya'akov the man of Kefar Sikhnin [a place not known today], and he recounted a saying of sectarianism in the name of Yeshu' the son of Pantiri, and it caused me pleasure, and I was caught by the words of sectarianism, for I violated that which is written in the Torah, 'Keep her ways far away from you, and don't come near the opening of her house, for she has brought many victims

---

① Source: Boyarin (2000). Cf. Rubenstein (2003), pp. 169 – 175; Shäfer (2007), pp. 15 – 22; 41 – 51.

② Bēma (Greek, "platform"): Raised platform in synagogue from which the Torah is read. By metonymy, bēma was also a place of judgement, being the extension of the raised seat of the judge.

down!' (Prov. 5:8)"

6.11 Maimonides, *Commentary on the Mishnah.* The Thirteen Principles of Faith①

We must remember in connection with this subject,② and indeed with all others, that our religion is based on the following thirteen principles:

The First Fundamental Principle is the existence of the Creator. There is a being who exists in the most perfect mode of existence, and He is the cause of the existence of all other beings. In Him is the source of their existence, and from Him their continued existence derives. If we could imagine the elimination of His existence, then the existence of every other being would be annulled and nothing would remain in being. But if we could eliminate the existence of all other beings, then His existence would not be annulled or diminished, for He depends for His existence on none beside Himself. Everything apart from Him, the Intelligences③ (that is, the angels), the bodies of the spheres, and whatever is beneath them—all depend for their existence on Him. This first fundamental principle is taught in the verse: "I am the Lord your God." (Exod. 20:2)

The Second Fundamental Principle is the unity of God. The Cause of

---

① Source: Alexander (1984). Cf. Jacobs (1964); Kellner (2006), Appendix Two; 宋立宏 (2015b)。

② Maimonides presented the Thirteen Principles in an attempt to define the term "Israelite" as used in Mishnah Sanhedrin 10:1 ("All Israelites have a share in the world to come...").

③ By "Intelligences" Maimonides means the "separate intellects" (*sekhalim nivdalim*): those disembodied intellects whose name derives from their being "separate" matter, as opposed to human intellects, which develop out of a material disposition, and which in Maimonides' Neoplatonized Aristotelianism move the heavenly spheres and constitute the intermediate stages of existence between God and our world. Maimonides was convinced that the Torah taught metaphysics and that the actual meaning of the biblical term "angel" was "separate intellect."

[the existence of] all things is one, not with the oneness of a genus or a species①, nor with the oneness of a single composite human being who may be divided into many discrete elements②. Nor is His oneness like that of a simple body which is numerically one, but capable of infinite subdivision and fragmentation. Rather, He is one with a oneness that is absolutely unique. This second fundamental principle is taught in the verse: "Hear, O Israel: the Lord our God, the Lord is One." (Deut. 6:4)

The Third Fundamental Principle is the denial of corporeality to God. This One is neither a body nor a force in a body.③ None of the accidents of bodies, such as motion and rest, appertain to Him either by essence or by accident. That is why the Sages denied to Him composition and separation when they said: "In heaven above there is neither sitting nor standing, neither *oref* [lit. 'shoulder'] nor *ippui* [lit. 'fatigue']" (Babylonian Talmud, Hagiga 15a); that is to say, neither "separation" [*oref*], nor "composition" [*ippui*], for the sense of *ippui* may be determined from the verse *Ve-afu be-khatef pelishtim* (Isa. 11:14), which means: "They shall push them with their shoulders so as to mass them together." The prophets said: "To whom will you compare God?" (Isa. 40:18); and again: "To whom will you compare me, whom do I resemble?" (Isa. 49:25). If God were a body, then He would be like other bodies. Wherever Scripture describes Him as having the attributes of bodies, such as movement, standing, sitting, speaking and so on, it speaks metaphorically, as the Sages have said: "The

---

① A genus (such as mammals) is one, but not simple, since it is composed of species; a species is one, but not simple, since it is composed of individuals.

② Such as the four elements (earth, air, water, fire).

③ I.e., God is neither a body nor a force which exists as the consequence of the existence of a body. An example of the latter in modern terms would be the force of gravity as we experience it.

Torah speaks in the language of men." (Babylonian Talmud, Berakhot 31b)① People have already had much to say on this subject.② This third fundamental principle is taught in the verse "You saw no image" (Deut. 4: 15), which means "You did not perceive Him as having an image," for, as we have stated, He is neither a body nor a force in a body.

The Fourth Fundamental Principle is God's pre-existence. This One whom we have described precedes all things absolutely. No other being has pre-existence in relation to Him. The proofs of this in Scripture are numerous. This fourth fundamental principle is taught in the verse: "The pre-existent God [*Elohei qedem*] is a refuge" (Deut. 33:27). ③

Know that one of the great principles of the Torah of Moses our Teacher is that the world is originated: God brought it into being and created it after absolute non-existence. The reason you see me dwelling so much on this question of the pre-existence of the world as taught by the philosophers, is to make possible the demonstration of God's existence, as I have explained and made clear in the *Guide of the Perplexed* [Ⅱ 15 – 19].

The Fifth Fundamental Principle is that God is the one Who should be worshipped and exalted, Whose greatness should be proclaimed, and Whom men should be called on to obey. We should not act thus towards anything beneath Him in existence, whether angels, or stars, or spheres, or elements,

---

① Maimonides wholly revised the meaning of this Talmudic statement. Its original use was to claim that not every apparently extra word in Scripture should be understood as teaching something taught nowhere else (on the basis of the rabbinic teaching that there are no unnecessary words in Scripture), since some apparently extra words are necessitated by the way in which Hebrew is actually spoken. Maimonides took it to mean that Scripture couched philosophical teachings in mythological language, suitable for the simple-minded or uneducated.

② Maimonides himself devoted the first fifty chapters of the *Guide of the Perplexed* to an analysis of biblical terms which seem to impute corporeality to God.

③ God here is described in terms which Aristotle could easily accept: God is presented as cause of the world, but not as its creator. It should be clear that a proper understanding of his principles requires a fairly lengthy course of study in Aristotelian philosophy.

or things compounded of them, for all these have been imprinted with their functions:[1] they have no independent judgment or free-will, but only love for God. We should not adopt intermediaries through whom to approach God, but should direct our thoughts towards Him and turn away from whatever is beneath Him. This fifth fundamental principle is the prohibition against idolatry. The greater part of the Torah is taken up with forbidding idolatry.

The Sixth Fundamental Principle is prophecy. It should be known that there exist in the human species certain persons of a vastly superior disposition and a high degree of perfection. If their souls are so trained that they receive the form of the intellect[2], then that human intellect will unite with the Active Intellect[3], from which a beneficent emanation will flow to it[4]. Such people are prophets; this process is prophecy; this is the true meaning of prophecy. A full explanation of this principle would be very lengthy. It is not our intention to offer proofs for each of the principles or to explain in what ways they are to be understood, for that would involve the sum of all the sciences. Rather we shall state them in the form of simple assertions. The verses of the Torah testifying to the prophecy of the prophets are numerous.

The Seventh Fundamental Principle is the prophecy of Moses our Teacher. We should believe that Moses was the father of all the prophets, both of those who came before him and those who followed him: all of them were inferior to him in rank. He was the one specially chosen by God out of the whole human species. He comprehended more of God than anyone in the past or the future ever comprehended or will comprehend. He reached such a state of exaltation beyond ordinary mortals that he attained

---

[1] I.e., it is forbidden to worship any entity other than God.
[2] I.e., actualize the potential intellects with which they were born.
[3] The tenth and last of the "separate intellects," or the Divine.
[4] I.e., the unification with the Active Intellect is the cause of the emanation upon the human intellect.

angelic status and was included in the order of the angels.① There remained no veil before him which he did not penetrate; no bodily hindrance stood in his way; no defect small or great marred him. The imaginative and sensual faculties in his perceptions were neutralized, his desiderative faculty was inoperative, and he remained pure intellect alone. It was for this reason it was said of him that he conversed with God without the mediation of an angel.

I had intended to explain here this extraordinary subject and to open up secrets locked away in the text of the Torah; to explain the meaning of the expression "mouth to mouth" (Num. 12:8), and the rest of the verse where it occurs, as well as the other verses dealing with the same subject. But I saw that this subject is very subtle and would require extensive treatment with introductions and illustrations. It would be necessary first to make clear the existence of the angels and the difference between their ranks and that of the Creator. The soul and all its faculties would have to be explained. The circle would have to be widened to include a discussion of the images which the prophets attribute to the Creator and his angels. For this subject alone a hundred pages would not suffice, even if I confined the discussion within the narrowest possible bounds. For this reason I shall leave it to its proper place, either in the "Treatise on the Explanation of the Midrashim [*derashot*]" which I have promised, or in the "Treatise on

---

① Maimonides here makes a number of unprecedented claims about Moses: (a) he is the "father of all the prophets," including the Patriarchs who preceded him; (b) no other prophet ever achieved his rank, nor will any prophet do so (including the Messiah); (c) unlike other prophets who, in effect, chose themselves, Moses was chosen by God from among all humans; (d) Moses' uniqueness was, apparently, a consequence of his having achieved such an exalted level of comprehension of God; (e) Moses became an angel, pure intellect only. None of these statements about Moses is commonplace in Jewish tradition. Maimonides deals with the special character of Mosaic prophecy in *Guide of the Perplexed*, II 39-40.

Prophecy" which I have begun to compose①, or in a commentary which I shall write on these fundamental principles.

I shall now come back to the point of this seventh fundamental principle and say that the prophecy of Moses our Teacher differs from the prophecy of all other prophets in four respects.

The first difference: To every other prophet that ever was God spoke only through a mediator, but to Moses without a mediator, as Scripture says: "Mouth to mouth I speak with him." (Num. 12:8)

The second difference: to every other prophet inspiration came only in a state of sleep, as Scripture says in various places: "In a dream of the night" (Gen. 31:24); "He had a dream" (Gen. 28:12); "By dreams and visions that come in the night" (Job 33:15); and there are many other verses of similar import. Or if inspiration came during the day, it was only after a deep sleep had fallen upon the prophet and his condition had become such that all his senses were inoperative and his mind was as empty as in sleep. This condition is called "vision" [*mahazeh*] and "apparition" [*mar'ah*], and is referred to in the phrase "Visions from God" [*mar'ot Elohim*] (Ezek. 8:3). But to Moses the word came in the daytime, when he was standing between the two cherubim, as God had promised him: "There I will meet with you and speak with you." (Exod. 25:22) God also said: "If there is a prophet among you, I the Lord will make myself known to him in a vision, and will speak with him in a dream. Not so with Moses my servant ... with him I speak mouth to mouth." (Num. 12:6–7)

The third difference: When inspiration came to any other prophet, even if in a vision or through the mediation of an angel, his faculties grew weak, his body became agitated, and a very great terror fell on him, so that he was almost crushed by it. This may be illustrated from the case of Daniel. When Gabriel spoke with him in a vision Daniel said: "No strength remained in

---

① Maimonides explains in *Guide of the Perplexed*, Introduction that he finally gave up the attempt to write these two works. For the relevant passage, see S. Pines' translation, vol. 1, pp. 9–10.

me, my appearance was altered beyond recognition, what strength I had deserted me." (Dan. 10:8) He also said: "I fell unconscious, face downwards on the ground." (Dan. 10:9) And again: "At the vision my anguish overcomes me." (Dan. 10:16) But it was not like this with Moses. The word came to him, but no agitation of any kind befell him, as Scripture says: "The Lord spoke to Moses face to face, as a man speaks to his friend." (Exod. 33:11) That is to say, just as a man does not fell disquiet when his friend speaks to him, so Moses was not disquieted when God's words came to him, even though it was "face to face." This was so because of the strength of his union with the Active Intellect, as we have said.

The fourth difference: To all other prophets inspiration came not by their own choice but by the will of God. Sometimes the prophet remained for a number of years without inspiration coming to him; sometimes the people asked the prophet to tell them something by inspiration, and he had to wait days or months to prophesy about it, or else he received no prophecy on the matter at all. We have seen cases where the prophet prepared himself by delighting his soul and by purifying his mind, as Elisha did when he said: "Now bring me a minstrel!" (2 Kgs. 3:15); and then inspiration came to him, though it was not inevitable that he would receive inspiration every time he prepared himself thus. But Moses our Teacher was able to say whenever he wished: "Stand still and I will hear what the Lord commands you." (Num. 9:8) And God said: "Tell Aaron your brother that he may not enter the sanctuary whenever he chooses." (Lev. 16:2) The Sages commented: "This prohibition against entering the sanctuary applied only to Aaron, but Moses was free to enter whenever he chose." (Sifra to Lev. 16:2)

The Eighth Fundamental Principle is that the Torah is from heaven. We should believe that the whole Torah which is in our possession today is the same Torah as was handed down to Moses, and that in its entirety it is from the mouth of the Almighty. That is to say, that the whole Torah came to him from God in a manner which is metaphorically called "speaking," though no one knows the real nature of that communication save Moses to whom it came. He fulfilled the function of a scribe receiving dictation, and he wrote the whole Torah, its histories, its narratives and its commandments, and that is why he is called a "copyist" [*mehoqeq* —Deut. 33:21]①. There is no difference between such verses as "The sons of Ham were Cush, Egypt, Put and Canaan" (Gen. 10:6) and "His wife's name was Mehetabel, daughter of Matred" (Gen. 36:39), on the one hand, and such verses as "I am the Lord your God" (Exod. 20:2) and "Hear, O Israel" (Deut. 6:4), on the other. It is all from the mouth of the Almighty; it is all the Torah of the Lord which is perfect, pure, holy and true.

The Sages regarded Manasseh as the greatest infidel and heretic that ever was, because he thought that there was both a kernel and a husk to the Torah, and that the histories and narratives have no value but were composed by Moses himself (Babylonian Talmud, Sanhedrin 99b). The Sages said that he who asserts that the *whole* Torah is from the mouth of the Almighty except for *one* verse which he claims was spoken not by God but by Moses himself, says, in effect, "The Torah is not from heaven" (Babylonian Talmud, Sanhedrin 99a). To such a one may be applied the verse: "He has despised the word of the Lord" (Num. 15:31). May God be exalted above all that infidels say! Rather, every letter of the Torah contains wisdom and wonders for him to whom God has granted understanding. You cannot comprehend the limit of its wisdom: "Its length is longer than the earth, its breadth broader than the sea." (Job 11:9) Man has only to follow the example of David, the anointed of the God of Jacob, the most pleasant singer of the hymns of Israel who prayed: "Open my eyes that I may see wonders in your Torah." (Ps. 119:18)②

So too the interpretation of the Torah which we have received is from the mouth of the Almighty, and the form of the Sukkah③ we make today,

---

① *Mehoqeq* here is usually translated "ruler", "leader" or "lawgiver", but an early Jewish tradition, found e.g. in the Targumim, took it as meaning "scribe" and saw in it a reference to Moses.

② I.e., each individual is required to try to understand the deeper meaning of the Torah.

③ The booth that Jews live in during the holiday of Sukkot.

the Lulav①, the Shofar, the Zizit②, the Tefillin③, and so on, are the very same as the forms which God told to Moses and which Moses passed on to us. He was a messenger who was "faithful" (*ne'eman*, cf. Num. 12:7) to his message. The verse of Scripture which teaches this eighth principle is: "By this you shall know that the Lord has sent me to do all these works, and that I have not done them on my own initiative" (Num. 16:28).

The Ninth Fundamental Principle is [the denial of the] abrogation [of the Torah]. This Torah of Moses will not be abrogated, nor shall another Torah come from God. Nothing may be added to it or taken from it, either from the written text or from the oral commentary, as Scripture says: "You shall not add to it nor take away from it" (Deut. 13:1). In the introduction to this work we have already explained what needs to be explained of this principle.

The Tenth Fundamental Principle is that God has knowledge of the deeds of men and does not disregard them. The view is not correct which says: "The Lord has abandoned the earth" (Ezek. 8:12); rather, as Scripture says, God is "great in counsel and mighty in deed, and his eyes are open to all the ways of men" (Jer. 32:19). Scripture also says: "The Lord saw that the wickedness of man was great in the earth" (Gen. 6:5). And again it says: "The cry of Sodom and Gomorrah is great" (Gen. 18:20). These verses teach this tenth fundamental principle.

The Eleventh Fundamental Principle is that God rewards him who obeys the commands of the Torah and punishes him who transgresses its prohibitions. The greatest of God's rewards is the world to come [*ha-olam ha-ba*], and the severest of his punishments is "cutting off" [*karet*]. In this chapter we have already said enough about this subject. The verse which teaches this principle is: "And yet, if it pleased you to forgive this sin of

---

① A bundle of palm-tree branches that are part of the ritual of Sukkot.
② The fringe worn on the corners of their garments by some Jews.
③ Small boxes containing prayers that male Jews wrap around their arms and foreheads when praying.

theirs...! But if not, erase me from the book that you have written"; and God replied: "It is the man who sinned against me that I shall erase from my book." (Exod. 32:32f) This is evidence that God takes cognizance both of the obedient and of the rebellious, so as to reward the one and punish the other.

The Twelfth Fundamental Principle concerns the Messianic Age. We should believe and affirm that the Messiah will come, and should not consider him as tardy: "Should he tarry, wait for him." (Hab. 2:3) No date may be fixed for his appearance, nor may the Scriptures be interpreted in such a way as to derive from them the time of his coming. The Sages have said: "May the wits of those who calculate the end be blasted!" (Babylonian Talmud, Sanhedrin 97b) We should have firm faith in him, honoring and loving him, and praying for his coming, in accordance with what has been said about him by all the prophets, from Moses to Malachi. Whoever has doubts about him, or makes light of his authority, contradicts the Torah, which clearly promises his coming, in the section [*parashah*, "weekly readings"] of *Balaam*① (Num. 22:2 – 25:9), and in the section *Nizzavim*② (Deut. 29:9 – 30:20). A general consequence of this principle is that Israel cannot have a king who is not descended from David, and, more particularly, from Solomon③. Whoever disputes the authority of this dynasty denies God and words of his prophets.

The Thirteenth Fundamental Principle is the resurrection of the dead. We have already explained this.

[The resurrection of the dead is one of the fundamental principles of the Torah of Moses our Teacher. He who does not believe it is devoid of religion, and has no bond with the Jewish people. However, resurrection is

---

① The *parashah* is usually called "Balaq". Maimonides is probably thinking of Num. 24:17.

② The passage of *Nizzavim* (standing) reiterates the covenant between God and the Israelites, the content of which is the Torah and the result of which is the establishment of Israel as God's people.

③ Maimonides' emphasis on the Solomonic descent of the Messiah may be aimed at the Christians, who (at Luke 3:31) traced Jesus' descent through David's "son" Nathan.

only for the righteous. As Genesis Rabbah says: "The power of the rain is for both the righteous and the wicked, but the resurrection of the dead is for the righteous alone." (cf. Genesis Rabbah 13:6) How can the wicked come back to life when they are dead even during their lifetime? The Sages said: "The wicked, even during their lifetime, are called dead, but the righteous, even when they are dead, are called alive." (Babylonian Talmud, Berakhot 18b) Know that man must assuredly die and be resolved into his constituent elements.]①

When all these principles are held as certain by a man and his faith in them is firm, then he belongs to the Community of Israel [*Kelal Yisra'el*], and there is an obligation to love him, to have compassion on him, and to perform for him all the acts of love and brotherhood which God has commanded us to perform one for another. Even if he has committed every possible sin because of lust, or because his lower nature got the better of him, though he will surely be punished to the extent of his rebellion, yet still he has a share in the world to come, and is regarded as "a sinner in Israel." However, if a man doubts one of these principles he has left the Community, has denied a basic principle, and is called a heretic, an Epicurean, and a "cutter of shoots"② (Babylonian Talmud, Hagiga 14b). There is an obligation to hate and to destroy him, and of him Scripture says: "Shall I not hate those who hate you, O Lord." (Ps. 139:21)

---

① The passage in brackets is found a little earlier in Maimonides' *Commentary on the Mishnah*, Sanhedrin 10. It appears to be the explanation of the doctrine of the resurrection to which he refers here.

② This phrase is used to describe the arch rabbinical heretic Elisha ben Abuya, also known as Aher ("Other"). See 6.9; 10.3.

6.12 Maimonides, Introduction to the *Mishneh Torah*. On the History of the Oral Torah and Its Transmission[①]

All the commandments given to Moses at Sinai were given along with their explanations, as it is said, "And I will give you the tablets of stone, the *torah* and the *mitzvah*" (Exod. 24:12): *torah* refers to the Written Torah—while *mitzvah* refers to its explanation. [Moses] commanded us to carry out the *torah* in accordance with the *mitzvah*. This *mitzvah* is what goes by the name "Oral Torah."

Moses, our master, wrote down the entire *torah* before he died in his own hand and gave a scroll to each tribe. One additional scroll, he deposited in the Ark to serve as a witness [to the true text], as it is said: "Take this scroll of the *torah*, and place it along the [inner] side of the ark of the covenant of the Lord your God that it may be there for a witness." (Deut. 31:26).

But the *mitzvah*, which is the explanation of the torah, he did not write down; he rather commanded it [orally] to the elders, Joshua and all the rest of Israel, as it is said: "Everything which I commanded you, that you shall observe to do; do not add to it or diminish from it" (Deut. 13:1)—which is why it is called the Oral Torah.

[Maimonides here enumerates the leading sages over the generations.]

All the above-mentioned sages were the great men of [their] generations. Some were academy heads; some were exilarchs; some were members of the Great Sanhedrin. Together with them, in each generation, were thousands and tens of thousands [of others] who heard [the tradition] from them and with them. Ravina and Rav Ashi were the last of the sages of the Talmud. It was Rav Ashi who compiled the Babylonian Talmud in the land of Shin'ar [Babylonia], some one hundred years after

---

① Sources: Walzer, Lorberbaum and Zohar (2000); Lerner (2000), pp. 133–139. Cf. 迈蒙尼德 (2015), 第 17—23 页。

Rabbi Yohanan compiled the Jerusalem Talmud.

The purpose of the two Talmuds is [to provide] explanation of the words of the Mishnah; explication of its profundities; and the innovations introduced in all the various courts from the days of Our Saintly Master① through the compilation of the Talmud. From the two Talmuds, the Tosefta, Sifra, Sifrei and the [other] supplements [to the Mishnah]—from all these [sources] emerge what is prohibited and what permitted, what is impure and what pure, what is liable and what exempt, what is fit and what unfit, as transmitted in direct succession from Moses, [who received it] from [God at] Sinai.

From these [sources] also emerge the measures that the sages and prophets of each generation decreed to make a fence round the Torah, in accordance with [the charge] they heard on the authority of Moses, who—in explaining [the verse] "you shall preserve my charge" (Lev. 18:30)—said: "Establish a safeguard for my charge." In addition, there emerge from [these sources] the customs and ordinances, ordained or practiced in each generation, as the court of that generation saw fit. For it is forbidden to deviate from them, as it is said, "You shall not deviate from anything they tell you, to the right or to the left." (Deut. 17:11)

In addition, legal judgments, [once] obscure, that were not received [on tradition] from Moses. [Rather] the Great Court of a particular generation deliberated on them, using the rules② whereby the Torah is expounded, and its elders [then] decided them, concluding that the law is such and such. All such [rulings made] from the days of Moses up until his own, Rav Ashi compiled in the Talmud.

The sages of the Mishnah compiled other works to interpret the words of the Torah. Rabbi Hoshayah, a disciple of Our Saintly Master, compiled an explanation of the book of Genesis. Rabbi Ishmael interpreted from

---

① "Our Saintly Master" refers to Rabbi Judah the Patriarch, who compiled the Mishnah.

② "The rules" refers to the thirteen rules for expounding Scripture.

"These are the names" until the end of Torah;① it is that which is called Mekhilta. Rabbi Akiba too compiled a Mekhilta, and other sages after them compiled collections of midrashim. All [of these works] were compiled prior to the Babylonian Talmud.

Thus, Ravina, Rav Ashi, and their colleagues were the last of Israel's great sages who transmitted the Oral Torah, who issued decrees, ordained ordinances, and instituted customs, and whose decrees, ordinances and customs gained acceptance among all [the people of] Israel, wherever they dwelt.

After [the term of] the court of Rav Ashi, who compiled and completed the Talmud in the days of his son, Israel was scattered still further, through all the lands of the earth, reaching the ends [of the inhabited world] and its remote regions. [Armed] conflict increased in the world and travel routes were disrupted by marauding troops. Study of the Torah diminished; and Israel no longer gathered to study at their academies by the thousands and tens of thousands as they had in times past.

Rather, individuals, "the remnants whom the Lord called" (Joel 3:5), would gather in every city and province, engage in [study of the] Torah, reflect upon all the compilations of the sages, and discern, from them, what course [the principles] of legal judgment [mandate].

Of all the post-talmudic courts that arose in the various provinces and established decrees, ordinances, or customs for the inhabitants of its province or [a group of] provinces, there was none whose enactments gained the acceptance of all Israel, because their settlements were scattered, travel routes were disrupted, and the provincial court in question consisted of [mere] individuals [lacking ecumenical authority], whereas the Great Court of Seventy [wherein such authority did reside] had been defunct for many years prior to the compilation of the Talmud.

Therefore, the inhabitants of one province are not compelled to follow the custom of another province; nor is one court told to uphold a decree that

---

① I.e., from the beginning of the book of Exodus through Deuteronomy.

another court enacted in its province. Similarly, if one of the Geonim taught that [on a certain issue] the course [mandated by the principles] of legal judgment is such and such and it becomes clear to another, subsequent court that such is not, in fact, the course [mandated by the principles] of legal judgment inscribed in the Talmud, one heeds not the earlier [authority] but the one to whose view reason inclines, be he the earlier or the later. The above applies [only] to inferences, decrees, ordinances, and customs introduced after the compilation of the Talmud; but whatever is included in the Babylonian Talmud, the whole House of Israel is duty-bound to follow. Every city and province is compelled to follow all customs followed by the sages of the Talmud, to uphold their decrees and to follow their ordinances.

For all the aforementioned things included in the Talmud have been accepted by all Israel. Moreover, the sages who established [those] ordinances, decrees, or customs, or who drew [those] inferences and taught that the law [*mishpat*] is such and such, were the entirety or majority of the sages of Israel, and the ones who heard the tradition [*ha-kabbalah*] on the rudiments of the entire Torah① in direct transmission extending back to Moses.

---

① I.e., the 613 commandments.

7 THE JEWISH LAWS

7.1 Exodus 20:1–18. The Decalogue①

(1) God spoke all these words,② saying:

(2) I the LORD am your God who brought you out of the land of Egypt, the house of bondage:(3) you shall have no other gods besides Me.

(4) You shall not make for yourself a sculptured image,③ or any likeness of what is in the heavens above, or on the earth below, or in the waters under the earth. (5) You shall not bow down to them or serve them. For I the

---

① The Decalogue, Hebrew "*aseret ha-devarim*," lit. "ten words," is the initial stipulation of the covenant with the Lord. "Decalogue," from the Greek for "ten words," is a more literal rendition of Hebrew than "Ten Commandments."

② The addressee is not specified. The present sequence of the narrative suggests that it was the people, as stated in Deut. 5:4 and 19, but according to Deut. 5:5 and, possibly, Exod. 20:15 – 18, God spoke only to Moses, who later communicated His words to the people. Talmudic exegesis resolves the inconsistency by explaining that the people heard the first two commandments, in which God speaks in the first person, directly from God and the remainder, in which God is spoken of in the third person, via Moses (b. Mak. 24a).

③ *Sculptured image.* There is no prohibition here of the plastic arts as such. Only images made for worship (v. 5) are prohibited. Non-idolatrous statues of certain creatures were permitted, such as the cherubs (Exod. 25:18 – 20) and the oxen supporting the water tank in Solomon's Temple (1 Kings 7:25); see also Num. 21:8 – 9.

LORD your God am an impassioned God①, visiting the guilt of the parents upon the children, upon the third and upon the fourth generations of those who reject Me, (6) but showing kindness② to the thousandth generation of those who love Me③ and keep My commandments.

(7) You shall not swear falsely by the name of the LORD your God; for the LORD will not clear one who swears falsely by His name.

(8) Remember④ the sabbath day and keep it holy. (9) Six days you shall labor and do all your work, (10) but the seventh day is a sabbath of the LORD your God: you shall not do any work⑤—you, your son or daughter, your male or female slave, or your cattle, or the stranger who is within your settlements. (11) For in six days the LORD made heaven and earth and sea, and all that is in them, and He rested on the seventh day; therefore the

---

① *Impassioned God.* Others, "jealous God." In the biblical view, this is an aspect of His passionate involvement with human beings and no more a character flaw than is human jealousy over marital infidelity. But postbiblical commentators found the implications of divine jealousy troubling, and Maimonides interpreted the term as merely an anthropomorphism based on the necessity of borrowing terms from human experience to describe God (*Guide of the Perplexed*, I :54).

② *Kindness.* Hebrew "*hesed*," better rendered "faithfulness." It refers to acts of kindness that are expected between parties in a relationship—husband and wife, parents and children, relatives, and allies—and to reciprocation of kindness (Gen. 40:14; Deut. 7:9; 1 Sam. 20:8; 2 Sam. 9:1; 10:2). Here, as frequently, it refers to God's covenantal faithfulness to Israel.

③ *Who love me.* The only time in the first four books of the Torah where the love of God is stressed. In Deuteronomy love of God is an important aspect of man's duties.

④ *Remember.* The Sabbath is understood to be already known to and practiced by the people. Jewish tradition dates the institution of its observance from the first appearance of the manna (Exod. 16:30) but emphasizes that the idea of the Sabbath was built into creation itself (Gen. 2:1 – 3).

⑤ *Work.* Jewish tradition defined this in detail, developing a catalog of thirty-nine main types of prohibited labor. They include the main agricultural and domestic activities that qualify as work, and from these categories later halakhic rules were developed.

LORD blessed the sabbath day and hallowed it.①

(12) Honor your father and your mother, that you may long endure on the land that the LORD your God is assigning to you.

(13) You shall not murder.

You shall not commit adultery.②

You shall not steal.

You shall not bear false witness against your neighbor.③

(14) You shall not covet your neighbor's house; you shall not covet your neighbor's wife, or his male or female slave, or his ox or his ass, or anything that is your neighbor's.

(15) All the people witnessed the thunder and lightning, the blare of the horn and the mountain smoking; and when the people saw it, they fell back and stood at a distance. (16) "You speak to us," they said to Moses, "and we will obey; but let not God speak to us, lest we die." (17) Moses answered the people, "Be not afraid; for God has come only in order to test you,④ and in order that the fear of Him may be ever with you, so that you do not go astray." (18) So the people remained at a distance, while Moses approached the thick cloud where God was.

---

① In place of this explanation of the origin of the Sabbath, the Decalogue in Deuteronomy states its purpose of providing rest to servants and cites the exodus as the reason for observing it (Deut. 5:14–15).

② *Adultery.* In the Bible this refers to voluntary sexual relations between a married or engaged woman and a man other than her husband. It did not refer to the extramarital relations of a married man. This prohibition was later widened by both rabbinic and Christian traditions.

③ *Bear false witness.* This covers both false accusation and false testimony in court. The penalty is stated in Deut. 19:16–21.

④ *In order to test you.* It is not clear what is tested. Another possible translation is "to give you an experience (of Him)," meaning that the theophany would give the people a vivid, sensory experience of God and the experience would instill "fear of God," a deterrent to sin.

7.2 Eye for Eye, or Monetary Compensation[①]

7.2.1 Exodus 21:22-27

(22) When men fight, and one of them pushes a pregnant woman and a miscarriage results, but no other damage ensues, the one responsible shall be fined according as the woman's husband may exact from him, paying as much as the judges determine. (23) But if other damage ensues, the penalty shall be life for life, (24) eye for eye, tooth for tooth, hand for hand, foot for foot, (25) bum for bum, wound for wound, bruise for bruise.

(26) When a man strikes the eye of his slave, male or female, and destroys it, he shall let him go free on account of his eye. (27) If he knocks out the tooth of his slave, male or female, he shall let him go free on account of his tooth.

7.2.2 Mishnah, Bava Kamma, 8:1

One who causes damage to his neighbor must compensate him on five counts: for damages; for pain; for healing; for loss of time; and for humiliation.

How do they compute compensation for damages? If he blinded his neighbor's eye, cut off his hand, broke his leg—they view the injured party as if he were a slave sold in the market and estimate how much he was worth before the injury and how much he is worth now.

How do they compute compensation for pain? If he burned his neighbor with a spit or a stake, even on his nail or other place which yields no wound—they estimate how much a person of similar status would

---

① Source: Corrigan, et al. (1998), pp. 10, 15-18.

demand to suffer that much pain.

How do they compute compensation for healing? If he struck his neighbor—he is obliged to pay for his healing. If sores appeared on his body—if they were caused by the blow, he must pay for the healing; if not, he is exempt from payment. If the wound healed and then opened repeatedly—he is obliged to pay for his healing. Once it has healed completely, he is no longer obliged for his healing.

How do they compute compensation for loss of time? They view him as if guarded cucumber patches for a living, for the damager has already given him compensation for his hand or leg.

How do they compute compensation for humiliation? All depends upon the status of the humiliator and the humiliated. One who humiliates a naked person (whose very nakedness is itself humiliating); one who humiliates a blind person (who cannot see that he is being humiliated); one who humiliates a sleeping person (who is unaware of the humiliation)—he is obliged to compensate him. But a sleeping person who humiliates another is exempt. If he fell from a roof, causing damages and humiliation—he is obliged to compensate the damage, but is exempt from compensating the humiliation, for it is said in Scripture: "And she put forth her hand and grabbed his shameful parts" (Deut. 25:11). He is obliged to compensate for humiliation only if he does so intentionally.

7.2.3 Mekhilta of Rabbi Ishmael, Mishpatim 8 (Exod. 21:23–25)

"The penalty shall be life for life" (Exod. 21:23)—this means that you must compensate life for a life, but you may not compensate a life with money.

Rabbi (Judah the Patriarch) says: "The penalty shall be life for life"—this implies monetary compensation!

You claim this implies monetary compensation? Perhaps it permits only death?

(Said Rabbi:) Just attend to Scripture's terminology: here, in discussing compensation, the term "determine" is used (Exod. 21:22) and elsewhere (Exod. 21:30, where monetary compensation is permitted for damages caused by cattle) "determine" is used. Just as there the reference is to monetary compensation, so here!

"Eye for eye" (Exod. 21:24)—this means monetary compensation.

You say monetary compensation? Perhaps it really means taking out his eye?

Rabbi Ishmael would say: Indeed, Scripture says: "One who kills an animal shall make restitution for it; but one who kills a human being shall be put to death." (Lev. 24:21) Scripture has juxtaposed damages to a human with damages to cattle and damages to cattle with damages to a human. Accordingly, just as damages to cattle are compensated with money, so too damages to humans (other than death itself) are compensated by money!

Rabbi Isaac says: Indeed (right after specifying that a goring ox must be killed), Scripture says: "If a ransom is imposed upon the owner." (Exod. 21:30) Now this yields a clear inference. Just as where Scripture imposes the death penalty it makes room for monetary compensation, in the present case (of bodily harm), where death is not mentioned, it is reasonable to suppose that the only compensation is monetary!

Rabbi Eliezer says: "Eye for eye"—shall I conclude that whether the damage is intentional or unintentional he only compensates with money? But, indeed, Scripture singles out one who intends to cause bodily harm, specifying that he must compensate in kind (by a wound to himself). For it is said: "Anyone who injures another shall suffer the same injury in return" (Lev. 24:19)—this is the general principle. "Eye for eye" (Lev. 24:20)—this is a specification. Where a general principle is immediately followed by a specification, the application of the principle is limited to the case stated in the specification.

Yet when it continues to say "the injury inflicted is the injury to be suffered" (Lev. 24:20) a general principle is restated.

Perhaps the point is that the two general principles are redundant?

Absolutely not! Rather, where a general principle introduces a specification which is then followed by another general principle, you can only draw inferences that have analogies to the specification. Just as the specification here is clear that wounds that are permanent, affecting major organs, are visible, and inflicted intentionally must be compensated only with money—so we conclude that all wounds that are permanent, affecting major organs, are visible, and inflicted intentionally are compensated with money!

Scripture says: "The injury inflicted is the injury to be suffered" (Lev. 24:20)—this applies only where he intended to harm him.

7.2.4 Babylonian Talmud, Bava Kamma, 86a

How do they compute compensation for humiliation? All depends upon the status of the humiliator and the humiliated. ①

Whose view is represented in the mishnaic tradition? It is neither that of Rabbi Meir nor that of Rabbi Judah. Rather, it is that of Rabbi Shimon.

For oral tradition transmits the following: "*They view all injured Jews as if they were freemen who lost their property, for they are the children of Abraham, Isaac and Jacob—these are the words of Rabbi Meir.*"

Rabbi Judah says: "They compensate a great person in accord with his greatness and an insignificant person in accord with his insignificance."

Rabbi Shimon says: "The rich are viewed as if they were freemen who lost their property; the poor are viewed as the least of these."

Now, in the light of this, who stands behind our mishnaic tradition? If you claim Rabbi Meir—our mishnaic tradition teaches *all depends upon the status of the humiliator and the humiliated*, but Rabbi Meir holds that they are all to be treated equally! And if you claim Rabbi Judah—our mishnaic tradition teaches *one who humiliates a blind person is obliged to compensate him*, but Rabbi Judah elsewhere holds that humiliation does

---

① The quoted sources are reproduced here in italics to distinguish them from the surrounding talmudic discussion.

not apply to the blind! Therefore, mustn't our authority be Rabbi Shimon?

You could even say that our mishnaic tradition is Rabbi Judah's! For when Rabbi Judah said that humiliation does not apply to the blind, he meant only that we do not hold him liable for humiliation, but he certainly is due compensation for humiliation!

But consider what is transmitted at the end of our mishnaic tradition: *"One who humiliates a sleeping person is obliged to compensate him; but a sleeping person who humiliates another is exempt."* Note that it does not transmit that a blind person who humiliates another is exempt. This implies that there is no difference one way or another with regard to a blind person (contrary to Rabbi Judah's view). Obviously, our mishnaic tradition represents the view of Rabbi Shimon!

7.3 Maimonides, Laws of the Study of Torah[1]

Comprising two positive commandments: 1. to study Torah; 2. to honor those who teach it and those who know it; and the explanation of these commandments [follows] in these chapters.

CHAPTER 1

1. Women and slaves are exempt from [the obligation] of the study of Torah. Concerning a minor, however, his father is obligated to teach him Torah, as it is said, "And you shall teach them to your children to speak of them." (Deut. 11:19) A woman is not obligated to teach her son, for [only] one who is obligated to study is obligated to teach.

---

[1] Source: Kaplan (2001). This translation is based on the Oxford manuscript of the *Book of Knowledge*, which contains a colophon by Maimonides himself that attests to the fact the manuscript was copied from his own autograph. Paragraphing follows that of the Oxford manuscript and not that of the printed editions. See also 迈蒙尼德 (2015),第 73—88 页。For the laws of honoring teachers and learned men in the *Shulhan Arukh*, see Leviant (1969), pp. 527 - 530.

2. Just as a man is obligated to teach his son, so is he obligated to teach the son of his son, as it is said, "Make them known to your sons and to the sons of your sons." (Deut. 4:9) And [this obligation applies] not only to one's son and the son of one's son, but a commandment [devolves] upon each and every Israelite sage to teach all the students even if they are not his sons, as it is said, "And you shall teach them diligently to your sons." (Deut. 6:7) On the basis of the tradition we have learned, "Your sons": this refers to your students, for students are called sons, as it is said, "And the sons of the prophets went forth." (2 Kings 2:3)

3. If this is so, why does the commandment refer to one's son and to the son of one's son? (Deut. 4:9) [To teach] that one's [own] son takes precedence over the son of one's son, and that the son of one's son takes precedence over the son of one's neighbor. Moreover, one is obligated to hire a teacher to teach one's son, but one is obligated to teach his neighbor's son only if it involves no expense.

4. One who was not taught by his father is obligated to teach himself when he reaches the age of discernment, as it is said, "And you shall study them and you shall observe them to perform them." (Deut. 5:1) And so you will find that in all circumstances study takes precedence over practice. For study leads to practice, but practice does not lead to study.

5. If a person needs to study Torah and he has a son [whom he is obligated] to teach Torah, he takes precedence over his son. But if his son understands and grasps what he studies better than he, his son takes precedence. However even though [in the above circumstance] his son takes precedence, he should not desist [from study]. For just as a commandment devolves upon him to teach his son, so is he commanded to teach himself.

6. A person should always [first] study Torah and [only] afterward marry. For if he will marry first, his mind will not be free for study. But if his inclination overpowers him to such an extent that his heart is not free, let him marry first and then study Torah.

7. When should a father begin to teach his son Torah? When the son

begins to speak his father teaches him "Moses commanded us the Torah, an inheritance, etc." (Deut. 33:4) and the first verse of the section of Shema (Deut. 6:4). Afterward he teaches him bit by bit several verses [at a time], until he is six or seven depending on his development, at which point he takes him to a teacher of children.

8. If it is the customary practice of the province [that people] hire teachers of children for pay, then he [the father] must pay his wages. And it is his duty to pay [a teacher's] wages to have him [his child] taught until he has read through the entire written Torah.

9. In a place where customarily teach the written Torah for pay—it is permissible [for a teacher] to teach for pay. But it is forbidden to teach the oral Torah for pay, as it is said, "Behold I [Moses] taught you statutes and ordinances as [that is, in the same manner as] the Lord my God commanded me." (Deut. 4:5) [This means that] "Just as I [Moses] studied [from God] for free, so you have studied from me for free. And similarly, when you will teach throughout the generations do so for free, just as you studied from me."

10. If a person cannot find anyone to teach him [the oral Torah] for free, he should study it [with someone] for pay, as it is said, "And buy the truth" (Prov. 23:23). Might one assume then that [in such circumstances] he can teach [the oral Torah] to others for pay? The verse continues, "and do not sell"—from this you may learn that it is forbidden for a person to teach [the oral Torah] for pay even if his master taught him [the oral Torah] for pay.

11. Every Israelite male is obligated to study Torah, whether poor or rich, whether in a state of bodily perfection or afflictions, whether a youth or a very old enfeebled man. Even a poor man who goes begging from door to door or even a married man with children is obligated to set aside for himself a fixed time for the study of Torah both in the day and in the night, as it is said, "And you shall meditate therein day and night." (Joshua 1:8)

12. Some of the great sages of Israel were hewers of wood, some were drawers of water, some were blind; and even so they occupied themselves

with the Torah during the day and the night. And they are included among the transmitters of the tradition from Moses our master.

13. Until when is a person obligated to study Torah? Until the day of his death, as it is said, "And lest they [the precepts] depart from your heart all the days of your life." (Deut. 4:9) And whenever one does not occupy himself with study, one forgets.

14. A person is obligated to divide the time allotted to study into three parts: One-third to the written Torah, one-third to the oral Torah, and one-third he should intelligently infer conclusions from premises and derive one matter from another, and he should compare one matter to another matter, and he should issue rulings through use of the [thirteen] hermeneutical principles① until he understands the essence of these principles and how he may derive the forbidden and the permitted and the like from those matters which he learned on the basis of tradition. And this [third] subject is termed Talmud.

15. How so? If a person is an artisan and occupies himself with his trade for three hours daily and with the Torah for nine hours daily, he should spend three hours in reading the written Torah, three hours in [reading] the oral Torah, and three hours in reflecting on how to infer one matter from another. And the words of the prophets are included in the written Torah, and their interpretation in the oral Torah. And those subjects termed Pardes② are included in the Talmud.

16. The above applies only to the period when a person begins his study. But once a person grows in wisdom and no longer needs to study the written Torah nor to occupy himself with the oral Torah, he should read the written Torah and the traditional teachings for fixed period, so that he should not forget any matter of the laws of the Torah, and should devote all

---

① For details of the Rabbinical hermeneutics, including the 13 principles, see Strack and Stemberger (1996), pp. 15 – 30; Birnbaum (1977), pp. 42 – 46; 傅有德 (2018), 第143—148页。

② The account of the chariot and the account of creation, which Maimonides elsewhere identifies with the divine science and natural science, respectively.

his days solely to Talmud in accordance with the breadth of his heart and the composure of his mind.

17. A woman who studies Torah will receive a reward, but it will not be like the reward received by a man. For she is not commanded [to study Torah]; and whoever performs an act that he is not commanded to do will not receive the same reward as one who performs an act and is so commanded, but will receive a lesser reward. Even though she will receive a reward, the sages have commanded that a person should not teach his daughter Torah. For the minds of most women are not directed to being taught, and they will turn words of Torah into words of folly, in accordance with the weakness of their understanding.

18. The sages have said: "One who teaches his daughter Torah, it is as if he teaches her frivolity." This [statement] applies only to [teaching her] the oral Torah, but concerning the written Torah, a man should not teach it to his daughter to begin with, but if he did teach it to her it is not as if he taught her frivolity.

CHAPTER 2

1. Teachers of the young are to be appointed in each province and district. And concerning any city in which there are not to be found young school children, the inhabitants of the city are to be excommunicated until they appoint teachers for the young. If they [still] do not appoint them, the city is to be laid waste, for the world is maintained only by the breath of school children.

2. Children are to be sent to study at about the age of six or seven, all in accordance with the strength of the son and his physical build. But a child younger than six is not to be sent. And the teacher may strike them [his pupils] to instill awe in them. But he may not strike them in a cruel or vindictive manner. Therefore he may not strike them with whips or sticks, but only with a small strap.

3. And the teacher should teach them the entire day and part of the night, in order to train them to study by day and by night. And the children

should not desist from study at all, except on the eves of the Sabbaths and the eves of holidays, toward the end of the day, and on holidays. But on the Sabbath they are not to study new material, but should review what they have studied. And one is not to cause children to desist [from their studies] even for the building of the Temple.

4. A teacher of children who leaves the children and goes outside, or who does other work while he is with them, or who is remiss in teaching them is included in the category of "Cursed be he who does the work of the Lord negligently" (Jer. 48:10). Therefore one should appoint as a teacher only a God-fearing individual who is both able to cover ground and be precise. An unmarried man should not teach children on account of their mothers who visit their sons. And, similarly, a woman should not teach child on account of their fathers who visit their sons.

5. Twenty-five children are to study with one teacher. If there were more than twenty-five children, if there are fewer than forty children a person is appointed alongside him to assist him in teaching them. If there are more than forty, one must appoint two teachers.

6. One may transfer a minor from one teacher to another teacher who is more able, whether in covering ground or in precision. When does the above apply? When both teachers are in the same city and there is no river separating them. But one is not to transfer a minor from one city to another, nor [even] from one side of the river to another, unless there is a sturdy bridge spanning the river, a bridge that is not likely to collapse quickly.

7. If one of the residents of an alley or even one of the residents of a courtyard wishes to set himself up as a teacher, his neighbors cannot prevent him. Similarly, [if there is] a teacher of children [who is already established], and his fellow comes along and opens up a school for children nearby him, so that other [new] children shall come to him or [even] so that children from the former should transfer to the latter, the former cannot prevent him, as it is said, "The Lord was pleased for His righteousness' sake to make the Torah great and glorious." (Isa. 42:21)

CHAPTER 3

1. With three crowns was Israel crowned—with the crown of Torah, with the crown of priesthood, and with the crown of kingship. The crown of priesthood was acquired by Aaron, as it is said, "And it shall be unto him and unto his seed after him the covenant of an everlasting priesthood." (Num. 25:13) The crown of kingship was acquired by David, as it is said, "His seed shall endure everlastingly, and his throne as the sun before Me." (Ps. 89:37) The crown of Torah [by contrast] is set before and available to all, as it is said, "Moses commanded us the Torah, an inheritance of the congregation of Jacob." (Deut. 33:4) Whoever so wishes may come and take it.

2. Lest you may say that the other crowns are greater than the crown of Torah, behold it is said, "By me [the Torah] kings reign and nobles decree justice. By me princes rule." (Prov. 8:15–16)

3. From this you may understand that the crown of Torah is greater than the crown of priesthood and the crown of kingship. The sages have said "An illegitimate who is a disciple of the sages is to take preference over a high priest who is an ignoramus," as it is said, "and it [the Torah] is more precious than rubies" (*peninim*) (Prov. 3:15); [that is], it is more precious than the high priest who enters within the innermost part of the sanctuary (*lipnai ve-lipnim*).

4. There is no commandment among all the commandments as weighty as the study of Torah. Rather, the study of Torah is equal to them all. For study leads to practice. Therefore study in all circumstances takes precedence over practice.

5. If a person is studying Torah and the opportunity to perform a commandment presents itself to him—if the commandment can be performed by others, let him not interrupt his study; but if not, let him perform the commandment and return to his study.

6. A person at the first stage of his judgment will be judged concerning his study and afterward concerning his other deeds. Therefore the sages have said: "Let a person occupy himself with the Torah even not for its own

sake; for as a result of [occupying himself with it] not for its own sake he will arrive at [occupying himself with it] for its own sake."

7. He whose heart lifts him up to perform this commandment fittingly and to be crowned with the crown of Torah should not turn his mind aside to other things and should not let it enter his heart that he will acquire Torah together with riches and honor at the same time. This is the way of Torah. A morsel of bread with salt you will eat, and on the ground you will sleep, and a life of pain you will lead, and [the while] you will toil in the Torah. It is not incumbent upon you to complete the work nor are you free to desist from it, but if you have piled up for yourself much Torah, you have piled up for yourself much reward. And the reward is in accordance with the pain.

8. Lest you will say, once I have gathered much wealth then I will return and study; once I have acquired sufficient for my needs then I will turn aside from my occupations and return and study—if this thought enters your heart, you will never acquire the crown of Torah. Rather make your Torah your fixed activity and your trade your casual activity; and do not say when I shall have leisure I will study, lest you never have leisure.

9. It is written in the Torah: "It is not in heaven ... and neither is it beyond the sea." (Deut 30:12–13) "It is not in heaven"—it [the Torah] is not to be found among those of arrogant spirit; "and neither is it beyond the sea"—nor is it to be found among those who cross the sea. Therefore the sages have said: "One who engages much in trade cannot become wise." And they have commanded and said: "Engage little in your occupation and occupy yourself with Torah."

10. Words of Torah are likened unto water, as it is said, "O, everyone who is thirsty, come for water." (Isa. 55:1) This teaches you that just as water does not accumulate on a slope, but flows away and gather only in a depression, so words of Torah are not to be found among those possessed of an arrogant spirit or a proud heart, but among one who is contrite and lowly in spirit, who sits in the dust at the feet of the sages, who removes temporal desires and pleasures from his heart, and who does a little work every day,

just enough for his livelihood, if he otherwise would have nothing to eat, and occupies himself the rest of his day and his night with Torah.

11. One whose heart prompts him to occupy himself with Torah and not to do any work, but to be supported by charity—such a person has desecrated the [divine] Name, and has cast shame on the Torah, and has extinguished the light of religion, and has brought evil upon himself, and has removed his life from the world to come, for it is forbidden to derive benefit through words of Torah in this world.

12. The sages have said: "Whoever derives benefit from words of Torah removes his life from the world." They further commanded and said: "Do not make of them [the words of Torah] a crown wherewith to make yourself great, nor a spade wherewith to dig." And they further commanded and said: "Love work, but hate lordship." And any Torah unaccompanied by work will in the end cease to be; and in the end this person will rob his fellow men.

13. It is an exalted rank for one to support himself by the work of his hands. And this was the manner of behavior of the early pietists. By this means a person will acquire all honor and good in this world and in the world to come, as it is said, "When you eat of the toil of your hands, happy you shall be and it shall be good with you" (Ps. 128:2): "happy"—in this world; "and it shall be good with you"—in the world to come which is wholly good.

14. Words of Torah will not abide with one who treats them slackly nor with those who study amidst luxury and amidst eating and drinking, but only with one who mortifies himself for their sake, who constantly subjects his body to pain, and deprives his eyes of sleep and his eyelids of slumber. The sages have said by way of metaphor: "'This is the Torah, if a person dies in a tent。'(Num. 19:14) [This is as if to say that] the Torah abides only with one who mortifies himself in the tents of wisdom." And similarly Solomon said in his wisdom: "If you are slack in the day of adversity, your strength is small indeed." (Prov. 24:10) He further said: "But my wisdom alone (*'af*) stayed with me." (Eccles. 2:9) [This is as if to say], "the wisdom

that I learned in wrath (*'af*) has stayed with me."

15. The sages have said: "A covenant is established for whoever toils away at his study in the synagogue that he will not forget it soon." And whoever modestly toils away at his study in private will become wise, as it is said, "And wisdom is with the modest." (Prov. 11:2) And whoever raises his voice while studying, his study will abide with him; but one who reads silently will soon forget.

16. Even though it is a commandment to study both in the day and in the night, a person learns most of his wisdom only at night. Therefore, he who wishes to acquire the crown of Torah should take heed of all his nights and not fritter away even one of them in sleeping and eating and drinking and conversation, and the like, but [should spend them] in study of Torah and words of wisdom. The sages have said: "The full measure of Torah is [acquired] only at night, as it is said, 'Arise, sing out in the night.' (Lam. 2:19)" And whoever occupies himself with the Torah at night, a thread of [divine] loving kindness is spun out for him during the day, as it is said, "By day the Lord shall command His loving kindness, and by night His song shall be with me, a prayer unto the Lord of my life." (Ps. 42:9) And any house where words of Torah are not to be heard at night will be consumed by fire.

17. "Because he has despised the word of the Lord" (Num. 15:31): this refers to one who has paid no attention at all to words of Torah. Similarly, whoever is able to occupy himself with Torah and does not so occupy himself, or whoever has read [the written Torah] and recited [the oral Torah] and has then turned aside to the vanities of this world and has set his study to the side and has abandoned it, is included among those who have despised the word of the Lord. The sages have said: "Whoever desists from the Torah on account of wealth will in the end desist from it on account of poverty. And whoever fulfills the Torah in a condition of poverty will in the end fulfill it in a condition of wealth."

18. And this matter is clearly set forth in the Torah, for it is said, "Because you did not serve the Lord your God in [a condition] of joy and

gladness of heart, having abundance of all things, therefore you will serve your enemy which the Lord will send against you in [a condition] of hunger and thirst and nakedness and lacking all things, and he will place an iron yoke, etc." (Deut. 28:47-48) And it is said, "That He might afflict you and try you to do good to you at your latter end." (Deut. 8:15)

CHAPTER 4

1. Torah should be taught only to a worthy student, whose deeds are fine, or to one of undetermined character. But if the student is walking in a path that is not good, he is to be brought back and guided in a straight path and examined, and afterward he is to be brought into the study house (*beit midrash*) and taught. The sages have said: "Whoever teaches a student who is not worthy, it is as if he cast a stone to Mercury, as it is said, 'As one puts a stone into a sling, so is he that gives honor to a fool.' (Prov. 26:8) And there is no honor but the Torah, as it is said, 'The sages shall inherit honor.' (Prov. 3:35)"

2. Similarly, a master (*rav*) who does not walk in a path that is good, even if he is a great sage and all the people are in need of him, he is not to be studied from until he returns to the good, as it is said, "For the priest's lips shall guard knowledge, and they shall seek Torah from his mouth, for he is [as] an angel of the Lord of Hosts." (Mal. 2:7) The sages have said: "If the master resembles an angel of the Lord of Hosts, then they shall seek Torah from his mouth. But if not, then they shall not seek Torah from his mouth."

3. How is teaching to be conducted? The master sits in front and the students face him, surrounding him like a crown, so that they may all see the master and hear his words. And the master should not sit on a chair while the students sit on the ground, but let them all sit on the ground or all sit in chairs. Formerly, the teacher used to sit and the students would stand. But before the destruction of the Temple it became the practice of everyone to teach the students while they were sitting.

4. If the master teaches the students directly, let him do so. But if he

teaches via an intermediary (*metargem*), the intermediary should stand between him and the students, and the master should address the intermediary, and the intermediary then declaim [what he heard] to all the students. And when [the students] pose a question to the intermediary, he [in turn] should pose it to the master; the master [thereupon] should reply to the intermediary, and the intermediary [in turn] reply to the questioner. The master should not raise his voice above the voice of the intermediary, nor should the intermediary raise his voice above the voice of the master when he poses a question to the master.

5. The intermediary is not permitted to detract from or add to or change [what the master said], unless the intermediary is the father or master of the sage. If the master tells the intermediary, "Thus did my master tell me" or "Thus did my revered father tell me," when the intermediary addresses these words to the people, he is to cite them in the name of the sage [quoted], and should mention the name of the master's father or master, and should say, "Thus did Rabbi so-and-so say." Even though the sage [when addressing the intermediary] did not mention the name [of his father or teacher, the reason he did not mention the name is] because one is forbidden to call one's master or father by his name.

6. If the master is teaching and the students do not understand, he should not get angry at them or chastise them, but should review and repeat the matter even one hundred times until they understand the depths of the law. Similarly, a student should not say "I understand" if he does not understand, but should ask again and again, even many times. And if the master gets angry at him or chastises him, he [the student] should say to him [the master]: "My master, it is Torah and I need to comprehend it, and my grasp is limited."

7. A student should not be embarrassed because of his fellow students who have comprehended the material after the first or second time [it was taught], while he does not comprehend until after [it has been taught] many times. For if he will be embarrassed on account of this matter, he will, as a result, enter and leave the study house without his having

comprehended anything. Therefore the early sages have said: "The one who is embarrassed cannot learn, and one who is irascible cannot teach."

8. When does the above apply: when the students have not understood the latter because of its profundity, or because their grasp is limited. But if it is clear to the master that the students are negligent and slack in [their study] of words of Torah, and it for that reason that they do not understand, he is obliged to chastise them and shame them with words [of reproach] in order to sharpen their wits. Concerning this matter, the sages have said: "Cast fear into the students."

9. Therefore, it is not fitting for a master to act in a light-hearted manner before his students, nor may he jest in their presence, nor may he eat or drink with them, in order that his awe rest upon them thereby, and that they speedily comprehend him.

10. One does not ask a question to a master who has just entered the house of study until his mind has become composed. Nor should a student ask a question upon his entry [to the house of study], until he sits down and rests. Nor may two students ask questions at the same time. Nor may the master be questioned about a subject other [than the one they are studying], but only about the subject with which they are currently occupied, so he will not be embarrassed. And a master may try to mislead the students, both by his questions and the deeds he performs in their presence, in order to sharpen their wits and in order to know whether they remember what he has taught them or not. And it need not be said that he has permission to ask them questions even concerning a subject with which they have not occupied themselves in order to spur them on.

11. One may not ask a question while standing, nor answer a question while standing. Nor [may questions be asked or answered] from a height or from a distance or while behind the elders. One may question the master only concerning the subject [with which they are currently occupied]; and one may ask a question only in a spirit of awe; and one may not ask about more than three laws in a particular subject.

12. Two [students] asked a question. One asked a question that is

directly pertinent to the subject, while the other asked a question that is not directly pertinent to the subject, one responds to the question that is directly pertinent to the subject. [A question] about an actual case and [a question] about a legal ruling, one responds to [the question about] the actual case; [a question] about a legal ruling and [a question] about a [legal] midrash,① one responds to [the question about] the legal ruling; [a question] about a [legal] midrash and [a question] about a nonlegal matter, one responds to [the question about] the [legal] midrash; [a question] about a nonlegal matter and [a question] about an a fortiori inference, one responds to [the question about] the a fortiori inference; [a question] about an a fortiori inference and [a question] about a *gezerah shavah*,② one responds to [the question about] the a fortiori inference.

13. If there are two questioners—one is a sage and the other is a student, one responds to the sage; if one of the questioners is a student and the other is an ignorant person, one responds to the student. If both questioners were sages or both students or both ignorant men, and if they both asked questions about legal rulings or about judicial questions or about judicial decisions or about cases, the discretion now rests in the hands of the intermediary.

14. No one is permitted to sleep in the house of study. And whoever dozes in the house of study, his wisdom will be torn into tatters. As Solomon stated in his wisdom, "And drowsiness shall clothe one in tatters" [Prov. 23:21]. And one should converse in the house of study only about words of Torah. Even if one sneezes, one does not say "be of good health" to him in the house of study; and it need not be said [that one does not speak there] about other matters. And the sanctity of the house of study is greater than the sanctity of synagogues.

---

① I.e., interpretation of a scripture verse.

② I.e., legal inference deriving from Scripture's use of the same phraseology in two different passages.

7.4 Maimonides, *Mishneh Torah*, Book 7, Chapter 10:1–19. Laws Concerning Gifts to the Poor[①]

1. We are obligated to be more scrupulous in fulfilling the commandment of charity[②] than any other positive commandment because charity is the sign of the righteous man, the seed of Abraham our Father, as it is said, "For I know him, that he will command his children ... to do righteousness" (Gen. 18:19). The throne of Israel is established and the religion of truth is upheld only through charity, as it is said, "In righteousness shall you be established" (Is. 54:14). Israel is redeemed only through charity, as it is written, "Zion shall be redeemed with judgment and they that return of her with righteousness" (Is. 1:27).

2. No man has ever become impoverished by giving charity and no evil or damage has ever resulted from charity, as it is said, "and the work of righteousness is peace" (Is. 32:17).

Whosoever displays mercy to others will be granted mercy himself, as it is said, "And He will grant you mercy, and have compassion upon you, and multiply you" (Deut. 13:18).

If someone is cruel and does not show mercy, there are sufficient grounds to suspect his lineage, since cruelty is found only among the other nations, as it is said, "They are cruel and will not show mercy" (Jer. 50:42).

All Jews and those attached to them are like brothers, as it is said, "You are sons to the Lord your God" (Deut. 14:1), and if a brother will not show mercy to his brother, then who will have mercy on him? And to whom can the poor of Israel look for help—to those other nations who hate and persecute them? They can look for help only to their brethren.

[①] Source: Twersky (1972), pp. 135–139. For the laws of charity in the *Shulhan Arukh*, see Leviant (1969), pp. 531–534.

[②] The Hebrew word *tzedakah* is translated throughout as both righteousness and charity. See *Guide*, III, ch. 53; also ch. 39.

3. Whosoever refuses to give charity is called *Belial*, the same term which is applied to idol-worshipers. With regard to idol-worshipers it is said, "Certain base fellows [lit. "children of *Belial*" (*bene beliyaal*)] have gone out" (Deut. 13:14), and with regard to those who refuse to give charity it is said, "Beware that there be not a base [*Belial*] thought in your heart" (Deut. 15:9); and he is called a wicked man, as it is said, "The tender mercies of the wicked are cruel" (Prov. 12:10); and he is called a sinner, as it is said, "And he cries to the Lord against you, and it be sin in you" (Deut. 15:9).

The Holy One, blessed be He, is close to the cries of the poor, as it is said, "You hear the cries of the poor" (paraphrase of Job 34:28). Therefore, one should heed their cries, for a covenant has been made with them, as it is said, "And when he will cry to Me I shall listen because I am merciful" (Ex. 22:26).

4. Whosoever gives charity to a poor man ill-manneredly and with downcast looks has lost all the merit of his action even though he should give him a thousand gold pieces. He should give with good grace and with joy and should sympathize with him in his plight, as it is said, "Did I not weep for him that was in trouble? Was not my soul grieved for the poor?" (Job 30:25) He should speak to him words of consolation and sympathy, as it is said, "And I gladdened the heart of the widow" (Job 29:13).

5. If a poor man requests money from you and you have nothing to give him, speak to him consolingly. It is forbidden to upbraid a poor person or to shout at him because his heart is broken and contrite, as it is said, "A broken and contrite heart, O God, You will not despise" (Ps. 51:19), and it is written, "To revive the spirit of the humble, and to revive the heart of the contrite" (Is. 57:10). Woe to him who shames a poor man. Rather one should be as a father to the poor man, in both compassion and speech, as it is said, "I am a father to the poor" (Job 29:15).

6. He who persuades and constrains others to give shall have a reward greater than that of the giver himself, as it is said, "And the work of righteousness shall be peace" (Is. 32:17). Concerning such that solicit charity

(for others) and their like, it is said, "And they that turn the many to righteousness [shall shine] as the stars" (Dan. 12:3).

7. There are eight degrees of charity, one higher than the other. The highest degree, exceeded by none, is that of the person who assists a poor Jew by providing him with a gift or a loan or by accepting him into a business partnership or by helping him find employment—in a word, by putting him where he can dispense with other people's aid. With reference to such aid, it is said, "You shall strengthen him, be he a stranger or a settler, he shall live with you" (Lev. 25:35), which means strengthening him in such manner that his falling into want is prevented.

8. A step below this stands the one who gives alms to the needy in such manner that the giver knows not to whom he gives and the recipient knows not from whom it is that he takes. Such exemplifies performing the meritorious act for its own sake. An illustration would be the Hall of Secrecy in the ancient sanctuary where the righteous would place their gift clandestinely and where poor people of high lineage would come and secretly help themselves to succor.

The rank next to this is of him who drops money in the charity box. One should not drop money in the charity box unless one is sure that the person in charge is trustworthy, wise, and competent to handle the funds properly, as was Rabbi Hananya ben Teradyon.

9. One step lower is that in which the giver knows to whom he gives but the poor person knows not from whom he receives. Examples of this were the great sages who would go forth and throw coins covertly into poor people's doorways. This method becomes fitting and exalted, should it happen that those in charge of the charity fund do not conduct its affairs properly.

10. A step lower is that in which the poor person knows from whom he is taking but the giver knows not to whom he is giving. Examples of this were the great sages who would tie their coins in their scarves which they would fling over their shoulders so that the poor might help themselves without suffering shame.

11. The next degree lower is that of him who, with his own hand, bestows a gift before the poor person asks.

12. The next degree lower is that of him who gives only after the poor person asks.

13. The next degree lower is that of him who gives less than is fitting but gives with a gracious mien.

14. The next degree lower is that of him who gives morosely.

15. There have been great sages who, before praying, would give a coin to the needy, because it is said, "I will behold your face in righteousness" (Ps. 17:15).

16. A species of charity is the maintenance of one's minor sons and daughters who have passed the age at which the father is obligated to support them, provided the purpose of such maintenance be that of educating the sons in sacred lore and of keeping the daughter in the right path, removed from shame. Similarly to be classed as charity is the maintenance of one's father and mother.

In giving charity, precedence should be accorded to one's own relatives.

He who lets poor people and orphans partake of food and drink at his table shall call upon the Lord and find, to his delight, that the Lord will answer, as it is said, "Then shall you call and the Lord will answer" (Is. 58:9).

17. The sages have enjoined that one's domestics should consist not of bondmen but of poor folk and orphans. Better to employ the latter and let the descendants of Abraham, Isaac, and Jacob benefit from one's possessions than to have that advantage go to the seed of Ham. Day by day, one who adds to the number of his bondmen augments the world's sin and iniquity. But hour by hour, one who takes the poor as members of his household increases virtue and merit.

18. A man should always exert himself and should sooner endure hardship than throw himself, as a dependent, upon the community. The sages admonished, "Make your Sabbath a weekday, sooner than become dependent." Even one who is learned and honored should, if impoverished, work at various trades, yes, despicable trades, in order to avoid dependency.

Better to strip the hides of beasts that have sickened and died than to tell people, "I am a great sage, my class is that of a priest, support me." Thus spoke the sages.

Outstanding scholars worked as hewers of wood, as carriers of beams, as drawers of garden water, as iron workers, as blacksmiths, rather than ask anything of the community and rather than accept any proffered gratuity.

19. He who, having no need of alms, obtains alms by deception will, ere he die of old age, fall into a dependency that is real. Such a person comes under the characterization: "Cursed is the man that trusts in man" (Jer. 17:5).

One, however, who does stand in need, and who, like an aged or sick or afflicted person, cannot live without help but who, in his pride, declines to accept help is a shedder of blood, guilty of attempts on his own life. Out of his misery, he gets naught but trespasses and sins.

But one, impoverished otherwise, who endures privation and exerts himself and lives a life of hardships rather than burden the community will, ere he die of old age, possess the means out of which he will succor others. Concerning such a person, it is written, "Blessed is the man that trusts in the Lord" (Jer. 17:7).

7.5 *Shulhan Arukh*

7.5.1 Yoreh De'ah: Laws about Converts[①]

268. How to make converts, men or women, and the laws about the marriage of a convert. Herein are twelve paragraphs.
  2. If a man wants to become a Jew they say to him: "What has prompted you to come to convert yourself? Don't you know that Jews are now oppressed, prostrate, mistreated, undergoing suffering?" If he answers:

---

① Source: Marcus (1999), p. 230.

"I know, and I am not worthy to join you," then they accept him without further delay and inform him of the principles of Judaism, namely, the unity of God, and the prohibition of idolatry. This they discuss with him at length. (Yebamot 47a.)[1]

7.5.2 Eben ha-Ezer: Laws of Propagation[2]

1. The laws about propagation, and that one should not be without a wife. Herein are fourteen paragraphs.
    6. Every Jew is commanded to get married at eighteen, and he who gets married earlier is observing the commandment in the very best way. But no one ought to get married before thirteen, for this would be lust. Under no circumstances should one pass his twentieth birthday without getting married, and if a person passes his twentieth birthday and doesn't care to get married, the court shall compel him to marry in order that he may fulfill the command of propagation. However, if he is busied with the Torah and concerned about it, and is afraid to get married lest he be troubled too much about making a living, and therefore have to neglect his study of the Torah, he is permitted to delay.

Gloss. [by Isserles] *But nowadays it is not the practice to compel a man to get married.*

---

[1] Practically all the laws of the *Shulhan Arukh* are of Talmudic origin.
[2] Source: Marcus (1999), p. 229.

7.5.3 Hoshen Mishpat 26:1–4. Prohibition Against Resorting to Non-Jewish Courts①

1. It is forbidden to appear for trial before gentile judges② and in their law courts—*i.e., at fixed judicial sessions at which magistrates adjudicate*—even in a lawsuit that they would judge in accordance with the laws of Israel. Even should both parties agree to be tried before them, it is forbidden. Whoever appears for trial before them is a wicked man: it is as if he reviled, blasphemed and rebelled against the Torah of Moses our teacher. **Gloss.** *The Jewish court has the right to impose on such a one the lesser ban* [niddui], *or the greater ban* [herem], *till he instructs the gentile authorities to drop proceedings against his fellow litigant. So, too, they may impose a ban* [herem] *on anyone who encourages one who goes to law before a gentile court. Even if the plaintiff does not go to law before a gentile court, but merely compels the defendant through the agency of the gentile court to appear with him for trial before a Jewish court—he deserves to be flogged. He who went before a gentile court and was found guilty under their laws, and then turned round and summoned the other party to appear before a Jewish court—some say his case should not be heard; others that it should be heard, unless he was the cause of some loss to his fellow litigant before the gentile court. The former opinion is, in my view, fundamental.*

2. If the power of the gentile courts is great, and the defendant a violent man, so that the plaintiff is unable to receive satisfaction from him through the Jewish courts, then he must first summon the defendant to appear before a Jewish court. Should he refuse, then the plaintiff may obtain permission from the Jewish court to seek redress through the gentile courts. **Gloss.** *The members of a Jewish court have the right to go before the gentile*

---

① Source: Alexander (1984), pp. 90–91.

② *Gentile judges.* Literally, "judges of star-worshippers" (*ovedei khokhavim*), that is, "idolaters."

courts and give evidence that one party is culpable in respect of another. This whole ruling applies only when the defendant refuses to submit to the Jewish court. Otherwise the Jewish court is forbidden to grant anyone permission to appear before a gentile court.

3. If anyone undertook by means of a *qinyan* [1] to appear with his fellow litigant for trial before a gentile court, it has no legal validity, and he is forbidden to appear for trial before them. If he gave an undertaking that, should he not appear before them, he would be bound to give such-and-such a sum to the poor, he is still forbidden to appear with his fellow litigant before the gentile court, though he is obliged to give the poor whatever he undertook to pay them. There is one authority who states that the Jewish court may not exact this pledge from him, but should merely inform him that the vow is binding on him.

4. Even if the plaintiff possesses a document in which it is written that he may summon the defendant under gentile law—he is still not permitted to summon him before the gentile courts. If the plaintiff handed over the document to the gentile court so that it might summon the defendant under its laws, he is obliged to reimburse the defendant for any loss he caused him, in excess of whatever the defendant is liable to pay under the laws of Israel.

Gloss. *This whole ruling applies only where one party can compel the other to appear before a Jewish court, but if a debtor proves violent, a creditor may hand over such a document to a gentile court.*

---

[1] *qinyan.* A symbolic way of making an agreement binding, in which one party hands over an object to another.

7.6 The Declaration of the Establishment of the State of Israel, May 14, 1948[①]

ERETZ-ISRAEL[②] was the birthplace of the Jewish people. Here their spiritual, religious and political identity was shaped. Here they first attained to statehood, created cultural values of national and universal significance and gave to the world the eternal Book of Books.

After being forcibly exiled from their land, the people kept faith with it throughout their Dispersion and never ceased to pray and hope for their return to it and for the restoration in it of their political freedom.

Impelled by this historic and traditional attachment, Jews strove in every successive generation to re-establish themselves in their ancient homeland. In recent decades they returned in their masses. Pioneers, ma'apilim[③] and defenders, they made deserts bloom, revived the Hebrew language, built villages and towns, and created a thriving community controlling its own economy and culture, loving peace but knowing how to defend itself, bringing the blessings of progress to all the country's

---

① Source: the website of the Israel Ministry of Foreign Affairs: http://mfa.gov.il/MFA/ForeignPolicy/Peace/Guide/Pages/Declaration%20of%20Establishment%20of%20State%20of%20Israel.aspx. Published in the *Official Gazette*, No. 1 of the 5th, Iyar, 5708 (14th May, 1948). David Ben-Gurion, chairman of the Jewish Agency Executive, read the Declaration of the Establishment of the State of Israel. The Jewish population of Palestine—except for Jerusalem, which was without electricity—heard the declaration ceremonies as they were broadcast from the Tel Aviv Museum.

② *Eretz-Israel.* Hebrew, "Land of Israel." This term indicates that the declaration's intent is not the land of the state of Israel, but the land that composed the ancestral home of the Jewish people.

③ *Ma'apilim* was the Hebrew name given to Jews who immigrated illegally to Palestine when immigration was severely limited during the British Mandate in the 1930s and 1940s. The term is of biblical origin, taken from the Hebrew word *va-ya'apilu*, which means "defiantly they marched" (Num. 14:44). The use of a biblical term for this defiant illegal immigration stressed that this was a return home, the continuation of an ancient and sacred history.

inhabitants, and aspiring towards independent nationhood.

In the year 5657 (1897), at the summons of the spiritual father of the Jewish State, Theodore Herzl, the First Zionist Congress convened and proclaimed the right of the Jewish people to national rebirth in its own country.

This right was recognized in the Balfour Declaration of the 2nd November, 1917, and reaffirmed in the Mandate of the League of Nations, which, in particular, gave international sanction to the historic connection between the Jewish people and Eretz-Israel and to the right of the Jewish people to rebuild its National Home.

The catastrophe which recently befell the Jewish people—the massacre of millions of Jews in Europe—was another clear demonstration of the urgency of solving the problem of its homelessness by reestablishing in Eretz-Israel the Jewish State, which would open the gates of the homeland wide to every Jew and confer upon the Jewish people the status of a fully privileged member of the comity of nations.

Survivors of the Nazi holocaust in Europe, as well as Jews from other parts of the world, continued to migrate to Eretz-Israel, undaunted by difficulties, restrictions and dangers, and never ceased to assert their right to a life of dignity, freedom and honest toil in their national homeland.

In the Second World War, the Jewish community of this country contributed its full share to the struggle of the freedom- and peace-loving nations against the forces of Nazi wickedness and, by the blood of its soldiers and its war effort, gained the right to be reckoned among the peoples who founded the United Nations.

On the 29th November, 1947, the United Nations General Assembly passed a resolution calling for the establishment of a Jewish State in Eretz-Israel; the General Assembly required the inhabitants of Eretz-Israel to take such steps as were necessary on their part for the implementation of that resolution. This recognition by the United Nations of the right of the Jewish people to establish their State is irrevocable.

This right is the natural right of the Jewish people to be masters of their own fate, like all other nations, in their own sovereign State.

ACCORDINGLY WE, MEMBERS OF THE PEOPLE'S COUNCIL [Mo'ezet ha-Am], REPRESENTATIVES OF THE JEWISH COMMUNITY OF ERETZ-ISRAEL AND OF THE ZIONIST MOVEMENT, ARE HERE ASSEMBLED ON THE DAY OF THE TERMINATION OF THE BRITISH MANDATE OVER ERETZ- ISRAEL AND, BY VIRTUE OF OUR NATURAL AND HISTORIC RIGHT AND ON THE STRENGTH OF THE RESOLUTION OF THE UNITED NATIONS GENERAL ASSEMBLY, HEREBY DECLARE THE ESTABLISHMENT OF A JEWISH STATE IN ERETZ- ISRAEL, TO BE KNOWN AS THE STATE OF ISRAEL [*Medinat Yisra'el*].

WE DECLARE that, with effect from the moment of the termination of the Mandate being tonight, the eve of Sabbath, the 6th Iyar, 5708 (15th May, 1948)①, until the establishment of the elected, regular authorities of the State in accordance with the Constitution which shall be adopted by the Elected Constituent Assembly not later than the 1st October 1948②, the People's Council shall act as a Provisional Council of State [*Mo'ezet Medinah Zemannit*], and its executive organ, the People's Administration [*Minhelet ha-Am*], shall be the Provisional Government of the Jewish State [*Ha-Memshalah Ha-Zemannit shel Ha-Medinah Ha-Yedudit*], to be called "Israel".

THE STATE OF ISRAEL will be open for Jewish immigration and for the Ingathering of the Exiles③; it will foster the development of the country for the benefit of all its inhabitants; it will be based on freedom, justice and peace as envisaged by the prophets of Israel; it will ensure complete

---

① The Declaration was approved at a festive session of the People's Council, comprised of representatives of *yishuv* (the Jewish community in Palestine) and the Zionist movement, on Friday, May 14, 1948, several hours before the British Mandate for Palestine came to an end.

② Israel still has no constitution, and progress towards it has been exceedingly slow.

③ This principle was set forth in legal and practical terms in the Law of Return, passed two years later (1950). See 7.7.

equality of social and political rights to all its inhabitants irrespective of religion, race or sex; it will guarantee freedom of religion, conscience, language, education and culture; it will safeguard the Holy Places of all religions; and it will be faithful to the principles of the Charter of the United Nations.

THE STATE OF ISRAEL is prepared to cooperate with the agencies and representatives of the United Nations in implementing the resolution of the General Assembly of the 29th November, 1947, and will take steps to bring about the economic union of the whole of Eretz-Israel.

WE APPEAL to the United Nations to assist the Jewish people in the building-up of its State and to receive the State of Israel into the comity of nations.

WE APPEAL—in the very midst of the onslaught launched against us now for months—to the Arab inhabitants of the State of Israel to preserve peace and participate in the upbuilding of the State on the basis of full and equal citizenship and due representation in all its provisional and permanent institutions.

WE EXTEND our hand to all neighbouring states and their peoples in an offer of peace and good neighbourliness, and appeal to them to establish bonds of cooperation and mutual help with the sovereign Jewish people settled in its own land. The State of Israel is prepared to do its share in a common effort for the advancement of the entire Middle East.

WE APPEAL to the Jewish people throughout the Diaspora to rally round the Jews of Eretz-Israel in the tasks of immigration and upbuilding and to stand by them in the great struggle for the realization of the age-old dream—the redemption of Israel.

PLACING OUR TRUST① IN THE "ROCK OF ISRAEL"②, WE AFFIX OUR SIGNATURES TO THIS PROCLAMATION AT THIS SESSION OF THE PROVISIONAL COUNCIL OF STATE, ON THE SOIL OF THE HOMELAND, IN THE CITY OF TEL‑AVIV, ON THIS SABBATH EVE, THE 5TH DAY OF IYAR, 5708 (14TH MAY, 1948).

David Ben-Gurion

Daniel Auster		*David Zvi Pinkas*
Mordekhai Bentov	*Rachel Cohen*	*Aharon Zisling*
Yitzchak Ben Zvi	*Rabbi Kalman Kahana*	*Moshe Kolodny*
Eliyahu Berligne	*Saadia Kobashi*	*Eliezer Kaplan*
Fritz Bernstein	*Rabbi Yitzchak Meir*	*Abraham Katznelson*
Rabbi Wolf Gold	*Levin*	*Felix Rosenblueth*
Meir Grabovsky	*Meir David Loewenstein*	*David Remez*
Yitzchak Gruenbaum	*Zvi Luria*	*Berl Repetur*
Dr. Abraham Granovsky	*Golda Myerson*	*Mordekhai Shattner*
Eliyahu Dobkin	*Nachum Nir*	*Ben Zion Sternberg*
Meir Wilner-Kovner	*Zvi Segal*	*Bekhor Shitreet*
Zerach Wahrhaftig	*Rabbi Yehuda Leib*	*Moshe Shapira*
Herzl Vardi	*Hacohen Fishman*	*Moshe Shertok*

7.7 The Law of Return (1950/1954/1970)③

1. Every Jew has the right to come to this country as an *oleh*

---

① *Trust.* In the religious tradition, "trust" connotes a belief in God and suggests a passive nod towards the "Redeemer of Israel." In Modern Hebrew, however, it (the Hebrew word is *bitakhon*, which also means security) refers principally to physical and military power.

② *Rock of Israel* [*be-Zur Yisra'el*]. From Psalms 19:15: "O LORD, my rock and my redeemer." See also 9.6. These opening words had prompted a debate among the members of the People's Council, reflecting the disagreements between its secular and religious members concerning the future image of the state. The debate ended in tacit acquiescence, presumably because of the reluctance to engage in such a discussion at that time. It should be mentioned, however, that the representatives of the *haredi* (ultra-Orthodox) community subsequently took exception to the entire Declaration, stating that it greatly offended their sensitivities.

③ Source: https://knesset.gov.il/laws/special/eng/return.htm.

[immigrant].

2. (a) *Aliyah* [immigration] shall be by *oleh*'s visa.

(b) An *oleh*'s visa shall be granted to every Jew who has expressed his desire to settle in Israel, unless the Minister of Immigration [1954: Minister of the Interior] is satisfied that the applicant—(1) is engaged in an activity directed against the Jewish people; or (2) is likely to endanger public health or the security of the State; [1954: or (3) is a person with a criminal past, likely to endanger public welfare.]

3. (a) A Jew who has come to Israel and subsequent to his arrival has expressed his desire to settle in Israel may, while still in Israel, receive an *oleh*'s certificate.

(b) The restrictions specified in section 2(b) shall apply also to the grant of an *oleh*'s certificate, but a person shall not be regarded as endangering public health on account of an illness contracted after his arrival in Israel.

4. Every Jew who has immigrated into this country before the coming into force of this Law, and every Jew who was born in this country, whether before or after the coming into force of this Law, shall be deemed to be a person who has come to this country as an *oleh* under this Law.

[1970: 4A. (a) The rights of a Jew under this Law and the rights of an *oleh* under the Nationality Law, 5712 – 1952, as well as the rights of an *oleh* under any other enactment, are also vested in a child and a grandchild of a Jew, the spouse of a Jew, the spouse of a child of a Jew and the spouse of a grandchild of a Jew, except for a person who has been a Jew and has voluntarily changed his religion.

(b) It shall be immaterial whether or not a Jew by whose right a right under subsection (a) is claimed is still alive and whether or not he has immigrated to Israel.

(c) The restrictions and conditions prescribed in respect of a Jew or an *oleh* by or under this Law or by the enactments referred to in subsection (a) shall also apply to a person who claims a right under subsection (a).

4B. For the purposes of this Law, "Jew" means a person who was born of a Jewish mother or has become converted to Judaism and who is not a member of another religion.]

5. The Minister of Immigration [1954: Minister of the Interior] is charged with the implementation of this Law and may make regulations as to any matter relating to such implementation and also as to the grant of *oleh*'s visas and *oleh*'s certificates to minors up to the age of 18 years.

[1970: Regulations for the purposes of sections 4A and 4B require the approval of the Constitution, Legislation and Judicial Committee of the Knesset.]

8 ETHICAL LITERATURE

8.1 Mishnah, Avot. Miscellaneous Moral Maxims

2:2 Rabban Gamaliel, son of Rabbi Judah the Patriarch, says: "Fitting is learning in the Torah along with a craft [*derekh eretz*]①, for the labor put into the two of them makes one forget sin. And all learning of the Torah which is not joined with labor is destined to be null and causes sin. And all who work with the community②—let them work with them [the community] for the sake of Heaven. For the merit of their fathers③ strengthens them, and their righteousness stands forever. And as for you, I

---

① *Craft.* Or, "*worldly occupation.*" "By this [*derekh eretz*] is meant trading or other means of making a living ... Since on the one hand a man learns from the Torah that you may not oppress, you may not rob, and on the other hand he is engaged in making a living, it will not even occur to him to steal, to rob, or to act with violence." (Mahzor Vitry)

② *All who work with the community.* That is, community leaders.

③ *Merit of their fathers* (*zekhut avot*). That is, the merit of the fathers of the community, namely, Abraham, Isaac, and Jacob. In Jewish theology, the *zekhut avot* concept implies that the good deeds of the ancestors contribute to the welfare of their descendants, and a Jew is best able to advance on the road to moral perfection if he or she starts with the accumulated spiritual heritage of righteous ancestors.

credit you with a great reward, as if you had accomplished it."①

2:4 Hillel says: "Do not withdraw from the community. And do not have confidence in yourself until the day you die. And do not judge your fellow until you are in his place. And do not say anything which cannot be heard, for in the end it will be heard.② And do not say: 'When I have time, I shall study,' for you may never have time."

2:5 Hillel used to say: "A boor [*bur*] will never fear sin, nor will an unlettered person [*am ha-aretz*]③ ever be pious [*hasid*], nor will a shy person learn, nor will an intolerant person teach, nor will anyone too busy in business get wise. Where there are no men, try to be a man.④"

2:9 Rabban Yohanan ben Zakkai said to his disciples: "Go and see what is the straight path to which someone should stick." Rabbi Eliezer

---

① *As for you, I credit you with a great reward, as if you had accomplished it.* "This is God speaking to those who bear the burden of communal work. For there are times when they are prevented from carrying out a commandment, because they are then engaged in some public task. And so the Lord, blessed be He, says to them that He will credit them with a great reward as if they had carried out that particular commandment, though they had in fact not done so: because they were busy in behalf of communal matters for the sake of Heaven." (Maimonides)

② The Hebrew word *lishmoa* can mean either "to hear" or "to understand." This mishnah, therefore, can also mean "And do not say anything which cannot be understood [with the hope] that in the end it will be understood." Based on this, Maimonides suggests that one's statements should be easily understood: "Let not the meaning of your words be far removed from their literal sense; say not, 'if a person probe deeply, he will see that what I said is right.' The mishnah warns against expression of this sort, by exhorting: let not your words require farfetched interpretation and extraordinary perception before they can be understood."

③ "A boor is someone in whom there is neither learning nor moral virtues; the *am ha-aretz* is one who has no intellectual capacities but does have some moral qualities." (Maimonides) Cf. Avot, 5:7; 5:10.

④ *Where there are no men, try to be a man.* "Where there is no one to take the initiative and assume responsibility, 'try to be a man,' to take on leadership." (Mahzor Vitry)

says: "A good eye."① Rabbi Joshua says: "A good friend." Rabbi Yose says: "A good neighbor." Rabbi Simeon says: "Foresight." Rabbi Eleazar says: "A good heart."② He said to them: "I prefer the opinion of Rabbi Eleazar ben Arakh, because in what he says is included everything you say."

3:2 Rabbi Hananiah, Prefect of the Priests, says: "Pray for the welfare of the government. For if it were not for the fear of it, one man would swallow his fellow alive."

3:7 Rabbi Simeon says: "If one is studying as he walks along the highway,③ and he interrupts his study and exclaims: 'How beautiful is that tree! How beautiful is that ploughed field!'—Scripture [Deut. 4:9] reckons it to him as though he were mortally guilty."④

3:9 Rabbi Haninah ben Dosa says: "For anyone whose fear of sin takes precedence over his wisdom, his wisdom will endure. And for anyone whose wisdom takes precedence over his fear of sin, his wisdom will not

---

① *A good eye.* That is, generosity, or liberality. Conversely, "an evil eye" means selfishness, grudge, and jealousy.

② *A good heart.* It means "that good conduct which comes from following the *via media*. This is the ideal and it includes contentment with one's portion, the love of good men, and other virtues (Maimonides)." "It seems to me that by 'a good heart' is meant the capacity for long-suffering, one's not being short-tempered. Such a person shuns anger, always makes reply softly; even when something evil is done to him, he puts up with it, and no bitterness comes from his mouth (Rabbi Jonah)."

③ According to Rashi, the study of Torah will protect the individual from the dangers of travel. To break off from such study puts one's life at risk.

④ "The reason for such strong condemnation is this: by nature man is drawn to vanity and idle matters; [if he does not resist his nature] he will be drawn on from such habits to throwing off the yoke of the Torah completely." (Meiri)

endure."①

3:13 Rabbi Akiba says: "Laughter and lightheadedness turn lewdness into a habit. Tradition [*masoret*]② is a fence for the Torah. Tithes are a fence for wealth. Vows are a fence for abstinence. A fence for wisdom is silence."

3:15 Everything is foreseen, and free choice is given. In goodness the world is judged.③ And all is in accord with the abundance of deed[s].

3:17 Rabbi Eleazar ben Azariah used to say: "Anyone whose wisdom is greater than his deeds—to what is he to be likened? To a tree with abundant foliage, but few roots. When the winds come, they will uproot it and blow it down, as it is said: 'He shall be like a tamarisk in the desert and shall not see when good comes but shall inhabit the parched places in the wilderness' (Jer. 17:6). But anyone whose deeds are greater than his wisdom—to what is he to be likened? To a tree with little foliage but

---

① "This is something the philosopher also agree with: if cultivation of good habits takes precedence over the pursuit of knowledge, and the habits are firmly fixed, when an individual engages in study, the study will reinforce these habits, he will get greater joy out of his learning, and will strive to perfect himself in it. But if the pursuit of evil is put before everything else, and the individual hopes that study will teach him self-restrain, then the learning becomes too much of a burden for him, and he will abandon it too." (Maimonides)

② *Tradition.* "This is a reference to those masoretic comments which are added to the margins of the Biblical books, and these are known as the Great Masorah. He who knows these notes well will know the correct interpretation of most of Scripture and will avoid error and confusion." (Mahzor Vitry) "This refers to the traditions of textual readings and punctuation of the Scripture which the Sages have handed on to their disciples, and these traditions are a fence for the written Torah. For you will not find variant readings in copies of Biblical books except in very few places. This is utterly unlike the situation with regard to copies of the Talmud, for in many passages there are variant readings." (Rabbi Jonah)

③ *In goodness the world is judged.* "The Lord's judgment of men is indeed a merciful one; it is not what strict justice requires. And so we are told of God's ways, long-suffering, and abundant in goodness and truth (Exod. 34:6); and our Sages, of blessed memory, said (Eruvin 22a), He is long-suffering toward the righteous and the wicked." (Maimonides)

abundant roots. For even if all the winds in the world were to come and blast at it, they will not move it from its place, as it is said: 'He shall be as a tree planted by the waters, and that spreads out its roots by the river, and shall not fear when heat comes, and his leaf shall be green, and shall not be careful in the year of drought, neither shall cease from yielding fruit.' (Jer. 17:8)"

4:1 Ben Zoma says: "Who is a Sage? He who learns from everybody, as it is said: 'From all my teachers I have gotten understanding.' (Ps. 119:99) Who is strong? He who overcomes his desire [*yetzer*],① as it is said: 'He who is slow to anger is better than the mighty, and he who rules his spirit than he who takes a city.' (Prov. 16:32) Who is rich? He who is happy in what he has, as it is said: 'When you eat the labor of your hands, happy will you be, and it will go well with you.' (Ps. 128:2) ('Happy will you be'—in this world, 'and it will go well with you'—in the world to come.) Who is honored? He who honors everybody, as it is said: 'For those who honor me I shall honor, and they who despise me will be treated as of no account.' (I Sam. 2:30)"

4:3 Ben Azzai used to say: "Do not despise anybody and do not treat anything as unlikely. For there is no man who does not have his time, and there is no thing that does not have its place."

4:15 Rabbi Matya ben Harash says: "Greet everybody first; and be a tail to lions② rather than a head to foxes."

4:18 Rabbi Simeon ben Eleazar says: "Do not try to make amends with your fellow when he is in angry, or comfort him when the corpse of his beloved is lying before him, or seek to find absolution for him at the moment at which he takes a vow, or attempt to see him when he is

---

① *Desire.* Here refers to *yetzer hara*, the human drive or the propensity to do evil. This drive is always in conflict with the *yetzer hatov*, the propensity to do good. Both inclinations are found in every human being.

② *A tail to lions.* "It's much better and more fitting for a person to be the disciple of someone who is wiser than he, than to be the master of someone who is inferior to him. The former will lead to his improvement, the latter to his deterioration." (Maimonides)

humiliated."

4:21　Rabbi Eliezer Haqqappar says: "Envy,① lust, and ambition drive a person out of this world."

5:7　There are seven traits to an unformed clod②, and seven to a sage. A sage does not speak before someone greater than he in wisdom. And he does not interrupt his fellow. And he is not at a loss for an answer. He asks a relevant question and answers properly. And he addresses each matter in its proper sequence, first, then second. And concerning something he has not heard, he says: "I have not heard the answer." And he concedes the truth. And the opposites of these traits apply to a clod.

5:10　There are four sorts of people. He who says: "What's mine is mine and what's yours is yours"—this is the average sort. (And some say:

---

①　*Envy.* "There is very nice parable about envy and excessive appetite. An envious man and a glutton were once met by Satan, who said to them: 'If one of you will ask for something, it will be given to him, but his fellow will get a double portion of it.' The glutton wanted both portions, his own and the other's. So he pressed his companion to ask first. Whereupon the envious fellow asked that they gouge out one of his eyes, so that the glutton should lose both." (Duran)

②　*Unformed clod* (golem). *Golem* comes from biblical Hebrew meaning a shapeless mass or an embryo (Ps. 193:16). Rabbinic Hebrew understands the word to denote something unfinished or, as it is used here, the kind of person contrasted with the wise. *Golem* gives Maimonides the opportunity to give differential definitions of five terms found in rabbinic literature that deal with folly and wisdom (Cf. Avot, 2:5; 5:10). They are *bur* (boor), *am ha-aretz* (unlettered man, or ignoramus), *golem* (clog), *hakham* (wise man, or sage), and *hasid* (pious man, or saint). For Maimonides, *bur* has neither intellectual nor moral virtues nor the ability to acquire them. He is like earth that can grow nothing. *Am ha-aretz* is a person who has moral virtues but no intellectual ones. Such a person is useful in and for society. *Golem* is a person who possesses both moral and intellectual virtues, but in a state of incompleteness and confusion. He is like an implement beginning to take shape in the hands of the craftsman but still lacking completion. *Hakham* refers to a person whose intellectual and moral virtues have reached their proper stage of perfection. *Hasid* refers to a person who, having achieved perfection in both moral and intellectual virtues, now prefers to stress the moral virtues.

"This is the sort of Sodom."①) "What's mine is yours and what's yours is mine"—this is an ignoramus [*am ha-aretz*]. "What's mine is yours and what's yours is yours"—this is a truly pious man [*hasid*]. "What's mine is mine and what's yours is mine"—this is a truly wicked man.

5:11 There are four sorts of personality: easily angered, easily calmed—his gain is canceled by his loss; hard to anger, hard to clam—his loss is canceled by his gain; hard to anger and easy to calm—a truly pious man; easy to anger and hard to calm—a truly wicked man.

5:13 There are four traits among people who give charity: he who wants to give, but does not want others to give—he begrudges what belongs to others②; he wants others to give, but he does not want to give—he begrudges what belongs to himself; he will give and he wants others to give—he is truly pious; he will not give and does not want others to give—he is truly wicked.

5:15 There are four traits among those who sit before the sages: a sponge, a funnel, a strainer, and a sifter. A sponge—because he sponges everything up; a funnel —because he takes in on one side and lets out on the other; a strainer—for he lets out the wine and keeps in the lees; and a sifter—for he holds back the coarse and collects the fine flour.

5:21 Judah ben Tema used to say: At five to Scripture, ten to Mishnah, thirteen to religious duties [*mitzvot*], fifteen to Talmud, eighteen to the wedding canopy, twenty to responsibility for providing for a family, thirty to fullness of strength, forty to understanding, fifty to counsel, sixty to old age, seventy to ripe old age, eighty to remarkable strength, ninety to a bowed back, and at a hundred—he is like a corpse who has already passed

---

① *The sort of Sodom.* "The men of Sodom did not want to take anything from anybody, but they also did not want any poor man to benefit from their possessions." (Mahzor Vitry)

② *Begrudges what belongs to others.* "He does not want others to practice charity, lest thereby their wealth increase; nor does he want them to enjoy a good name." (Mahzor Vitry)

and gone from this world.①

8.2 Shmuel Hanagid, A Gift from the Battlefield (1046) ②

Yehosef:
Here is a book for you,
Culled from the best of Araby's③ rich tongue,
And copied by me while the sword is drawn
And the spear gleams deadly in our hands.
Death orders about armies,
Requisitioning now this, now that one's youth,
But even as the grave yawns wide around me,
I can't stop educating you:

---

① The numbers in this list have been determined in different ways. Rashi holds that the age of marriage at eighteen was deduced from the word *adam*, primordial "man." It is used eighteen times from the beginning of the Torah until the creation of woman. Twenty as the age to begin pursuing a livelihood is suggested by the age of enlistment in the ancient army of Israel, as indicated in Numbers 1:3. Since the Levites began their service in the Tabernacle at the age of thirty, this must be the age of full strength. The Levites were responsible for carrying the sacred instruments of the Tabernacle (Num. 4:47). They ceased their work at the age of fifty but still served in some capacity (Num. 8:25 - 26). Thus, their service must have been counsel. Hence fifty is the age for such counsel. Psalms 90:10 contains the words "The days of our years are three-score years and ten, /Or even by reason of strength four-score years." From this we learn that the fullness of age comes at seventy and the strength of age at eighty.

② Source: Halkin (2000). Cf. Weinberger (1973), p. 65. Yehosef, Shmuel Hanagid's son, was ten when he received his father's gift, of which he writes: "And he [Hanagid] copied out a selection of Arabic poems in his own hand and sent them from his camp, which was preparing for an offensive in Nisan 4806 [March - April 1046]. And he commanded me to read them, so that I might become familiar with them and increase my facility in Arabic." It was written during the 1046 campaign. The fact that a Hebrew poet in a largely Berber military bivouac copied and sent his son a book of Arabic verse says much about the age. It also illustrates the value attached by Hanagid to his son's education.

③ Lit. "Kedar and Ephah." Cf. Gen. 25:13, 4. Both terms are metaphors for Arabs.

I'd rather see you with some learning
Than all my enemies routed from the field!

So take this book and study it.
It's time you broke with the gross stutterers
You call your friends. Mark what I say:
The cultured man is like a fruiting tree,
Even the leaves of which bear remedies;
The ignorant one, like the forest cordwood,
Good only for consigning to the flames.

8.3 Bahya ibn Pakuda, On Asceticism, Its Kinds and Advantages (*Sefer Hovot ha-Levavot*)[1]

What are the definitions of special asceticism, and how are the people of the law bound to practice it? The sages have given different definitions of this term. One of them said, "Asceticism is the absence from anything which may distract a man from God." Another said, "Asceticism is the avoidance of this world and putting little hope in it." Still another said, "Asceticism is tranquility of the soul and the severance of all its ties of attachment to the things which give it only pleasure and rest." "Asceticism is confidence in God," said one. "Asceticism is breaking one's hunger, covering one's nakedness, and the avoidance of all attachment to the rest," said another. "Asceticism is freeing the heart from all creatures, and the love of solitude." "Asceticism is gratitude for God's graces and endurance of His trials;" and finally, "Asceticism is the soul's abstention from every pleasure and bodily comfort except the natural needs which are absolutely necessary, and the driving away of all the rest from the soul." This last definition fits the asceticism practiced by the people of the Law better than the other

---

[1] Cf. Lazaroff (1970).

definitions mentioned above.

As to the obligation of the people of the law to practice asceticism, it springs from the following reason: the purpose of the Law is to give the mind mastery over the entire soul, with its desires for the pleasures of the body, and to establish the superiority of the mind. It is well known that the dominance of the instinct over the mind is the root of every sin and the cause of all the vices. When that happened, not only did the people turn to this world, but they also turned away from their religion. Thus the instinct robbed them of the mainstay of their immunity to sin and deprived them of the way of their forefathers, which was one of moderation in this world, satisfaction with but little of it, and contentment with their mere sustenance in it. The instinct made them love worldly goods, and desire their increase; made them boastful of them, desirous of enjoying and ennobling themselves with them, until they started to sink into this ocean. Then the instinct forced them to suffer the waves that crashed over them, deafening their ears and blinding their eyes. A few are so preoccupied with the pleasures that are in their reach that these pleasures have become their religion and their law, and they distract them from their Lord, until they perish through them, as it is said (Jer. 2:19): "Thine Own wickedness shall correct thee, and thy back-slidings shall reprove him: Know therefore and see that it is an evil and a bitter thing, that thou hast forsaken the Lord thy God, neither is my fear in thee, saith the Lord God of hosts." However, most of them are denied their pleasures and thus they become their only concern. Their soul becomes attached desiring them constantly and longing for them day and night, as it is said (Ps. 36:5): "He deviseth iniquity upon his bed; he setteth himself in a way that is not good; he abhorreth not evil." As long as they live, they are in a state of grief, failures unable to achieve their hopes, losers in the bargain, lost souls, men who always make a bad choice because they are ignorant of the value of the goods and what they are worth in exchange, as it is said (Ps. 106:20): "Thus they exchanged their glory for the likeness of an ox that eateth grass."

Incited by their ruling habits, allured by what are now their fixed necessities, they keep filling their spare time with the consequences of their seduction and continue to strengthen their hearts' attachment to them. The more they repeat this, the further they go from the light of truth. The further they go from the light, so long abandoned by them, the more accustomed they grow to the instinct, which they have just discovered. Thus darkness covers them and the world seems in their eyes greater and greater. They think much of the cultivation of the world and adorn it by destroying their own minds. The more construction is added to the world, the more destruction is added to their minds, until they consider their error the right and its fallacy the truth. This they establish as their law and custom, bequeathing it from father to sons, raising their offspring by it, commanding the peoples to follow it—and their rulers vie in enforcing it. Thus stupidity has the upper hand and the place where they are is full of folly. Corruption has become the accepted thing in the world, moderation is rare, and abstention from its luxuries is considered an excess. They imitate each other until the moderate man is considered impotent, the man who refuses to run after the world is considered a failure, he who is content with a sufficiency is a weakling, and he who strives for the world is considered a prudent man. They praise and honor each other for their achievements in this world; they make friendly relations with others only for its sake; they are angry or happy because of it alone. They toil solely for the reward of this world, and their stomachs are their gods, their clothes are their religion, and the adornment of their houses is their Law. Thus they wander in the abyss of ignorance. They run in the path of failure, loaded with the weight of their desires. They ask for the reward of the pious while they do the deeds of sinners; they ask to be ranked with the virtuous while they follow the way of the wicked, as said our ancient sages (Sotah 22b): "They commit the transgression of Zimri and expect a reward like that given to Phinehas."[1]

---

[1] Numbers 25. Phinehas killed Zimri when the latter was in the process of having sexual relations with a Midianite woman.

Since the instinct has conquered most of the people of the Law in the manner described above, they must fight back with special asceticism, whose conditions we have mentioned at the beginning of this chapter. They must confront the instinct with it if they are to go back to the limits of moderation prescribed by the Law, which constitutes their well-being in the world and in religion. This fact necessitated the existence of a special group among the people of the Law, a group of people who would practice this special asceticism and fulfill its conditions so that the rest of the people of the Law would benefit by it when their souls incline to animal desires and their nature drags them down to follow their instinct.

8.4 Maimonides, The Fourth Chapter of *Eight Chapters*. On Medical Treatment for the Diseases of the Soul[①]

Good actions are those balanced in the mean between two extremes, both of which are bad;[②] one of them is an excess and the other a deficiency. The virtues are states of the soul and settled dispositions in the mean between two bad states [of the soul], one of which is excessive and the other deficient. Certain actions necessarily result from these states [of the soul]. For example, moderation is the moral habit in the mean between lust and insensibility to pleasure. Thus, moderation is one of the good actions, and the state of the soul that produces moderation is a moral virtue. Lust is the first extreme and total insensibility to pleasure the other extreme; both of them are completely bad. The two states of the soul necessarily giving rise to lust (the excessive state) and insensibility (the deficient state) are both moral vices. In like manner, liberality[③] is the mean between miserliness and extravagance; courage is the mean between rashness and cowardice; wit is

---

① Source: Weiss and Butterworth(1975).

② The concept of the golden mean, or middle path, goes back to Aristotle. See *Nicomachean Ethics*, ii, chs. 6 – 9, 1106a 24 – 1109b 27.

③ *Liberality* (*sakhā'*) refers to the right attitude in spending money on oneself.

the mean between buffoonery and dullness; humility is the mean between haughtiness and abasement; generosity[1] is the mean between prodigality and stinginess; contentment is the mean between greed and laziness; gentleness is the mean between irascibility and servility; modesty is the mean between impudence and shyness; and so too, with the rest of them. If the meanings are understood, it is not absolutely necessary that names be assigned to them.

People often err concerning these actions and think that one of the two extremes is good and a virtue of the soul. Sometimes they think the first extreme is good, as when they think rashness is a virtue and call rash men courageous. If they see an exceedingly rash and bold person in a perilous situation who intentionally throws himself into danger but is saved by chance, they praise him for it and call him courageous. Sometimes they think the other extreme is good and say that someone who depreciates himself is gentle; or that a lazy man is contented; or that someone insensible to pleasure because of the dryness of his nature is moderate. Due to this kind of error, they also think that extravagance and prodigality are among the praiseworthy actions. Now all this is erroneous, for in truth one praises the mean, and a man needs to aim at it and continuously weigh all his actions with a view to this mean.

Know that these moral virtues and vices are acquired and firmly established in the soul by frequently repeating the actions pertaining to a particular moral habit over a long period of time and by our becoming accustomed to them. If those actions are good, we shall acquire the virtue; if they are bad, we shall acquire the vice. Since by nature man does not possess either virtue or vice at the beginning of his life (as we shall explain in the eighth chapter), he undoubtedly is habituated from childhood to actions in accordance with his family's way of life and that of the people of his town. These actions may be in the mean, excessive, or defective—as we have indicated.

---

[1] *Generosity* (*karam*) is the right disposition in giving good things to other people.

Should his soul become sick, he must follow the same course in treating it as in the medical treatment for bodies. For when the body gets out of equilibrium, we look to which side it inclines in becoming unbalanced, and then oppose it with its contrary until it returns to equilibrium. When it is in equilibrium, we remove that counterbalance and revert to that which keeps the body in equilibrium. We act in a similar manner with regard to moral habits. We may, for example, see a man whose soul has reached a condition in which he is miserly toward himself. This is one of the vices of the soul, and the action he performs is one of the bad actions—as we have explained in this chapter. Thus, if we wanted to give medical treatment to this sick person, we would not order him to be liberal. That would be like using a balanced course for treating someone whose fever is excessive; this would not cure him of his sickness. Indeed, this man [with a miserly soul] needs to be made to be extravagant time after time. He must repeatedly act in an extravagant manner until the condition that makes him miserly is removed from his soul, and he just about acquires an extravagant disposition or comes close to it. Then we would make him stop the extravagant actions and order him to perform liberal actions continually. He must always adhere to this course and not go toward the excess or deficiency. Similarly, if we were to see him acting in an extravagant manner, we would order him to perform miserly actions repeatedly.

But we would not make him repeat miserly actions as many times as we made him repeat extravagant actions. This subtlety is the rule of therapy and is its secret. For a man can more easily turn from extravagance to liberality than from miserliness to liberality. Likewise, it is easier to turn from being insensible to pleasure to being moderate than from being lustful to being moderate. Therefore we make the lustful man repeat actions which lack pleasure more than we make the insensible man repeat lustful actions; we require the coward to practice rashness more than we require the rash man to practice cowardice; and we train the stingy man in prodigality more than we train the prodigal man in stinginess. This is the rule for the medical treatment of moral habits, so memorize it.

Because of this teaching, the virtuous men would not let a disposition of their souls remain in the mean, but would incline a little toward the excess or the defect as a precaution. I mean, they would, for example, incline from moderation a little toward insensibility to pleasure, from courage a little toward rashness, from generosity a little toward prodigality, from humility a little toward abasement, and likewise with the rest. This is the meaning expressed in their saying, inside the line of the law.① What the virtuous men did at certain times and also what some individuals among them [always] did in inclining toward one extreme—for example, fasting, rising at night, abstaining from eating meat and drinking wine, keeping away from women, wearing garments of wool and hair, dwelling on mountains, and secluding themselves in desolate places—they did only with a view to medical treatment, as we have indicated. Again, if they saw that due to the corruption of the people of the city they would be corrupted through contact with them and through seeing their deeds and that social intercourse with them would bring about the corruption of their own moral habits, then they withdrew to desolate places where there are no evil men. As the prophet said, peace be upon him: "O that I were in the desert." (Jer. 9:1)

When the ignorant saw these virtuous men perform such actions, but without knowing their intention, they thought those actions to be good and aimed at performing them, claiming to be like those virtuous men. They set about afflicting their bodies with every kind of affliction, thinking they were acquiring virtue and doing something good and would thereby come near to God—as if God were an enemy of the body and desired its ruin and destruction. They were not aware that those actions are bad and that one of the vices of the soul is thereby acquired. Such men can only be compared to someone ignorant of the art of medicine who sees that skillful physicians have given deathly sick people the pulp of colocynth, scammony, aloe, and

---

① Cf. *Mishneh Torah*, Laws Concerning Character Traits, I 5, where those identified here as "virtuous men" (*fudalā*) are called "pious men" (*hasidim*). Ibn Tibbon translates *fudalā* throughout as *hasidim*.

similar things to drink, while forbidding them any food, and that they are cured of their disease and completely escape destruction. Such an ignorant man then says: "Since these things cure disease, it is even more appropriate and fitting that they preserve or augment the health of a healthy man." He therefore proceeds to take them continuously and follows the regimen of the sick; as a result he undoubtedly becomes sick. Similarly, those with sick souls are undoubtedly so from taking medication while they are healthy.

This perfect Law which perfects us makes no mention of such things. As [the Psalmist] who knew it testified about it: "The Law of the Lord is perfect, making wise the simple, restoring the soul." (Ps. 19:8)① Indeed, its goal is for man to be natural by following the middle way. He shall adhere to the mean when he eats whatever is his to eat, when he drinks whatever is his to drink, and when he has sexual intercourse with whomever is his to have sexual intercourse. He shall dwell in a city and follow justice and equity; he shall not inhabit caves or mountains, nor wear garments of hair and wool, nor torment his body or make it weary or afflict it. That is forbidden in the tradition which has come down to us. He [God] said about the Nazirite: "He [the priest] shall make atonement for him because he sinned against the soul." (Num. 6:11) They said: "Now then, against which soul did he sin? His own, because he withheld himself from wine. Is there not here an argument from the lesser to the greater? If whoever afflicts himself regarding wine needs atonement, how much the more does the one who afflicts himself regarding everything [need atonement]."(B.T., Ta'anit 11a; Nedarim, 10a; Nazir, 19a, 22a; Bava Kamma, 91b)

In the traditions of our prophets and those who transmit our Law, we see these men aiming at the mean and at preserving their souls and bodies in accordance with what the Law requires. God (may He be exalted) answered through His prophet those who asked if they should continue fasting one day in the year or not. They said to Zechariah: "Should I weep

---

① The original verse reads: "The Law of the Lord is perfect, restoring the soul; the testimony of the Lord is sure, making wise the simple."

in the fifth month, separating myself, as I have done for so many years?" (Zech. 7:3) And He answered them: "When you fasted and mourned in the fifth and in the seventh month these seventy years, did you at all fast unto Me, even unto Me? And when you eat and you drink, are you not the ones who eat and who drink?" (Zech. 7:5–6) Then He commanded them to follow only the mean and virtue, and not to fast. This is what he said to them: "Thus spoke the Lord of hosts saying: Execute true judgment and show loving-kindness and compassion, every man to his brother, etc." (Zech. 7:9) After that he said: "Thus says the Lord of hosts: The fast of the fourth month and the fast of the fifth and the fast of the seventh and the fast of the tenth shall be for the house of Judah joy and gladness and cheerful seasons. Love truth and peace." (Zech. 8:19) Know that "truth" refers to the rational virtues because they are immutably true (as we mentioned in the second chapter) and that "peace" refers to the moral virtues through which there is peace in the world.

I return to my purpose. If it be said by the men of our Law who imitate the [other] religious communities—and I speak only of them—that they torment their bodies and renounce their pleasures only to discipline the powers of the body so as to incline a little to one side (in the way we have explained in this chapter that a man ought to do), this is an error on their part, as we shall explain. The Law forbids what it forbids and commands what it commands only for this reason, i.e., that we move away from one side as a means of discipline. God therefore enjoined the following upon us: the prohibition of all forbidden foods, the prohibition of forbidden sexual intercourses, the ban concerning the prostitute, the requirement of a marriage contract and betrothal, and even so [sexual intercourse] not always being permitted but forbidden during the periods of menstruation and birth, and the further limitation upon sexual intercourse instituted by our elders who prohibited it during the daytime, as we explained in Sanhedrin.[①] The purpose of all this is that we move very far away from the extreme of lust

---

[①] Commentary on the Mishnah, Sanhedrin, VII 4.

and go a little from the mean toward insensibility to pleasure so that the state of moderation be firmly established within our souls. The same applies to everything occurring in the Law with respect to the paying of tithes (Deut. 14:22 – 29; 26:12 – 13), the gleanings of the harvest (Lev. 19:9; 23:22), the forgotten sheaves (Deut. 24:19), the corner of the field (Lev. 19:9; 23:22), the fallen grapes (Lev. 19:10), the gleanings of the vineyard (Lev. 19:10), the decree of the Sabbatical year (Deut. 15:1 – 2) and the Jubilee year (Lev. 25:8 – 55), and charity sufficient for what the needy lack①. These come close to prodigality so that we move very far away from the extreme of stinginess and approach the extreme of prodigality, the purpose being to establish generosity firmly within us.

If you consider most of the commandments in this way, you will find that all of them discipline the powers of the soul. For example, they eliminate revenge and vengeance by His saying: "You shall not take revenge nor bear a grudge" (Lev. 19:18), "You shall surely release it" (Exod. 23:5)②, and "You shall surely help to lift them up, etc." (Deut. 22:4)③; these aim at weakening the power of rage and irascibility. Similarly, "You shall surely bring them back" (Deut. 22:1)④, aims at removing the state of avarice. Similarly, the following aim at removing the state of impudence and instilling that of modesty: "You shall rise before the aged and honor the old man" (Lev. 19:32), "Honor your father" (Exod. 20:12), and "You shall not turn aside from the thing they shall tell you" (Deut. 17:11). Moreover, He also moves [us] away from the other extreme, i.e., shyness, for in order that

---

① This refers not simply to giving charity to the poor, but to giving a man what he "lacks," which partially depends upon his previous circumstances. Thus, if a rich man is impoverished, what he "lacks" must be restored to him—even a horse to ride upon and a servant to run before it. *Mishneh Torah*, Laws Concerning Gifts to the Poor, Ⅶ 3. See 7.4.

② The complete verse reads: "If you see the ass of your enemy lying under its burden, you shall refrain from leaving him with it; you shall surely release it with him."

③ The complete verse reads: "You shall not see your brother's ass or his ox fallen down by the way, and hide yourself from them; you shall surely help him to lift them up."

④ The complete verse reads: "You shall not see your brother's ox or his sheep driven away, and hide yourself from them; you shall surely bring them back to your brother."

shyness be eliminated and we remain in the middle way, He said: "You shall surely rebuke your neighbor and not bear sin because of him" (Lev. 19: 17) and "You shall not fear the face of any man" (Deut. 1:17).

Only a manifestly ignorant individual would come and wish to add to these things and, for example, prohibit eating and drinking, in addition to the stipulated prohibition about food; and prohibit marriage, in addition to what is prohibited concerning sexual intercourse; and give all of his money to the poor or to the Temple property, in addition to what the Law says about charity, Temple properties, and valuations.① His actions are bad and he does not know that he goes all the way to one extreme, completely leaving the mean. The sages have a statement about this subject in the Jerusalem Talmud, in the ninth [tractate] of Nedarim, and nothing more marvelous than it has yet reached me. They censure those who become like prisoners by imposing oaths and vows on themselves, and they literally say there: "Rav Aidi [said] in the name of Rabbi Isaac: Is what the Torah has prohibited for you not enough, that you prohibit other things for yourself" (J.T. Nedarim IX 1)? This is precisely the meaning we have presented, neither more nor less. Thus, it has become clear to you from everything we have discussed in this chapter that it is necessary to aim at the mean in actions and not depart from it toward one of the two extremes, except with a view to medical treatment and to opposing something with its contrary.

When the man knowledgeable in the art of medicine sees his temperament changing ever so slightly, he does not neglect the disease and let it take possession of him so that he would need an extremely strong medicine. When he knows that one of his bodily organs is weak, he takes continual care of it, avoids things harmful to it, and aims at what is useful to it so that this organ becomes healthy or so that it does not become

---

① "Temple property" is property dedicated to the Temple; "valuation" refers to the monetary value of an individual's life which he may vow to dedicate to the Temple. The latter sum is fixed by the individual's age and could never exceed 50 shekels. A man is forbidden to dedicate more than one-fifth of his wealth to the poor. *Mishneh Torah*, Laws Concerning Valuations and Dedicated Objects, I 3 and VIII 12.

weaker. Similarly, the perfect man needs to inspect his moral habits continually, weigh his actions, and reflect upon the state of his soul every single day. Whenever he sees his soul inclining toward one of the extremes, he should rush to cure it and not let the evil state become established by the repetition of a bad action—as we have mentioned. Thus, as we said above, he should attend to the defective moral habit in himself and continually seek to cure it, for a man inevitably has defects. Indeed, the philosophers have said that it would be very difficult to find someone disposed by nature toward all of the moral and rational virtues. This has also been said frequently in the books of the prophets. He said: "Behold, He puts no trust in His servants, etc." (Job 4:18) "And how can one born of woman be just?" (Job 25:4)① Solomon said absolutely: "There is no man who is just upon the earth, who does only good and does not sin." (Eccles. 7:20)②

You know that God, may He be exalted, said to the master of the first and the last men, Moses our master, peace be upon him: "Because you did not believe in Me to sanctify Me" (Num. 20:12), "Because you rebelled against My word" (Num. 20:24), "Because you did not sanctify" (Deut. 32:51). His sin, peace be upon him, in all this was that he inclined toward one of the two extremes away from one of the moral virtues—i.e., gentleness—when he inclined toward irascibility and said: "Hear now you rebels" (Num. 20:10). God disapproved of a man like him becoming irascible in the presence of the community of Israel when irascibility was not proper. For this individual something like that was a profanation of the Name, because they would imitate his every movement and speech and would wish thereby to attain the happiness of this world and the other [world]. How could irascibility, which (as we have explained) is among the bad actions, stem from him and not originate from one of the evil states of the soul?

---

① The original verse reads: "How can man be just with God; and how can one born of woman be clean?" The speaker is Bildad.

② Maimonides reverses the word order of the first two words in the verse and thus renders it more smoothly.

We shall now explain the significance of His saying, "You rebelled against My word."(Num. 20:24) He [Moses] was not addressing the vulgar nor men without virtue, but people the least significant of whose women was like Ezekiel ben Buzi, as the sages have mentioned.[1] They would reflect upon everything he would say or do. Thus when they saw him irate, they [in effect] said: "He, peace be upon him, has no moral vice, and if it were not that he knew God has become angry with us about our searching for water and that we have exasperated Him, may He be exalted, he would not have become irate." We do not find that God, may He be exalted, was irate or angry when He spoke to [Moses] about this matter. Rather, He said to him: "Take the rod ... and you shall give the congregation and their cattle drink."(Num. 20:8) We have departed from the purpose of the section, but we have solved one of the difficulties of the Torah. It is often spoken about and someone often asks: "What sin did he commit?" Examine what we have said and what others have said about it, and the truth will lead the way.

I return to my purpose. If a man continually weighs his actions and aims at the mean, he is in the highest of human ranks. In that way, he will come close to God and will attain what belongs to Him. This is the most perfect of the ways of worship. The sages, may their memory be blessed, referred to this goal, commented on it, and said: "Everyone who appraises his paths merits and sees the salvation of the Holy One, blessed be He. As it is said: ' And to him who sets his way aright will I show the salvation of God.' (Ps. 50:23) Do not read *wesam derekh*, but *wesham derekh*." (B.T., Moed Qatan, 5a)[2] *Shumah* means "assessing" and "appraising," and this is precisely the meaning that we have explained in this entire chapter. This is the extent of what we saw to be necessary with respect to this subject.

---

[1] Mekhilta on Exod. 15:2; Deuteronomy Rabbah VII 9.

[2] The biblical verse is from Ps. 50:23 and, according to this interpretation of the sages, would read: "And to him who appraises his way (*wesham derekh*) will I show the salvation of God."

8.5 Eleazar of Worms, On Hasidic Piety

The root of (proper) fear (means) that it is difficult for (the Pietist) to perform (a virtuous act) and yet he still resists (the lures of) his passions and evil impulse because of the fear of (God's) name. His only fear is that he might not be (as) perfect (in his devotion) to the Lord as was Abraham. (When Abraham did not hesitate to obey the Lord even by sacrificing Isaac, God said to him:) "For you are one who fears the Lord." (Genesis 22:12) This was the most demanding of Abraham's trials (and by resisting it, Abraham manifested his fear of God.)

8.6 Moses Sofer, An Ethical Will (1836)

With God's help, the 15th of Kislev 5597 (November 24, 1836).

Since man does not know how long he is destined to labor for the Almighty, treasure your knowledge of God's teaching ever more, so as to elevate the house of our Lord, and so that you, my sons, daughters, sons-in-law, and grandchildren, and their children, may truly live!

May your mind not turn to evil and never engage in corruptible partnership with those fond of innovations, who, as a penalty for our many sins, strayed from the Almighty and His law! Do not touch the books of Rabbi Moses [Mendelssohn] from Dessau, and your foot will never slip! Study and teach your children the entire Holy Scripture with Rashi's explanations, the Torah with Ramban's [Nachmanides] exegesis, for this is the main source of religion. Should hunger and misery lead you into temptation, then the Almighty will protect you; resist temptation and do not turn to the idols or to some god of your own making! The daughters may read German books[①], but only those which have been written in our own

---

① Most likely, books in Yiddish.

way, according to the interpretations of our teachers(may they rest in peace), and absolutely no others! By all means, stay far from the theater. That I absolutely forbid you!

Be warned not to change your Jewish names, speech, and clothing—God forbid—and your motto shall be: "And Jacob came in peace to the city of Shechem" (Gen. 33:18).

Do not be concerned that I have left you no fortune or wealth; for the Father of the orphans compassionately protects all those without father or mother; He will not forsake you either! Do not use God's teaching to make crown for yourselves or even a bread-winning tool! And even less—God forbid—shall you use it to wander around preaching for money or soliciting a job. Never say: "Times have changed!" We have an old Father—praised be His name—who has never changed and never will change... . The order of prayer and synagogue shall remain forever as it has been up to now, and no one may presume to change anything of its structure ...

8.7 Israel Salanter, The Struggle of the Moral Person (1881)①

Let us now explain the words of the Talmud, Tractate Sukkah 52a: "The Evil Urge appears to the righteous like a huge mountain, while to the wicked it appears like the thread of a hair ... The righteous weep, saying: How can we conquer such a huge mountain? And the wicked weep, saying: How is it possible that we cannot conquer such a thread of hair?"

Now to understand the Sages' words we must first consider what we find there: "Whoever is greater than his colleague, has a more powerful Evil Urge." It would appear, at first glance, to the contrary: that a righteous person who fears God has the desire to further improve himself. If so (contrary to the Sages) wouldn't the Evil Urge have been diminished within him? Nevertheless—we shall see that matters are otherwise.

---

① Source: Corrigan, et al. (1998), p. 262.

Consider a person who does not fear (his inner, unconscious motives). The Evil Urge will first attach itself to external (i.e., conscious) motives in order to corrupt them, but it will pay little attention to inner motives. This is already written in the midrash: "The wicked are full of regrets." The reason for their regret is that external motives do not accumulate to take possession of a person. (Their desire to sin exists) only at the moment an object of desire is before them—as they said: "The eye sees and the heart desires." And therefore when the object of desire is gone and his external motives have calmed, at that moment are aroused the inner motives which have not been perverted, and they bring him to such profound regret that he wants to forsake the acts motivated by the external motives.

But in the case of a person who fears (his inner, unconscious, motives), the external motives appear impeccable. For this reason, the Evil Urge attempts first to effect its influence on the inner motives. And the more a man is righteous, the Urge will penetrate that much more deeply into his inwardness, and the person will not be aware of this or of the evil influences upon him.

But the person who fears (his inner motives) with a total wholeness will labor and prove himself through his laudatory external motives, most essentially through the gift of the Torah, in order to transform at its very root the Evil Urge which inhabits the inner motives, and to repair these inner motives, no matter how difficult this weighs upon one.

Now this is the point of stating that, to the wicked, the Evil Urge appears like a thread of hair, because (the purity of) his inner motives was never so perverted. Therefore, only a bit of stock-taking and study of Torah and Musar will enable him to awaken and strengthen the inner motives which will overcome the external motives and transform even them to good. But the righteous, whose inner motives have been perverted by the Evil Urge—he truly has his work cut out for him to use his laudable external motives alone in order to overpower the inner motives and to repair them. That is why they seem like an enormous mountain to him.

9 THE JEWISH LITURGY

9.1 The Shema

Deuteronomy 6: 4 – 9

Hear, O Israel, the LORD is our God, the LORD alone.
Blessed be the name of his glorious majesty forever and ever.
You shall love the LORD your God with all your heart, and with all your soul and with all your might. Take to heart these instructions with which I charge you this day. Impress them upon your children. Recite them when you stay at home and when you are away, when you lie down and when you get up. Bind them as a sign on your hand and let them serve as a symbol on your forehead; inscribe them on the doorposts of your house and on your gates.

Deuteronomy 11: 13 – 21

If, then, you obey the commandments that I enjoin upon you this day, loving the LORD your God and serving Him with all your heart and soul, I will grant the rain for your land in season, the early rain and the late. You shall gather in your new grain and wine and oil—I will also provide grass in the fields for your cattle—and thus you shall eat your fill. Take care not to be lured away to serve other gods and bow to them. For the LORD's anger will flare up against you, and He will shut up the skies so that there will be no rain and the ground will not yield its produce; and you will soon perish from the good land that the LORD is assigning to you. Therefore impress these My words upon your very heart: bind them as a sign on your hand and let them serve as a symbol on your forehead, and teach them to your children—reciting them when you stay at home and when you are away, when you lie down and when you get up; and inscribe them on the doorposts of your house and on your gates—to the end that you and your children may endure, in the land that the LORD swore to your fathers to assign to them, as long as there is a heaven over the earth.

Numbers 15: 37 – 41

The LORD said to Moses as follows: Speak to the Israelite people and instruct them to make for themselves fringes on the corners of their garments throughout the ages; let them attach a cord of blue to the fringe at each corner. That shall be your fringe; look at it and recall all the commandments of the LORD and observe them, so that you do not follow your heart and eyes in your lustful urge. Thus you shall be reminded to observe all My commandments and to be holy to your God. I the LORD am your God, who brought you out of the land of Egypt to be your God: I, the LORD your God.

9.2 The Amidah (Shemoneh Esreh or Eighteen Benedictions) [1]

1. Blessed are you, O Lord our God and God of our fathers, God of

---

[1] Source: Alexander (1984), pp. 72 – 74. Cf. Birnbaum (1977), pp. 81 – 96; Elbogen (1993), pp. 24 – 54.

Abraham, God of Isaac, God of Jacob, the great, mighty and revered God, God most high, generous and kind, owner of all things. You remember the pious deeds of the patriarchs, and in love will bring a redeemer to their children's children, for your name's sake, O King, Helper, Savior and Shield. Blessed are you, O Lord, the Shield of Abraham.

2. O Lord, you are for ever mighty. You bring back the dead to life. You have the power to save. Out of lovingkindness you sustain the living; with great compassion you revive the dead. You support the falling, heal the sick, free the captives, and keep faith with those who sleep in the dust. Who is like you, Lord of mighty deeds, and who may be compared to you, O King, who brings death and life, and causes salvation to spring forth? You are to be trusted to bring the dead back to life. Blessed are you, O Lord, who revives the dead.

3. You are holy, and your name is holy, and holy beings praise you every day. Blessed are you, O Lord, the holy God.

4. You favor mankind with knowledge, and teach mortals understanding. Favor us with the knowledge, understanding and discernment that come from you. Blessed are you, O Lord, gracious Giver of knowledge.

5. Turn us back, O our Father, to your Torah; draw us near, O our King, to your service. Bring us back in perfect repentance to your presence. Blessed are you, O Lord, who delights in repentance.

6. Forgive us, O our Father, for we have sinned; pardon us, O our King, for we have been disobedient; for you pardon and forgive. Blessed are you, O Lord, ever gracious and ready to forgive.

7. Look on our misery, champion our cause, and redeem us swiftly for your name's sake, for you are a mighty Redeemer. Blessed are you, O lord, the Redeemer of Israel.

8. Heal us, O Lord, and we shall be healed; save us and we shall be saved; for it is you we praise. Send us complete healing for all our ills, for you, O divine King, are a trustworthy and compassionate Physician. Blessed are you, O Lord, who heals the sick of his people Israel.

9. O Lord our God, bless this year and all its varied produce for our good. Send a blessing on the earth; satisfy us with your goodness, and make this year as blessed for us as former good years. Blessed are you, O Lord, who blesses the years.

10. Sound the great Shofar for our freedom. Raise the banner to rally our exiles, and gather us in from the four corners of the earth. Blessed are you, O Lord, who gathers the dispersed of his people Israel.

11. Restore our judges as at first, our counselors as in former times. Remove from us sorrow and sighing. Rule over us, O Lord, you alone, in kindness and compassion, and vindicate us in judgment. Blessed are you, O Lord, the King who loves righteousness and justice.

12. For slanderers may there be no hope. May all wickedness perish in an instant. May all your enemies be swiftly cut off. Uproot, smash, overthrow and humble swiftly in our days the arrogant kingdom. Blessed are you, O Lord, who breaks the enemies and humbles the arrogant.①

13. Towards the righteous and the pious, towards the elders of your people, the house of Israel, towards the remnant of their scholars, towards the righteous proselytes②, and towards us also may your compassion be stirred, O Lord our God. Grant a rich reward to all who sincerely trust in your name; set our portion with them for ever, so that we may not be put to shame; for we have trusted in you. Blessed are you, O Lord, the support and security of the righteous.

14. To Jerusalem, your city, return in mercy, and dwell in it, as you

---

① An early manuscript fragments from Cairo Geniza: "And for apostates [*meshummadin*] let there be no hope; and may the arrogant kingdom be quickly uprooted, in our days. And may the Nazarenes [*nozerim*] and the heretics [*minim*] perish quickly; and 'may they be erased from the Book of Life; and may they not be inscribed with the righteous' (Ps. 69:29). Blessed are you, Lord, who humble the arrogant." *Nozeri* is the common rabbinic term for a Christian.

② I.e., proselytes who have accepted Judaism out of inner conviction.

have promised. Rebuild it soon in our days as an everlasting structure, and swiftly establish in it the throne of David. Blessed are you, O Lord, who rebuilds Jerusalem.

15. Cause the scion of David your servant to spring up swiftly, and let his horn be exalted through your saving power, for we wait for your salvation all day long. Blessed are you, O Lord, who makes the horn of salvation to flourish.

16. Hear our supplication, O Lord our God. Spare us and pity us; receive our prayers with compassion and favor; for you are a God who listens to prayers and petitions. O our King, do not turn us out of your presence empty-handed, for you hear with compassion the prayers of your people Israel. Blessed are you, O Lord, who hears prayer.

17. O Lord our God, receive with pleasure your people Israel and their prayers. Restore the service to the sanctuary of your House. Accept with love and approval the fire-offerings of Israel and their prayers, and may the service of your people Israel be ever pleasing to you. May our eyes witness your return in mercy to Zion. Blessed are you, O Lord, who brings back his Shekhinah to Zion.

18. We give thanks to you, for you are the Lord our God and the God of our fathers for ever and ever; you are the Rock of our life, the Shield of our salvation in every generation. We will give thanks to you and praise you for our lives that are held in your hand, for our souls that are in your care, for your miracles that are with us every day, and for your wonders and your benefits that we experience every moment—morning, noon and night. You are all-good, for your mercy has no end; you are all-compassionate, for your kindness knows no limit: we have always put our hope in you. For all this, O our King, may your name be continually blessed and exalted for evermore. May all that lives give thanks to you and praise your name in sincerity, O God, our salvation and our help. Blessed are you, O Lord, whose name is All-Good, and to whom it

is proper to give thanks.
19. Grant peace, well-being, blessing, grace, lovingkindness and compassion to us and to all Israel, your people. Bless us, O our Father, all of us together, with the light of your face; for by the light of your face you have given us, O Lord our God, the Torah of life, love and kindness, righteousness, blessing, mercy, life and peace. May it be good in your sight to bless your people Israel at all times and at every hour with your peace. Blessed are you, O Lord, who blesses his people Israel with peace.

9.3 Aleinu[①]

It is incumbent upon us to praise the Master of all, to exalt the Creator of the universe, who has not made us like the nations of the world and has not placed us like the families of the earth; who has not designed our destiny to be like theirs, nor our lot like that of all their multitude. We bend the knee and bow and acknowledge before the supreme King of kings, the Holy One, blessed be he, that it is he who stretched forth the heavens and founded the earth. His seat of glory is in the heavens above; his abode of majesty is in the lofty heights. He is our God, there is none else; truly, he is our King, there is none besides him, as it is written in his Torah: "You shall know this day, and reflect in your heart, that it is the Lord who is God in the heavens above and on the earth beneath, there is none else."[②]

We hope therefore, Lord our God, soon to behold thy majestic glory, when the abominations shall be removed from the earth, and the false gods exterminated; when the world shall be perfected under the reign of the Almighty, and all mankind will call upon thy name, and all the wicked of the earth will be turned to thee. May all the inhabitants of the world realize

① Cf. Elbogen (1993), pp. 71 – 72.
② Deuteronomy 4:39.

and know that to thee every knee must bend, every tongue must vow allegiance. May they bend the knee and prostrate themselves before thee, Lord our God, and give honor to thy glorious name; may they all accept the yoke of thy kingdom, and do thou reign over them speedily forever and ever. For the kingdom is thine, and to all eternity thou wilt reign in glory, as it is written in thy Torah: "The Lord shall be King forever and ever."[1] And it is said: "The Lord shall be King over all the earth; on that day the Lord shall be One, and his name One."[2]

9.4 The Mourner's Kaddish[3]

Glorified and sanctified be God's great name throughout the world which he has created according to his will. May he establish his kingdom in your lifetime and during your days, and within the life of the entire house of Israel, speedily and soon; and say, Amen.

May his great name be blessed forever and to all eternity.

Blessed and praised, glorified and exalted, extolled and honored, adored and lauded be the name of the Holy One, blessed be he, beyond all the blessings and hymns, praises and consolations that are ever spoken in the world; and say, Amen.

May there be abundant peace from heaven, and life, for us and for all Israel; and say, Amen.

He who creates peace in his celestial heights, may he create peace for us and for all Israel; and say, Amen.

---

[1] Exodus 15:18.
[2] Zechariah 14:9. This verse alludes to Deuteronomy 6:4, the Shema.
[3] Cf. Elbogen (1993), pp. 80–84.

9.5 Passover Liturgy. Selections from Passover Haggadah[①]

The Introduction

This is the bread of distress[②] which our forefathers ate in the land of Egypt. Let all who are hungry enter and eat; let all who are needy come to Passover feast.[③] This year we are here; next year may we be in the Land Israel.[④] This year we are slaves; next year may we be free men.

[①] Source: Biale and Miles (2015). Cf. Birnbaum (1953); Tabory (2008); 宋立宏 (2015a).

[②] I.e., *matzah*, unleavened bread that is obligatory to eat on the first night of Passover. The phrase "bread of distress" is borrowed from Deuteronomy 16:3, where the Israelites are told to eat it in remembrance of the hasty departure from Egypt. The Aramaic word *anya* can mean both "distress" or "poverty."

[③] Exodus 12:4 enjoins sharing of the Passover meal with those who cannot provide their own.

[④] In the biblical period, Passover (the sacrifice of the paschal lamb) and the Feast of Unleavened Bread (eating the *matzah*) were pilgrimage holidays during which the Israelites were supposed to journey to Jerusalem to celebrate them.

The Four Questions①

Why does this night differ from all other nights?

On all other nights we eat either leavened and unleavened bread; why on this night only unleavened bread?

On all other nights we eat all kinds of herbs; why on this night only bitter herbs?②

On all other nights we need not dip our herbs even once; why on this night must we dip them twice?③

On all other nights we eat either sitting up or reclining; why on this night do we all recline?

The Reply

We were Pharaoh's slaves in Egypt, and the Lord our God brought us forth

---

① Exodus 13:14 addresses the idea that children in the future will ask about the purpose of Passover ritual. The Four Questions are quoted in the Mishnah (Pesahim 10:4) with one variation. Instead of asking why all the participants recline this night, the question in Mishnah reads: "On all nights we eat meat roasted, stewed or boiled; why do we eat only roast this night?" Obviously, the questions asked by the young child at the Seder table date back to ancient times when the paschal lamb was offered in Jerusalem and roasted. With the destruction of the Temple and the cessation of the sacrificial offerings there naturally came a change in the formula, and the question about the paschal lamb was replaced by the question about the custom of reclining.

② The bitter herbs, or *maror*, represent the bitterness of slavery in Egypt.

③ This refers to dipping a vegetable (*karpas*) into salt water, which represents the tears of the enslaved Israelites, and dipping bitter herbs in *haroset*, a sweet, fruity, pasty concoction that symbolizes the mortar that was used to build Pharaoh's storehouses.

from there with a mighty hand① and an outstretched arm②. And if the Holy One, blessed be he, had not brought our forefathers forth from Egypt, then we, our children, and our children's children would still be Pharaoh's slaves in Egypt.

So, even though all of us were wise, all of us full of understanding, all of us elders, all of us knowing in the Torah, we should still be under the commandment to tell the story of the departure from Egypt. And the more one tells the story of the departure from Egypt, the more praiseworthy he is.

[**History of the Jews**]

In the beginning our fathers were idolaters, but now the Omnipresent has drawn us to his service, as it is said: "And Joshua said unto all the people: 'Thus saith the Lord, the God of Israel: Your fathers dwelt of old time beyond the River③, even Terah, the father of Abraham, and the father of Nahor; and they served other gods. And I took your father Abraham beyond the River, and led him throughout all the land of Canaan, and multiplied his seed, and gave him Isaac. And I gave unto Isaac Jacob and Esau; and I gave unto Esau Mount Seir, to possess it; and Jacob and his children went down into Egypt.'" (Josh. 24:2 – 4) ④

---

① Deuteronomy 6:21.
② Deuteronomy 5:15.
③ I.e., to the east of the Euphrates.
④ This passage recounts the history of the Jews and emphasizes that, despite their roots in idolatry, the Jews are now called to worship only God.

The Midrash on Deuteronomy 26:5–8: Introduction

Blessed be He who keeps his promise to Israel[1], blessed be he. For the Holy One, blessed be he, premeditated the end of the bondage, thus doing that which he said to Abraham in the Covenant between the Sections,[2] as it is said: "And he said unto Abram: 'Know of a surety that thy seed shall be a stranger in a land that is not theirs, and shall serve them; and they shall afflict them four hundred years; and also that nation, whom they shall serve, will I judge; and afterward shall they come out with great substance.'" (Gen. 15:13–14)

And it is this promise that has stood by our fathers and by us. For it was not one man only who stood up against us to destroy us; in every generation they stand up against us to destroy us, and the Holy One, blessed be he, saves us from their hand.

Go forth and learn what Laban, the Aramean, sought to do to Jacob, our father.[3] While Pharaoh decreed death only for the male children, Laban sought to uproot all.

---

[1] This refers to the promises of the land of Canaan, numerous offspring, and blessing given to the ancestors in Genesis.

[2] A reference to the covenant ceremony in Genesis 15:9–17, which involves sections (parts) of animals.

[3] In Genesis 31, Laban, Jacob's father-in-law, attempts to keep Jacob and his family (and their possessions) as part of his own household. The reference here likely alludes to attempts by other kingdoms to dominate the Jews of Palestine in the Second Temple period.

The Midrash[①]

For it is said: "An Aramean would have destroyed my father, and he went down into Egypt, and sojourned there, few in number; and he became there a nation, great, mighty, and populous" (cf. Deut. 26:5).

"And he went down into Egypt": compelled by the word of God.

"And sojourned there": teaching us that Jacob did not go down to Egypt to settle but to sojourn there.[②] As it is said: "And they said unto Pharaoh: 'To sojourn in the land are we come; for there is no pasture for thy servants' flocks; for the famine is sore in the land of Canaan. Now therefore, we pray thee, let thy servants dwell in the land of Goshen.'" (Gen. 47:4)

"Few in number": as it is said: "Thy fathers went down into Egypt with threescore and ten persons; and now the Lord thy God hath made thee as the stars of heaven for multitudes." (Deut. 10:22)

"And he became there a nation": teaching us that the Israelites were distinguishable there.[③]

"Great and powerful": as it is said: "And the children of Israel were fruitful, and increased abundantly, and multiplied, and grew exceedingly strong; and the land was filled with them." (Exod. 1:7)

"And populous": as it is said: "I caused thee to increase, even as the growth of the field. And thou didst increase and grow up, and thou camest to excellent beauty: thy breasts were fashioned, and thy hair was grown; yet

---

① The Haggadah now begins a typical rabbinic commentary and expansion (midrash) on Deuteronomy 26:5–8.

② The rabbinic commentary emphasizes that they had no intention of assuming political authority.

③ I.e., they did not assimilate. This was a pressing concern in the time of the rabbis well. However, cf. Genesis 41:45.

thou wast naked and bare." (Ezek. 16:7)[1]

"And the Egyptians considered us evil; they afflicted us, and laid upon us hard bondage." (Deut. 26:6)

"And the Egyptians considered us evil":[2] as it is said: "Come let us deal shrewdly with them, lest they multiply, and it come to pass, that, when there befalleth us any war, they also join themselves unto our enemies, and fight against us, and get them up out of the land." (Exod. 1:10)

"And afflicted us": as it is said: "Therefore they did set over them taskmasters to afflict them with their burdens. And they built for Pharaoh store-cities, Pithom and Raamses." (Exod. 1:11)

"And laid upon us heavy bondage": as it is said: "And the Egyptians made the children of Israel to serve with rigour." (Exod. 1:13)

"And we cried unto the Lord, the God of our fathers, and the Lord heard our voice, and saw our affliction, and our toil, and our oppression." (Deut 26:7)

"And we cried unto the Lord, the God of our fathers": as it is written: "And it came to pass in the course of those many days that the king of Egypt died; and the children of Israel were groaning under the bondage and cried out, and their cry for help from the bondage rose up to God." (Exod. 2:23)

"And the Lord heard our voice": as it is said: "And God heard their groaning, and God remembered His covenant with Abraham, with Isaac and with Jacob." (Exod. 2:24)

"And saw our affliction": this is enforced separation [of husbands from having sexual relations with their wives], as it is said: "And God saw the children of Israel, and God knew." (Exod. 2:25)

"And our travail": this is the sons, as it is said: "Every son that is born you shall cast into the river, and every daughter you shall save alive."

---

[1] This passage from Ezekiel imagines Israel through the metaphor of a beautiful young woman redeemed from ignominious origins.

[2] Literally, "dealt ill with us."

(Exod. 1:22)

"And our oppression": this is the persecution, as it is said: "Moreover I have seen how the Egyptians oppress them." (Exod. 3:9)

"And the Lord brought us forth out of Egypt with a mighty hand, and with an outstretched arm, and with great terribleness, and with signs, and with wonders." (Deut. 26:8)

"And the Lord brought us forth out of Egypt": not by the hands of an angel, and not by the hands of a seraph, and not by the hands of a messenger, but the Holy One, blessed be he, himself, in his own glory and in his own person. As it is said: "For I will go through the land of Egypt in that night, and will smite all the first-born in the land of Egypt, both man and beast; and against all the gods of Egypt I will execute judgments: I am the Lord." (Exod. 12:12)

"For I will go through the land of Egypt in that night": I, and not an angel. "I will smite all the first-born in the land of Egypt": I, and not a seraph. "And against all the gods of Egypt I will execute judgments": I, and not a messenger. "I am the Lord": I am He, and no other. ①

"With mighty hand": this is the pestilence, as it is said: "Behold, the hand of the Lord is upon thy cattle which are in the field, upon the horses, upon the asses, upon the camels, upon the herds, and upon the flocks; there shall be a very grievous pestilence." (Exod. 9:3)

"And with an outstretched arm": this is the sword, as it is said: "Having a drawn sword in his hand stretched out over Jerusalem." (I Chron. 21:16)

"And with great terribleness": this is the revelation of the Divine Presence,② as it is said: "Or hath God assayed to go and take Him a nation from the midst of another nation, by trials, by signs, and by wonders, and

---

① This passage is a midrash within a midrash. The text turns away from the exposition of Deuteronomy 26:8 to expound on the proof text, Exodus 12:12.

② This interpretation involves a play on the Hebrew words for "terribleness" and "appearance," which sound similar.

by war, and by a mighty hand, and by an outstretched arm, and by great terrors, according to all that the Lord your God did for you in Egypt before thine eyes?" (Deut. 4:34)

"And with signs": this is the rod [of Moses], as it is said: "And thou shalt take in thy hand this rod, wherewith thou shalt do the signs." (Exod. 4:17)

"And with wonders": this is the blood, as it is said: "And I will show wonders in the heavens and in the earth, blood, and fire, and pillars of smoke." (Joel 3:3)

Another explanation [of Deut. 26:8]: "A mighty hand" refers to two [plagues],① "an outstretched arm" refers to two, "and with great terribleness" refers to two, "and with signs" refers to two, "and with wonders" refers to two.

These make up the ten plagues which the Holy One, blessed be he, brought upon the Egyptians in Egypt, and they are these: blood, frogs, lice, beasts, pestilence, boils, hail, locusts, darkness, the slaying of the first-born.

Redemption

Blessed art thou, O Lord, our God, king of the universe, who redeemed us and who redeemed our fathers from Egypt, and has brought us to this night, to eat thereon unleavened bread and bitter herbs. So, O Lord our God and God of our fathers, bring us to other festivals and holy days that come toward us in peace, happy in the building of thy city and joyous in thy service. And there may we eat of the sacrifices and the paschal② offerings, whose blood will come unto the walls of thy altar for acceptance.③ Then shall we give thanks to thee with a new song, for our redemption and the

---

① Each of these phrases in Hebrew consists of two words. Since the total comes to ten, it is taken as an allusion to the ten plagues.

② Pertaining to Passover.

③ A reference to the customary pouring of the blood of a sacrifice at the base of the altar.

liberation of our soul. Blessed art thou, O Lord, Redeemer of Israel.

9.6 Solomon Ibn Gabirol, "At Dawn I Come to You"[①]

At dawn I come to You, my Rock, my Strength;
   I offer You my dawn and evening prayers.
Before Your majesty I stand in fear,
   because Your eye observes my secret thoughts.
What is there that man's mind and mouth[②]
   can make? What power is there in my body's breath?
And yet the songs of man delight You. Therefore I
   shall praise You while God's breath (*nishmat*) remains in me.[③]

9.7 Solomon Alkabetz, "Lekhah Dodi (Come, My Beloved)"[④]

Come, my beloved,[⑤] to meet the bride; let us welcome the Sabbath.

---

① Source: Scheindelin (2016), pp. 306 – 307. Cf. Cole (2007), p. 91. This poem has been adopted by many modernized prayer books, usually as an introduction to the morning service (*Shaharit*). It is a *reshut* ("permission") to the *nishmat* for the Day of Atonement. *Reshut* is a type of piyyut, introducing the poet to the congregation, or introducing the prayer that he is about to chant. *Nishmat* refers to a prayer whose opening words *nishmat kol hai* mean "the breath of every living being." It is recited in *Shaharit* on Sabbath and festivals and at the Passover *seder*.

② *man's mind and mouth*. Possibly an allusion to an Arabic maxim *innamā l-insān/ al-qalb wa l-lisān*, meaning "Man is just the heart and the tongue."

③ As is customary in this type of poem, the final line of the poem leads into the *nishmat* prayer.

④ Source: Birnbaum (1977), pp. 243 – 248. Cf. Cole (2012), pp. 133 – 135; 352 – 360.

⑤ The Song of Songs 7:12.

"Observe" and "Remember,"① in a single command, the One God announced to us. The Lord is One, and his name is One,② for fame, for glory and for praise.

Come, my beloved, to meet the bride; let us welcome the Sabbath.

Come, let us go to meet the Sabbath, for it is a source of blessing. From the very beginning it was ordained; last in creation, first in God's plan.

Come, my beloved, to meet the bride; let us welcome the Sabbath.

Shrine of the King, royal city, arise!③ Come forth from thy ruins. Long enough have you dwelt in the valley of tears!④ He will show you abundant mercy.

Come, my beloved, to meet the bride; let us welcome the Sabbath.

Shake off your dust, arise! Put on your glorious garments, my people, and pray: "Be near to my soul, and redeem it through the son of Jesse, the Bethlehemite."⑤

Come, my beloved, to meet the bride; let us welcome the Sabbath.

Bestir yourself, bestir yourself, for your light has come; arise and shine! Awake, awake, utter a song;⑥ the Lord's glory is revealed upon you.

Come, my beloved, to meet the bride; let us welcome the Sabbath.

---

① An explanation of the variation between Exodus 20:8, which says "Remember the Sabbath," and Deuteronomy 5:12, which says "Observe the Sabbath." According to rabbinic tradition, God miraculously uttered both words simultaneously.

② Zechariah 14:9. The verse evokes the Shema as well.

③ A reference to the messianic hope for the rebuilding of the Temple and the city of Jerusalem.

④ "The valley of tears" (Psalms 84:7) is the Exile.

⑤ The Messiah, who will be a descendant of David, the son of Jesse the Bethlehemite.

⑥ The phrase evokes Judges 5:12.

Be not ashamed nor confounded. Why are you downcast? Why do you moan? The afflicted of my people will be sheltered within you; the city shall be rebuilt on its ancient site.

Come, my beloved, to meet the bride; let us welcome the Sabbath.

Those who despoiled you shall become a spoil, and all who would devour you shall be far away. Your God will rejoice over you as a bridegroom rejoices over his bride.

Come, my beloved, to meet the bride; let us welcome the Sabbath.

You shall extend to the right and to the left, and you shall revere the Lord. Through the advent of a descendant of Perez[①] we shall rejoice and exult.

Come, my beloved, to meet the bride; let us welcome the Sabbath.

Come in peace, crown of God, come with joy and cheerfulness; amidst the faithful of the chosen people come O bride; come, O bride.

Come, my beloved, to meet the bride; let us welcome the Sabbath.

---

① According to Ruth 4:18-22, Perez, the son of Judah and Tamar (see Genesis 38) is an ancestor of David, who, in turn, is the ancestor of the Messiah.

10 THE YOKE OF THE TORAH

10.1 Ecclesiastes (Kohelet) 12:12

A further word: Against them, my son, be warned! The making of many books is without limit and much study is a wearying of the flesh.

10.2 A Greek Inscription Found at the Amphiareion, Oropus in Attica (300–250 BCE). A Jew Undertaking Incubation in a Pagan Temple[1]

... under which Moschus is to serve Phrynidas(?) for a year(?), and to be free, dependent on no one. If anything happens to Phrynidas before the time (of the *paramonē*)[2] elapses, let Moschus go free wherever he wishes. For good fortune. Witnesses: Athenodorus(son) of Mnasikon of Oropus, Biottus(son) of Eudicus of Athens, Charinus(son) of Anticharmus of Athens, Athenades

---

[1] Source: Noy, et al. (2004), pp. 177–180. It is suggested that Moschus, the earliest Jew known from the Greek mainland, and his father may have come to Greece as slaves after the campaign of Alexander the Great in Palestine (334–333 BCE). This is possible, but he could well have been born in Greece.

[2] *Paramonē* refers to the obligation on a slave, whose manumission has been deferred, to remain in service for a stipulated time. The missing part of the inscription most probably included the date of the manumission and a reference to the condition of the fictional sale to the god Amphiaraus.

(son) of Epigonus of Oropus, Hippon (son) of Aeschylus of Oropus.

Moschus (son) of Moschion, a Jew, (set this up), having seen a dream with the god Amphiaraus and Hygeia① commanding (him), in accordance with what Amphiaraus and Hygeia ordered, to write it on a stele and set it up by the altar②.

10.3 Babylonian Talmud, Hagiga 15a–b. The Story of a Sinful Master of Torah③

Aher gazed and cut the shoots. ④ *About him scripture says, "Let not your month lead you into sin, [and do not say before the malakh (angel/ messenger) that it was an error, else God may be angered by your talk and destroy the work of your hands]."* (Ecclesiastes 5:5 = Tosefta Hagiga 2:3)

What did he see? He saw Metatron⑤, to whom was given permission one hour each day to sit and write the merits of Israel. He said, "It is taught that 'On high there is no sitting and no jealousy and no rivalry and no back⑥ and no weariness.' Perhaps—Heaven forbid—there are two divine powers?!" Immediately they brought out Metatron and struck him with

---

① *Hygeia.* The Greek personification of health. She is often said to have been a daughter of Asclepius, the god of medicine.

② *Altar.* According to Pausanias (1.34.4), the altar of the Amphiareion had five different parts: the first was dedicated to Heracles, Zeus, and Apollo the Healer; the second to the heroes and to wives of heroes; the third to Hestia, Hermes and Amphiaraus and the children of Amphilochus; the fourth to Aphrodite and Panacea, Iaso and Athena the Healer; and the fifth to the nymphs, Pan, and to the rivers Achelous and Cephisus. It is possible then that Moschus had placed his inscription near the third part of the altar dedicated to Amphiaraus.

③ Source: Rubenstein (2003), pp. 232–236.

④ For Aher and "cut the shoots," see 6.9.

⑤ A high-ranking angel.

⑥ The sense of "no back" derives from Ezekiel's vision in which the animals bearing the chariot of God have faces on all four sides, hence no backs (Ezek 1:1–28).

sixty lashes of fire. He was given permission to burn the merits of Aher.① A heavenly voice went out and said to him, "*Return, rebellious children* (Jer. 3:22)—except Aher."

He (Aher) said, "Since that man (=since I) has been banished from that world (=the next world), I will go and enjoy myself in this world." Aher went out to evil ways (literally, "evil growth"). He found a certain prostitute. He propositioned her. She said to him, "Are you not Elisha ben Abuya, whose name went out throughout the world?" He uprooted a radish on the Sabbath and gave it to her. She said, "It is another (*aher*)." ②

After he went out into evil ways, Aher asked R. Meir, "What is written, *The one no less than the other is God's doing* (Ecclesiastes 7:14)?" He(Meir) said, "Everything that God made, He made its counterpart. He made mountains, he made hills. He made seas, he made rivers." He (Aher) said to him, "Akiba, our master, did not say this. [Rather], He made righteous, he made wicked. He made the Garden of Eden, he made Gehenom.③ Each and every person has two portions, one in the Garden of Eden and one in Gehenom. The righteous man, having earned merit, takes his portion and the portion of his fellow in the Garden of Eden. The wicked man, having been found guilty, takes his portion and the portion of his fellow in Gehenom." ④

Rav Mesharshia said, "What is the verse [that supports this idea]? *They shall have a double share in their land.* (Isa. 61:7) And it is written, *Shatter them with double destruction* (Jer. 17:18)." ⑤

After he went out into evil ways Aher asked R. Meir, "What is written, *Gold or glass cannot match its value, nor vessels of fine gold be exchanged*

---

① Measure-for-measure punishment. Elisha caused Metatron to be burned with fire, so Metatron burns out Elisha's merits.

② This incident explains the tradition that Elisha "cut the shoots" of the Tosefta.

③ I.e., Gehenna, the underworld.

④ This theology of transferring merits and sins is completely exceptional in rabbinic literature.

⑤ Isaiah refers to the righteous, Jeremiah refers to the wicked.

for it (Job 28:17)?" He (Meir) said, "This refers to matters of Torah which are difficult to acquire like vessels of gold and vessels of fine gold and easy to lose like vessels of glass." He (Aher) said to him, "By God! Are they even like clay vessels that have no value?"① He (Aher) said to him, "Akiba your master, did not say thus. Rather just as vessels of gold and vessels of glass, even if they are broken, they can be restored, so a sage, even though he sins, can be restored." He said to him, "Then you too should repent." He said to him, "No, I have already heard from behind the curtain, *Return, rebellious children* (Jer. 3:22)—except Aher."

Our sages taught: It once happened that Aher was riding his horse on the Sabbath going on his way and R. Meir was walking after him to learn Torah from his mouth. He said to him, "Meir, return (*hazor*) back, since I have already measured by the footsteps of my horse that the Sabbath boundary is here." He said to him, "Then you too should repent (*hazor*)." He said to him, "No, I have already heard from behind the curtain, *Return, rebellious children* (Jer. 3:22)—except Aher."

He (Meir) took hold of him (Aher) and

He brought him to the study-house. He said to a child, "Tell me your study verse." He said to him, "*There is no peace—said the Lord—for the wicked* (Isa. 48:22)."

He brought him to another study-house. He (the child) said to him, "*Though you wash with natron and use much lye, [your guilt is ingrained before me—declares the Lord God]* (Jer. 2:22)."

He brought him to another study-house. He (the child) said to him, "*And you, who are doomed to ruin* (Jer. 4:30)."

He brought him to thirteen study-house. They recited for him in similar ways. The child in the thirteenth said, "*And to the wicked* (ulerasha) *God said: Who are you to recite my laws [and mouth the terms of my covenant, seeing that you spurn my discipline, and brush my words aside?]* (Ps. 50:

---

① If Torah can be compared to various types of vessels, then it must be comparable to worthless clay vessels as well.

16)." That child stuttered so it sounded as if he said, "And to Elisha (*ule'elisha*) God said ..." Some say he (Aher) took a knife and cut him up and sent him to thirteen study-houses.① And some say, he (Aher) said to him, "If I had a knife with me I would cut you up."

When Aher died, they (the angels?) said, "Let him not be punished and let him not enter the world to come. Let him not be punished since he studied Torah regularly. Let him not enter the world to come since he sinned."

R. Meir said, "When I die I shall cause smoke to rise from his grave." When R. Meir died, smoke rose up from Aher's grave.

R. Yohanan said, "Is it a mighty deed to burn one's master with fire? One was among us, and yet we cannot save him? If I were to take him by the hand, who would tear him away from me? When I die I will extinguish the smoke from his grave." When R. Yohanan died, the smoke ceased from the grave of Aher. (The eulogizer said of him [Yohanan], "Even the guard of the gate [of Gehenom] could not stand before you, our master.")

The daughter of Aher came before Rabbi [Judah the Patriarch]. She said to him, "My master, support me." He said to her, "My daughter, whose daughter are you?" She said to him, "The daughter of Aher." He said, "Is there still his seed in the world? *He has no offspring or descendant among his people, no survivor where he once lived* (Job 18:19)."② She said to him, "My master. Remember his Torah and do not remember his deeds." Fire came down from heaven and tried to burn Rabbi. Rabbi wept and said, "If this [happens] for those who dishonor her [Torah], how much the more so for those who respect her?"

How did R. Meir learn Torah from Aher? Did not Rabbah bar bar Hanna say that R. Yohanan said, "What is the meaning of *For the lips of a priest guard knowledge, and men seek rulings from his mouth; for he is a malakh* (messenger/angel) *of the Lord of hosts* (Mal. 2:7)? If the master is

---

① Cf. the stories in Judges 19 and I Samuel 11.
② This passage refers to the wicked.

similar to the '*malakh* of the Lord of hosts,' then they should seek Torah from his mouth, and if not, do not seek Torah from his mouth."

Resh Laqish said, "R. Meir found a verse and expounded it: *Incline your ear and listen to the words of the sages; pay attention to my wisdom* (Prov. 22:17). It does not say 'to their wisdom' but 'to my wisdom.'" ①

R. Hanina said, "From here: *Take heed, daughter, and note, incline your ear; forget your people and your father's house* (Ps. 45:11)." (The verses contradict each other! There is no difficulty. One is about an adult, one a child.)②

When Rav Dimi came up [from Israel] he said, "They say in the West [Israel]: Eat the date and throw the peel away."

Rava expounded: "What is written, *I went down to the nut grove to see the budding of the vale* (Song 6:11)? Why are words of Torah compared to a nut? To tell you that just as a nut, even though it is dirtied with mud and filth, its inside is not soiled, so too a sage, even though he sins, his Torah is not soiled."

Rabba bar Rav Sheila came upon Elijah. He said to him, "What is the Holy One, Blessed be he, doing?" He said to him, "He recites traditions from the mouths of all the sages, but he does not recite from the mouth of R. Meir." He said to him, "Why?" He said to him, "Because he learned traditions from the mouth of Aher." He said to him, "So what? R. Meir found a pomegranate. He ate the inside and threw away the peel." He said to him, "Now He (God) says: 'Meir, my son, says,' *When a human being suffers, the Shekhinah—what expression does it say? 'I am light(=pained) in my head. I am light in my hand.' If it says 'I am saddened' on account of the blood of the wicked who are killed, how much the more so for the*

---

① One should separate God's wisdom (Torah) from "their wisdom," the baleful advice of sinning masters.

② That is, an adult is able to discern good teaching from bad ("pay attention to my wisdom" taken to mean that an adult listener will heed only the wisdom, and not the wickedness), whereas a child cannot (thus, Aher's daughter, presumably a minor, must disregard all he said).

blood of the righteous that is spilled? (=Mishnah Sanhedrin 6:5)'"

10.4 From the Cairo Geniza. An Egyptian Woman Seeks to Rescue Her Husband from a Sufi Monastery (*c.*1355–1367) ①

In your name, You, Merciful.

To the high Seat of our lord, the Nagid,② may his splendor be exalted and his honor be great.

The maidservant, the wife of Basir, the bell maker, kisses the ground and submits that she has on her neck three children because her husband has become completely infatuated with [life on] the mountain with al-Kurani,③ in vain and to no purpose, a place where there is no Torah, no prayer, and no mention of God's name in truth. He goes up the mountain and mingles with the mendicants, although these have only the semblance, but not the essence, of religion.

The maidservant is afraid there may be there some bad man who may induce her husband to forsake the Jewish faith, taking with him the three children.

The maidservant almost perishes because of her solitude and her search for food for the little ones. It is her wish that our Master go after her husband and take the matter up with him according to his unfailing wisdom. What the maidservant entreats him to do is not beyond his power, nor the high degree of his influence.

The only thing that the maidservant wants is that her husband cease to

---

① Source: Goitein (1988), pp. 471–474.

② The Nagid [head of the Jewish community in Egypt], to whom the letter is addressed, can only be David II Maimonides, who followed his father Joshua ben [son of] Abraham II ben David I ben Abraham I ben Moses Maimonides in 1355 as head of the Jewish community in Egypt.

③ The Sufi master is no doubt Yusuf al-Aljami al-Kurani, who died in Cairo in January 1367.

go up the mountain and that he may show mercy toward the little ones. If he wishes to devote himself to God, he may do so in the synagogue, regularly attending morning, afternoon, and evening prayers, and listening to the words of the Torah, but he should not occupy himself with worthless things.

Furthermore, he presses the maidservant to sell their house, to leave the Jewish community, and to stay on the mountain, [which would mean that] the little ones would cease to study the Torah. [It would be helpful] if our Lord gave orders to the maidservant in that matter and instructed her concerning it,[1] for his wisdom is unfailing. And Peace.

Our lord—may God prolong his life—is in charge of a vast region; thus his high aspiration could not fail to hinder the above mentioned from going up the mountain and to induce him to attend the synagogue and to occupy himself with the upkeep of the family.

P.S. Our lord has promised the little one a medicine for the ear, for he suffers from it. There is no harm in trying it out, seeing that even the barber is playing with it without experience and mercy.

10.5　*Or Ha-Me'ir* 5: 42b–c. A Hasidic Parable Attributed to Ba'al Shem Tov[2]

This parable is told. There was once a musician, well-known for the great beauty of his music, who came to play before the king. One particular melody was so loved by the king that he ordered the musician to play it for him several times each day. An so it was. After a time, however, the musician began to weary of the tune; no longer could he play it with the

---

[1]　Since the house, or a part of it, was certainly mortgaged to the sum promised in her marriage contract, it could not be sold without her permission.

[2]　Source: Green and Holtz (1993), pp. 118–119. The parable is quoted in the name of the Ba'al Shem Tov. The author of the *Or Ha-Me'ir* offers the suggestion that man must be blind to this world in order to see the other—an explanation which seems to escape rather than confront the frightening reality of this parable.

same passion and excitement as before.

The king, to rekindle his musician's love for his favorite tune, ordered that a man be brought in from the market, one who had never heard the tune before. Seeing someone who had never heard him play, the musician's vigor was renewed, and he played the tune in all its beauty, thus the king ordered a new man brought each day.

After some time, the king sought other counsel, for to find a new audience each day was not an easy matter. It was decided that the musician should be blinded, so that he never see a human form again. Now the blind musician sat before the king, and whenever the king sought to hear his favorite tune he would simply say: "Here comes someone new, one who has never heard you play before!" And the musician would play his tune with the greatest joy.

The parable is not explained.

10.6 Solomon Maimon, "My Emergence from Talmudic Darkness" (1793)[1]

My father had in his study a cupboard containing books. He had forbidden me indeed to read any books but the Talmud. This, however, was of no avail: as he was occupied the most of his time with household affairs, I took advantage of the opportunity thus afforded. Under the impulse of curiosity I made a raid upon the cupboard and glanced over all the books. The result was, that, as I had already a fair knowledge of Hebrew, I found more pleasure in some of these books than in the Talmud. And this result was surely natural. Take the subjects of the Talmud, which, with the exception of those relating to jurisprudence, are dry and mostly unintelligible to a child—the laws of sacrifice, of purification, of forbidden meats, of feasts, and so

---

[1] Source: Maimon (1888), pp. 27 – 28, 33 – 35, 89 – 93, 107 – 108, 253 – 257. Cf. Maimon (2018).

forth—in which the oddest rabbinical conceits are elaborated through many volumes with the finest dialectic, and the most absurd questions are discussed with the highest efforts of intellectual power; for example, how many white hairs may a red cow have, and yet remain a *red* cow;① what sorts of scabs require this or that sort of purification; whether a louse or a flea may be killed on the Sabbath—the first being allowed, while the second is a deadly sin;② whether the slaughter of an animal ought to be executed at the neck or the tail;③ whether the high priest put on his shirt or his socks first;④ whether the *Yabam*, that is, the brother of a man who died childless, being required by law to marry the widow,⑤ is relieved from his obligation if he falls off a roof and sticks in the mire.⑥ *Ohe jam satis est*:⑦ Compare these glorious disputations, which are served up to young people and forced on them even to disgust, with history, in which natural events are related in an instructive and agreeable manner, with a knowledge of the world's structure, by which the outlook into nature is widened, and the vast whole is brought into a well-ordered system; surely my preference will be justified ...

I must now say something of the condition of the Jewish schools in general.⑧ The school is commonly a small smoky hut, and the children are scattered, some on benches, some on the bare earth. The master, in a dirty

---

① See Babylonian Talmud, Avodah Zarah, 24a.
② See Babylonian Talmud, Sabbath, 14a.
③ See Babylonian Talmud, Hulin, 27a.
④ See Babylonian Talmud, Sanhedrin, 49b.
⑤ *Yabam*. The brother of the deceased. This refers to the so-called "levirate marriage"(from Latin "levir," "brother-in-law"). See Deuteronomy 25:5 – 6.
⑥ See Babylonian Talmud, Yebamot, 53b; Bava Kamma, 27a. The hypothetical case discussed in the Talmud involves a man falling off a roof and, without intent, penetrating his widowed sister-in-law. The rabbis rule that such an incident does not constitute sexual intercourse.
⑦ Latin, "Alas, it is enough already!" (Horace)
⑧ Maimon's description of Jewish schools here is an early classic of the enlightened critique of traditional Jewish education.

blouse sitting on the table, holds between his knees a bowl, in which he grinds tobacco into snuff with a huge pestle like the club of Hercules, while at the same time he wields his authority. The ushers give lessons, each in his own corner, and rule those under their charge quite as despotically as the master himself. Of the breakfast, lunch, and other food sent to the school for the children, these gentlemen keep the largest share for themselves. Sometimes even the poor youngsters get nothing at all; and yet they dare not make any complaint on the subject, if they will not expose themselves to the vengeance of these tyrants. Here the children are imprisoned from morning to night, and have not an hour to themselves, except on Friday and a half-holiday at the Newmoon.

As far as study is concerned, the reading of Hebrew at least is pretty regularly learned. On the other hand, with the mastery of the Hebrew language very seldom is any progress made. Grammar is not treated in the school at all, but has to be learnt *ex usu*,① by translation of the Holy Scriptures, very much as the ordinary man learns imperfectly the grammar of his mother-tongue by social intercourse. Moreover there is no dictionary of the Hebrew language. The children therefore begin at once with the explanation of the Bible. This is divided into as many sections as there are weeks in the year, in order that the Books of Moses, which are read in the synagogues every Saturday, may be read through in a year. Accordingly every week some verses from the beginning of the section proper to the week are explained in school, and that with every possible grammatical blunder. Nor can it well be otherwise. For the Hebrew must be explained by means of the mother-tongue. But the mother-tongue of the Polish Jews is itself full of defects and grammatical inaccuracies; and as a matter of course therefore also the Hebrew language, which is learned by its means, must be of the same stamp. The pupil thus acquires just as little knowledge of the language, as of the contents, of the Bible.

In addition to this the Talmudists have fastened all sorts of

---

① "Out of practice."

extraordinary conceits on the Bible. The ignorant teacher believes with confidence, that the Bible cannot in reality have any other meaning than that which these expositions ascribe to it; and the pupil must follow his teacher's faith, so that the right understanding of words necessarily becomes lost. For example, in the first Book of Moses it is said, "Jacob sent messengers to his brother Esau, etc.."[①] Now, the Talmudists were pleased to give out, that these messengers were angels. For though the word *Malachim* in Hebrew denotes messenger as well as angels, these marvel-mongers preferred the second signification, because the first contains nothing marvelous. The pupil therefore holds the belief firm and fast, that *Malachim* denotes nothing but angels; and the natural meaning of messengers is for him wholly lost. A correct knowledge of the Hebrew language and a sound exegesis can be attained only gradually by independent study and by reading grammars and critical commentaries on the Bible (such as David Kimhi's and Ibn Ezra's), but of these very few rabbis make use ...

By means of the instruction received from my father, but still more by my own industry, I had got on so well, that in my eleventh year I was able to pass as a full rabbi. Besides I possessed some disconnected knowledge in history, astronomy, and other mathematical sciences. I burned with desire to acquire more knowledge, but how was this to be accomplished in the want of guidance, of scientific books, and of all other means for the purpose? I was obliged therefore to content myself with making use of any help that I could by chance obtain, without plan or method.

In order to gratify my desire of scientific knowledge, there were no means available but that of learning foreign languages. But how was I to begin? To learn Polish or Latin with a Catholic teacher was for me impossible, on the one hand because the prejudices of my own people prohibited to me all languages but Hebrew, and all sciences but the Talmud and the vast array of its commentators, on the other hand because the prejudices of Catholics would not allow them to give instruction in those

---

① Genesis 32:4.

matters to a Jew. Moreover I was in very low temporal circumstances. I was obliged to support a whole family by teaching, by correcting proofs of the Holy Scriptures, and by other work of a similar kind. For a long time therefore I had to sigh in vain for the satisfaction of my natural inclination.

At last a fortunate accident came to my help. I observed in some stout Hebrew volumes, that they contained several alphabets, and that the number of their sheets was indicated not merely by Hebrew letters, but that for this purpose the characters of a second and a third alphabet had also been employed, these being commonly Latin and German letters ... I gradually learnt the Latin and German characters.

By a kind of deciphering I began to combine various German letters into words; but as the characters used along with the Hebrew letters might be something quite different from these, I remained always doubtful whether the whole of my labor in this operation would not be in vain, till fortunately some leaves of an old German book fell into my hand. I began to read. How great were my joy and surprise, when I saw from the connection, that the words completely corresponded with those which I had learned ...

I still always felt a want which I was not able to fill. I could not completely satisfy my desire for scientific knowledge. Up to this time the study of the Talmud was still my chief occupation. With this, however, I found pleasure merely because of its form, for this calls into action the higher powers of the mind; but I took no interest in its matter. It affords exercise in deducing the remotest consequences from their principles, in discovering the most hidden contradictions, in hunting out the finest distinctions, and so forth. But as the principles themselves have merely an imaginary reality, they cannot by any means satisfy a soul thirsting after knowledge.

I looked around therefore for something, by which I could supply this want. Now, I knew that there is a so-called science, which is somewhat in vogue among the Jewish scholars of this district, namely the Kabbalah, which professes to enable a man, not merely to satisfy his desire of knowledge, but also to reach an uncommon perfection and closeness of communion with God. Naturally therefore I burned with desire for this science. As however it cannot, on account of its sacredness, be publicly taught, but must be taught in secret, I did not know where to seek the initiated or their writings ...

[Maimon eventually obtained some old German books on the natural sciences.] I pocketed the few books, and returned home in rapture. After I had studied these books thoroughly, my eyes were all at once opened. I believed that I had found a key to all the secrets of nature, as I now knew the origin of storms, of dew, of rain, and such phenomena. I looked down with pride on all others, who did not yet know these things, laughed at their prejudices and superstitions, and proposed to clear up their ideas on these subjects and to enlighten their understanding.

But this did not always succeed. I labored once to teach a Talmudist, that the earth is round, and that we have antipodes. He however made the objection, that these antipodes would necessarily fall off. I endeavored to show that the falling of a body is not directed towards any fixed point in empty space, but towards the center of the earth, and that the ideas of Over and Under represent merely the removal from and approach to this center. It was of no avail; the Talmudist stood to his ground, that such an assertion was absurd ...

[Having made his way to the centers of the Enlightenment in Germany, and after great travail, Maimon acquired the rudiments of German secular culture.] I had received too much education to return to Poland, to spend my life in misery without rational occupation or society, and to sink back into the darkness of superstition and ignorance, from which I had hardly delivered myself with so much labor. On the other hand, to succeed in Germany was a result on which I could not calculate, owing to my ignorance of the language, as well as of the manners and customs of the people, to which I had never yet been able to adapt myself properly. I had learnt no particular profession, I had not distinguished myself in any special science, I was not even master of any language in which I could make myself perfectly intelligible. It occurred to me, therefore, that for me there was no alternative left, but to embrace the Christian religion, and get myself baptized in Hamburg. Accordingly I resolved to go to the first clergyman I should come across, and inform him of my resolution, as well as of my motives for it, without any hypocrisy, in a truthful and honest fashion. But as I could not express myself well orally, I put my thoughts into writing in German with Hebrew characters, went to a schoolmaster, and got him to copy it in German characters. The purport of my letter was in brief as follows:

> I am a native of Poland, belonging to the Jewish nation, destined by my education and studies to be a rabbi; but in the thickest darkness I have perceived some light. This induced me to search further after light and truth, and to free myself completely from the darkness of superstition and ignorance. In order to this end, which could not be attained in my native place, I came to Berlin, where by the support of some enlightened men of our nation I studied for some years—not indeed after any plan, but merely to satisfy my thirst for knowledge. But as our nation is unable to use, not only such planless studies, but even those conducted on the most perfect plan, it cannot be blamed for becoming tired of them, and pronouncing their encouragement to be useless. I have therefore resolved, in order to secure temporal as well as eternal happiness, which depends on the attainment of perfection, and in order to become useful to myself as well as others, to embrace the Christian religion. The Jewish religion, it is true, comes, in its articles of faith, nearer to reason than Christianity. But in practical use the latter has an advantage over the former; and since morality, which consists not in opinions but in actions, is the aim of all religion in general, clearly the latter comes nearer than the former to this aim. Moreover, I hold the mysteries of the Christian religion for that which they are, that is, allegorical representations of the truths that are most important for man. By this means I make my faith in them harmonize with reason,

but I cannot believe them according to their common meaning. I beg therefore most respectfully an answer to the question, whether after this confession I am worthy of the Christian religion or not. In the former case I am ready to carry my proposal into effect; but in the latter, I must give up all claim to a religion which enjoins me to lie, that is, to deliver a confession of faith which contradicts my reason.

The schoolmaster, to whom I dictated this, fell into astonishment at my audacity; never before had he listened to such a confession of faith. He shook his head with much concern, interrupted the writing several times, and became doubtful, whether the mere copying was not itself a sin. With great reluctance he copied it out, merely to get rid of the thing. I went then to a prominent clergyman, delivered my letter, and begged for a reply. He read it with great attention, fell likewise into astonishment, and on finishing entered into conversation with me.

"So," he said, "I see your intention is to embrace the Christian religion, merely in order to improve your temporal circumstances."

"Excuse me, Herr Pastor," I replied, "I think I have made it clear enough in my letter, that my object is the attainment of perfection. To this, it is true, the removal of all hindrances and the improvement of my external circumstances form an indispensable condition. But this condition is not the chief end."

"But," said the pastor, "do you not feel any inclination of the soul to the Christian religion without reference to any external motives?"

"I should be telling a lie, if I were to give you an affirmative answer."

"You are too much of a philosopher," replied the pastor, "to be able to become a Christian. Reason has taken the upper hand with you, and faith must accommodate itself to reason. You hold the mysteries of the Christian religion to be mere fables, and its commands to be mere laws of reason. For the present I cannot be satisfied with your confession of faith. You should therefore pray to God, that He may enlighten you with His grace, and endow you with the spirit of true Christianity; and then come to me again."

"If that is the case," I said, "then I must confess, Herr Pastor, that I am not qualified for Christianity. Whatever light I may receive, I shall always make it luminous with the light of reason. I shall never believe that I have fallen upon new truths, if it is impossible to see their connection with the truths already known to me. I must therefore remain what I am—a stiff-necked Jew. My religion enjoins me to *believe* nothing, but to *think* the truth and to *practice* goodness. If I find any hindrance in this from external circumstances, it is not my fault. I do all that lies in my power."

With this I bade the pastor goodbye ...

10.7 Rahel Levin Varnhagen, On Being Jewess

10.7.1 Letter to David Veit (1795)

I imagine that just as I was thrust into this world some supermundane being plunged these words into my heart with a dagger. "Yes, have sensibility, see the world as only a few see it, be great, noble; nor can I free you of incessant, eternal thought. But I add *one* thing more: Be a Jewess!" And now my whole life is a slow bleeding to death. But keeping still I can prolong it. Every attempt to stop the bleeding is to die anew, and immobility is only possible for me in death itself. These ravings are true, they can be translated. You may smile, or weep from compassion, I can ascribe every evil, every misfortune, every vexation that has befallen me from *that*; and I don't care if I look ridiculous in someone else's eyes. This opinion is my essence, and I must give you clear proof of it before I die.

10.7.2 Statement on the Deathbed as Recorded by Karl August Varnhagen von Ense

"What a history!" she exclaimed with deep emotion. "Here I am, a fugitive from Egypt and Palestine, who has found your help, love, attention! Divine guidance has led me to you, dear August, and you to me! With sublime rapture I am contemplating my origins and this fateful nexus between the oldest memories of mankind and the latest developments linking poles far apart in time and space. What for a long period of my life has been the source of my greatest shame, my most bitter grief and misfortune—to be born a Jewess—I would not at any price now wish to miss. Will it be the same with my illness, shall I once find delight in it, never wanting to miss it again? O dear August, what consoling insight, what a meaningful parable! Let us continue on this way!" And then, weeping, she went on: "Dear August, my heart is refreshed in its innermost depths; I thought of Jesus and cried over his passion. I have felt, for the first time in my life, that he is my brother. And Mary, how she must have suffered! She witnessed the pain of her beloved son, and did not succumb, but kept standing at the cross! I could not have been able to do that; I would not have been strong enough. May God forgive me, I confess how weak I am."

10.8 Kadya Molodowsky, *Merciful God* (1945)[1]

Merciful God,
Choose another people,
Elect another.[2]
We are tired of death and dying,

---

[1] Sources: Molodowsky (1999): 352 – 355; Hellerstein (2014): 324 – 328. The Hebrew epithet *Eyl khanun* (Merciful God) comes from the penitential prayer "Shlosh-esre middot" (The Thirteen Attributes of Mercy), recited on several occasions in the liturgical calendar—including during the *selihot* (penitential) prayers recited during the High Holidays season and on Yom Kippur. This prayer is based on two Biblical verses, Exodus 34:6 – 7.

[2] The Yiddish is ambiguous. The word can be read as either the adverb *dervayl* (variant of *dervayle*, "meanwhile, for the time being"), or as the familiar imperative of the verb *derveyln* (to elect).

We have no more prayers.
Choose another people,
Elect another.
We have no more blood
To be a sacrifice.
Our house has become a desert.
The earth is insufficient for our graves,
No more laments for us,
No more dirges
In the old, holy books.

Merciful God,
Sanctify another country,
Another mountain.
We have strewn all the fields and every stone
With ash, with holy ash.
With the aged,
With the youthful,
And with babies, we have paid
For every letter of your Ten Commandments.

Merciful God,
Raise your fiery brow,
And see the peoples of the world—
Give them the prophecies and the Days of Awe.[1]
Your word is babbled in every language—
Teach them the deeds,
The ways of temptation.

---

[1] *Days of Awe.* The ten days beginning with Rosh Hashana (New Year) and ending with Yom Kippur (Day of Atonement).

Merciful God,
Give us simple garments
Of shepherds with their sheep,
Blacksmiths at their hammers,
Laundry-washers, skin-flayers,
And even the more base.
And do us one more favor:
Merciful God,
Deprive us of the Divine Presence of genius.[1]

---

[1] The Yiddish reads: "*Nem tsu fun undz di shekhine fun gaones.*" The phrase "*shekhine fun gaones*" is ambiguous. *Gaones* denotes "scholarship, brilliance, ingenuity, genius," and evokes a host of connotations in the Jewish tradition. In one sense, "genius" refers to possessing a unique, special quality of exceptionality; but the term also invokes its usage as a title held by the heads of the great Babylonian yeshivot in Late Antiquity and, by extension, a title for extraordinary rabbis, like Elijah, the Gaon of Vilna (1720—1797), who exemplified the hyper-learnedness of Talmudic scholarship and spiritual leadership. *Shekhine* denotes "Divine Presence," or "Divine Manifestation."

11 SECULAR FORMS OF JEWISHNESS

11.1 I. L. Peretz, "The Golem" (1893)

Great men were once capable of great miracles.

When the ghetto of Prague was being attacked, and they were about to rape the women, roast the children, and slaughter the rest; when it seemed that the end had finally come, the great Rabbi Loeb put aside his *Gemara*, went into the street, stopped before a heap of clay in front of the teacher's house, and molded a clay image. He blew into the nose of the *golem* [1]—and it began to stir; then he whispered the Name into its ear, and our *golem* left the ghetto. The rabbi returned to the House of Prayer, and the *golem* fell upon our enemies, threshing them as with flails. Men fell on all sides.

Prague was filled with corpses. It lasted, so they say, through Wednesday and Thursday. Now it is already Friday, the clock strikes twelve, and the *golem* is still busy at its work.

"Rabbi," cries the head of the ghetto, "the *golem* is slaughtering all of Prague! There will not be a gentile left to light the Sabbath fires or take down the Sabbath lamps."

Once again the rabbi left his study. He went to the altar and began singing the psalm "A song of the Sabbath."

The *golem* ceased its slaughter. It returned to the ghetto, entered the

---

[1] For *golem*, see 8.1 (Avot 5:7); 1.7.2.

House of Prayer, and waited before the rabbi. And again the rabbi whispered into its ear. The eyes of the *golem* closed, the soul that had dwelt in it flew out, and it was once more a *golem* of clay.

To this day the *golem* lies hidden in the attic of the Prague synagogue, covered with cobwebs that extend from wall to wall. No living creature may look at it, particularly women in pregnancy. No one may touch the cobwebs, for whoever touches them dies. Even the oldest people no longer remember the *golem*, though the wise man Zvi, the grandson of the great Rabbi Loeb, ponders the problem: may such a *golem* be included in a congregation of worshipers or not?

The *golem*, you see, has not been forgotten. It is still here! But the Name by which it could be called to life in a day of need, the Name has disappeared. And the cobwebs grow and grow, and no one may touch them.

What are we to do?

11.2 Bialik, "Bring Me in Under Your Wing"(1905)

Bring me in under your wing,
be sister for me, and mother, [1]
the place of you, rest for my head,[2]

---

[1] While "wing" here is intentionally ambiguous, the situation of the poem conjures immediate associations of phrases from Scripture and the liturgy. See especially the famous hymn for a burial "El Malei Rahamim"(God Full of Mercy): "God full of mercy, who dwells on high, bring rest beneath the wings of the Shekhinah ... to the souls of our beloved." The "sister" of line 2 recalls Song of Songs 5:2: "Open to me, my sister, my love, my dove, my undefiled." See also Psalms 17:8: "Keep me as the apple of the eye, hide me under the shadow of thy wings." The verse from Psalms refers to God, though the poem makes it clear that the addressee is feminine, and so the dominant association is with an earthly beloved, with a mother figure, or with a philosophical-theological figure along the lines of Sophia or the Shekhinah.

[2] The Hebrew for "place of rest" is *heik*, meaning "bosom" or "lap" (cf. Deuteronomy 13:7 and Micah 7:5).

a nest for my unwanted prayers.[1]

At the hour of mercy, at dusk,[2]
we'll talk of my secret pain:
They say, there's youth in the world—
What happened to mine?

And another thing, a clue:
my being was seared by a flame.
They say, there's love in the world—
What do they mean?

The stars betrayed me—there
was a dream, which also has passed.
Now in the world, I have nothing,
Not a thing.[3]

Bring me in under your wing,
be sister for me, and mother,

---

[1] The "unwanted" prayers (in Hebrew, literally, "rejected" or "neglected") establish the place of liminality—of religious longing that finds no answer.

[2] In the Kabbalistic context dusk is actually an hour of danger and severity, except on Sabbath, when favor and grace become manifest. It's possible that Bialik here is intentionally, and ironically, reversing the polarity of the association—as his prayers have already been rejected.

[3] In the Kabbalistic contexts, *nothing* is a complex term (cf. Matt [1995b]), and the Hebrew for this line—*ein li davar* (literally, "I have nothing," or "I have not a word")—is more complex still. For one, it recalls the verse from Psalms 19:4 "There is no speech, there are no words [*ein devarim*]." The phrase also echoes Bialik's famous essay "Revealment and Concealment in Language" (Bialik [1975]), which describes the words we use in daily language as husks (a term that conjures associations with the Kabbalistic *kelippot*), the centers of which are empty. Though it is true that the speaker has "nothing," in the Kabbalistic context "nothing" is also the ultimate generative principle.

the place of you, rest for my head,

a nest for my unwanted prayers.

11.3 Bialik and Ravnitzky, *The Book of Legends*. On the Binding of Isaac

"And it came to pass after these things that God tried Abraham" (Gen. 22:1). After what things? According to R. Yohanan, citing R. Yose ben Zimra, after the things Satan had to say. [Following the feast given] upon the "child's having grown and being weaned" (Gen. 21:8), Satan spoke up to the Holy One, "Master of the universe, out of the entire feast that this old man, upon whom You bestowed fruit of the womb at the age of one hundred—out of the entire feast he prepared, could he not have spared, say, one turtledove, one fledgling, as an offering to You.

The Holy One replied, "Is it not true that Abraham prepared the feast in honor of his son? Still, if I say to him, 'Sacrifice your son to Me,' he will sacrifice him at once." Satan said, "Try him." At once "God tried Abraham."

"And He said: 'Take, I beg thee (*na*), thy son.'" (Gen. 22:2) R. Simeon bar Abba said: The word *na* can imply only entreaty. The matter may be illustrated by the parable of a king of flesh and blood who had to face many wars, in all of which he had one mighty warrior who invariably achieved victory. In the course of time, he faced a war particularly severe. The king said to the mighty warrior, "I beg you, stand to with me in this war, that mortals should not say, 'The earlier wars were of no substance.'"

Likewise, the Holy One said to Abraham, "I have tried you with many tests, and you have stood up to them all. Now, I beg you, stand to with Me in this test, that it not be said, 'The earlier ones were of no substance.'"

"Take now thy son." (Gen. 22:2) Abraham: "I have two sons [which one do you mean]?" God: "Thine only son." (ibid.) Abraham: "[Both are only sons]—Isaac is the only son I have from his mother, and Ishmael is the only son I have from her who is his mother." God: "The son whom thou lovest." (ibid.) Abraham: "Master of the universe, are there separate compartments in one's inmost self for love? I love both of them." God: "Very well, then—Isaac." Why did God drag out His command to such length? So that Abraham's mind might not be stunned [by such a heartrending demand].

"And offer him up there for a burnt offering upon one of the mountains" (Gen. 22:2). Abraham asked, "Which mountain?" God: "Wherever you see My glory standing and waiting for you."

Abraham meditated in his heart, saying: What am I to do? Shall I tell Sarah? Women tend to think lightly of God's commands. If I do not tell her and simply take off with him—afterward, when she does not see him, she will strangle herself. What did he do? He said to Sarah, "Prepare food and drink for us, and we will rejoice today." She asked, "Why today more than other days? Besides, what is the rejoicing about?" Abraham: "Old people like ourselves, to whom a son was born in our old age—have we not cause to rejoice?" So she went and prepared the food. During the meal, Abraham said to Sarah, "You know, when I was only three years old, I became aware of my Maker, but this lad, growing up, has not yet been taught [about his Creator]. Now, there is a place far away where youngsters are taught [about Him]. Let me take him there." Sarah: "Take him in peace."

"And Abraham rose up early in the morning." (Gen. 22:3) Why early in the morning? Because he said: It may be that Sarah will reconsider what she said yesterday and refuse to let Isaac go. So I'll get up early and go while she is still asleep. Moreover, it is best that no one see us.①

"And he [himself] saddled his ass." (Gen. 22:3) Love disregards dignity! How many menservants, how many maidservants did that righteous man have, yet he himself saddled his ass in his eagerness [to do God's will].

"And took two of his young men with him." (Gen. 22:3) These were

---

① They may find out what he is about to do and seek to dissuade him.

Ishmael and Eliezer. He said: while I am offering up Isaac, these two will take care of our gear. At once, rivalry set in between Ishmael and Eliezer. Ishmael said, "Now that my father is about to bring his son as a burnt offering, I, being my father's firstborn, will be heir." Eliezer replied, "But he has exiled you and sent you into the wilderness! Whereas I am the servant who waits on him day and night—I am to be his heir." But the holy spirit replied to both of them, "Neither the one nor the other is to be the heir."

"And rose up, and went." (Gen. 22:3) On the way, Satan ran ahead of Abraham, appeared before him in the guise of an old man, and asked, "Where are you going?" Abraham: "To pray." Satan: "Why should one going to pray have fire and a knife in his hand, and kindling wood on his shoulder?" Abraham: "We may abide there a day or two, and we will have to slaughter an animal, bake bread, and eat." Satan: "Old man, do you think I was not there when the Holy One said to you, 'Take now thy son'? Old man, you are out of your mind. A son who was given you at the age of one hundred—and you are setting out to kill him!" Abraham: "Even so." Satan: "And should He test you even more severely, will you still stand firm?" Abraham: "Yes, even more and more severely." Satan: "But tomorrow He will call you murderer for shedding the blood of your son." Abraham: "Even so."

Seeing that his efforts were in vain, Satan left Abraham and, disguising himself as a young man, stood at Isaac's right and said, "Where are you going?" Isaac: "To study Torah." Satan: "While still alive or after your death?" Isaac: "Is there a man who can study after his death?" Satan: "O hapless son of a hapless mother! How many fasts did your mother fast, how many prayers did she utter until at last you were born! And now this old man has gone mad in his old age and is about to slit your throat." Isaac: "Nevertheless, I shall not deviate from the will of my Maker and from the bidding of my father." Satan: "If so, shall all those fine tunics your mother made [for you] become a legacy for Ishmael, for him who hates your family? Apparently you give no thought [to what would follow upon your death]." As the proverb has it, "If the whole word does not enter [the listener's mind], half of it does." For Isaac turned to his father and said: "Father, listen to what this one is saying to me!" Abraham replied, "Pay no attention to him!"

When Satan saw that neither Abraham nor Isaac heeded what he had to say, he proceeded to turn himself into a wide stream. At once [having to cross the stream], Abraham went down into the water until it reached to his knees and then said to his lads: Follow me. They went down after him. Halfway across the stream, the water came up to his neck. In that instant, Abraham lifted his eyes heavenward and said: Master of the universe, You chose me. You appeared to me, saying: "I am unique and you are unique. Through you shall My Name become known in My world—so bring your son Isaac before Me as a burnt offering. And I did not hold back. As You see, I am occupied with your bidding." But now "I am come into deep waters."(Ps. 69:3) If either I or Isaac were to drown, who will fulfill Your commands, and by whom will the uniqueness of Your Name be proclaimed? The Holy One replied: As you live! My Name shall be proclaimed in the world through you.

The Holy one rebuked the stream and it dried up, so that they found themselves standing on dry land.

What did Satan do? He said to Abraham, "This is what I heard from behind the [heavenly] curtain: 'A lamb will be the burnt offering—Isaac is not to be the burn offering.'" But such is the punishment of a liar—even when he tells the truth, no one listens. [Hence Abraham gave Satan no heed.]

"Then on the third day Abraham lifted up his eyes, and saw." (Gen. 22:4) Why on the third day? Why not on the first, or on the second? That the nations of the world might not say: God deranged Abraham so that he cut his son's throat.

"And saw the place from afar." (Gen. 22:4) [But since the place was hollowed out], how could it have been seen from afar?① The place was originally hollowed out. But when the Holy One decided to cause His presence to dwell there and to make it His sanctuary, He said: It is not fitting for a king to dwell in a valley, but only on a high and lofty mountain, resplendent in beauty and visible to all. So He beckoned the valley's environs to come together and provide a suitable place for the Presence.

Then Abraham asked Isaac, "Do you see what I see?" Isaac replied, "I see a mountain, radiant in majesty, with a [mysterious] cloud hovering over it." Abraham asked the two lads, "Do you see anything?" They replied, "We see nothing other than stretches of wilderness." Abraham: "O people the like of asses! As the ass sees but does not comprehend, so it is with you. 'Abide ye here, people like the ass.' " (Gen. 22:5)②

"Abraham took the wood of the burnt offering and laid it upon Isaac his son" (Gen. 22:6), as upon one [condemned] who is made to carry the cross upon his shoulder.

"And Isaac said … 'Behold, the fire and the wood, but where is the lamb for the burnt offering?' " (Gen. 22:7) In that instant, fear and dread terror fell upon Isaac, when he saw in Abraham's hand nothing at all fit for an offering. So, suspecting what was intended, he asked, "Where is the lamb for the burnt offering?" Abraham replied, "The Holy One has chosen you." Isaac said, "If He has so chosen, my life is given to Him, but I grieve for mother." Nevertheless, "they went both of them together" (Gen. 22:8)— one to bind, the other to be bound; one to slaughter, the other to be slaughtered.

"And they came to the place" (Gen. 22:9)—both carrying stones [for the

---

① In Gen. 22:2, Moriah is spoken of as "land," presumably not elevated; in 2 Chron. 3:1, it is described as "mount." In the comment that follows, the inconsistency is explained by assuming that Moriah had been lowland, but because God was to appear there, the land (*morayah*), in reverence of God, elevated itself to the height of a mountain.

② The verse usually reads: "Abide ye here with the ass." But by a slight change in vowels, the word *im* ("with") may be read *am* ("people").

altar], both carrying the fire, both carrying the wood. For all that, Abraham acted like one making wedding preparations for his son, and Isaac like one making a wedding bower for himself.

Then Isaac said, "Father, hurry, do the will of your Maker, burn me into a fine ash, then take the ash to my mother and leave it with her, and whenever she looks at it she will say, 'This is my son, whom his father has slaughtered.' ... Father, what will you do in your old age [without me]?" Abraham replied, "My son, we know that we can survive you for but a short time. He who comforted us in the past will comfort us until the day we die."

When Abraham was about to begin the sacrifice, Isaac said, "Father, bind my hands and my feet, for the urge to live is so willful that when I see the knife coming at me, I may flinch involuntarily [causing the knife to cut improperly] and thus disqualify myself as an offering. So I beg you, bind me in such a way that no blemish will befall me." So Abraham "bound his son well" (Gen. 22:9). Then Isaac said to Abraham, "Father, don't tell mother about this while she is standing over a pit or on a rooftop, for she might throw herself down and be killed."

"And he placed him on the altar." (Gen. 22:9) Abraham's eyes were directed at Isaac's, and Isaac's at the heaven of heavens. Tears were flowing from Abraham's eyes, until his entire body was all but afloat in them. He took the knife in order to cut Isaac's throat deeply enough so that a quarter of a *log* of blood would issue from him.① At that instant Satan appeared and shoved Abraham's arm aside, so that the knife fell out of his hand. When he reached out to pick it up, his mouth fell wide open with weeping as a great cry of anguish erupted from him. Then, his eyes blinking frantically, he looked up to the Presence and pleaded in a rising voice, "I lift mine eyes to the mountains; whence will my help come?" (Ps. 121:1) At that, the Holy One appeared above the angels and flung open the firmament. Isaac lifted up his eyes, and, as he beheld the chambers of the

---

① The amount of blood required for ritually valid slaughtering of animals (*shehitah*).

chariot, he trembled and shuddered. The ministering angels stood in rows upon rows, crying and weeping, as they said to one another, "Behold, one who is unique is about to slaughter, and one also unique is about to be slaughtered. Master of the universe, the oath 'Thus shall be thy seed' (Gen. 15:5)—what is to become of it?" The Holy One said to the angel Michael, "Why are you standing still? Do not let Abraham go on!" "Then the angel of the Lord called unto him out of heaven, and said: 'Abraham, Abraham,'" (Gen. 22:11) twice, as who cries out in distress, "What [dreadful] thing are you about to do?"

When Abraham turned his face toward the angel, the angel said again, "What are you about to do? 'Do not lay thy hand upon the lad!'" (Gen. 22:12) Abraham asked, "Who are you?" Michael replied, "I am an angel." Abraham: "When the Holy One told me to offer my son, He Himself spoke to me; so too, if He now wishes something else, He Himself should speak to me."

At once the Holy One flung open the firmament, as well as the thick cloud [covering it], and said, "By Myself I swear." (Gen. 22:16) Abraham replied, "You have sworn, and I too swear that I will not go down from this altar until I say all that I need to say." God: "Say it." Abraham: "Did you not say to me, 'Count the stars... so shall thy seed be' (Gen. 15:5)?" The Holy One: "Yes." Abraham: "Out of whom?" God: "Out of Isaac." Abraham: "When You commanded me to sacrifice Isaac, I should have replied: Yesterday You told me, 'In Isaac shall thy seed be called' (Gen. 21:12); now You say to me, 'Offer him there for a burnt offering' (Gen. 22:2). Nevertheless, I restrained my impulse and did not reply as I should have done. Even so now [I say to You], When Isaac's children shall sin and find themselves in distress, be You mindful on their behalf of the binding of Isaac; let it be reckoned in Your presence as though his ash were in fact heaped upon the altar—be then filled with compassion for his children, forgive them, and redeem them from their distress." The Holy One replied, "You had your say, and now I will have Mine. Isaac's descendants will sin in My very presence, and I will have to judge them on New Year's Day.

However, should they implore Me to seek out some merit on their behalf, and to remember on their behalf the binding of Isaac, let them blow in My presence the horn of this creature." Abraham: "The horn of what creature?" God: "Turn around." At once "Abraham lifted up his eyes, and looked, and behold a ram." (Gen. 22:13)

R. Eliezer said: The ram came from the mountains, where he had been grazing. R. Joshua differed: An angel brought him from the Garden of Eden, where he had been grazing beneath the tree of life and drinking out of the waters that passed under it, and the fragrance of that ram went forth throughout the world. When was the ram placed in the Garden? During twilight at the end of the six days of creation.

Throughout that day, Abraham saw the ram become entangled in a tree, break loose, and go free; become entangled in a bush, break loose, and go free; then again become entangled in a thicket, break loose, and go free. The Holy One said, "Abraham, even so will your children be entangled in many kinds of sin and trapped within successive kingdoms—from Babylon to Media, from Media to Greece, from Greece to Edom." Abraham asked, "Master of the universe, will it be forever thus?" God replied, "In the end they will be redeemed at [the sound of] the horns of this ram, as is said, 'The Lord shall blow the horn [shofar] when He goes forth in the whirlwinds at Teman [Edom].'" (Zech. 9:14)

11.4 Franz Kafka, "My Father's Bourgeois Judaism" (1919)

I found little means of escape from you in Judaism. Here some escape would, in principle, have been thinkable, but more than that, it would have been thinkable that we might both have found each other in Judaism or even that we might have begun from there in harmony. But what sort of Judaism was it I got from you? In the course of the years I have taken roughly three different attitudes to it.

As a child I reproached myself, in accord with you, for not going to the synagogue enough, for not fasting, and so on. I thought that in this way I was doing a wrong not to myself but to you, and I was penetrated by a sense of guilt, which was, of course, always ready to hand.

Later, as a young man, I could not understand how, with the insignificant scrap of Judaism you yourself possessed, you could reproach me for not (if for no more than the sake of piety, as you put it) making an effort to cling to a similar insignificant scrap. It was indeed really, so far as I could see, a mere scrap, a joke, not even a joke. On four days in the year you went to the synagogue, where you were, to say the least, closer to the indifferent than to those who took it seriously, [you] patiently went through the prayers by way of formality, [you] sometimes amazed me by being able to show me in the prayer book the passage that was being said at the moment, and for the rest, so long as I was in the synagogue (and this was the main thing) I was allowed to hang about wherever I liked. And so I yawned and dozed through the many hours (I don't think I was ever again so bored, except later at dancing lessons) and did my best to enjoy the few little bits of variety there were, as, for instance, when the Ark of the Covenant was opened, which always reminded me of the shooting galleries where a cupboard door would open in the same way whenever one got a bull's eye, only with the difference that there something interesting always came out and here it was always just the same old dolls with no heads. Incidentally, it was also very frightening for me there, not only, as goes without saying, because of all the people one came into close contact with, but also because you once mentioned, by the way, that I too might be called up to read the Torah. That was something I went in dread of for years. But otherwise I was not fundamentally disturbed in my state of boredom, unless it was by the *bar mitzvah*,① but that meant no more than some ridiculous learning by heart, in other words, led to nothing but something like the ridiculous passing of an examination, and then, as far as you were concerned, by little, not very significant incidents, as when you were called up to read the Torah and came well out of the affair, which to my way of feeling was purely social, or when you stayed on in the synagogue for the prayers for the dead,② and I was sent away, which for a long time, obviously because of being sent away and lacking, as I did, any deeper interest, aroused in me the more or less unconscious feeling that what was about to take place was something indecent.—That was how it was in the synagogue, and at home it was, if possible, even more poverty-stricken, being confined to the first evening of Passover which more and more developed into a farce, with fits of hysterical laughter, admittedly under the influence of the growing children. (Why did you have to give way to that influence? Because you brought it about in the first place.) And so there was the religious material that was handed on to me, to which may be added at most the outstretched hand pointing to "the sons of the millionaire Fuchs," who were in the synagogue with their father at high holidays③. How one could do anything better with this material than get rid of it as fast as possible was something I could not understand; precisely getting rid of it seemed to me the most effective act of "piety" one could perform ...

---

① *bar mitzvah* (Aramaic/Hebrew, "son of the commandment"). In Talmudic usage, an adult Jewish male, who is subject to the full rigor of the commandments. Nowadays commonly used of the ceremony marking the attainment of legal majority. According to Jewish tradition, the legal age of majority is 13 years; from this age a male Jew is responsible for his own actions, whereas previously his father bore responsibility for him. It has become customary to mark the occasion by calling him up to the reading of the Torah.

② I.e., the mourner's Kaddish, see 9.4.

③ *High holidays.* Term used to refer to the solemn festivals of New Year (Rosh ha-Shana) and the Day of Atonement (Yom Kippur).

11.5 Woody Allen, Fragment Two of the Scrolls (1974)

... And Abraham awoke in the middle of the night and said to his only son, Isaac, "I have had a dream where the voice of the Lord sayeth that I must sacrifice my only son, so put your pants on." And Isaac trembled and said, "So what did you say? I mean when He brought this whole thing up?"

"What am I going to say?" Abraham said. "I'm standing there at two am in my underwear with the Creator of the Universe. Should I argue?"

"Well, did he say why he wants me sacrificed?" Isaac asked his father.

But Abraham said, "The faithful do not question. Now let's go because I have a heavy day tomorrow."

And Sarah who heard Abraham's plan grew vexed and said, "How doth thou know it was the Lord and not, say, thy friend who loveth practical jokes, for the Lord hateth practical jokes and whosoever shall pull one shall be delivered into the hands of his enemies whether they pay the delivery charge or not." And Abraham answered, "Because I know it was the Lord. It was a deep, resonant voice, well modulated, and nobody in the desert can get a rumble in it like that."

And Sarah said, "And thou art willing to carry out this senseless act?" But Abraham told her, "Frankly yes, for to question the Lord's word is one of the worst things a person can do, particularly with the economy in the state it's in."

And so he took Isaac to a certain place and prepared to sacrifice him but at the last minute the Lord stayed Abraham's hand and said, "How could thou doest such a thing?" And Abraham said, "But thou said ..."

"Never mind what I said," the Lord spoke, "Doth thou listen to every crazy idea that comes thy way?" And Abraham grew ashamed. "Er—not really ... no... "

"I jokingly suggest thou sacrifice Isaac and thou immediately run out to do it."

And Abraham fell to his knees, "See, I never know when you're kidding."

And the Lord thundered, "No sense of humor. I can't believe it."

"But doth this not prove I love thee, that I was willing to donate mine only son on thy whim?"

And the Lord said, "It proves that some men will follow any order no matter how asinine as long as it comes from a resonant, well-modulated voice."

And with that, the Lord bid Abraham get some rest and check with him tomorrow.

11.6 Yaakov Malkin, "The Faith of Secular Jews" (1998)

What do secular Jews believe?

FREE JEWS—that is, Jews free from the dominion of Halakhic religion, free from an exclusive religious interpretation of *mitzvot*, from a religious interpretation of Jewish celebration, traditions and culture, Jews free of one inflexible view of the Bible and post-biblical literature—such Jews believe in:

THE FREEDOM TO CHOOSE the ways of realizing one's Jewishness. Jews may not be the "Chosen People," but Jewishness involves the obligation to choose. Jewish culture has no one "form of practice"; the free Jew determines how, and through what forms, he or she will participate in the ethnic solidarity which distinguishes Jewish identity.

FREE JEWS BELIEVE IN GOD as the hero of their central book and of other classic works of Jewish literature. This literature created God—both in human images and in the formless abstractions of philosophical thought. God has been perceived by Jews as a living functioning agent in all the eras of our history and culture. In the minds of most twentieth century secular Jews, God continues to function as the emblem of a long literary tradition—though without any practical authority in our personal or political life.

FREE JEWS BELIEVE IN THE BIBLE as a literary and historical

anthology which stands at the core of Jewish culture and identity. This book became the basis for all Judaisms. Within the Bible can be found all the literary genres of Western literature. The corpus of the Bible—books of literature, laws, history, chronicles, philosophy, and rhetoric—represents the first thousand years of Judaism as the pluralistic national culture of the Jewish people.

FREE JEWS BELIEVE IN HUMANISM AND DEMOCRACY as essential to Judaism. The ethics of humanism were defined by Hillel, and this is the light by which the secular Jew reads the laws and principles guiding his/her life. Hillelian values allow for a humanist reading of the Ten Commandments, the teachings of the Prophets, the controversies over interpretations of the Talmudic law. These values advocate the sanctity of majority rule—which the Talmud too upholds, ① even when contradicting the voice of God. Belief in human rights is fundamental to the secular Jew. These rights take precedence over all religious demands and restrictions. In Israel, they form the basis of the law, a law which strives to reinterpret Jewish heritage free from the anachronisms of Halakhic rulings.

FREE JEWS BELIEVE IN PLURALISM as fundamental to Jewish identity and culture throughout its history. In the biblical period, monotheism and polytheism coexisted and clashed, as did various Jewish views regarding the ethical nature of God. In the Hellenistic period, a plurality of views found expression in Jewish culture and were battled over in civil wars. The Middle Ages offered a plurality of secular and religious Jewish literatures and of ethnic traditions, and the simultaneous existence of rationalism and mysticism.

FREE JEWS BELIEVE IN OPENNESS TO OTHER CULTURES. This openness and exchange characterized Judaisms throughout history. It was Judaism's receptiveness to Egyptian, Mesopotamian, Hellenistic, Muslim, Christian, European, and American cultures that enabled it to spread its influence and to endure. Cross-fertilization and cultural flexibility render

---

① See 6.5; 6.6.

Judaism one of the most influential—and influenced—cultures in the West.

FREE JEWS BELIEVE IN HOLIDAY CELEBRATIONS as expressions of unique family and community values. In each period, in each context, free Jews redefine the practice of Jewish holidays, "pouring new content into old vessels." The Sabbath and the national holidays are celebrated by secular Jews in forms free from the rigidity and exclusivity of religious interpretation. These secular celebrations play a central role in Jewish family and community life, and become points of reference and enrichment for Jewish culture.

FREE JEWS BELIEVE IN THE UNIQUENESS OF THE JEWS AS A NATION. This belief is rooted in the acceptance of all nations as unique and entitled to a self-determined identity. The definition of the Swiss nation will not be applicable to the Welsh or the Gypsy nations. So too, the definition of the Jews as a nation has its own uniqueness, determined by the unique history of Judaism, and by the fusion of its history and cultural heritage. The uniqueness of Judaism is the consequence of the way Jewish states and its exiled communities have evolved, of its pluralistic culture, and of the interrelations between that culture and other national languages and cultures.

FREE JEWS BELIEVE THAT JUDAISM IS PART OF WORLD CULTURE. Rather than stress the exclusivity of Judaism, secular Jews recognize that the masterpieces of biblical literature, together with the great works of Greece, had a determining influence on the development of Western culture. The Ten Commandments are recognized as the ethical basis of Western morality. The Bible underlies, too, for example, the invention of the week and the Sabbath as egalitarian concepts which enable leisure for all. The innovation of the synagogue as both religious center and a center for learning and social relations—influenced the Western concept of community.

FREE JEWS BELIEVE IN JEWISH EDUCATION as the vanguard of the socialization of all Jewish women and men, of all ages. Secular Judaism teaches pluralism and humanism; it also teaches that these humanizing forces are possible only within a national and cultural context. Jewish education is a source of individual, family and community enrichment—and cohesion. It enables Jews to know and formulate their national culture. It stresses the participatory role of the individual in the interpretation and modes of practice which, in their many interrelated forms, define the Jews as a nation. Most important, secular Jews see education as one of the factors which determine the quality of individual life, and of the community within which the secular Jew functions as a free and committed part of the Jewish nation.

11.7　Irene Eber, On the Memory of the Holocaust (2004)[①]

Transforming remembered multidimensional scenes charged with emotions, imbued with sounds and half-remembered smells, and seen by the inner eye as movements and color, into words flattened onto paper is ultimately unsatisfactory. Nor can one be, in the final analysis, satisfied with the depiction of the many faces of fear, anguish, the sorrow of loss, or the estrangement felt when returning to the world where displacements were only partial or had not occurred. Wallace Fowlie, in considering the writing of autobiography, notes a "curious escape from life into words, this leap from an intention ... to the expression of the intention,"[②] which leads to a sense of foolishness. It is not only foolishness, I would add, but also inevitable dismay at the inadequacy of words, their shortcomings when compared to the intensity of the memory they are meant to convey.

　　The task of the historian is to rescue from oblivion, to document, to explain, to find meaning, to make sense of portions of the past. And while I have attempted as faithfully and as honestly as I could to preserve and

---

　　① Source: Eber (2004), "Postscript," pp. 209 – 211. Cf. 宋立宏(2017). This postscript is not translated in the Chinese version (伊爱莲[2013]).

　　② Wallace Fowlie, "On Writing Autobiography," in James Olney, ed., *Studies in Autobiography* (New York, 1988), p. 165.

document a small fragment, the destruction of Jewish Mielec and its people, I am at a loss where meaning or sense is concerned. A changing and evolving culture, a tradition—call it Yiddish culture, together with its guardians and those who perpetuated it—was destroyed, rooted out. To be sure, today a building here or there, a cemetery, a synagogue, remnants and reminders, might be renovated and, a plaque affixed, become a tourist attraction. But all such restoration and making presentable is, in effect, "museumification;" the life that was has become a museum piece. Instead of a living, changing culture we have lifeless museums and exhibits in glass cases with neat labels attached.

We also have the re-created Holocaust with the latest technology in Holocaust centers. The proliferation of such centers in American cities is astounding. No longer mere museums with presumably boring exhibits, some of these centers are firmly lodged in the computer age, where the visitor is not a spectator but is required to participate, as if in a video game, in a simulation game of the Holocaust. They, however, also want to show "the real thing," whether it is a nicely refurbished Polish cattle car or paving stones from the Warsaw ghetto or death masks of beheaded Jewish prisoners that had been ordered by the Vienna Museum of Natural History during the Nazi period.①

Joseph R. Levenson reminds us that "preserving the past by recounting it, or displaying its bequests, is not perpetuating it." And he tells the story of the Baal Shem, who, when confronted by a difficult task, went to a certain place in the forest, lit a fire, and prayed, and his task was accomplished. A generation later, the place in the forest and the prayers were still known, and in the generation thereafter only the place in the forest was remembered. But in the generation of Rabbi Israel of Rizhin, the place, how to light the fire, and how to say the prayer were forgotten. All he

---

① The death mask exhibit was reported by Mariam Niroumand, *Die Tageszeitung*, August 7, 1997, p. 10.

could do was tell the story.①

But are the stories museums tell enough? Should we congratulate ourselves for having labels on glass cases, plaques on buildings, and even monuments? We need these in order to remember, goes the argument. Yet, how much are we forgetting while we remember? And exactly what is it that we remember when we leave a Holocaust center, aside from its technological perfection?

By attempting to translate life into words, I fear that I too have contributed to forgetting. I have, inevitably, left so much out. And as at the beginning of this writing so now at its end, the meaning of wanton destruction continues to elude me. To me, my words seem hollow. Sadly I agree with the Chinese poet who wrote this couplet a long time ago:

Always dissatisfaction remains when the end is reached
—dare we then be complacent and cherish our conceit?②

11.8　Adi Nes, "Abraham and Isaac" (2006)

See **Figure 13.**

---

① The story was retold according to Gershom Scholem's version (see Scholem [1974], pp. 349–350. Scholem heard the story told by S. J. Agnon). Joseph R. Levenson, *Confucian China and Its Modern Fate: A Trilogy* (Berkeley, 1968), pp. 124–125. Martin Buber has a slightly different version of this story. See his *Tales of the Hasidim: The Later Masters* (New York, 1948), pp. 92–93.

② The couplet was translated by E. R. Hughes, in *The Art of Letters: Lu Chi's "Wen Fu," A.D. 302* (New York, 1951), p. 106. (陆机《文赋》的原文为"恒遗恨以终篇,岂怀盈而自足?")

12 JEWISH VOICES FROM THE MARGINS

12.1 The Prophets' Warning to the Israelites

12.1.1 Amos 5:21–24; 7:10–17

(21) I loathe, I spurn your festivals,
I am not appeased by your solemn assemblies.
(22) If you offer Me burnt offerings—or your meal offerings—
I will not accept them;
I will pay no heed
To your gifts of fatlings.
(23) Spare Me the sound of your hymns,
And let Me not hear the music of your lutes.
(24) But let justice well up like water,
Righteousness like an unfailing stream.[①]

(10) Amaziah, the priest of Bethel, sent this message to King Jeroboam of Israel: "Amos is conspiring against you within the House of Israel. The country cannot endure the things he is saying. (11) For Amos has said,

---

[①] Others, "But let justice roll down like waters/And Righteousness like an ever-flowing stream."

'Jeroboam shall die by the sword, and Israel shall be exiled from its soil.'"

(12) Amaziah also said to Amos, "Seer[①], off with you to the land of Judah! Earn your living there, and do your prophesying there. (13) But don't ever prophesy again at Bethel; for it is a king's sanctuary and a royal palace." (14) Amos answered Amaziah: "I am not a prophet, and I am not a prophet's disciple. I am a cattle breeder and a tender of sycamore figs. (15) But the LORD took me away from following the flock, and the LORD said to me, 'Go, prophesy to My people Israel.' (16) And so, hear the word of the LORD. You say I must not prophesy about the House of Israel or preach about the House of Isaac; (17) but this, I swear, is what the LORD said: Your wife shall play the harlot in the town, your sons and daughters shall fall by the sword, and your land shall be divided up with a measuring line. And you yourself shall die on unclean soil; for Israel shall be exiled from its soil."

12.1.2　Micah 3:9–12; 6:6–9

(9) Hear this, you rulers of the House of Jacob,
You chiefs of the House of Israel,
Who detest justice
And make crooked all that is straight,
(10) Who build Zion with crime,
Jerusalem with iniquity!
(11) Her rulers judge for gifts,
Her priests give rulings for a fee,
And her prophets divine for pay;
Yet they rely upon the LORD, saying,
"The LORD is in our midst;
No calamity shall overtake us."

---

① Cf. I Sam. 9:9, "Formerly in Israel, when a man went to inquire of God, he would say, 'Come, let us go to the seer,' for the prophet of today was formerly called a seer."

12 JEWISH VOICES FROM THE MARGINS

(12) Assuredly, because of you
Zion shall be plowed as a field,
And Jerusalem shall become heaps of ruins,
And the Temple Mount
A shrine in the woods.

(6) With what shall I approach the LORD,
Do homage to God on high?
Shall I approach Him with burnt offerings,
With calves a year old?
(7) Would the LORD be pleased with thousands of rams,
With myriads of streams of oil?
Shall I give my first-born for my transgression,
The fruit of my body for my sins?
(8) "He has told you, O man, what is good,
And what the LORD requires of you:
Only to do justice
And to love goodness,
And to walk modestly with your God;①
(9) Then will your name achieve wisdom."

---

① This didactic saying is one of the most influential and often quoted sayings in prophetic literature. It was considered as a possible compendium of all the Mitzvot:

R. Simlai when preaching said: Six hundred and thirteen commandments were communicated to Moses on Mount Sinai. Three hundred and sixty five of them are negative commandments, corresponding to the number of days in the solar year. The remaining two hundred forty eight are positive commandments, corresponding to the number of limbs in the human body ... Micah came and reduced them to three [principles], as it is written, He has told you, O human, what is good, and what the LORD requires of you: only to do justice, and to love goodness, and to walk humbly with your God. "To do justice," this concerns justice; "and to love goodness," this concerns *"gemilut hasadim"* (acts of kindness); "and to walk humbly with your God," this concerns walking in funeral and bridal processions (b. Makkot 23b – 24a).

12.2 Shmuel Hanagid on War and the Good Life

12.2.1 "First War"①

First war resembles
a beautiful girl
we all want to flirt with
and believe.

Later it's more
a repulsive old whore
whose callers are bitter
and grieve.

12.2.2 "The Gazelle that Stutters"②

Where is the gazelle that stutters and where did go
The fawn perfumed with pure myrrh and frankincense?③

---

① Source: Cole (1996), see also Carmi (1981), p. 291. This title is not Hanagid's as poets of his age did not name individual poems. The poem is based on the Arabic attributed to Imru al-Qais (500 – 542): "War [at first] is a beautiful girl urging young men to sign away their lives. As the fire breaks into flames she becomes a headless hag who offers a broken promise and an [unkissable] stinking corpse." Al-Ma'ari (973 – 1057) has an interesting twist on this: "If the intellect is unstable/it is overwhelmed by the world, /a weak man embraced by a whore. /If the mind becomes disciplined, /the world is a distinguished woman/who rejects her lover's advances."

② Source: Weinberger (1973). Cf. Scheindlin (1986), pp. 77 – 89.

③ The terms "gazelle" and "fawn" are both taken from the Song of Songs. These are metaphors for the ornately dressed cupbearers, who by stuttering were able to draw attention to themselves.

The moon has covered up the light of the stars.
My love, arise and overlay the light of the moon!
He chirped with a tender voice and relied upon him
Who gave speech to turtle-doves and swallows when they approached.①
He wanted to say, "evil" (*ra*) but instead said to me, "touch" (*ga*)!
I drew near according to his word;
He desired to say, "stop" (*surah*) but uttered, "belly" (*sugah*).②
I hastened to it, fenced about with lilies.

12.2.3 "Invitation"③

I would lay down my life for the fawn
who, rising at night to the sound of
melodious harp and flute, saw a cup in
my hand and said: "Drink your grape's
blood from my lips."④ And the
moon was like a C⑤ inscribed in golden
ink upon the robes of night.

---

① Cf. Jeremiah 8:7: "Even the stork in the sky knows her seasons, /And the turtledove, swallow, and crane /Keep the time of their coming."

② The stuttering cup-bearer confused the Hebrew letter "resh" with the "gimel."

③ Source: Carmi (1981), p. 298. See also Scheindlin (1986), pp. 68–71; Cole (1996), p. 15.

④ Cf. Deuteronomy 32:14: "You drank fine wine from the blood of grapes." A similar image is found in the Arabic poetry of Ibn Shuhaid (992–1035, Cordoba): "I kissed his throat, /a white jewel/drank the vivid red of his mouth/and so passed the night with him/deliciously until darkness smiled, /showing the white teeth of dawn."

⑤ In Hebrew, the letter *yod* [the tenth letter of the Hebrew alphabet—a crescent]. The image of the moon like a letter is also common in Arabic poetry of the time, e.g.: "The air was clear, and the moon was bound in brightness, which shone toward the west, like a blue page with a silver dot, under a golden N."

12.3　Judah Halevi, "My Heart is in the East"①

My heart is in the East—
and I am at the edge of the West.
How can I possibly taste what I eat?
How could it please me?
How can I keep my promise
or ever fulfill my vow,②
when Zion③ is held by Edom④
and I am bound by Arabia's chains?⑤
I'd gladly leave behind me
all the pleasures of Spain—
if only I might see
the dust and ruins of your Shrine.

---

　① For a commentary on this most famous poem of Judah Halevi, see Scheindlin (2008), pp. 168 – 171.
　② The poet had made a vow to leave Spain for Zion.
　③ Jerusalem.
　④ Christians. At this time, Jerusalem was held by Crusaders who forbade Jews to reside within its precincts.
　⑤ "Arabia's chains" refers to Muslim rule in Spain and the entire Islamic ethos that went with it, but it also alludes to the Arabic meters, which Halevi elsewhere refers to as "shackles."

12.4 Judaism in Confucian Culture

12.4.1 弘治碑（公元 1489 年）①

夫一赐乐业②立教祖师阿无罗汉③,乃盘古阿耽④十九代孙也。自开辟天地,祖师相传授受,不塑于形象,不谄于神鬼,不信于邪术。其时神鬼无济,像态无佑,邪术无益。思其天者轻清在上,至尊无对,天道不言,四时行而万物生。观其春生夏长,秋敛冬藏,飞潜动植,荣悴开落,生者自生,化者自化,形者自形,色者自色。祖师忽地醒然,悟此幽玄,实求正教,参赞真天,一心侍奉,敬谨精专。那其间立教本至今传,考之在周朝一百四十六年也。一传而至正教祖师乜摄⑤,考之在周朝六百十三载也。生知纯粹,仁义俱备,道德兼全。求经于昔那山⑥顶,入斋四十昼夜,去其嗜欲,亡绝寝膳,诚意祈祷,虔心感于天心,正经一部,五十三卷,有自来矣。其中至微至妙,善者感发人之善心,恶者惩创人之逸志。再传而至正教祖师蔼子剌⑦,系出祖师,道承祖统,敬天礼拜之道,足以阐祖道之蕴奥。然道必本于清真礼拜:清者精一无二,真者正而无邪,礼者敬而已矣,拜下礼也。人于日用之间,不可顷刻而忘乎天,惟寅午戌而三次礼拜,乃真实天道之理。祖贤一敬之修何如,必先沐浴更衣,清其天君,正其天官,而恭敬进于道经⑧之前。道无形象,俨然

---

① 现存最早一块记载开封犹太人历史的石碑,又称《重建清真寺记》碑。石碑立于明朝弘治二年(公元1489年)。碑高153厘米,宽80厘米,厚5厘米;碑上共有36行,每行56—58字不等。现存开封市博物馆,字迹已模糊不清。此处释文根据梵蒂冈图书馆所藏拓片,见 https://digi.vatlib.it/view/MSS_Borg.cin.497,感谢复旦大学陈拓博士让我注意到这件拓片。另参考陈垣(1980),李景文等(2011)。按,犹太人可能最早在中文世界用"清真寺"称呼自己的寺院,参见刘迎胜:《关于元代中国的犹太人》,《元史论丛》第六辑,北京:中国社会科学出版社,1997 年。
② 以色列。
③ 亚伯拉罕。
④ 亚当。
⑤ 摩西。
⑥ 西奈山。
⑦ 以斯拉。
⑧ 托拉经卷,即《摩西五经》。

天道之在上。姑述敬天礼拜纲领而陈之:

始焉鞠躬敬道,道在鞠躬也。中立不倚敬道,道在中立也。静而存养,默赞敬道,不忘之天也。动而省察,鸣赞敬道,不替之天也。退三步也,忽然在后,敬道后也。进三步也,①瞻之在前,敬道前也。左之鞠躬敬道,即善道在于左也。右之鞠躬敬道,即不善道在于右也。仰焉敬道,道在上也。俯焉敬道,道在尔也。终焉而拜道,敬在拜也。噫!敬天而不尊祖,非所以祀先也。春秋祭其祖先,事死如事生,事亡如事存,维牛维羊,荐其时食,不以祖先之既往而不敬也。每月之际四日斋,斋乃入道之门,积善之基。今日积一善,明日积一善,善始积累。至斋,诸恶不作,众善奉行。七日善终,周而复始,②是易有云,吉人为善,惟日不足之意也。四季之时七日戒,众祖苦难,祀先报本。亡绝饮食,一日大戒,③敬以告天,悔前日之过失,迁今日之新善也。是易圣人于益之大象有曰,风雷益,君子以见善则迁,有过则改,其斯之谓与!

噫!教道相传,授受有自来矣。出自天竺④,奉命而来,有李、俺、艾、高、穆、赵、金、周、张、石、黄、李、聂、金、张、左、白七十姓⑤等,进贡西洋布于宋,帝曰:归我中夏,遵守祖风,留遗汴梁。宋孝隆兴元年⑥癸未,列微⑦五思达领掌其教,俺都剌始建寺焉。元至元十六年⑧己卯,五思达重建古刹清真寺,坐落土市字街东南,四至三十五丈。殆我大明太祖高皇帝开国初,抚绥天下军民,凡归其化者皆赐地以安居乐业之乡,诚一视同仁之心也。以是寺不可无典守者,惟李诚、李实、俺平徒、艾端、李贵、李节、李昇、李纲、艾敬、周安、李荣、李良、李智、张浩等,正经熟晓,劝人为善,呼为满剌。其教道相传,至今衣冠礼乐,遵行时制,语言动静,循由旧

---

① 陈垣释文作"进五步也",据梵蒂冈拓片改。
② 安息日(Sabbath)。
③ 赎罪日(Yom Kippur)。
④ 所谓天竺,不过以旧有名词,拟西域极远处,就像以盘古比附亚当,令人易明。
⑤ 似应为十七姓。其中两李、两金、两张,姓同而族异。
⑥ 公元1163年,即金世宗大定三年。选择"宋孝隆兴元年"而不用"金世宗大定三年"作为纪年符号,看来是受到正统思想的影响。因为金、元两朝均以少数民族入主中原,不被中原人承认为正统。明代兴起即以驱逐异族复兴汉族统治为标榜,当然自承宋王朝纪年而用宋不用金。
⑦ 利未。
⑧ 公元1279年。

章,人人遵守成法,而知敬天尊祖,忠君孝亲者,皆其力也。俺诚医士,永乐十九年①奉周府定王传令,赐香重修清真寺,寺中奉大明皇帝万万岁牌。永乐二十一年②以奏闻有功,③钦赐赵姓,授锦衣卫指挥,升浙江都指挥佥事。正统十年④,李荣、李良自备资财,重建前殿三间。至天顺五年⑤,河水濆没,基址略存,艾敬等具呈,按照先奉本府承河南布政使司劄付等因至元年古刹清真寺准此。李荣复备资财,起盖深邃,明金五彩妆成,焕然一新。成化年⑥高鉴、高锐、高鋐,自备资财,增建后殿三间,明金五彩妆成,安置道经三部,外作穿廊,接连前殿,乃为永远之计。此盖寺前后来历也。天顺年⑦石斌、李荣、高鉴、张瑄,取宁波本教道经一部,宁波赵应捧经一部赍至汴梁归寺。高年由贡士任徽州歙县知县,艾俊由举人任德府长史。宁夏金瑄,先祖任光禄寺卿,伯祖胜,任金吾前卫千兵;瑄置买供卓铜炉瓶烛台;乃弟瑛,弘治二年,舍资财,置寺地一段;瑛与钟,托赵俊置碑石。俺都剌立基址启其端,李荣、高鋐建造成其事,有功于寺。诸氏舍公帑,经龛、经楼、经卓、连笼、栏杆、供卓、付檐诸物器皿,亦为妆彩画饰周围之用,壮丽一方。

愚惟三教,各有殿宇,尊崇其主。在儒则有大成殿,尊崇孔子;在释则有圣容殿,尊崇尼牟⑧,在道则有玉皇殿,尊崇三清。在清真,则有一赐乐业殿,尊崇皇天。其儒教与本教,虽大同小异,然其立心制行,亦不过敬天道,尊祖宗,重君臣,孝父母,和妻子,序尊卑,交朋友,而不外于五伦矣。噫嘻!人徒知清真寺礼拜敬道,殊不知道之大原出于天,而古今相传,不可诬也。虽然,本教尊崇如是之笃,岂徒求福田利益计哉?受君之恩,食君之禄,惟尽礼拜告天之诚,报国忠君之意。祝颂大明皇上,德迈禹汤,圣并尧舜,聪明睿智,同日月之照临,慈爱宽仁,配乾坤之广大,国祚绵长,祝圣寿于万年,皇图巩固,愿天长于⑨地久,风调雨顺,共享太平之福。勒之金石,用传永久云。

---

① 公元1421年。
② 公元1423年。
③ 对"奏闻有功"的考证,见李景文等(2011),第372页。
④ 公元1445年。
⑤ 公元1461年。
⑥ 公元1465—1487年。
⑦ 天顺为中国明朝第六个皇帝明英宗二次登基后的年号(公元1457年—1464年)。
⑧ 照原碑,当作"牟尼"。
⑨ 照原碑。

开封府儒学增广生员金钟撰

祥符县儒学廪膳生员曹佐书

开封府儒学廪膳生员傅儒篆

弘治二年①,岁在己酉,仲夏吉日,清真后人宁夏金瑛、祥符金礼并立。瓦匠吴亮、吴海②。

12.4.1a A Stele Inscription Recording the Reconstruction of the Pure and True Temple [Synagogue] (1489) ③

Abraham, the patriarch who founded the religion of Israel, was of the nineteenth generation from Pangu④ Adam. From the opening up of the cosmos, the patriarchs handed down successively the traditions that they had received. They made no images, flattered no spirits and ghosts, and placed no credence in heterodox practices. At that time, the spirits and ghosts could not aid [them], images afforded [them] no protection, and heterodox practices availed [them] nothing.

So [Abraham] meditated upon Heaven: "[It is] ethereal and pure above, most honorable and beyond compare. The Dao of Heaven 'does not speak, yet the four seasons run their course thereby, and all creatures are born thereby.'"⑤ It is evident that things come to life in the springtime, grow during the summer, are harvested in the autumn, and are stored up in the winter. [Living things] fly, swim, walk, and grow. They luxuriate and then decompose, they bloom then fall. Processes of generations go on by themselves; processes of transformation proceed by themselves; things take on shape and form in and of themselves; variety generates variety of its own

---

① 公元1489年。

② 国内通行释文作"吴遵",这里根据梵蒂冈图书馆藏拓片改作"吴海"。

③ Source: Lipman (2001) with few minor revisions. For discussions, see also Leslie (1972), pp. 79–102; Plaks (1999).

④ A giant sometimes represented as the first man in Chinese myth.

⑤ *Analects of Confucius* 17:19.

accord. The patriarch suddenly awoke as if from sleep, enlightened into these profound mysteries. He began truly to seek the orthodox teaching with a view to assisting true Heaven. With all his heart he served [it], and gave himself up wholly to respectful veneration. Then he laid the foundation of the teaching which has been handed down to this day. Examination reveals that this was in the 146th year of the Zhou dynasty.①

Through transmission, [the teaching] reached Moses, also a patriarch of the orthodox teaching. Examination reveals that he lived in the 613th year of the Zhou.② From birth he was gifted with pure and genuine insight. His human-heartedness and righteousness were entirely perfected; his Dao and inherent virtue were complete together. He sought for the Scriptures at the top of Mount Sinai, and [to this end] he fasted forty days and nights. He put away lustful passions and denied [himself] both sleep and food, worshiping with perfect sincerity. His devotion touched the mind-heart of Heaven, and the orthodox Scripture, in fifty-three sections, had its origin from this. Its contents are extremely subtle and mysterious; the good men [recorded there] incite goodness in human hearts, while the evil men [recorded there] repress and warn the unregulated willfulness of humankind.

Thereafter the teaching was transmitted to Ezra, another patriarch of the orthodox teaching. A descendant of the patriarchs, [he received from them] the complete Dao and the continuous lineage. His Way of honoring Heaven and ritual worship revealed the mysteries of the ancestral Dao.

The Dao must be based on purity, truth, ritual, and worship. Purity means it is one, pure, and inimitable; truth signifies rectitude without heterodoxy; ritual denotes reverence itself; and worship is the act of obeisance [bowing]. In the midst of daily occupations, people must not forget Heaven even for a moment, but rather morning, noon, and night, three times a day, should undertake ritual and worship. This is the

---

① Tenth century BCE.
② Sixth century BCE.

fundamental principle of the true Dao of Heaven.

What was the common practice of the patriarchal worthies in their cultivation of balanced reverence? First they had to bathe and change their garments; then they purified their Heavenly minds and regulated their Heavenly naturalfaculties. Then, with great respect they entered before the Scriptures of the Dao. The Dao has no form or figure but is just like the supremacy of the Dao of Heaven.

The simpleoutline of ritual procedure in the worship of venerating Heaven is as follows: First, the worshiper bends the body to honor the Dao, and the Dao is present in bending the body. Then he stands erect, without leaning, to honor the Dao, and the Dao is present in standing erect. In meditation he preserves [his ability to] nurture [himself]; by silent praise he venerates the Dao, for Heaven should never be forgotten. In movement he examines his conduct, and by vocal praise he honors the Dao, for Heaven knows no substitute. He retreats three paces, and immediately [the Dao is] behind him, so he honors the Dao behind him. He advances three steps and perceives [the Dao] before him, so he honors the Dao before him. Turning to the left he bends his body to venerate the Dao, which is good, for the Dao is on his left. Turning to the right he bends his body to venerate the Dao, which is not good,① for the Dao is on his right. He looks upward to venerate the Dao, and the Dao is above [him]. He looks downward to venerate the Dao, and the Dao is near [him]. In conclusion, he bows to the Dao, and his reverence lies in the bowing.

To revere Heaven without paying homage to the ancestors is not the proper way to sacrifice to the ancients. In the spring and autumn ancestral sacrifices, he should "serve the dead as if serving the living, serve those gone as if serving those present."② He should offer oxen and sheep, and seasonal food, and should not fail to honor the ancestors because they had

---

① Turning to the right during the prayer would put the Dao (God) on the worshiper's right, which is a position of inferiority in Chinese social rituals.

② *Doctrine of the Mean*, 19:5.

already passed on.

In every month there should be four days' observance. [Weekly] observance is the gateway to the Dao, and the foundation upon which good works are stored up. Today a good deed is stored up, tomorrow another good deed, and from this beginning, the doing of good deeds becomes a habit. At the time of observance, no evil is done, but all sorts of good actions are performed. Thus the seven days are brought to a good ending, and a new period commences①. As the *Book of Changes* (*I Ching*) says, "The fortunate person, doing good, finds the day insufficient for his intentions." At the four seasons of the year are observances of seven days in consideration of the calamities experienced by the ancestors, and sacrifices are made to the forefathers in order to repay the source [of all good we have received by the ancestors' merit]. Cutting off from all food and drink, there is rigid abstinence for one whole day②, reverently calling upon Heaven for repentance of previous faults and for moving toward new good deeds in the present. Is this not the meaning of the forty-second hexagram of the *Book of Changes*, as the sage explains: "The wind and thunder unite, and the Lordly Man sees the good and approaches [it], acknowledges his faults and corrects them"?

Truly, the Dao of our teaching has been passed down, its transmission and reception in order. It came from India, coming according to the command [of Heaven?]. The clans of Li, An, Ai, Gao, Mu, Zhao, Jin, Zhou, Zhang, Shi, Huang, Li, Nieh, Jin, Zhang, Zuo, and Bai, seventy [seventeen?] lineages in all, bore tribute of western cloth to the Song [emperor]. He said, "You have come to my Zhongxia [kingdom]—revere and preserve your ancestral ways; hand them down in Bianliang [Kaifeng]."

In the *guiwei* year, the first year of the Longxing reign period of the Xiaozong emperor of the Song dynasty [1163 CE], Levi the ustad [rabbi]

---

① Sabbath.
② Yom Kippur.

was charged with leading the teaching, and Andula ['Abd-Allah?①] began to build the synagogue. In the *jimao* year, the sixteenth year of the Zhiyuan reign period of the Yuan dynasty [1279], the ustad rebuilt the ancient synagogue, the Pure and True Temple. It was situated southeast of Earth-market Street, and each of its four sides was thirty-five *zhang* in length.

When Emperor Gao, [whose temple name was] Taizu, of the great Ming [dynasty], founded the empire, he first calmed the armies and people of the world. To all who responded to his transformation [of the empire], he bestowed land for settlement where they could live peacefully and happily follow their occupations. Truly he possessed a heart that looked upon all with equal benevolence.

Because this temple could not be without leaders, those who were well versed in the orthodox Scriptures and who exhorted others to do good were designated as Manla②—Li Cheng, Li Shi, An Pingdu, Ai Duan, Li Gui, Li Jie, Li Sheng, Li Gang, Ai Jing, Zhou An, Li Rong, Li Liang, Li Zhi, and Zhang Hao. The Dao of their teaching has been transmitted continuously, [so that] to the present, the robes and headdress, the rites and music, all conform to the fixed order of the seasons. The phrases and words, the movements and pauses, all accord with ancient rules. [The fact that] all the [Jewish] people observe and preserve the established laws, know how to honor Heaven and venerate the ancestors, and show themselves loyal to their lord and filial to their parents is entirely due to the work of the Manla.

In the nineteenth year of the Yongle reign period [1421], the physician An Cheng was given a present of incense and permitted to rebuild the synagogue by order of prince Ding of Zhou. A tablet wishing long life to the emperor of Great Ming was placed in the synagogue. In the twenty-first year of the Yongle reign period [1423], [An Cheng] was granted the surname Zhao and the rank of a commissioner in the Embroidered Uniform Guard by imperial decree, because he made a report to the throne and was

---

① Literally, "the slave of God," a name that a Central Asian Jew or Muslim might hold.
② I.e., mullahs, community leaders.

adjudged meritorious for it. He was promoted to be assistant commissioner of the Regional Military Commission in Zhejiang.

In the tenth year of the Zhengtong reign period [1445], Li Rong and Li Liang prepared private funds and rebuilt the front hall [of the temple], three *jian* in size.

In the fifth year of the Tianshun reign period [1461], the river floods swept [the entire synagogue] away, leaving only the foundations. Ai Jing and others petitioned the provincial commissioner, requesting [and receiving] permission to reconstruct the synagogue according to the [model of the] ancient synagogue of the Zhiyuan reign period [i.e., 1279 CE], which had been approved by the prefect, the provincial governor, et al. Li Rong again prepared private funds and began the building on a spacious scale—brightly gilt and painted in colors, its splendor was entirely renewed.

During the Chenghua reign period [1465 – 1487], Gao Jian, Gao Rui, and Gao Hong prepared private funds and constructed an additional rear hall, three *jian* in size, brightly gilt and painted in colors. [They] placed [therein] three copies of the Scriptures. On the exterior [they] constructed a corridor to connect [it] to the front hall. Truly this was a permanent contribution. This then is the complete history of the synagogue.

In the Tianshun reign period [1457 – 1464], Shi Bin, Li Rong, Gao Jian, and Zhang Xuan went to Ningbo and brought back a copy of our teaching's Scriptures. Zhao Ying of Ningbo brought another copy to Bianliang [Kaifeng] and respectfully presented it to our temple.

Gao Nian, a graduate with the *gongshi* degree, was appointed magistrate of Ji county, Hui prefecture [Anhui province].

Ai Jun, a provincial graduate (*juren*), was appointed annalist of Prince De's house.

Jin Xuan of Ningxia had an ancestor who had been president of state banquets, while his uncle [Jin] Sheng had been a commander of the Jinwu regiment in the Imperial Escort. [Jin] Xuan bought and placed [in the synagogue] the table of offerings, with its bronze censer, and the pairs of flower vases and candlesticks. His younger brother [Jin] Ying prepared funds in the second year of the Hongzhi reign period [1489] to purchase a portion of the temple's land. Moreover, [Jin] Ying and [Jin] Zhong [who composed this inscription] deputed Zhao Jun to purchase this inscriptional stone. Andula ['Abd-Allah?], who laid the foundation and began the work, Li Rong, and Gao Hong, who completed the construction, all have achieved merit for the temple. All families contributed to the common fund for providing shrines for the Scriptures, a tripartite archway before the Scriptures, and the table for [reading] the Scriptures. Also they provided the [two] racks, the balustrade, the ceremonial tables, the frontal drapes, and all the various articles, utensils, and vessels. Moreover, the painting and decorations beautified the entire compound.

Reflecting on the three teachings [of China—Confucianism, Buddhism, and Daoism], each has its temples in which they honor their Lord. Thus, the Confucians have the Temple of the Great Perfection to honor Confucius; the Buddhists have the Temple of the Holy Countenance to honor Shakyamuni; the Daoists have the Temple of the Jade Emperor to honor the Three Purities. So the Pure and True [the Jews, in Chinese, *Qingzhen*] have the Temple of Israel to honor August Heaven.

Although there are some minor discrepancies between their Confucian doctrine and our own, in their main focus of ideas and established practices both are exclusively concerned with honoring the Dao of Heaven, respecting ancestors, valuing the relations of ruler and subject, obedience to parents, harmony within families, correct ordering of social hierarchies, and good fellowship among friends—nothing more than the "five cardinal relationships" of humankind. Alas! People know only that ritual and obeisances in the Pure and True Temple honor the Dao, but they do not know that the great source Dao lies in Heaven, and it has been transmitted since antiquity without possibility of falsehood.

Although the followers of our teaching sincerely devote themselves to its practice, could it be only to obtain prosperous fields and profitable business? Since we receive the benevolence of our lord [the emperor] and consume his generous emoluments, we expend our sincerity in rituals and worship and calling upon Heaven, our intention always to repay [the favors of] our empire and [express] loyalty to our lord [the emperor].

We invoke blessings on the emperor of the Great Ming Dynasty, that his virtue may surpass that of Yu and Tang and his sageliness equal that of Yao and Shun. May his intelligence and intuitive wisdom radiate like the descending rays of the sun and moon, and his merciful love and wide benevolence match the vast breadth of Heaven and Earth. For the continuous dignity of the empire we pray that the age of the sovereign may extend to ten thousand years; for the strengthening of the empire, we pray for him a perpetual Heaven and age-long Earth. May the winds be harmonious and the rains favorable, so that together we may enjoy the blessings of universal peace.

We carve this on metal [-hard] stone, so that it may be transmitted through the ages.

Composed by Jin Zhong, Confucian scholar and Zengguang licentiate of Kaifeng city.

Written by Cao Zuo, Confucian scholar and Linshan licentiate of Xiangfu county.

Seal characters by Fu Ru, Confucian scholar and Linshan licentiate of Kaifeng city.

On a fortunate day in the second summer month of the *jiyou* year, the second year of the Hongzhi reign period [1489], jointly raised up by Jin Ying of Ningxia and Jin Li of Xiangfu [in Kaifeng], descendants of the Pure and True [the Jews].

Wu Liang and Wu Hai, stone masons.

12.5 Rabbi Yoel Teitlbaum of Satmar on the Holocaust (1961)

During the recent years we have gone through many hardships and sufferings as bitter as wormwood,① of measure never known since Israel has become a nation, and "unless the Lord had left us a remnant [behold, we would have been as Sodom, and resembled Gomorrah]."②

... Now it has always been the Jewish custom, that at every trouble that came up they tried to find out the cause thereof, namely, what sin was it that had brought it forth, so they could come to repent and return to the Lord, as we find in the Bible and the Talmud ...

... Now in our generation, one doesn't have to dig very far to find out what was the sin that brought this horror upon us, for it is explicitly written in the words of our Sages, based on Scripture. They taught [that the Lord adjured the Children of Israel], that if they breach the oaths—not to surmount the Walls③ and not to push on the Redemption—"I shall abandon you to be slaughtered as the gazelles and the hinds of the field."④ And, due to our sins, thus it was. For the heretics and nonbelievers [=the Zionists] made all sorts of endeavors to breach these oaths, to surmount the Walls and to take themselves freedom and sovereignty before time has come, which is the essence of "pushing on the Redemption." And they drew the majority of the Jews to this impure idea.

... And it is explicated in the Talmud, Shevuot 39, that in all sins the sinner alone is punished, but in the sin of breach of oath—the punishment is upon the sinner, his family and the entire world. From this saying, that the whole world suffers due to the individual sinner's action, we can learn how severe is the sin of breach of oath. *A fortiori* in this breach of oath, which was made in many actions and in great multitude, for in the last several years it seemed that nearly most of the Jews assisted their actions in various ways, and did it openly and publicly, while but few had the merit of proper protest. This is why this suffering came upon us, which the Sages

---

① See Prov. 5:4ff.
② Is. 1:9.
③ i.e., not to carry out a mass immigration.
④ Babylonian Talmud, Ketubot, 111a, based on Song 2:7, 3:5, 8:4.

described as being abandoned to slaughter, God forbid. And [it is said that] "every calamity comes down to the world because of the Wicked, but begins its affliction with the Righteous."①

12.6 Ellen M. Umansky, "Re-Visioning Sarah: A Midrash on Genesis 22"②

It was morning. Sarah had just awakened and reached over to touch her husband, Abraham, to caress him, but Abraham wasn't there. Neither, she discovered, was Isaac, her only son, Isaac, whom she loved more than anyone or anything in the world. She quickly dressed and went outside, hoping they'd be nearby. But they were gone, and so was Abraham's ass and his two young servants. It wasn't unusual for Abraham to take Isaac somewhere, but never this early and never without saying good-bye. And so she waited, and wept, and screamed.

Hours passed. It was hot and Sarah thought about going inside to escape the heat of the sun. But what if I miss them, she thought. I want to make sure that I catch the first glimpse of them, even if they're far away. And so she stood and waited ... and waited ... and waited. She felt anxious, nervous, upset. "Where could they be?" "Where has Abraham taken my son?" The sun began to set. She started to shiver, partly from the cold, mostly from fear. Again she cried, and wailed, and moaned. Isaac had been God's gift to her, a sign of His love and a continuing bond between them. She had laughed when God told her she was pregnant. She was old and no longer able to bear a child. But God had given her Isaac and filled her breasts with milk and for the first time in her life Sarah was happy.

She looked around her and saw the fields, now empty, and in the distance saw the mountains, sloping upwards into the sky. And then she

---

① See Babylonian Talmud, Bava Kamma, 60a.
② Source: Umansky (1992).

saw them ... Abraham walking with his ass and his servants and Isaac far behind, walking slowly, his head turning from side to side, his hands oddly moving as though he were trying to make sense of something, and Sarah knew in that instant where Abraham and Isaac had been and why they had gone. Though she could barely make out the features of Isaac's face, she could tell from his movements and his gestures that he was angry, that he wanted nothing to do with his father who had tried to kill him. Abraham was almost down the mountain by now and soon would be home. He'd to explain, to make her understand *his* side of the story. But Sarah wanted no part of it. She was tired of hearing Abraham's excuses and even more tired of hearing what *he* thought God demanded. And so Sarah turned and went inside and prayed that if only for one night, Abraham would leave her alone.

12.7 Jacob Neusner, Stranger at Home (1981)[①]

Once upon a time, when I was a young man, I felt helpless before the world. I was a Jew, when being Jewish was a bad thing. As a child, I saw my old Jewish parents, speaking a foreign language and alien in countless ways, isolated from America. And I saw America, dimly perceived to be sure, exciting and promising, but hostile to me as a Jew. I could not get into a good college. I could not aspire to medical school. I could not become an architect or an engineer. I could not even work for an electric utility.

When I took my vacation, I could not go just anywhere, but had to ask whether Jews would be welcome, tolerated, embarrassed, or thrown out. Being Jewish was uncomfortable. Yet I could not give it up. My mother and my father had made me what I was. I could hide, but could not wholly deny, not to myself even if to others, that I was a Jew. And I could not afford the price in diminished self-esteem of opportunity denied, aspiration

---

① Source: Neusner (1981), pp. 66 – 67.

deferred, and insult endured. Above all, I saw myself as weak and pitiful. I could not do anything about being a Jew nor could I do much to improve my lot as a Jew.

Then came Hitler and I saw that what was my private lot was the dismal fate of every Jew. Everywhere Jew hatred was raised from the gutter to the heights. Not from Germany alone, but from people I might meet at work or in the streets I learned that being Jewish was a metaphysical evil. "The Jews" were not accepted, but debated. Friends would claim we were not all bad. Enemies said we were. And we had nothing to say at all.

As I approached maturity, a still more frightening fact confronted me. People guilty of no crime but Jewish birth were forced to flee their homeland, and no one would accept them. Ships filled with ordinary men, women and children searched the oceans for a safe harbor. And I and they had nothing in common but one fact, and that fact made all else inconsequential. Had I been there, I should have been among them. I, too, should not have been saved at sea.

Then came the war and, in its aftermath, the revelation of the shame and horror of holocaust, the decay and corrosive hopelessness of the Displaced Persons camps, the contempt of the nations, who would neither accept nor help the saved remnants of hell.

At the darkest hour came the dawn. The State of Israel saved the remnant and gave meaning and significance to the inferno. After the dawn, the great light: Jews no longer helpless, weak, unable to decide their own fate, but strong, confident, decisive.

And then came the corrupting doubt; if I were there, I should have died in hell. But now has come redemption and I am here, not there.

How much security in knowing that if it should happen again I shall not be lost. But how great a debt paid in guilt for being where I am and who I am!

Appendices

A. James Kugel, "Four Assumptions of the Biblical Interpretation"[1]

Readers always approach texts with certain assumptions, and the assumptions change depending on what they are reading; not every text is thought to *mean* in the same way. Thus, when we read a poem in which the poet says to his beloved, "I faint! I die!" we know he's not really dying; likewise, when he says he's wallowing in love in the same way that a cooked fish is wallowed in galantine sauce, well ... we know this isn't really intended as an exact description of his emotional state. And it is not just poems. Novels and short stories, form letters and radio commercials and last wills and testaments—all sorts of different compositions come with their own conventions, and we as readers are aware of those conventions and interpret the texts accordingly. We expect to be amused by a stand-up comedian's recitation of his woes, and so we laugh in all the right places; yet if a somewhat similar monologue is spoken by a patient at his group therapy session, people will probably not laugh, in part because they bring an entirely different set of expectations to his "text." (Also, they don't want to hurt his feelings.)

  It is a striking fact that all ancient interpreters seem to have shared very much the same set of expectations about the biblical text. No one ever sat

---

[1] Source: Kugel (2008), pp. 14–17.

down and formulated these assumptions for them—they were simply assumed, just like our present-day assumptions about how we are to understand texts uttered by poets and group-therapy patients. However, looking over the vast body of ancient interpretations of different parts of the Bible, we can gain a rather clear picture of what their authors were assuming about the biblical text—and what emerges is that, despite the geographic and cultural distance separating some of these interpreters from others, they all seem to have assumed the same four basic things about *how* the Bible was to be read:

1. They assumed that the Bible was a fundamentally cryptic text: that is, when it said A, often it might really mean B. Thus, when it said, "And it came to pass after these things," even though that might look like the familiar transitional phrase, what it might really mean was "after these *words.*" Indeed, this text, they felt, was so cryptic that it did not even say what the words were—it had left it to the interpreters themselves to remember the book of Job and so figure out the rest. Similarly, when the Bible repeated "and the two of them walked together," the second occurrence of this phrase had a hidden meaning: Abraham and Isaac had agreed and now proceeded as if of one mind.

2. Interpreters also assumed that the Bible was a book of lessons directed to readers in their own day. It may seem to talk about the past, but it is not fundamentally history. It is instruction, telling us what to do: be obedient to God just as Abraham was and you will be rewarded, just as he was. Ancient interpreters assumed this not only about narratives like the Abraham story but about every part of the Bible. For example, Isaiah's prophecies about the Assyrian crisis contained, interpreters believed, a message for people in their own time (five or six centuries later). Likewise, when the book of Nahum had referred metaphorically to a "raging lion," the text was not talking about some enemy in Nahum's own day, but about Demetrius

III, who was the king of Syria six hundred years later, in the time of the ancient interpreters. Similarly, the Bible's laws were understood as being intended for people to obey in the interpreters' own time, even though they had been promulgated in a very different society many centuries earlier.

3. Interpreters also assumed that the Bible contained no contradictions or mistakes. It is perfectly harmonious, despite its being an anthology; in fact, they also believed that everything that the Bible says ought to be in accord with the interpreters' own religious beliefs and practices (since they believed these to have been ordained by God). Thus, if the Bible seemed to imply that God was not all-knowing or that Abraham had been callous and deceitful with his son, interpreters would not say that this story reflected beliefs about God or basic morality that had changed since ancient times. Instead, they stoutly insisted that there must be some way of understanding the Bible's words so as to remove any such implications: that cannot be what the Bible really intended! And of course the Bible ought not to contradict itself or even seem to repeat itself needlessly, so that if it said "and the two of them walked together" twice, the second occurrence cannot be merely repetitive; it must mean something different from the first. In short, the Bible, they felt, is an utterly consistent, seamless, perfect book.

4. Lastly, they believed that the entire Bible is essentially a divinely given text, a book in which God speaks directly or through His prophets. There could be little doubt about those parts of the Bible that openly identify the speaker as God: "And the LORD spoke to Moses, saying ..." "Thus says the LORD, the God of Israel ..." But interpreters believed that this was also true of the story of Abraham and the other stories in Genesis, even though the text itself never actually said there that God was the author of these stories. And it was held to be true of the rest of the Bible too—even of the book of Psalms, although the psalms themselves are prayers and songs

addressed *to* God and thus ought logically not to have come *from* God. Nevertheless, most interpreters held the psalms to be in some sense of divine origin, written under divine inspiration or guidance or even directly dictated to David, their traditional author.

How these assumptions came into existence is hard to say for sure, and in any case that question need not detain us here; the fact is, they did come into existence, even before Israel's ancient library of sacred texts began to be called the Bible, in fact, even before its precise table of contents had been determined.

What are modern readers to make of these assumptions? Many readers will balk at the ancient interpretation of the Abraham and Isaac story given above. But it is simply in the nature of assumptions in general that they are *assumed*, not consciously adopted. Once biblical interpretation had started along the path of these Four Assumptions, it developed a logic, and a momentum, of its own. This was simply how the Bible was to be understood. The power and persuasiveness of these assumptions may be clearer if one considers that, to a remarkable degree, they continue to color the way people read the Bible right down to the present day (even if nowadays they may lead to somewhat different conclusions from those advanced by the ancient interpreters). Thus, many modern-day Jews and Christians continue to look to the Bible as a guidebook for daily life (Assumption 2); they do not read it as if it were just a relic from the ancient past. In fact, a significant number of contemporary Jews and Christians seek to act on a daily basis in accordance with the Bible's specific exhortations and laws, and many view the Bible's prophecies as being fulfilled in the events of today's world (another aspect of Assumption 2). Without quite saying so, quite a few readers also generally assume that the Bible has some sort of coherent message to communicate and that it does not contradict itself or contain mistakes (Assumption 3). Many also believe that the Bible's meaning is not always obvious (Assumption 1)—it even seems *deliberately* cryptic sometimes, they say. And the idea of divine inspiration, in fact, the conception of the Bible as a whole as the word of God (Assumption 4), is an article of faith in a great many denominations.

Thus, whatever one thinks of the Four Assumptions, there is no denying their staying power. What is more, some of the interpretations they gave rise to have demonstrated a comparable durability: to a degree not generally recognized, these interpretations are still with us and have actually succeeded in changing the meaning of quite a few biblical stories. As will be seen presently, the story of Adam and Eve only became "the Fall of Man" thanks to these ancient interpretive assumptions; the book of Genesis says nothing of the kind. The same is true of many other things that people have always believed the Bible says—that Abraham was the one who discovered that there is only one God, that David was a pious king who wrote the book of Psalms, or that the Song of Solomon speaks of God's love for His people. The Bible says these things only if it is read in accordance with the Four Assumptions.

B. David Stern, "The Brutality of Repentance"[1]

The Torah reading that is most commonly associated with Rosh Hashanah and the meaning of the holiday is the Akedah, the Binding of Isaac. In Jewish tradition, that story has come to symbolize what absolute obedience to God's commandments means, not only in terms of Abraham's own character as a perfectly righteous man but also more functionally, in the practical significance of his deed for subsequent generations of his descendants. Abraham's silent, unquestioning obedience to God's command that he sacrifice his son earned, according to the tradition, a *zekhut*[2] or merit—heavenly Brownie points, as it were—that we—Abraham's descendants—are able to invoke on our own behalf on Rosh Hashanah, the

---

[1] Source: Stern (2012).
[2] See 8.1 (Avot 2:2).

Day of Judgment, when we seek God's forgiveness for our own misdeeds and failings, because we lack sufficient merits or good deeds of our own to justify our being forgiven. Even if there are those among us who find Abraham's obedience to be misguided, the relevance of Abraham's behavior and its practical import for Rosh Hashanah is clear, at least as it appeared to our ancestors.

In contrast, the relevance of the *first* day's Torah reading to Rosh Hashanah is not obvious. What could the story of the expulsion of Hagar and Ishmael, Abraham's other son, ever have to do with Rosh Hashanah? What can it teach us about the Day of Judgment? Truth be told, the reason why we read the story of Hagar and Ishmael on the first of the two days of Rosh Hashanah is not clear. The first Rabbinic text to mention Genesis 21 as the beginning of the reading on Rosh Hashanah is Tosefta Megillah 3:3, but it gives no explanation for the choice. Some later sages explained that the reason was because Genesis 21 begins, *Va-Adonai pakad et Sarah /And God took note (or remembered) Sarah*, and the theme of remembrance is key to the Day of Judgment. Others have suggested that the story of the birth of Isaac is a corollary to Rosh Hashanah's other theme as the birthday of the world's creation. And part of the reason must surely lie in the fact that the narrative of Isaac's birth is the natural beginning to the story of the Akedah that follows in the next chapter in Genesis. It is not the story of Isaac's birth, however, that most of us remember about the Torah reading of the first day of Rosh Hashanah. Rather, what sticks in our minds, if not our throats, is the far more troubling narrative of the expulsion of Hagar and Ishmael. What relevance can that story have to Rosh Hashanah?

Part of the answer may lie in the connection between the two stories in the two chapters, the expulsion of Hagar and Ishmael and the Akedah. Somewhat strangely, the classical commentators do not remark much on their connection, but modern commentators and readers have often seen clear parallels between them. For one thing, both are stories in which Abraham either loses or is threatened with the loss of an only son—that is, the only son of the child's mother—in the case of Ishmael, Hagar,

Abraham's *pilegesh* or concubine (although she is actually Sarah's maidservant, not Abraham's); and in the case of Isaac, Sarah herself. In both stories, the two sons are saved by an angel. (See Gen. 21:17 and 22:11, whose wordings are virtually identical save for the name of the addressee.) And in both stories, when Abraham gets ready to fulfill God's command, we are told, *Va-yashkeim Avraham ba-boker /Early next morning, Abraham* ... (Gen. 21:14 and 22:3). As the commentators on the Akedah comment, the reason why the Bible tells us that Abraham got up early in the morning was not to teach us that he was an early riser (or couldn't sleep) but to indicate his readiness to perform God's commandment—whether it was to sacrifice his son or to cast him out into the desert. Through these various repetitions and parallels, the Bible seems to be drawing our attention to the connections between the two stories, although, as usual, it never specifies what they really are.

On the other hand, for all their parallels, there are also profound differences between the two stories. Probably the biggest difference is their mode of representation, the way they present their stories and characters to the reader. As many have noted, the most striking thing about the Akedah as it is presented in the Torah is what the text does not tell us: it does not tell us why God commands Abraham to sacrifice Isaac. It does not tell us what Abraham felt or thought. Nor does it tell us what Isaac thought or felt. (Isaac, in any case, has only one line, the famous "where's the animal to be sacrificed, Daddy?") We do not know when the Akedah took place; in point of fact, we do not even know where the land of Moriah is (or the mountain of Moriah, though the tradition ascribed it to the Temple mount). And just as we do not know why God commands Abraham to sacrifice Isaac, we do not know why the angel tells Abraham not to. And where does the ram come from? We do not know.

These are just some of the silences and holes in the text; there are many more. And yet it is fair to say that the power of the story comes from the very fact of these silences. As the great literary scholar Eric Auerbach pointed out more than sixty years ago, the Akedah is "fraught with background." The less the text tells us, the more we, the story's readers, are tempted to fill in the silences and blanks. Of course, we can't do this honestly. Instead, the Torah essentially asks us to accept the story the way it is and to submit to its truth silently, just as Abraham silently submits to God's command.

The story of Hagar and Ishmael is presented in virtually the opposite way. It tells us much about the characters and their feelings and motivations. *Va-teire Sarah et ben Hagar ha-mitzrit asher yaldah l'Avraham m'tzacheik /And Sarah saw the son of Hagar the Egyptian whom she had born to Abraham "m'tzacheik."* This is what angers Sarah and sets off her demand that Hagar be expelled. Of course, we already know that Sarah doesn't like Hagar. Four chapters back, at the beginning of Genesis 16, after Sarah realizes that she is barren and gives Hagar her maidservant to Abraham as a surrogate—a legitimate practice in the Ancient Near East—and after Hagar becomes pregnant, we are told that *Va-takeil g'virtah be-'eineha /Her mistress, Sarah, was lowered in her eyes.* Apparently, Hagar's pregnancy went to her head, and she flaunted it before Sarah, who was outraged at her behavior. With Abraham's consent, Sarah then proceeds to torture Hagar until she makes her flee from their house into the desert where an angel ultimately saves her and convinces her to return to Abraham's house and to give birth to her son.

Essentially, this story is the model for the later story, a kind of doublet, the main difference between them being that in the earlier story, Hagar brings her expulsion upon herself through her own behavior; even if her punishment seems somewhat excessive to her arrogance, it's her own doing. In our story, however, we have no idea what Hagar did to bring her punishment upon herself and her son. All the text says is that Sarah saw Hagar's son *m'tzacheik*. This word is somewhat enigmatic—it means "laughing" or "playing"—but why exactly laughing or playing should bring upon Ishmael and Hagar what amounts to a death-sentence is not obvious. The classical commentators tell us that the word is the same as *m'sacheik*, and that it is either an allusion to idol worship—Ishmael was an idolater—or that he was making fun of Isaac or ridiculing Sarah and saying that she had become pregnant from Abimelekh, the Philistine king (who had taken her from Abraham in a previous chapter) and not from Abraham. Still other commentators propose that the word has a sexual connotation, either fondling or molestation.

None of these answers, though, is entirely satisfying because the surrounding text itself doesn't lead naturally to any of them. I would suggest that what the word really means—especially in light of the next verse where Sarah demands that Abraham expel Hagar and Ishmael because she does not want the son of that maidservant to share in the inheritance with Isaac—is that *m'tzacheik* is "being Yitzhak," Isaac-ing, as it were, acting as though he were the favored son. This is what Sarah cannot abide.

Abraham, we are told, was distressed at Sarah's demand, and understandably so, because Ishmael after all is also his son. But then, even more amazingly, God tells Abraham *not* to be distressed and to obey Sarah, his wife. He then adds that He, God, will take care of Hagar and Ishmael, and make Ishmael into a great nation. Yet sending Hagar and Ishmael off into the barren desert seems a strange way, even for God, to take care of someone, and this very perplexity is also complicated by what follows: Abraham obeys God, gets up early in the morning (eagerly, that is), and sends Hagar and Ishmael off into the desert with a little bread and some water, apparently enough only for a day, because, as we're then told, Hagar and Ishmael run out of water and food very quickly, and Hagar leaves Ishmael under a bush in the desert to die.

Now, if Abraham truly believed God that He would take care of Hagar and Ishmael, why does he see fit to give them *any* bread and water? God will take care of them. Yet if the reason he gives it to them is because he doesn't want to rely on miracles, why does he give them only enough for a day? It's almost as if, by giving them a *little* sustenance for the road, Abraham is really assuaging his own guilty conscience for sending them to what seems to be their inevitable deaths.

And this is what indeed happens. Hagar gets lost in the desert, the two run out of food and water, she realizes they are going to die, she hides her son because she can't bear watching him die, she weeps, and apparently Ishmael cries even louder because it is his voice that God hears, after which He subsequently orders the angel to save them.

In this story, then, completely unlike the Akedah, we are told an immense amount about the characters and their actions even if their motivation and meaning are sometimes ambiguous because the information we're given is either contradictory or unclear. The real problem is that the more we are told about the characters, the less we find them sympathetic or exemplary. Abraham initially seems to feel the right thing when Sarah first demands that he expel Hagar and he balks at doing it, but then God—for reasons that seem paradoxical at the least (nearly killing someone is a strange way to protect them)—orders Abraham not to follow his better instincts, and *then*, Abraham, a little too eagerly, follows his *worse* instincts, and as we've already said, sends Hagar and Ishmael off with a little food but clearly not enough to sustain them for very long. We are more sympathetic to Hagar and Ishmael—they don't at all appear to deserve the way they are treated—but it's sympathy for pure victims. Hagar seems to resign herself entirely to death; she doesn't try to do anything to save herself and her son, and though it's understandable that she doesn't want to watch Ishmael die, hiding him under a bush seems a little too cavalier.

And most problematically of all, there is Sarah. Back in Genesis 16 when Sarah persecutes Hagar until she flees, Sarah's anger is at least given some justification, even if the punishment she inflicts upon Hagar is excessive. We can understand how sensitive and vulnerable the barren Sarah must have felt when she was unable to conceive for so long, and Hagar appears to have slept with Abraham one night and instantly gotten pregnant. But now, four chapters later, Sarah has been granted her greatest wish; she has a son; she knows that her son will be Abraham's real heir(God has told them so repeatedly); and yet, she is still jealous of Hagar, and jealous of Ishmael for her own son, Isaac. As my friend and colleague Sara

Horowitz once pointed out in her own *Rosh Hashanah dvar Torah*①, this jealousy is a kind of unnecessary spitefulness. Even though Sarah now has what she wants, she still can't bear to see someone else have it, too. We all know this kind of spite. We all have felt it, and felt deeply embarrassed when we felt it.

The Bible is famous for not pulling punches when it portrays its characters. Jacob begins as a trickster, and ends up a wizened but slightly embittered patriarch; his sons kidnap and sell their brother; most of what we know about the Israelites after they leave Egypt is how they disobey God and His commands, and are repeatedly ungrateful for the kindnesses He does them. The story of Hagar and Ishmael's expulsion, however, is, I think, one of the Bible's most unsparing and honest portrayals of its characters, and especially so in comparison with the very idealized portrayal of Abraham and Isaac in the story of the Akedah that follows. In the parashah② that we read on the first day of Rosh Hashanah, no one comes out looking very good; all the characters look very human, very much, all too much, like ourselves, even though we hardly wish to recognize ourselves when we behave like Abraham and Sarah in this story.

And that, I would propose, may be the meaning that this parashah can hold for us on the first day of Rosh Hashanah, on the day before we read the Akedah. As I noted at the outset, we read the Akedah in order to invoke Abraham's righteousness and the merit or *zekhut* of his righteousness for our own sake on this Day of Judgment. But Abraham's *zekhut*, the *zekhut avot*, the merit of our ancestors, does not work automatically—alas! It helps, but you also need to do *teshuvah*, to repair your own ways, and to do that, you first need to look at yourself as closely, unsparingly, even harshly, as the Bible looks at Abraham and Sarah in the earlier parashah. Repentance begins with brutal honesty.

---

① *dvar Torah* ("word of Torah"), also known as a *Drasha* in Ashkenazic communities, is a talk on topics relating to a *parashah* of the Torah—typically the weekly Torah portion.

② *Parashah* ("section"). In the reading of Torah, a section of the *Sidrah* (Aramaic, "arrangement"), one of the fifty-four divisions of the Torah.

Terms and Sources

aggadah (pl. **aggadot**; Aramaic, "narrative" or "story"; its Hebrew form is "haggadah"): Name given to those sections of *Talmud and *Midrash containing homiletic expositions of the Bible, stories, legends, folklore, anecdotes, or maxims. In contradistinction to *halakhah*.

Akiba(*c.* 50 – 135 CE): Distinguished rabbi in ancient Palestine. A major legal scholar, who established an academy in Bne Brak, Akiba ben Joseph was also a legendary mystic and martyr. He was tortured and killed by the Romans in 135 CE.

Aleinu ("it is [incumbent] upon us"): Prayer recited towards the end of all services, named for its opening words: "It is incumbent upon us to praise the Master of all ..." It is the proclamation of God as King over a united humanity. An old tradition claims Joshua as its author. It might date from before the destruction of the Second Temple, which would make it one of the oldest known prayers. It is reported that it was the death-song of Jewish martyrs in the Middle Ages. *Aleinu* has been the occasion of repeated attacks on account of the passage: "They bow to vanity and emptiness and pray to a god that cannot save." Through fear of the official censorship, the passage in question has been excluded from the prayer. Source: Birnbaum (1977).

Allen, Woody (b. 1935): American comedian, filmmaker, writer, and actor. He pretends that his parody of the Akedah is a translated fragment of the *Dead Sea Scrolls, documents in the form of scrolls discovered in a cave near the Dead Sea in 1947. Source: Allen (1974).

Almoli, Shelomo (before 1485 – after 1542): Grammarian, physician, philosopher, and kabbalist. Probably born in Spain, Almoli passed his early years in Salonika, but before 1515 settled in Constantinople, where he spent the rest of his life, apparently earning his livelihood as a physician. He planned to write an encyclopedic work which would present the reader with a compendium of all that was new and noteworthy in human knowledge, but little of it was ever published. His most popular book, however, is *Mefasher Ḥelmin* (Salonika, 1515), often republished under its Hebrew title *Pitron Ḥalomot* ("Interpretation of Dreams"). In it he classifies dreams by categories and gives rules for their interpretation.

Alphabet of Ben Sira: An anonymous medieval text dated to anywhere between 700 and 1000 CE. Claiming falsely to have been written by the Second Temple author Ben Sira, this nonrabbinic book of legends is a compilation of two lists of proverbs, 22 in Aramaic and 22 in Hebrew, both arranged as alphabetic acrostics. Each proverb is followed by haggadic commentary.

am ha-aretz ("people of the land"): In Rabbinic Hebrew, a person without knowledge of *Torah; applied pejoratively to those who did not belong to the class of the *ḥakhamim*.

Amidah ("standing"): The main statutory prayer. In rabbinic usage it is often referred to simply as the Prayer (*Tefilla*), or as the Eighteen (Shemoneh Esreh), referring to the original number of benedictions. It is prescribed for recitation three times daily, in the evening (*Ma'ariv*), morning (*Shaharit*) and afternoon (*Minhah*), whether one is praying with a congregation or in private. The structure is more or less fixed, the main variations depending on the occasion: weekday, Sabbath or festival. The form of Amidah given in this book is for weekday services. In traditional and Orthodox prayer books the wording is now basically fixed (although considerable divergences are recorded well into the Middle Ages); however, the wording is varied slightly at different times of the year and in certain special circumstances. The other modernist movements, while retaining the traditional structure, have revised the wording to a greater or lesser extent, primarily to make the language more gender-inclusive and to accommodate some changes in current theological beliefs (such as bodily resurrection). In private devotion the prayer is said silently; in congregational worship it is said silently and then, in the morning and afternoon services, it is traditionally repeated aloud by the reader. The weekday Amidah now contains nineteen benedictions; their basic structure is as follows (the name of the benediction is given first, with its Hebrew form in brackets; the closing words [*hatima*], which function as titles of God and sum up the message of the benediction, follow): 1. Patriarchs (*avot*): Shield of Abraham. 2. Mighty deeds (*gevurot*): Reviver of the dead. 3. Holiness of the Name (*kedushat ha-Shem*): The holy God. 4. Knowledge (*da'at*): Gracious giver of knowledge. 5. Repentance (*teshuva*): He who desires repentance. 6. Forgiveness (*selicha*): Gracious one who abundantly pardons. 7. Redemption (*geulla*): Redeemer of Israel. 8. Healing (*refu'a*): Healer of the sick of his people Israel. 9. Blessing of the years (*Birkat ha-shanim*): He who blesses the years. 10. Ingathering of exiles (*kibbuts galuyot*): He who gathers in the scattered ones of his people Israel. 11. Restoration of justice (*hashavat ha-mishpat*): King who loves righteousness and justice. 12. Blessing of the heretics (*birkat ha-minim*): He who breaks foes and humbles the arrogant. 13. For the pious (*al ha-tsaddikim*): Trusted support of the righteous. 14. Rebuilding of Jerusalem (*binyan Yerushalaim*): Rebuilder of Jerusalem. 15. Messiah (*Mashiach ben David*): Who makes the horn of salvation to sprout. 16. Hearkening to prayer (*shome'a tefilla*): Hearkening to prayer. 17. Worship (*avodah*): Who restores his presence to Zion. 18. Thanksgiving (*hoda'a*): You whose name is Goodness, and to whom it is fitting to give thanks. 19. Peace (*shalom*): He who blesses his people Israel with peace. On Sabbath benedictions 4—16 are replaced by a single benediction that speaks of the sanctity of the Sabbath day, and concludes with the *hatima* "Who sanctifies the Sabbath."

Amora'im ("speakers"; from Aramaic "amora" with Hebrew plural ending): The rabbis of the third to fifth centuries CE in Israel and Babylonia who composed the two *Talmudim.

Amos: Biblical book, first of the Twelve Minor Prophets. The first of the biblical prophets to write, Amos was a shepherd from the Judaean town of Tekoa, southeast of Jerusalem. His career lasted from 783 to 743 BCE during a period of great prosperity, especially in the Northern Kingdom of Israel. Unlike other prophets of his time, he was not a professional prophet but was "taken away from following the flock" (7:15). God sends Amos to prophesy against the wealthy citizens of the North. The priest Amaziah puts him on trial for disturbing the public order and has him packed off to the backwoods of the Southern Kingdom, from which he came. In criticizing a sacrificial religion devoid of social justice, he—like many of the prophets who followed him—harks back to the desert period, when he imagined Israel did not worship God with sacrifices (the account in the *Torah suggests the opposite). The Book of Amos ends with a prophecy of regeneration. Even though the destruction of the Northern and Southern Kingdoms still lay in the future, Amos's prophesies of destruction and renewal set the stage for those later prophets who lived during these catastrophes.

Apocrypha ("things hidden away"): Apocryphal books are books of uncertain or disputed canonicity; they are to be "hidden away," that is, not read in public. The Apocrypha is the collection of Jewish books that are included in the Greek or Latin Old Testament of the church but not in the Hebrew *Tanakh of the Jews.

Ark: Receptacle for *Torah scrolls, the most prominent and distinctive feature of a synagogue. The English term ark is derived from the biblical account of the "ark of the covenant" (Exodus 37), in which the tablets of the covenant were kept, and which had the form of a chest or ark. The synagogue ark is generally located in such a way that a worshipper looking towards it is facing east or towards Jerusalem (in Jerusalem, towards the site of the Temple), which is the canonical direction for saying the *Amidah. One or more Torah scrolls are kept inside the ark, and the opening of the ark is a solemn moment in services at which the scroll is read. The congregation rises whenever the ark is opened, and remains standing as long as the ark stays open.

Ashkenazim: Jews originally from—or descendants of Jews from—northern France, Germany, and Eastern Europe. Before World War II, *Yiddish was the common language of the Eastern European Ashkenazim, and they maintained rituals, customs, liturgy, *synagogue architecture, methods of study, and pronunciation of Hebrew different from the *Sephardim.

Augustine (354 – 430): A Latin Father of the Church and perhaps the most significant Christian thinker after St. Paul. As a young man he was attracted to the ideas of Manichaeism, a dualistic doctrine of opposing good and evil powers promoted by the Persian prophet Mani (d.*c.* 276). Augustine met the Manichaean bishop Faustus in around 383 in Carthage, and later wrote *Contra Faustum Manichaeum* (*Against Faustus the Manichaean*), an extensive polemical tract in 33 books refuting Manichaeism. Faustus denied that the Hebrew prophets predicted Christ. In book 12, Augustine argued that the Hebrew scripture revealed "types" of Christ, and Cain typified the Jews as Abel typified Christ. Augustine insisted that the task of the Jews was to carry the books known to Christians as the Old Testament that would prove the truth of Christianity if they were read properly as prophecies of the coming of

Christ. Augustine also formulated the Church policy toward Jews that became authoritative for many centuries to come: The Jews fully deserved to be crushed and humiliated, because of their obstinacy in rejecting Jesus as their messiah. Yet they should not be completely destroyed; instead, they should be permitted to survive in a state of humiliating poverty and social exclusion so that they might be punished for their stubborn refusal to acknowledge the message of their own Scriptures and might serve as an everlasting testimony to the superiority of Christianity and the fate of the nonbeliever.

Avot ("fathers"): A tractate of the *Mishnah which, because of its exclusive focus on ethical and moral exhortations and its complete neglect of legal matters, is unlike any other tractate. Its opening two chapters are a chain of tradition depicting the transmission of the *Torah from God to Moses, and from Moses ultimately to the rabbis of the Mishnah. A sixth chapter is a later addition. The six Chapters of the Fathers (*Pirkei Avot*) included in the Prayerbook are recited on Saturday afternoons during the summer, one chapter each Sabbath. *Avot* is the most popular rabbinic composition of all times, inspiring hundreds of commentaries over the centuries. Sources: Goldin (1957); Neusner (1988).

Avot de-Rabbi Nathan (*"The Fathers according to Rabbi Nathan"*): A collection of elaborations and interpretation of biblical texts presented in the form of a commentary on the Mishnaic tractate *Avot*. The text is preserved in two versions, A and B. However, a recent study has shown that version A in fact survives in two principal branches which are quite distinct from each other. While the "origins" of this text may belong to the end of the Tannaitic period(late second century CE), the extant versions themselves can hardly be dated earlier than the sixth century CE at the very earliest. Source: version A by Goldin (1955).

Ba'al Shem Tov ("master of the good name," or "possessor of a good reputation"): Title under which Israel ben Eliezer (*c.* 1700 – 1760), the founder of *Hasidism, is usually known. (The shorter form Ba'al Shem and the acronym Besht are also widely used.) "Ba'al Shem," Master of the Name, is an old title given to wonder-workers who achieve magical results by their mastery of divine and angelic names, typically associated with amulets, spells and mystery cures. The Ba'al Shem Tov seems first to have acquired a reputation as such a wonder-worker in his native district of Podolia and in the neighboring regions of Volhynia and Galicia. Little is known for certain about his life, however; much that was written about him in his time and later belongs to the genre of hagiography (saints' lives), and invests him with supernatural powers. In 1740 he opened a school and attracted many followers to his teaching of a Judaism that distanced itself from the stultifying dryness (as he saw it) that characterized the Talmud study of his day and instead embraced joy, ecstatic prayer. His theology is based in large part on that of Isaac *Luria, which it reinterprets in significant ways. It is panentheistic; in other words God is present in all things. The Ba'al Shem Tov is said to have described how he once ascended to the hall of the Messiah, and asked him when he would come. The reply was that when the Ba'al Shem Tov's teachings were thoroughly spread in the world, then all the *kelipot* ("husks", *see* *Luria) trapping the divine sparks would be ended and the era of salvation would begin.

Bahya ibn Pakuda (flourished second half of the eleventh century): Spanish philosopher and moralist. Almost nothing is known of his life other than that he was a judge (*dayyan*). His *Book of Directions to the Duties of the Heart* (*Sefer Hovot ha-Levavot*), composed in Judeo-Arabic, has come to be seen as a classic of Jewish thought. The title of the work is derived from the contrast between the outward observance of the various practical commandments, the "duties of the limbs," and the inward, spiritual "duties of the heart." Bahya warns against attending to the former to the neglect of the latter. This scheme is not original—it is derived from the works of Muslim mystics and Bahya's ideas are deeply indebted to Arab Neoplatonism—but it represents a new departure in the Jewish tradition, and the book achieved enormous popularity, being translated into Hebrew in the twelfth century. He advocates asceticism—the negation of material pleasures—as a great virtue, something that one finds only episodically in *Talmudic literature. In fact, many of the stories, anecdotes and epigrams that he included in his work can be traced to writings of Muslim ascetics and mystics, mainly Sufis. Source: Biale and Miles (2015).

baraita (pl. **baraitot**; Hebrew, "external" or "outside"): Traditions and teachings of the *tanna'im, not embodied in the *Mishnah but often quoted in the *Gemara or found in *Tosefta.

Bialik, Hayim Nahman(1873 - 1934): The poet laureate of modern Hebrew. Born to an Orthodox family and educated at a famous yeshiva, he had full command of the entire Hebrew register of learning. After moving to Odessa in 1891, he broke with traditional Judaism, and he devoted himself to the creation of a national, secular Jewish culture. His attitude to traditional Judaism, however, was ambivalent. On the one hand, he was angered at what he felt to be the moribund state of traditional Jewish society; on the other hand, he was painfully aware of the dilemma of modern Jews whose struggle for the right to determine their own destiny seemed to require a desperate rejection of divine law. The cultural renaissance sponsored by Zionism and the revival of Hebrew as the national idiom of the Jewish people, he insisted, cannot thrive without taking root in the spiritual treasures of Israel's past. He increasingly espoused the concept of what he called *kinus*, or ingathering and extension of the great works of the (traditional) Jewish past into the (secular) Jewish present. Bialik exemplified his conception of *kinus* when in 1908 he began to publish (together with editor Y. H. Ravnitzky) *Sefer Ha-Aggadah*, a collection of legends and imaginative homiletic literature drawn from the *Midrash and *Talmud. This monumental project, which underwent numerous editions, served as a wellspring of modern Hebrew literature. In 1924, he settled in Tel Aviv, where he lived for the rest of his life. Sources: Bialik and Ravnitzky (1992); Cole (2012).

Cairo Geniza: The Jews considered it sacrilegious to destroy any document in which the name of God appeared, lest the name itself be mutilated. Because references to God were common even in writings not dealing directly with religious matters, the practice of storing old writings rather than destroying them was extended to anything written in Hebrew letters and created a disinclination to discard any written material at all. Consequently the custom grew up of burying them in a cemetery. While awaiting burial they were often stored in a specially designated room or container in the synagogue, known as the *geniza* ("hiding away"). The grave in which they are buried is also marked with the same word.

The Cairo Geniza is the name given to the manuscripts and printed papers, mostly very damaged, that were recovered from an old synagogue in Fustat (Old Cairo) towards the end of the nineteenth-century. The majority were removed to Cambridge University; others are found in various European and American libraries and in private collections. They number some 200,000 pieces, some over 1,000 years old, and together constitute the largest and most important haul of Jewish manuscripts ever discovered. Many of the manuscripts are documents (letters, legal deeds, etc.), that enable the everyday life of medieval communities and individuals to be reconstructed in extraordinary detail; others are long-lost literary works.

Carlebach, Shlomo (1925 – 1994): A key figure in an observed revival of the values and ethos of *Hasidism in American Jewry. In the 1960s, Rabbi Shlomo Carlebach became a renowned writer and singer of religious music and a pioneer in his approach to the modern *baal teshuvah* ("returnee") movement, encouraging Jews to reembrace their heritage and follow more observant religious practices. His influence persists through his teachings and the so-called Carlebach-style services that include much singing and dancing.

Dead Sea Scrolls: Collection of ancient manuscripts which were discovered in 1947 by an Arab shepherd looking for a lost sheep. The bulk of the scrolls are thought to represent the library of a Jewish sect at Qumran which was situated close to the Dead Sea. They were hidden in nearby caves for safekeeping when the Qumran settlement was destroyed by the Romans in 70 CE, towards the end of the Jewish revolt against Roman rule in Palestine. The texts were preserved by the dry climate of the area, and some of them date back to the second century BCE. Many of the works found were previously unknown, being sectarian writings, although all the books of the Hebrew Bible except the Book of Esther are represented in whole or in part. The scrolls depict the Qumran sect as a righteous community of people of light and those outside as wicked people of darkness who are to be hated and avoided. The Community Rule (1QS) was among the first seven Dead Sea Scrolls discovered in Qumran Cave 1 in 1947. (Additional fragmentary copies of the work were found in Qumran Caves 4 and 5.) The Rule is a collection of rules and ideals for life within a distinct sectarian community, which consist of the community's application of biblical law (e. g., purity laws) and regulations particular to the sectarian way of life (e. g., initiation rites, communal property). The Rule further outlines many of the central theological and ideological bases of the sectarian community. Sources: Vermes (2004); Jassen (2013).

Decalogue (Greek, "ten words"; in Hebrew "*aseret ha-devarim*"): Precepts revealed by God to Moses and engraved on two tablets of stone, also known as the Ten Commandments. The text is preserved twice in the Bible, with different wording (Exodus 20:1 – 17, Deuteronomy 5:6 – 21), particularly with regard to the *Sabbath. The expression "Ten Commandments" is not found in the Bible, but we do find the phrase "ten words" (Exodus 34:28), applied to a different list (see also Deuteronomy 10:4). The Decalogue does not appear in the liturgy to avoid the heretical belief that only the Ten Commandments were of divine origin and that the other parts of the *torah did not come from God.

Duran, Simeon ben Zemah (1361 – 1444): Rabbinic authority known by the acronym Rashbats. He studied in his native Majorca and in Aragon, Spain. Source: Goldin (1957).

Eber, Irene (1930 – 2019): Holocaust survivor, Sinologist, and scholar on Jews in the Far East. Born in Germany, then expelled to her father's hometown of Mielec, Poland, then hidden in a chicken coop for almost two years in Nazi-occupied Poland, she eventually self-fashioned out of this traumatic past and metamorphosed herself into one of the founders of Sinology in Israel, teaching at the Hebrew University of Jerusalem for many years. In 1980, at the age of fifty, Eber returned to Mielec. Her journey back would unleash a life's worth of memories, and the result is her autobiography *The Choice*. Source: Eber (2004).

Ein Sof (Hebrew, "The Infinite"): In the *Kabbalah, the name given to God in his purest essence—that is, God as a "no thing."

Eleazar of Worms (*c.* 1176 – 1238): A leading figure of the so-called German pietism (*Hasidut Ashkenaz*). These German pietists (*Hasidei Ashkenazi*) believed in a piety beyond the letter of the law, which they called *din shamayim* ("the heavenly law"). This heavenly law was characterized by strong asceticism and altruism, as well as elaborate rituals of punishment that strongly resembled the Christian penitential practices of the same age. It must be emphasized that very little of this teaching is explicitly prescribed by *Talmudic literature. The cause as well as the result of these practices was an intense fear of God, considered the highest religious value by members of the *Hasidei Ashkenaz*. Source: Biale and Miles (2015).

gaon (pl. **geonim**; Hebrew, "pride" or "eminence"): Title of the heads of the Babylonian academies in the post-Talmudic period (roughly 750 – 1150 CE). This period of Jewish religious history has come to be known as the geonic period; it was the time in which the teachings of the Babylonian *Talmud began to be developed and codified and to be spread around the Jewish world, reaching as far as Spain. In modern times the title has sometimes been applied to outstanding scholars.

Gemara: *See* *Talmud.

Genesis Rabbah : *See* *Midrash. Source: Freedman and Simon (1939).

Gilboa, Amir (1917 – 1984): Ukraine-born Israeli poet. He came to Palestine in 1937 as an illegal immigrant, and fought in World War II in the Jewish Brigade of the British Army (1942) and later in Israel's Independence War. His work combines traditional elements with colloquial usages, and personal with national motifs. In "Isaac," he adapts the biblical story of the binding of Isaac to understand the martyrdom of Jews in his own day. Gilboa transported Abraham and Isaac from the land of Israel to the forests of Europe. But now it is not Isaac who faces sacrifice, but Abraham, reflecting the experience of Gilboa's generation, who had abandoned their parents in Nazi Europe while they survived in Palestine, the prestate name for Israel. Source: Carmi (1981).

Ginzberg, Louis (1873 – 1953): Talmudic and rabbinic scholar. Born in Kovno, Lithuania, Ginzberg attended the Lithuanian *yeshivot of Slobodka and Tels, then studied at the universities of Berlin, Strasbourg, and Heidelberg. In 1899 he immigrated to the United States, where he became an editor of the rabbinic section of the *Jewish Encyclopedia* in 1900. From 1903 to 1952, he taught *Talmud at the Jewish Theological Seminary of America in New York. The major thrust of Ginzberg's scholarship focused on the origins of *aggadah*, *halakhah*, and *geonic literature. His introductions, commentaries, and extended analyses of various texts opened scholarly and popular access to many basic works. In his *The Legends of the Jews* (7 vols. 1909 – 1938), Ginzberg analyzed the origin and development of the legend in *Midrashic literature by interweaving rabbinic, Hellenistic, early Christian, *kabbalistic, and other textual sources. Not only was it an attempt to collect all Jewish legends, it also became the first comprehensive and critical attempt to analyze the legends and trace their development and place in both Jewish tradition and world folklore. What impelled Ginzberg's work was a conception of Aggadah as the folk literature of the Jewish people. Ginzberg's *Legends,* thus, had a dual purpose—first, to present to an American audience the wealth of Jewish legends in a readable, interesting form; and second, to use this occasion as a pretext to collect legends from every conceivable source and to analyze and trace their parallels, influences, and sources. To this day *Legends of the Jews* remains the single indispensable reference work on Aggadah. It is still the first book to which a student or scholar turns to learn the main lines of the postbiblical understanding of a biblical episode and its sources. Source: Ginzberg (2003).

Gordis, Robert (1908 – 1992): American Jewish scholar and rabbi who taught for over half a century at the Jewish Theological Seminary of America as Professor of Bible. He also held leading positions within the Conservative movement and composed many of its most important *responsa.

Gouri, Hayyim (b. 1923): Israeli poet and journalist. Born in Tel Aviv, he served in the Palmach, was sent on various missions by the Haganah to the displaced persons' camps in Europe, and later saw active service in the Israeli forces during the War of Independence and succeeding campaigns. His poetry often reflects the volatile moods of the country. Source: Carmi (1981).

Haggadah (pl. **Haggadot**; Hebrew, "telling"): The text that is used to conduct the *Passover *seder.* The commandment to "tell" the exodus from Egypt is found in Exodus 13:8, and the core of the Haggadah consists of rabbinic elaborations on the biblical exodus story. This part of the ritual goes back to early rabbinic times; other elements were added gradually, and early medieval Haggadot, recovered from the *Cairo Geniza, display a good deal of diversity. Today's printed Haggadot are more or less standardized, but there is a new trend to revise the text to suit the needs of different groups, such as

Reform and Reconstructionist Jews, feminists or secular kibbutzim. Since every home has to have at least one copy, and some boast many, the Haggadah is one of Judaism's most popular books. Large numbers of manuscripts exist, some of them lavishly illustrated—it has been one of the fields where traditionally Jewish artists have been allowed to exercise their skills. It is estimated that well over 5,000 different editions of the Haggadah have been printed to date.

Hai Gaon (or Hai ben Sherira, 939 – 1038): Last outstanding Babylonian *gaon of a great Talmudic academy, remembered for the range and profundity of the exceptionally large number of *responsa he wrote.

hakham (pl. *hakhamim*; Hebrew, "wise men"): Sage, learned person, scholar of the Torah. *Talmid hakham* ("student [disciple] of a sage") usually designates a scholar; also, the learned class, opposite of *'am ha-aretz.*

halakhah (pl. *halakhot*; Hebrew, "way" or "path"): An accepted decision in rabbinic law. Also refers to those parts of the *Talmud concerned with legal matters. In contradistinction to *aggadah.*

halakhic midrashim: A group of individual rabbinic texts that interpret different books of the Pentateuch. The name reflects the fact that these books deal largely, though by no means exclusively, with matters of *halakhah,* the interpretation and application of biblical laws. Apparently because of their concern with *halakhah*, these texts were compiled exclusively on the biblical books of Exodus, Leviticus, Numbers, and Deuteronomy; Genesis, because it contains little of an overtly legal character, was not included in the scope of the *halakhic midrashim.* The best known are the *Mekhilta de R. Ishmael* and *Mekhilta de R. Shimon b. Yohai* (both on Exodus), *Sifra* (on Leviticus), *Sifrei* (on Numbers and Deuteronomy). With regard to date, since the rabbis cited in them are generally *tanna'im* along with some first-generation *amora'im*, the *halakhic midrashim* are generally assumed to have been compiled sometime in the third century CE. If this dating is correct, the *halakhic midrashim* represent, after the *Mishnah, *Tosefta, and perhaps one or two other texts, the earliest stage of rabbinic writings. Unlike the Mishnah, however, they underline the relationship between scripture and *halakhah*, that is, between written Torah and oral Torah.

haredim (Hebrew, "fearful"): The most conservative and observant among Orthodox Jews. The term derives from the Biblical verb *hared* which appears in Isaiah 66:2; its plural *haredim* appears in Isaiah 66:5 and is translated as "[one who] trembles" at the word of God. The word connotes an awe-inspired fear and anxiety to perform the will of God. Haredim affect a distinctive style of dress: the men wear beards and sidelocks and black coats and hats, while married women have shaved heads, covered by a wig or headscarf, and wear modest clothing that hides most of their bodies. Haredim in Israel are increasingly violent in their hostility to modernizing trends, and particularly to secular Zionism.

hasid (pl. **hasidim**; Hebrew, "pious"): The term designates members of pietistic groups, notably during the Second Commonwealth and in thirteenth century Germany. More recently, it designates members of the movement known as *Hasidism, founded by Israel *Ba'al Shem Tov (Besht) at the end of the eighteenth century in Eastern Europe.

Hasidism: Revivalist movement, based on the teachings of *Ba'al Shem Tov, which began under the leadership of Dov Baer of Mezhirech in the mid-eighteenth century in Poland. Hasidism addressed itself to those Jews who were left spiritually and physically impoverished by the Chmielnicki Massacres (1648 – 1649). In place of scholarly elitism, the Ba'al Shem Tov's followers put forward an interpretation of *Kabbalah which taught that God was to be found in all aspects of life, since the world existed within Him, and He could be served through everyday activities. This mystical panentheism attracted scholars to the movement and also appealed to the mass of uneducated Jews. People were encouraged to cleave to God and experience Him in ecstatic joy through song, dance and even the use of tobacco and alcohol. At the center of each Hasidic community was a charismatic leader, the Tzaddik, who was believed to work miracles and act as a channel for divine energy (*ruah ha-kodesh*) to flow into the world. *Hasidim sought the tzaddik's blessings for all their undertakings and told stories about his wonderful deeds. They set up their own autonomous synagogues, created a new liturgy based on the *Lurianic rite, introduced changes in ritual, neglected the set times for prayers because prayer had to be a matter of inner feeling, and adopted specific modes of dress. The opponents of the new movement, known as Mitnaggedim("opponents"), charged them with being innovators, destroyers of tradition, and dangerous revolutionaries. They burnt their books, pronounced a ban against them and had some of their leaders imprisoned. As Hasidism spread, however, it ceased to be a religion of protest and came closer to institutionalized Orthodoxy. Today it is a major conservative force in opposing the encroachments of modernity on traditional Jewish life. Hasidism is now divided into a number of separate and often conflicting groups, based mainly in the United States (Satmar, Lubavitch, Bobov) and Israel (Belz, Bratslav, Ger, Vizhnitz).

Havdalah (Hebrew, "separation"): A prayer recited at the end of the *Sabbath and festivals to indicate the distinction between the sacred day that has ended and the weekday that is beginning. Havdalah corresponds to *Kiddush, which proclaims the sanctity of the Sabbath day at its beginning.

Heschel, Abraham Joshua (1907 – 1972): Religious philosopher. Scion of a Hasidic dynasty in Poland, he studied philosophy in Berlin, escaped the Nazis and immigrated to America, where he ended up professor of Jewish ethics and mysticism at the Jewish Theological Seminary in New York. His theology was based on his interpretation of Hasidic spirituality in light of modernity, and he also became a passionate advocate for applying the prophets' call for social justice to contemporary problems. *The Sabbath* (1951), excerpted in this book, takes a step backward from the myriad Sabbath laws to meditate on the broader spiritual meaning of this weekly holiday. Heschel concludes that Judaism is about the sanctification of time rather than place. Source: Heschel (1951).

Ibn Gabirol, Solomon (1021 or 1022 –c. 1070): Hebrew poet and philosopher in Muslim Spain. Solomon Ibn Gabirol comes down to us as one of the most complicated intellectual figures in the history of post-biblical Hebrew literature. Unlike his worldly predecessor *Shmuel Hanagid, the first important poet of the period, Ibn Gabirol was a reclusive, mystically inclined writer whose modern-sounding medieval poems range from sublime descriptions of the heavenly spheres to poisonous jabs at court life and its pretenders. His major philosophical work, *The Fountain of Life*, which later came to exercise an important influence on Christian scholastic thought, is a work of pure metaphysics, divorced from any particular religious context.

Josephus, Flavius (*c.* 37 –*c.* 100): Historian and apologist. Born of a priestly family in Jerusalem, Josephus was, by his own account, a gifted student who acquired a broad exposure to the different Jewish schools of thought existent in his own time. He served as a general in the great Jewish revolt against the Romans but was defeated and taken prisoner. After the war Josephus moved to Rome, where he wrote, mainly in Greek, about Judaism arguing for the spiritual value and practical utility of the Jewish religion and its ethical superiority to Hellenism. The first four books of his multivolume *Jewish Antiquities* retell the events of the *Pentateuch with frequent additions and modifications that reflect the biblical interpretations he learned in his youth; they are a rich source of information about ancient exegesis. Josephus' approach, however, is that of a Hellenistic writer who, never forgetting his audience, adapts his writing to their taste. In addition, he wrote a lengthy account of the Jewish revolt against Rome (*The Jewish War*), a brief autobiography (*Life*), and a defense of Judaism against various detractors (*Against Apion*). Sources: Josephus in Loeb Classical Library; Feldman (2013).

Judah Halevi (1075–1141): Hebrew poet and religious thinker. Born in Spain, where he spent most of his life, Judah died in the Land of Israel. Passionate yearning for Zion (an unusual subject for Hebrew poetry at the time) is a major theme in his verse. His religious poetry is sublime, and several of his creations have earned a place in the liturgy. Besides his abundant corpus of poetry, Judah is also the author of an Arabic prose work, commonly known *The Khazar* (the full title is *The Book of the Khazar: A Book of Argument and Demonstration in Defense of the Despised Faith*; it is sometimes referred to by its Hebrew title, *Kuzari*). It is an account of Judaism, setting out its merits in comparison to Christianity and Islam and to Aristotelian philosophy, and insisting on national experience and the continuity of Jewish tradition as outweighing the dogmatic claims of the other contenders. "My Heart is in the East" is one of the most famous poems in all of Hebrew literature, and its theme and lyric concision have spoken to Jews throughout the Diaspora for centuries. Source: Cole (2007).

Kabbalah (Hebrew, "received tradition"): A Jewish mystical theology, systematized in southern France and in Spain in the twelfth through the thirteenth century, whose aim is to uncover the *Torah's secrets, thereby providing a direct connection to God and an understanding of his relationship to his creation. This connection may be established by uniting the *sefirot*—that is, emanations from the *Ein Sof* (Godhead).

Kaddish (Aramaic, "sanctification"): Aramaic prayer that begins "Glorified and sanctified be God's great name throughout the world which he has created according to his will." The word *Kaddish* is the second word of this sentence. Its main themes are praise of God and prayer for the coming of his kingdom. It is recited traditionally at the end of each section of every service and on some other occasions. There are five forms of the

Kaddish: the short or "half Kaddish (or *Kaddish le'ela*), which punctuates the service at certain fixed points; the full Kaddish (*Kaddish titkabbal*), said after major sections of the service; the rabbis' Kaddish (*Kaddish de-rabbanan*), said after the recitation or study of a passage of rabbinical literature; the mourner's Kaddish (*Kaddish yehe shelama*); and the great Kaddish (*Kaddish de-etchadita*), said at a funeral or on concluding the study of Talmudic tractate. The wording has been varied in some modern liturgies. Although is commonly considered a mourner's prayer, the Kaddish contains no mention of death or of grief, but is a glorification of God and a prayer for the coming of his reign on earth. The recitation of this prayer by mourners, both at the cemetery and subsequently, represents an act of submission to the divine will, and is popularly thought to bring merit to the soul of the departed. Source: Birnbaum (1977).

Kafka, Franz (1883 – 1924): Czech-born German-Jewish novelist. Although estranged from the bourgeois Judaism of his father, Kafka identified positively with Judaism, shown by his interest in secular Jewish culture and Zionism, which provided a counter-Jewish identity for many middle class Jewish youths of his day. Kafka wrote this autobiographical letter to his father in 1919, which he never actually sent, at the age of thirty-six. Source: Mendes-Flohr and Reinharz (2011).

Kiddush (Hebrew, "sanctification): A prayer recited over wine at the beginning of *Sabbath or a festival to sanctify the holy day. Wine is the symbol of joy, for it is "wine that cheers man's heart" (Psalm 104:15). The use of wine in connection with the Kiddush is spoken of in the *Talmud, where the biblical command "remember the Sabbath" is interpreted to mean "remember it over wine" (Pesahim 106a). When the wine is not available, the Kiddush is pronounced over two loaves of bread which are in memory of the double portion of manna that was gathered on Fridays (Exodus 16:22).

Lekhah Dodi ("Come, My Beloved"): One of the best known Jewish religious poems. Written by the Safed kabbalist Rabbi Solomon Alkabetz (1505 –c. 1576), this poem became a favorite text of synagogal composers; a great number of melodies were set to it. Alkabetz belonged to a mystic brotherhood that had the custom of going out into the fields dressed in white towards sunset each Friday to greet the *Sabbath, which they identified with the *Shekhinah. Each stanza consists of four parts, three of which have the same rhyme, while the fourth part ends in a common rhyme throughout the poem. Stanzas one, two, and nine deal with the value of the Sabbath and stanzas three through eight with Jerusalem and redemption. Much of the poem is a poetic expression of Israel's Messianic hope. Borrowing and slightly adapting a number of phrases and images from the Bible, Alkabetz wove them together into an essentially new creation expressing the millennial hope that Jerusalem, too long a dweller in the valley of tears, will soon rise from the dust and be magnificently rebuilt. The agent of the redemption is, of course, to be the Messiah, referred to in the fourth stanza as "the Bethlehemite" and in the eighth as "a descendant of Perez." The Sabbath is personified here and compared to a bride, in the same sense as Israel is likened to a bride (Jeremiah 2:2). The poem is sung in the Friday evening service of welcoming the Sabbath; as the last stanza is sung, congregants turn towards the entrance of the synagogue (west) and bow to greet the Sabbath. A motive for this practice is that the Shekhinah that accompanies the Sabbath is in the west. Turning to the door also has its origin in King Solomon's innovation of making two gates in the Temple, one for bridegrooms and the other for mourners to enter. The purpose was to alert the people with whom to rejoice or whom to comfort. After the destruction of the Temple, the sages transferred this custom into synagogue.

Leviticus Rabbah: See *Midrash.

Luria, Isaac (1534 – 1572): Kabbalist, also known as the Ari ("lion," and an acronym of "the divine Rabbi Isaac"). Born in Jerusalem and brought up in Egypt, he settled in Safed in 1570 and died there in an epidemic two years later. Little is known for certain about the last two years of his life, which had a truly revolutionary effect on Jewish mystical theology. Luria left little in his own hands, but his disciples wrote down and published his teachings. The best known of these is the *Etz Hayyim* ("Tree of Life") of Hayyim Vital (1543 – 1629). Living as he did in the century following the epoch-making event of the completion of the Christian reconquest of Spain, when many Jews had been forced to become Christians and many others had become exiles, Luria was deeply troubled by the urgent need for messianic redemption. Luria and his disciples did not claim to depart from the *sefirotic system of the *Zohar, but they gave it a new vocabulary and a new theological framework.

Lurianic Kabbalah provides a myth of creation. Like the big bang theory of modern physics, Luria's cosmos began when God withdrew himself (*tzimtzum*) away from a central point within himself, creating an empty space (*halal ha-panui*). This empty Space was necessary for the creation of the world because God could not create something other than himself within himself. God then emanated light into the empty space, which arranged itself in vessels (*kelim*) that then received additional divine light. But the vessels contained defects, the "roots of stern judgment" (*shorshei ha-dinim*), that prevented the vessels from holding the light. Then, in a divine catastrophe, the vessels shattered (*shevirat ha-kelim*), and the light was scattered throughout the empty space in the form of sparks (*nitzotzot*). These sparks were trapped in the shards of the vessels, called *kelipot* ("husks"), which became the basis for the material world. In an effort to rescue these sparks, God radiates new light, forming the *sefirot*, which Luria called "faces" (*partzufim*). Man's role is to redeem the scattered sparks, a process called *tikkun* ("repairing" or "restoring"). Restoring the sparks requires not only performance of the commandments; one also has to do so with special formulas or meditations, called *kavvanot* (literally, "intentions"). According to Luria, the messianic age will come when all the sparks have been restored to God and the divine harmony returned to its primordial state. Although focused heavily on the process of creation, Lurianic Kabbalah has a strong messianic flavor that reflected the eschatological atmosphere in sixteenth century Safed.

Maccabees: Name of four books that are not found in the Hebrew Bible but have been preserved in Greek in Christian tradition. All were written by Jews. 2 Maccabees is essentially a greatly abridged (and somewhat garbled) version of a now lost history of the Maccabean revolt written by a certain "Jason of Cyrene" (otherwise unknown); this abridgement was probably completed in the first half of the first century BCE. Source: Suggs, Sakenfeld and Mueller (1992).

Mahzor Vitry: A liturgical work compiled by Rabbi Simhah of Vitry, France, a pupil of *Rashi. It contains the prayer texts, many *piyyutim* (liturgical poems) and *zemiroth* (table songs) for Sabbaths and festivals, as well as *Pirkei *Avot* and several Talmudic selections concerning religious behavior. It is of fundamental importance for the history of Jewish liturgy. Source: Goldin (1957).

Maimon, Solomon (*c.* 1753 – 1800): Philosopher. Born in Sukoviboeg, Poland, he received a traditional Talmudic education. In search of secular learning, Maimon abandoned his family and rabbinic office, and went to Germany, where he gradually acquired a profound knowledge of German culture and philosophy. Kant noted that of all His critics nobody understood his work as well as Maimon. Deeply impressed and influenced throughout his life by the strict rationalism of *Maimonides (whose name he borrowed as his own surname), Maimon devoted much of his writing to engaging with earlier Jewish thinkers, including Baruch Spinoza (1632 – 1677). In his autobiography (*Lebengeschichte*), published in German in 1793, Maimon describes his estrangement from traditional Judaism. Although he presents it as process immanent to his experience of Judaism, his estrangement undoubtedly gained articulation and self-consciousness from his contact with non-Jewish culture. His autobiography was widely read throughout the nineteenth and twentieth centuries by German intellectuals—non-Jewish and Jewish—who derived their concepts of traditional Judaism from it. Source: Maimon (1888).

Maimonides, Moses (*c.* 1138 – 1204): Rabbi, codifier, philosopher, and physician; the most prominent Jewish thinker in the post-Talmudic era, also known by the acronym Rambam (Rabbi Moses ben Maimon). Born in Cordoba, Maimonides wandered with his family through North Africa; they settled in Cairo, where he later headed the Jewish community. Maimonides' first important work was his Arabic *Commentary on the Mishnah* (1168), in which he attempts to define the fundamental beliefs of Judaism—those teachings to which a Jew must assent if he is to have a share in the world to come. The 13 fundamental principles of the Jewish faith set out by him are arguably the nearest Judaism has ever come to a formal creed, or "dogma." However, although these principles were very influential they were never really accepted as a practical criterion of orthodoxy. *Eight Chapters* is part of Maimonides' *Commentary on the Mishnah.* No tractate of the *Mishnah deals with ethics as such. In order to give a coherent account of this subject, Maimonides wrote a long Introduction to *Pirkei *Avot*, a special treatise in his view on the therapy of the soul that shows the way to perfection and happiness. This Introduction, a self-contained unit with surprisingly few quotations from *Avot*, has come to be known as *Eight Chapters.* His greatest achievements, however, were the halakhic code of law, *Mishneh Torah* (1178), and the philosophical treatise *The Guide of the Perplexed* (1190). The *Mishneh Torah* ("Repetition of the Law"), written in Hebrew, systematically organizes the whole of Jewish law. The *Guide*, written in Arabic, was designed for readers whose faith had been undermined by philosophical criticism. The book aimed to harmonize philosophy and Judaism, thus enabling a renewed, but also a refined, religious faith. Although his philosophical views were the subject of fierce opposition, his influence on the development of Judaism was enormous. Sources:

Maimonides (1963); Twersky (1972); Weiss and Butterworth (1975).

Malkin, Yaakov (b.1926): Israeli educator, professor of aesthetics and rhetoric at the University of Tel Aviv. He founded in Jerusalem a College of Pluralistic Judaism to promote dialogue between secular and Orthodox Jews. In a booklet sponsored by the College, Malkin outlines for the broader public his "credo." In this selection, he presents the beliefs of secular—"free"—Jews. Source: Neusner and Avery-Peck (2001).

Meiri, Menahem ben Solomon (1249 –c. 1316): Talmudist from Perpignan, in southern France. He is mainly remembered as the author of commentaries on the tractates of the Talmud. As a Talmudic commentator with a strongly rationalistic turn of mind he is held by many to be second only to *Rashi. His introduction to *Avot* contains a significant essay tracing the chain of tradition from Moses to his own day. Source: Goldin (1957).

Mekhilta ("treatise"): *See *halakhic midrashim*.

Micah: Biblical book, sixth of the Twelve Minor Prophets. Micah seems to have lived in the 8th century BCE. His prophecy begins with a condemnation of political, social and religious abuses that if continued will bring about the downfall of the two states of Samaria and Judah, and continues with a vision of universal peace, with Jerusalem as the capital, under a ruler from Bethlehem.

Midrash (pl. **Midrashim**; Hebrew, "interpretation" or "exegesis"): A body of work that complied, mainly in the Land of Israel, between the third and eleventh centuries CE, preserving excerpts from sermons, and lectures and other comments on the words of Scripture, which are woven together into something resembling a commentary. The word "midrash" is derived from the verb root *derash* ("inquiry"), which denotes searching out and discovering other meanings and information from *Scripture. In the sixteenth century the so-called Midrash Rabbah was published, presenting originally independent Midrashim on each of the five books of the Torah as well as the five *megillot* ("scrolls")—the Song of Songs, Ruth, Esther, Ecclesiastes, and Lamentations. Thus these ten Midrashim have acquired a kind of canonical status. Each volume is identified by the name of the corresponding book from the Bible, followed by the word *Rabbah* (Hebrew, "great"). As a series, these works were edited and redacted between the fifth and tenth centuries CE. Final touches to *Numbers Rabbah* and *Esther Rabbah* were made as late as the thirteenth century. *Genesis Rabbah* is the oldest (425 CE) of the series. Source: Freedman and Simon (1939).

Mishnah ("repetition"): An anthology of legal statements on various topics produced by the rabbis of the second century CE and edited by Rabbi Judah the Patriarch. It is the text around which both *Talmudim are organized. The subject matter of the Mishnah is arranged under six major headings called orders (*sedarim*), which in turn are subdivided into sixty-three tractates (*massehtot*). Each tractate is divided into chapters (*perakim*), and each of these is divided in turn into smaller units to which the same term *mishnah* is applied. Thus Mishnah Shabbat 6:4 refers to the Mishnah, tractate Shabbat ("the Sabbath"), chapter 6, paragraph 4. The first order, "Seeds" (*Zera'im*), is mainly concerned with agricultural laws, but it opens with a tractate devoted to prayers and blessings. Next comes "Set Feasts" (*Mo'ed*), that is the regulations for Sabbaths, festivals and other special days. The third order, "Women" (*Nashim*), contains tractates on marriage, divorce and other aspects of personal status. "Damages" (*Nezikin*), the fourth order, is concerned with the civil and criminal law, while the remaining orders, "Holy Things" (*Kodashim*) and "Purities" (*Toharot*), deal respectively with temple sacrifices and the rules of ritual impurity. These headings serve to define the interests of the *Halakhah in early rabbinic Judaism. The rabbis whose opinions are cited in the Mishnah are known as *Tanna'im. The Mishnah appears more interested in studying the *halakhah* than in determining actual practice. It records innumerable disagreements without resolving them; it prefers representative case rather than general principles of law; it discusses some laws that seem not to be of practical application. While there are many discussions of laws in the Torah the main focus is not directly on the Torah itself but on teaching, established practice, precedent and custom. The Mishnah is written in a type of Hebrew that is different from that of the Bible and presents many signs of Greek influence, including numerous Greek words. Source: Neusner (1988).

mitzvah (pl. **_mitzvot_**): Commandment, precept, law, religious duty, sometimes also obligation. The term usually refers to the precepts of the written Torah, yet there are specific instances in which it is used for rabbinically ordained rituals.

Molodowsky, Kadya (1894–1975): Modern *Yiddish poet. She participated in nearly every aspect of Yiddish literary culture that existed in her lifetime, first in Poland, where she lived until 1935, when she emigrated, and then in America. Before her emigration, she taught young children in the Yiddish schools of Warsaw. In New York, she supported herself by writing for the Yiddish press and founded a literary journal, _Svive_ ("Surroundings"), which she edited for nearly thirty years. Briefly during the early 1950s, Molodowsky wrote and edited Yiddish publications in the new state of Israel. She returned there in 1971 to receive the Itzik Manger Prize, the most prestigious award in Yiddish letters. Her poetry was influenced not only by the Russian symbolists and Yiddish modernists, but also by traditional sources such as the Bible and the _tekhines_, the women's prayers in Yiddish. Source: Molodowsky (1999).

Nahmanides, Moses (1194–1270): Scholar and communal leader. Also known as Moses ben Nahman, Ramban(an acronym). He was born and lived in Girona, Spain, and had close connections with Barcelona, where he took part in an important disputation with a representative of Christianity. In

1267 he settled in the Land of Israel, where he died. Nahmanides' Commentary to the *Pentateuch is one of the most popular commentaries. It was also the first Biblical Commentary to use the teachings of the *Kabbalah. His interpretation on Genesis 1:26 is that God calls, as it were, on all that He had made to participate with Him in creating man, hence the plural is used. Man is the apex of creation. In his person there is united the properties of all things on earth and all beings in heaven. He has a body created out of dust but he also has a soul which spurs him on to acquire wisdom and perfection. Source: Jacobs (1973).

Neusner, Jacob (1932 – 2016): American academic scholar of Judaism. His statement in this book, written as a kind of "generational statement," vividly captures the emotional force of the Holocaust and Israel as symbolic realities for those American Jews born after 1930. The close historical coincidence of the destruction of European Jewry and the creation of the State of Israel has had a powerful symbolic resonance among contemporary Jews.

Or Ha-Me'ir ("The Burning Light"): A major homiletical work on the weekly Torah lections by Rabbi Ze'ev Wolf of Zhitomir, one of the foremost disciples of Rabbi Dov Baer, the Maggid ("Preacher") of Mezhirech, who is a chief disciple of *Ba'al Shem Tov. First printed in 1798, shortly after the author's death, the book, which provides an original view of the religious and theological ideas that characterized the movement of *Hasidism in its early stages, became one of the basic Hasidic texts.

Pagis, Dan (1930 – 1986): Israeli poet, born in Bukovina of German-speaking parents. He spent some of his early years in a Nazi concentration camp in the Ukraine, from which he escaped before the end of the war. He then settled in Palestine where he learnt Hebrew and ended up the foremost authority on the poetics of Hebrew literature in the High Middle Ages and the Renaissance. Though originally German-speaking, he deliberately cultivated modern Hebrew as his only poetic language. His references to the Holocaust are sometimes oblique and filtered through his use of biblical images and imaginary conversation with a ghost of himself who has erroneously survived. Source: Pagis (1981).

pardes (Persian, "paradise" or "orchard"): (1) In the *Talmud (Hagiga 14b) and *Tosefta (Hagiga 2:3 – 4), refers to four second-century rabbis who entered the *pardes*, presumably the realm of heavenly secrets. One interpretation of this text is that the four rabbis were in search of mystical knowledge in the form of a journey through the heavenly palaces. (2) An acronym made up from the four consonants of the word (*P-R-D-S*) and used as a mnemonic for the four categories of biblical interpretation: *Peshat*, literal meaning; *Remez*, allegorical meaning; *Drash*, midrashic meaning (See *Midrash); *Sod*, mystical or secret meaning.

Passover (*Pesah*): A major Jewish festival observed for eight days in the Diaspora and seven days in the land of Israel. The festival commemorates the Exodus of the children of Israel from Egypt and points ahead to the final redemption of the world in the age of the Messiah; hence, it is also called the Festival of Freedom. It is also the time of the barley harvest and the end of the rainy season. The lunar calendar must be adjusted by the addition of an extra month, where necessary, so that Passover always falls in the spring. Spring has always been regarded as suggestive of the beginning and survival of the Jewish people. No leavened bread (*hametz*) may be eaten for the whole festival, and a day before Passover begins, all leaven is cleared out of the home after a search for any crumbs that may be hidden in nooks and crannies. The festival begins on the evening before the fifteenth of Nisan, the night of the Exodus, with a ritual family meal (*seder*). Matzah is eaten at the meal to remind the participants of the bread of slavery eaten in Egypt, and Passover is also known as *hag ha-matzot*, "the festival of unleavened bread." The end of Passover is the time when the Israelites crossed over the Red Sea. The mystics saw Passover as a celebration of the marriage of the Community of Israel, symbolizing the female aspect of God, with Her husband the male aspect. The name of the festival originates in the last of the ten plagues, when the Egyptian firstborn children were slain by God, who "passed over" the houses of the Israelites, which had the blood of the Pascal lamb smeared on their doorposts, and spared their firstborn (Exod. 12:27).

Pentateuch: The first five books of the Hebrew Bible—Genesis through Deuteronomy—also known as the Five Books of Moses or by the Hebrew word *Torah (understood as "teaching").

Peretz, I. L. (1851 – 1915): Yiddish and Hebrew Writer. Born in Poland, he was exposed while still a boy to that conflict of ideas which was to dominate his mature life as writer and intellectual leader: the conflict between traditionalism, as embodied in a powerful *Hasidic inheritance, and modernism, the new trend of secular-progressivist thought that was beginning to sweep through the world of East European Jewry. He later became an official of the Jewish community in Warsaw and stood at the intellectual center of Yiddish culture and literature. The legend of the Golem comes from the idea of an unfinished being—a body without a soul—that can be brought to life through the use of the name of God. This legend, which gained great popularity among German Jews sometime in the fifteenth century, has inspired many works of art including films and literature. Source: Howe and Greenberg (1989).

Philo of Alexandria (*c.* 20 BCE –*c.* 40 or 50 CE): The first Jewish philosopher whose works have survived. This Greek-speaking Egyptian Jew is the author of a multivolume series of commentaries on the *Pentateuch. Philo was heir to an already existing tradition of interpreting the Bible allegorically, a tradition that appears to have flourished in Alexandria, Egypt. Philo championed this approach; for him, although biblical stories recounted historical events, they likewise had an "undermeaning" *(huponoia)* by which Abraham, Jacob, and other biblical figures were understood to represent abstractions or spiritual realities whose truth applied to all times and places. Philo explained many biblical texts in keeping with then-current Greek philosophical ideas. He sought to show both Hellenized Jews and the sophisticated non-Jews of Alexandria that the Bible was a philosophical work that could stand comparison to the best in Greek writing. Although Philo's allegorical explanations of Scripture were certainly widely known in the Jewish world, his works played almost no role in the later history of Jewish biblical interpretation. They were, however, extraordinarily important to Christianity, and through the writings of Clement of Alexandria, Eusebius, and other Christian scholars gained a place for his ideas and methods in much Christian biblical interpretation. Sources: Philo in Loeb Classical Library; Runia (2013).

Pirkei de-Rabbi Eliezer ("Chapters according to Rabbi Eliezer"): A *midrashic work, written in rabbinic Hebrew, that retells much of the *Pentateuch and discourses on other themes. Its allusions to Islamic culture and to Arab rule over the land of Israel certainly suggest that this work was put into its final form after the Arab conquest—according to some, as late as the eighth or ninth century CE. At the same time, the text preserves many ancient traditions. At times these traditions are presented by the work in a form that suggests that their author had read these pseudepigraphic texts not in the Greek or other translations through which these texts have survived in Christian churches, but in a Hebrew or Aramaic version now lost. The midrashic material presented here overlaps a good deal with that found in *Targum Pseudo-Jonathan, but the precise relationship between these two texts remains the subject of conjecture.

piyyut (from Greek): A liturgical hymn, or the genre in general. The word is thought o be derived from post-classical Greek *pi-i-tis*, a poet, or *pi-i-ma*, a poem. The piyyutim constitute the richest and most inventive corpus of Hebrew poetry, and among their composers (known as payyetanim) are many or the best-known Hebrew poets. The origins of piyyut are obscure; it seems to have originated in the Land of Israel in late antiquity, perhaps in association with the beginnings of a fixed synagogue liturgy in Hebrew. The names of literally thousands of payyetanim are known, and tens of thousands of their creations survive. Throughout the Middle Ages voices were raised against the use of piyyutim; *Maimonides, for instance, found in their recitation "the major cause for the lack of devotion of the masses." Similar considerations led the nineteenth century reformers to excise most of the piyyutim from the liturgy: they were found to be obscure, theologically dubious, and an impediment to concentration on the prayers. All modernist prayer books, however, contain some piyyutim today.

Plaskow, Judith (1947 –): American Jewish feminist. For Plaskow, the *Torah, and Jews' conception of their own history, have been written by and in the language of a male patriarchy in a manner that sanctions the marginalization of women, and must be reclaimed by redefining its content to include material on women's experiences: "Jewish feminists, in other words, must reclaim Torah as our own. We must render visible the presence, experience, and deeds of women erased in traditional sources. We must tell the stories of women's encounters with God and capture the texture of their religious experience." In addition to supplementing Torah with new material reflecting women's perspectives, Plaskow calls for new *Midrash reconstructing women's understanding of Torah in light of and in continuity with contemporary needs and perspectives. Source: Plaskow (2005).

proof texts: Quotations from *Scripture or other writings used to support a particular point of view. Since these excerpts may be taken out of context, they may not actually reflect original intent.

rabbi (Hebrew, "my master"): Ordained scholar who is traditionally licensed to interpret and expound *halakhah. This ordination is known as Semikhah ("laying on [of hands]," as the term was originally used of a ritual of laying one's hand on a sacrificial victim before it was slaughtered). Rabbis are also known as rav ("master") or *hakham ("wise men" or "sage"). Since it is forbidden to take payment for teaching or issuing rulings about halakhah, rabbis in the past were not paid for their activities and had to support themselves. Today, they are salaried synagogue officials, with wide preaching and pastoral duties. Officially, they are not paid for their religious role, however, but are financially compensated for not being able to work in another profession because of their rabbinic commitments. Women have been ordained as rabbis by Reform and Conservative seminaries, but Orthodox Judaism has still opposed the ordination of women.

Rashi (1040 – 1105): Acronym of Rabbi Solomon ben Isaac; the most prominent Jewish exegete of both the Bible and the Talmud. Born in Troyes, where he lived all his life, his reputation extended throughout the Jewish world. Rashi's commentary on the Bible draws freely on the Midrash. Written in a simple, terse style, this commentary emphasizes the ethical and the homiletical although it by no means neglects the simple and literal meaning (*peshat*). It is this very emphasis on the ethical and the legendary (*derash*), however, that endeared him to the average reader. His work acquired enormous popularity, partly because it could be used for teaching children. It was widely copied and studied, and was in due course one of the first Hebrew works to be printed; it became itself the object of numerous commentaries, and is often found printed in editions of the Hebrew Bible alongside the biblical text. His commentary to the Babylonian Talmud opened up that obscure and difficult text to generations of readers. Source: Rosenbaum and Silbermann (1929).

responsum (pl. **responsa**; Latin, "response [s]"): (1) Written opinion (*teshuvah*) given to question (*she'elah*) on aspects of Jewish law by qualified authorities. There are estimated to be some 300,000 medieval responsa, and they constitute the case law of the medieval *halakhah, exercising a vital formative influence on the evolution of the religious law. (2) Collections of such queries and opinions in book form (*she'elot uteshuvot*). These responsa began to appear after the editing of the Babylonian *Talmud.

Sabbath (in Hebrew "*Shabbat*"): The weekly day of rest observed from sunset on Friday until nightfall on Saturday. The Sabbath is central to the Bible. It is the day which God blessed, having rested from the work of Creation which He performed in six days. The Sabbath is the only festival mentioned in the *Decalogue, and it is especially emphasized in God's words to Moses in Exodus 31:12 – 17. In the repetition of the Decalogue (Deut. 5:15), the Sabbath is also linked to the Exodus and the miraculous deliverance from slavery to freedom that that narrative expresses. A Jew must imitate God by resting on Sabbath from all work. Public desecration of the Sabbath was punishable by death according to biblical law (Num. 15: 32 – 36); the rabbis, in fact, considered the public desecration of Sabbath a sin equal to idolatry. The *Mishnah enumerates thirty-nine principal categories of work forbidden on the Sabbath (Shabbat 7:2), each of which is further subdivided. No Sabbath laws, however, are permitted to stand in the way of saving human life in cases of illness or danger. Jews often employed non-Jews to perform some of these labors for them; in Eastern Europe such an employee was known as *shabbes goy.*

Sabbath is also a day of celebration. The mother lights two candles on Friday evening to bring added light into the home. The liturgy welcomes the Sabbath queen, and when the head of the household returns home from synagogue, he is accompanied by two angels, who come to inspect whether the Sabbath preparations have been made. The family then recite the evening *kiddush over wine. The end of the holy day is marked by the *Havdalah ceremony. The day is a foretaste of the World to Come in the Messianic age, when the peace and tranquility of Sabbath will characterize the whole world. If all the Jews were able to keep a Sabbath day completely, the Messiah would come. The mystics saw the union of the male and female aspects of God as taking place on Sabbath, which is therefore an auspicious time for sexual union between husband and wife.

The idea of the weekly Sabbath passed into the other monotheistic religions, although the Christian Sunday originally had a different emphasis and only later became a "day of rest"; the Muslim Friday is not a day of rest at all but a day of communal prayer. A number of Christian sects, however, observe Saturday as their Sabbath.

Salanter, Israel (1810 – 1883): Founder of the Musar movement, a pietistic movement deriving its name from the Hebrew word for moral instruction (*musar*) and advocating moral earnestness as a necessary supplement to the observance of *mitzvot and Talmudic learning. The movement arose in mid-nineteenth-century Lithuania, becoming by the turn of the century a dominant trend within its *yeshivot. It was a response to the increasing laxity in the observance of the *halakhah that resulted from the secular influences on Lithuanian Jewry. Unlike *Hasidism, of which it was in some sense a rival, the Musar movement did not discourage the academic study of the *Talmud, but urged that it should be complemented by deep personal piety and by meditation on ethical texts, many of which were revived and republished as a result of this renewed interest. Study of these texts was a feature of the "Musar houses" (*musar shtibl*), where both professional scholars and members of the wider public would retire for a period of self-scrutiny every day, and they were chanted aloud to special tunes so as to fix them in people's minds. The selection in this book is from his *The Tree Bearing Fruit*, a collection of writings published in 1881.

Scripture: Texts that various religious groups consider sacred. *Hebrew Scripture* refers to the *Tanakh.

sefirah (pl. ***sefirot***; Hebrew, "counting" or "enumeration"): According to *Kabbalah, the ten enumerations of the *Ein Sof (Godhead) that together make up God's creative nature: *Keter* ("crown"), *Hokhmah* ("wisdom"),

Binah ("understanding"), *Hesed* ("mercy"), *Gevurah* ("power"), *Tiferet* ("beauty"), *Netzah* ("eternity"), *Hod* ("majesty"), *Yesod* ("foundation"), and *Malkhut* ("kingdom")—also called *Shekhinah* ("dwelling"). This last *sefirah* is particularly important because it serves as the mediator between the divine world and the lower worlds.

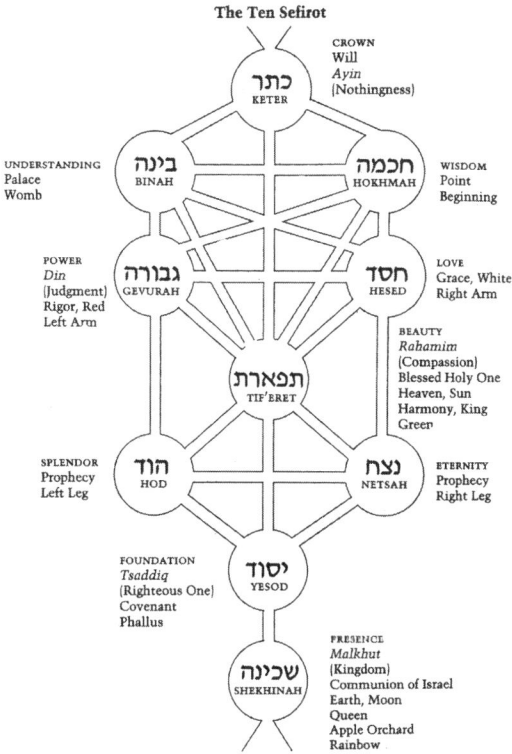

Sephardim (Hebrew, "Spaniards"): Jews of Spain and Portuguese origin who, at the end of the fifteenth century, were expelled from the Iberian peninsula and spread throughout North Africa, the Ottoman Empire, the Americas, Italy, and Holland. *See* *Ashkenazim.

Septuagint: The ancient Greek translation of Hebrew Scripture. Starting in the third century BCE, Hebrew Scripture began to be translated into Greek, apparently for the use of Greek-speaking Jews in Hellenistic centers like Alexandria, Egypt. A legend eventually sprang up about this translation to the effect that seventy, or seventy-two, Jewish elders were commissioned to do the translation of the *Pentateuch (Torah), each in an isolated cell; when the translations were compared, they all agreed in every detail, for the translators had been divinely guided. As a result, this translation came to be known as the *Septuaginta*, "seventy" in Latin (usually abbreviated as LXX). Subsequently, the name "Septuagint" also came to include the old Greek translation of the other books of the Hebrew Bible, a translation made in stages from the third to the first century BCE. It served as the base for the philosophical-exegetic works of *Philo and the historical-exegetic writings of *Josephus. Many of the terms used by LXX translators became part and parcel of the language of the New Testament. For example, *christos*, originally a Greek rendering of the Hebrew *mashiach*, "anointed," became accepted appellation of Jesus of Nazareth. Furthermore, the New Testament quotes the LXX frequently. The Septuagint differs from the Hebrew Bible in certain ways: (1) the Greek text varies at many points from the corresponding Hebrew text; (2) the order of the Biblical books is not the same—the threefold division of *Tanakh is not followed in the LXX; (3) several books not found in the Hebrew are included in the LXX—these books are known as the *Apocrypha. Source: Brenton (1986).

Shekhinah (Hebrew, "dwelling"): The divine presence in the world, specifically among the people of Israel. Followers of *Kabbalah identify the *Shekhinah* with the tenth of the *sefirot*, where it represents the feminine principle (the "Divine Daughter"). Contemporary feminists frequently use this word as a feminine noun for God.

Shema (Hebrew, "hear"): The paragraph beginning "Hear, O Israel" from Deuteronomy 6:4–9. According to the *Mishnah, this paragraph is combined with Deuteronomy 11:13–21 and Numbers 15:37–41 to form a single prayer. This is the central prayer of the Jewish liturgy, an affirmation of monotheism. The liturgical use of the central verses of the Shema can be traced back to the Second Temple period.

Shmuel Hanagid (993 – 1056): One of the finest Hebrew poets of all time and a rabbinic scholar of note. He was born in Cordoba and was among those who fled the capital when the Berber hordes destroyed it in 1013. A renowned Talmudist and statesman, he was the first Spanish Jew to be granted the title Nagid (Hebrew or Aramaic, "prince"), an honorific title bestowed on the leaders of the medieval community in Muslim Spain and Egypt. He was appointed vizier shortly after the accession to the throne (1038) of Badis, the Berber ruler of Granada. In this capacity the Nagid, or Isma'il ibn Nagrela as he was known in Arab circles, commanded the armies of Granada in a series of victorious campaigns against Seville and her allies, which lasted from 1038 to 1056. The many poems he sent to his son from the battlefield constitute a unique poetic diary of his tempestuous life. He died after a strenuous campaign and was succeeded as vizier and commander by his son, Yehosef. Ten years later Yehosef Hanagid was assassinated and the Jewish community of Granada was massacred by the Muslims. Hanagid's vast knowledge of Hebrew and Arabic culture is apparent in his technical mastery and in his rich repertoire of forms and motifs. He excels in the fusion of epic and lyrical elements.

Shofar (Hebrew, "horn"): Horn of the ram (or any other ritually clean animal excepting the cow) sounded for the memorial blowing on Rosh Hashanah (the Jewish New Year), and other occasions. The sounding on Rosh Hashanah serves as a reminder of the horn of the ram that was sacrificed by Abraham in place of Isaac. Generally speaking, shofar is blown to awaken people from their spiritual slumber.

Shulhan Arukh ("prepared table"): The latest and most widely accepted of the authoritative codes of *halakhah. First published in 1565, the *Shulhan Arukh* was compiled by Joseph Caro (1488 – 1575), an exile from Spain who finally settled in Safed in Galilee. It is a concise summary of Caro's larger work, the *Beit Yosef* ("house of Joseph"), which took the form of an elaborate commentary on the law code of Jacob ben Asher (c. 1270–1340) known as the *Arba'ah Turim* ("four rows"). Designed for the needs of students and as a handy reference book, the *Shulhan Arukh* completely overshadowed the earlier work in popular esteem, and has never been superseded. It was compiled with the needs of Caro's fellow *Sephardim in mind, but an *Ashkenazi contemporary, Moses Isserles (c. 1525–1572), appended his glosses, known as Mappah ("tablecloth"), providing Ashkenazi rules and customs where these differed. Isserles' glosses served a number of purposes. They clarified Caro's meaning; they included the opinions of recent Ashkenazi authorities whom Caro had ignored; and they gave much greater place to custom (*minhag*) than Caro had allowed. Isserles' glosses were widely regarded as an essential supplement to the *Shulhan Arukh*, and have been printed along with Caro's text. Following the pattern introduced by Jacob ben Asher, Caro divides the laws under four headings. The first section, Orah Hayyim ("path of life"), deals with the ritual obligations of daily life, including worship and prayer and the observance of Sabbath and holy days. Yoreh De'ah ("teacher of knowledge"), the second section, contains dietary regulations, family purity, charity, prohibition against idolatry, respect for parent and teacher, circumcision and mourning. Eben ha-Ezer ("stone of help") concerns itself with rules of personal status, marriage and divorce. Finally, Hoshen Mishpat ("breast-plate of judgment") covers civil and criminal law, inheritance, loans, and appointment of judges.

Sifra ("book"): *See* *halakhic midrashim.

Sifre: *See* *halakhic midrashim.

Sofer, Moses (1762–1839): Leading opponent of Modernism in all its forms (including political emancipation and Enlightenment ideas, as well as religious reforms), also known as the Hatam Sofer. Born in Frankfurt, he was appointed rabbi Pressburg (Bratislava, in the Austro-Hungarian Empire) in 1806. His outlook is encapsulated in the slogan "innovation is forbidden in the Torah" (in Hebrew, *hadash asur min ha-torah*). Source: Biale and Miles (2015).

synagogue (Greek, "assembly"): (1) A Jewish house of worship and place for study and education. It is the central institution of Jewish communal worship and study since antiquity. The structure of the building has changed, though in all cases the ark containing the Torah scrolls faces the ancient Temple site in Jerusalem. (2) A Jewish congregation.

tagin (Aramaic, "crowns"): Three short vertical strokes or flourishes added to the upper left hand of particular Hebrew letters in the Torah scrolls and other biblical manuscripts.

Talmud (Hebrew, "study"): The foundation text of rabbinic Judaism. There are actually two Talmuds. The rabbis of Israel in the third to fourth centuries CE produced the Yerushalmi, the Jerusalem Talmud (although it was produced in Galilee, not Jerusalem), also called the Palestinian Talmud or the Talmud of the land of Israel, while the rabbis of Babylonia in the third to sixth centuries produced the Bavli, the Babylonian Talmud. Both contain a mixture of *halakhah and *aggadah. Each is set out in the form of a commentary (known as *Gemara [Aramaic, "study"]) on the text of *Mishnah: typically a passage of the Mishnah is quoted, and a detailed discussion—which may actually wander far from the content of the Mishnaic passage—follows. Thus Yerushalmi Peah 8:9, 31b designates the Jerusalem Talmud's commentary to Mishnah Tractate Peah, chapter 8, paragraph 9, found on folio 21, column b in the first edition (Venice, 1523). The Bavli too follows the order of the Mishnah but is simply referred to by the folio number of the standard printed edition, for example, Bavli Shabbat 34a. The two Talmuds overlap in almost all the topics dealt with in the second, third, and fourth orders of the Mishnah; though the Babylonian Talmud has no discussion on the first order (Seeds), and the Jerusalem

Talmud has no discussion on the fifth (Holy Things). Very little of the *amoraic treatment of the sixth order of the Mishnah (Purities) is preserved. Both Talmuds gradually achieved the status of authoritative and sacred texts, though only the Babylonian Talmud ever really dominated the academic and legal curriculum of traditional Jewish study over the ages. Source: Neusner (2006).

Tanakh: An acronym for the three parts that make up the cornerstone of Judaism: Torah ("teaching"), Nevi'im ("prophets"), and Ketuvim ("writings"). This threefold division, which differs from the usual Christian arrangement of the books, is very old, and is thought to reflect the stages in which the text was codified. When Jews speak of the Bible, they are referring to Tanakh.

Tanna'im ("teachers," or "repeaters"; from Aramaic "tanna" with Hebrew plural ending): The rabbis of Palestine in the second century CE whose statements are contained primarily in the *Mishnah but also in other rabbinic works.

Targum (pl. **Targumim**; Aramaic, "translation"): Name applied to various translations of biblical books into Aramaic, a Semitic language related to Hebrew and spoken widely throughout the ancient Near East from the eighth century BCE onward. Their origin is thought to be in synagogal practice, when a vernacular translation was given in conjunction with the Hebrew reading to help the public understand the Hebrew words. Some of the Targumim adhere closely to the actual words of the Hebrew and to what might be called their plain meaning, while others import a greater or lesser amount of explanatory material and even mini-sermons, but all of them represent an interpretation of what the Hebrew text means. The best-known Targum of the Torah is the one attributed to Onkelos (a shadowy figure of whom nothing is known). A straightforward, relatively unadorned rendering of the Hebrew, this became the favorite Targum for

Babylonian Jews, and is still printed in many Bibles facing the Hebrew text. Jews in the Land of Israel and associated areas used a variety of translations of the Torah, the best-known being the Targum Pseudo-Jonathan (also known as the Jerusalem Targum, or Yerushalmi). The various Targumim from the Land of Israel, like Targum Pseudo-Jonathan, paraphrase the Hebrew and contain frequent exegetical expansions of the biblical text, from a few words to entire paragraphs, not found in the original. The process of translating biblical texts into Aramaic must have begun long before any of our extant Targumim was composed; such translation began perhaps as early as the time of the return from Babylonian exile. Thus, any dating of a targum is likely to be misleading, since at least some of the interpretations contained within that targum may go back to a period far earlier than the targum's own composition.

Teitlbaum, Yoel (1886 – 1979): Satmar rabbi. He fled from the Holocaust to Jerusalem and then to New York. There he rebuilt his Hasidic community, which soon became the greatest Hasidic movement and the leading force of extremist *haredim. In response to the foundation of the State of Israel, he published his anti-Zionist book, *Va-Yoel Moshe* (literally: "And Moses was content," based on Exod. 2:21; the title alludes to the author's first name, Yoel, and to his ancestor, Rabbi Moshe Teitlbaum, the founder of the Hasidic dynasty from which the Satmar emerged). The book became the essential work of radical haredi anti-Zionism. According to Teitelbaum, Zionism and the establishment of the State of Israel constitute a violation of the three oaths which the people of Israel were made to swear (Babylonian Talmud, Ketubot, 111a). This has delayed the coming of the Messiah and complete redemption, and resulted in all the troubles affecting the Jewish people in the twentieth century. The Holocaust also was a divine punishment for the sins of Zionism. Source: Neusner and Avery-Peck (2001).

Ten Commandments. *See* *Decalogue.

Torah (understood as "teaching"): A Hebrew word used in the Bible to describe, inter alia, a particular statute or procedure, or a collection thereof; the phrase "Torah of Moses" or "Torah of God" that appears in later biblical books may designate the contents of the *Pentateuch as a whole. In any case, the term *Torah* was used in postbiblical Hebrew to designate (1) the *Pentateuch (in this sense the word *torah* was translated into Greek as *nomos* [law, way of life] and appears in the New Testament phrase, "the Law and the Prophets," meaning [more or less] the Bible); (2) somewhat more loosely, the Bible as a whole; and (3) still more loosely, the entire corpus of rabbinic learning, including Bible, *Mishnah, *Talmud, *Midrash.

Tosefta (Aramaic, "supplement"): Tannaitic *baraitot* compiled as a supplement to the *Mishnah a generation after the Mishnah was written, according to the tradition. It follows the Mishnah's structure, comprising the same six orders and sixty-three tractates. The Tosefta is about four times the size of the Mishnah.

Umansky, Ellen M.: American Jewish feminist. Like many other contemporary Jewish feminists, she encourages the creation of new *midrashim as a way to revision traditional literature through the lens of female experience. In this way women are reinterpreted from "objectified Others" to normative Jews whose experience of God, Torah, and Israel can add to, challenge, and transform previously held religious convictions. Source: Umansky (1992).

Varnhagen, Rahel Levin (1771 – 1833): German intellectual and salon host. Born into a prosperous Jewish merchant family in Berlin, she was raised in Orthodox Jewish surroundings. She was noted for her scintillating intelligence, and her home became the informal center of literary, social and political luminaries of her day. In 1819, after repeated romantic disappointments, she married a man fourteen years her junior, a minor Prussian diplomat named Karl August Varnhagen von Ense, and she converted to his religion,

Protestantism. Sources: Mendes-Flohr (2011); Robertson (1999).

yeshiva (pl. **yeshivot;** Hebrew, "sitting"): In general, a talmudic academy. It can also refer to an Orthodox rabbinical seminary or a day school for children that provides both religious and secular instruction.

Yiddish: A middle-high Germanic fusion language that contains Hebrew and Slavic elements, spoken by Ashkenazic Jews and written with Hebrew characters. In Eastern Europe before the Holocaust, it was the main language of Ashkenazic community. *See* *Ashkenazim.

Zohar ("splendor"): The classic text of *Kabbalah. Mostly written in an artificial Aramaic, the book has the form of a commentary on the *Torah, outwardly resembling the *Midrash and purporting to go back to the time of the *Tanna'im. It is made up of a number of parts, not all by the same author. The main author is known to be Moses of León (d. 1305), but kabbalists maintain an old belief that the true author is a Tanna, Simeon bar Yohai, who is often mentioned in the work. The Zohar is a vehicle for the theosophical ideas of the Kabbalah, centering on the doctrine of the ten *sefirot*, produced by emanation from the ultimate and unknowable *Ein Sof*. It spread from Spain around the Mediterranean, and after it was printed in Italy in the late 1550s it became even more widely accessible. Indeed, Zohar is one of only two books (the Bible is the other) called "holy" (*kadosh*) in the Jewish canon (interestingly, the *Talmud is never given this description). The Zohar is not one book, but like the Talmud a vast work with many parts: in addition to the main section, which is arranged according to chapters of the Torah, there are twenty-three other divisions. Like the Talmud it lacks an organized doctrine and is dependent upon free association: if a word or an idea triggers another similar phrase or thought, the discussion moves freely on. Nineteenth century rationalism was strongly opposed to the reverence paid to the Zohar. Source: Biale and Miles (2015).

参考书目/Bibliography

阿丁·施坦泽兹(Adin Steinsaltz)诠释:《阿伯特——犹太智慧书》,张平译,北京:中国社会科学出版社,1996年。

亚丁·史坦萨兹(Adin Steinsaltz):《塔木德精要》,朱怡康译,台北:启示出版,2015年。

埃里希·奥尔巴赫:《摹仿论——西方文学中现实的再现》,吴麟绶、周新建、高艳婷译,北京:商务印书馆,2014年。

陈垣:《开封一赐乐业教考》,载《陈垣学术论文集》,北京:中华书局,1980年,第255—302页。

大卫·比尔:《犹太世俗主义》,载宋立宏主编:《从西奈到中国》,北京:三联书店,2012年,第191—202页。

傅有德等:《犹太哲学史》,北京:中国人民大学出版社,2008年。

傅有德:《犹太教的释经传统与思维方式》,载宋立宏主编:《犹太流散的表征与认同——徐新教授从教40年纪念文集》,北京:社会科学文献出版社,2018年,第135—150页。

哈维瓦·伊沙伊:《诗人什穆埃尔·哈纳吉德——犹太民族与阿拉伯叙事的奇特交汇》,宗笑飞译,载傅有德主编:《犹太研究》,第14辑,济南:山东大学出版社,2016年,第220—226页。

李景文、张礼刚、刘百陆、赵光贵编校,张倩红审定:《古代开封犹太人:中文文献辑要与研究》,北京:人民出版社,2011年。

摩西·迈蒙尼德:《论知识》,董修元译,济南:山东大学出版社,2015年。

宋立宏:《自由与救赎之书:逾越节〈哈加达〉》,载宋立宏:《罗马与耶路撒冷》,杭州:浙江大学出版社,2015年,第172—183页。

宋立宏:《犹太教有教义吗?——一个观念史反思》,载宋立宏:《罗马与耶路撒冷》,杭州:浙江大学出版社,2015年,第235—264页。

宋立宏:《汉学、犹太身份与大屠杀记忆——对以色列汉学家伊爱莲的理解》,《国际汉学》2017年第4期,第24—32页。

魏道思拉比:《犹太文化之旅》,刘幸枝译,南昌:江西人民出版社,2009年。

徐新、凌继尧主编:《犹太百科全书》[修订版],上海:上海人民出版社,1998年。

徐新:《论贾布奈革命——犹太知识分子掌握民族领导权的起点》,《学海》2005年第3期,第41—49页。

雅各·纽斯纳:《犹太教》,周伟驰译,上海:上海古籍出版社,2008年。

雅各·纽斯纳:《犹太拉比典籍要点指南》,张圣佳译,新北:圣经资源中心,2014年。

亚伦·奥本海默:《犹太教:从圣殿到文本》,载宋立宏主编:《从西奈到中国》,北京:三联书店,2012年,第217—228页。

约瑟夫:《犹太古史记》,二版,纽约、台中:信心圣经神学院,2016年。

张平译注:《天下通道精义篇——犹太处世书》,北京:北京大学出版社,2003年。

张平译注:《密释纳,第1部 种子》,济南:山东大学出版社,2011年。

张平译注:《密释纳,第2部 节期》,济南:山东大学出版社,2017年。

钟志清:《现代希伯来文学对"以撒献祭"母题的阐释》,《圣经文学研究》2014年第1期,第167—185页。

周平:《〈犹太古史〉所罗门传:希伯来传统与希腊化双重视野》,北京:社会科学文献出版社,2011年。

Agnon, S. Y., *Present at Sinai: The Giving of the Law,* trans. Michael Swirsky. Philadelphia: Jewish Publication Society, 1994.

Alexander, Philip S., ed. *Textual Sources for the Study of Judaism.* Manchester: Manchester University Press, 1984.

Almoli, Shelomo, *Dream Interpretation from Classical Jewish Sources,* trans. Yaakov Elman. Hoboken NJ: KTAV Publishing House, 1998.

Alon, Gedalyahu, "Rabban Johanan B. Zakki's Removal to Jabneh." In *Jews, Judaism and the Classical World: Studies in Jewish History in the Times of the Second Temple and Talmud.* Jerusalem: Magnes Press, 1977, pp. 269–313.

Baskind, Samantha and Larry Silver, *Jewish Art: A Modern History.* London: Reaktion Books, 2011.

Berlin, Adele, and Marc Zvi Brettler, eds. *The Jewish Study Bible.* Oxford: Oxford University Press, 2004.

Biale, David, ed. *Cultures of the Jews: A New History.* New York: Schocken Books, 2002.

Biale, David, and Jack Miles, eds. *The Norton Anthology of World Religions: Judaism.* New York: W.W. Norton & Company, Inc., 2015.

Bialik, H. N., "Revealment and Concealment in Language." In *Modern Hebrew Literature,* ed. Robert Alter. New York: Behrman House, 1975, pp. 127-137.

Bialik, Hayim Nahman, and Yehoshua Hana Ravnitzky, eds. *The Book of Legends, Sefer Ha-Aggadah: Legends from the Talmud and Midrash,* trans. William G. Braude. New York: Schocken Books, 1992.

Bickerman, Elias J., "The Warning Inscription of Herod's Temple." *Jewish Quarterly Review,* New Ser., Vol. 37, No. 4. (1947): 387-405.

Birnbaum, Philip, trans. *Daily Prayer Book: Ha-Siddur Ha-Shalem.* New York: Hebrew Publishing Company, 1977.

Birnbaum, Philip, *Encyclopedia of Jewish Concepts.* New York: Hebrew Publishing Company, 1979.

Bowker, John, *The Targums and Rabbinic Literature: An Introduction to Jewish Interpretations of Scripture.* Cambridge: Cambridge University Press, 1979.

Boyarin, Daniel, "Talmudic Texts and Jewish Social Life." In *Religions of Late Antiquity in Practice,* ed. Richard Valantasis. Princeton: Princeton University Press, 2000, pp. 133-142.

Brenton, Lancelot C. L., *The Septuagint with Apocrypha: Greek and English.* Peabody, MA: Hendrickson Publishers, 1986.

Carmi, T., ed. *The Penguin Book of Hebrew Verse.* London: Penguin Books, 1981.

Chametzky, Jules, John Felstiner, Hilene Flanzbaum, and Kathryn Hellerstein, eds. *Jewish American Literature: A Norton Anthology.* New York: W. W. Norton, 2001.

Cohen, Arthur A., and Paul Mendes-Flohr, eds. *Contemporary Jewish Religious*

Thought: Original Essays on Critical Concepts, Movements, and Beliefs. New York: Free Press, 1987.

Cohen, Shaye J. D., *From the Maccabees to the Mishnah,* third ed. Louisville, Kentucky: Westminster John Knox Press, 2014. (沙亚·科亨:《古典时代犹太教导论》,郑阳译,北京:中国社会科学出版社,2012年。)

Cole, Peter, trans. *Selected Poems of Shmuel HaNagid.* Princeton: Princeton University Press, 1996.

Cole, Peter, trans. *The Dream of the Poem: Hebrew Poetry from Muslim and Christian Spain 950–1492.* Princeton: Princeton University Press, 2007.

Cole, Peter, trans. *The Poetry of Kabbalah: Mystical Verse from the Jewish Tradition.* New Haven: Yale University Press, 2012.

Corrigan, John, Carlos M. N. Eire, Frederick M. Denny, Martin S. Jaffee, eds. *Readings in Judaism, Christianity, and Islam.* Upper Saddle River, New Jersey: Prentice Hall, 1998.

Dan, Joseph, ed. *The Teachings of Hasidism.* New York: Behrman House, 1983.

Dan, Joseph, ed. *The Heart and the Fountain: An Anthology of Jewish Mystical Experiences.* New York: Oxford University Press, 2002.

De Lange, Nicholas, *The Penguin Dictionary of Judaism.* London: Penguin Books, 2008.

Eber, Irene, *The Choice: Poland, 1939–1945.* New York: Schocken Books, 2004. (伊爱莲:《抉择:波兰,1939—1945》,吴晶译,北京:学苑出版社,2013年。)

Elbogen, Ismar, *Jewish Liturgy: A Comprehensive History,* trans. Raymond P. Scheindlin. Philadelphia: The Jewish Publication Society, 1993.

Feldman, Louis H., "The Akedah." In *Outside the Bible: Ancient Jewish Writings Related to Scripture,* eds. Louis H. Feldman, James L. Kugel, and Lawrence H. Schiffman. Philadelphia: Jewish Publication Society, 2013, pp. 1156–1162.

Freedman, H., and Maurice Simon, eds. *Midrash Rabbah,* 10 vols. London: Soncino Press, 1939.

Ginzberg, Louis, *Legends of the Jews: Bible Times and Characters from the Creation to Moses in the Wilderness,* second edn. Philadelphia: Jewish Publication Society of America, 2003.

Goitein, S. D., *A Mediterranean Society: The Jewish Communities of the Arab World as Portrayed in the Documents of the Cairo Geniza, Vol. V. The Individual.* Berkeley: University of California Press, 1988.

Goldin, Judah, trans. *The Fathers According to Rabbi Nathan.* New Haven: Yale University Press, 1955.

Goldin, Judah, trans. *The Living Talmud: The Wisdom of the Fathers and Its Classical Commentaries.* New York: New American Library, 1957.

Gordis, Daniel, *Israel: A Concise History of a Nation Reborn.* New York: Ecco, 2016.（丹尼尔·戈迪斯:《以色列:一个民族的重生》,王戎译、宋立宏校译,杭州:浙江人民出版社,2018年。）

Goshen-Gottstein, Alon, "Four Entered Paradise Revisited." *Harvard Theological Review* 88 (1995): 69–133.

Green, Arthur, and Barry W. Holtz, eds. *Your Word is Fire: The Hasidic Masters on Contemporary Prayer.* Woodstock, Vermont: Jewish Lights Publishing, 1993.

Halbertal, Moshe, *People of the Book: Canon, Meaning, and Authority.* Cambridge Mass.: Harvard University Press. 1997.

Halkin, Hillel, *Grand Things to Write a Poem On: A Verse Autobiography of Shmuel Hanagid.* Jerusalem: Gefen Publishing House, 2000.

Heilman, Samuel C., *The People of the Book: Drama, Fellowship, and Religion.* Chicago: University of Chicago Press, 1987.

Heinemann, Joseph, with Jakob J. Petuchowski, eds. *Literature of the Synagogue.* New York: Behrman House, 1975.

Hellerstein, Kathryn, *A Question of Tradition: Women Poets in Yiddish, 1586–1987.* Stanford, California: Stanford University Press, 2014.

Heschel, Abraham Joshua, *The Sabbath: Its Meaning for Modern Man.* New York: Farrar, Straus and Giroux, 1951.（A.J.赫舍尔:《安息日的真谛》,邓元蔚译,上海:上海三联书店,2013年。）

Holtz, Barry W., ed. *The Schocken Guide to Jewish Books: Where to Start Reading about Jewish History, Literature, Culture and Religion.* New York: Schocken Books, 1992.

Howe, Irving, and Eliezer Greenberg, eds. *A Treasury of Yiddish Stories.*

New York: Penguin Books, 1989.

Jacobs, Louis, *Principles of the Jewish Faith: An Analytical Study.* New York: Basic Books, 1964.

Jacobs, Louis, *Jewish Biblical Exegesis.* New York: Behrman House, 1973.

Jacobs, Louis, *The Schocken Book of Jewish Mystical Testimonies.* New York: Schocken Books, 1997.

Jassen, Alex P., "Rule of the Community." In *Outside the Bible: Ancient Jewish Writings Related to Scripture,* eds. Louis H. Feldman, James L. Kugel, and Lawrence H. Schiffman. Philadelphia: Jewish Publication Society, 2013.

Josephus, *Josephus,* eds. and trans. H. St. J. Thackeray, R. Marcus, A. Wikgren, and L. H. Feldman. Cambridge, MA: Harvard University Press, Loeb Classical Library, 1926–1965.

Kaplan, Lawrence, "Moses Maimonides' Law of the Study of Torah." In *Judaism in Practice: From the Middle Ages through the Early Modern Period,* ed. Lawrence Fine. Princeton: Princeton University Press, 2001, pp. 171–185.

Keller, Sharon R., ed. *The Jews in Literature and Art.* Köln: Könemann, 1992.

Kellner, Menachem, *Must a Jew Believe Anything?* second edn. Oxford: The Littman Library of Jewish Civilization, 2006.

Kloppenborg, John S., "The Theodotos Synagogue Inscription and the Problem of First-Century Synagogue Buildings." In *Jesus and Archaeology*, ed. James H. Charlesworth. Grand Rapids, MI: Eerdmans, 2006.

Kugel, James L., *Traditions of the Bible: A Guide to the Bible as It Was at the Start of the Common Era.* Cambridge, MA: Harvard University Press, 1998.

Kugel, James L. *How to Read the Bible: A Guide to Scripture, Then and Now*. New York: Free Press. 2008.

Lazaroff, Allan, "Bahya's Asceticism against its Rabbinic and Islamic Background." *Journal of Jewish Studies,* 21 (1970): 11–38.

Lerner, Ralph, *Maimonides' Empire of Light: Popular Enlightenment in an Age of Belief.* Chicago: University of Chicago Press, 2000.

Leslie, Donald D., *The Survival of the Chinese Jews: The Jewish Community of Kaifeng.* Leiden: E. J. Brill, 1972.

Leviant, Curt, ed. *Masterpieces of Hebrew Literature: A Treasury of 2000 Years of Jewish Creativity.* New York: Ktav Publishing House, 1969.

Levine, Lee I., *The Ancient Synagogue: The First Thousand Years,* second edn. New Haven: Yale University Press, 2005.

Lipman, Jonathan, N., "Living Judaism in Confucian Culture: Being Jewish and Being Chinese." In *Judaism in Practice: From the Middle Ages through the Early Modern Period,* ed. Lawrence Fine. Princeton: Princeton University Press, 2001, pp. 265–277.

Maimon, Solomon, *An Autobiography,* trans. J. Clark Murray. Urbana: University of Illinois Press, 2001 [1888].

Maimon, Solomon, *The Autobiography of Solomon Maimon: The Complete Translation,* eds. Yitzhak Y. Melamed and Abraham P. Socher, trans. Paul Reitter. Princeton: Princeton University Press, 2018.

Maimonides, Moses, *The Guide of the Perplexed,* 2 vols., trans. Shlomo Pines. Chicago: University of Chicago Press, 1963.（摩西·迈蒙尼德:《迷途指津》,傅有德、郭鹏、张志平译,济南:山东大学出版社,2000年。）

Marcus, Jacob Rader, *The Jew in the Medieval World: A Source Book, 315-1791,* revised edn. ed. Marc Saperstein. Cincinnati: Hebrew Union College Press, 1999.

Matt, Daniel C., *The Essential Kabbalah: The Heart of Jewish Mysticism.* New York: Harper Collins, 1995a.

Matt, Daniel C., "*Ayin:* The Concept of Nothingness in Jewish Mysticism." In *Essential Papers on Kabbalah,* ed. Lawrence Fine. New York: New York University Press, 1995b, pp. 67-108.

Mellinkoff, Ruth, *The Mark of Cain.* Berkeley: University of California Press, 1981.

Mendes-Flohr, Paul, and Jehuda Reinharz, eds. *The Jew in the Modern World: A Documentary History,* third ed. New York: Oxford University Press, 2011.

Molodowsky, Kadya, *Paper Bridge: Selected Poems of Kadya Molodowsky,* ed. and trans. Kathryn Hellerstein. Detroit: Wayne State University Press, 1999.

Neusner, Jacob, *Stranger at Home: "Holocaust," Zionism, and American Judaism.* Chicago: University of Chicago Press, 1981.

Neusner, Jacob, *The Mishnah: A New Translation.* New Haven: Yale University Press, 1988.

Neusner, Jacob, *The Babylonian Talmud: A Translation and Commentary.* On CD-ROM. Peabody, MA: Hendrickson Publishers, 2006.

Neusner, Jacob, and Alan J. Avery-Peck, eds. *The Blackwell Reader in Judaism,* Oxford: Blackwell Publishing, 2001.

Noy, David, Alexander Panayotov, and Hanswulf Bloedhorn, eds. *Inscriptiones Judaicae Orientis, Volume I: Eastern Europe,* Tübingen: Mohr Siebeck, 2004.

Nulman, Macy, *The Encyclopedia of Jewish Prayer: Ashkenazic and Sephardic Rites.* Northvale, New Jersey: Jason Aronson Inc., 1993.

Pagis, Dan, *Points of Departure,* trans. Stephen Mitchell. Philadelphia: Jewish Publication Society of America, 1981.

Philo, *Philo*, eds. and trans. F. H. Colson and G. H. Whitaker. Cambridge, MA: Harvard University Press, Loeb Classical Library, 1929–1962.

Plaks, Andrew H., "The Confucianization of the Kaifeng Jews: Interpretations of the Kaifeng Stelae Inscriptions." In *The Jews of China, Volume One: Historical and Comparative Perspectives,* ed. Jonathan Goldstein. Armonk, New York: M. E. Sharpe, 1999, pp. 36–49.（浦安迪："中国犹太人的儒化：开封石碑碑文释解"，钟志清译，载《浦安迪自选集》，北京：三联书店，2011年，第445—460页。）

Plaskow, Judith. *The Coming of Lilith: Essays on Feminism, Judaism, and Sexual Ethics, 1972–2003.* Boston: Beacon Press, 2005.

Plaut, W. Gunther, Bernard J. Bamberger, and William W. Hallo, *The Torah: A Modern Commentary.* New York: Union of American Hebrew Congregations, 1981.

Rabinovich, Itamar, and Jehuda Reinharz, eds. *Israel in the Middle East: Documents and Readings on Society, Politics, and Foreign Relations, Pre-*

1948 to the Present, second edn. Waltham, Mass.: Brandeis University Press, 2008.

Reynolds, J., and R. Tannenbaum, *Jews and Godfearers at Aphrodisias: Greek Inscriptions with Commentary.* Cambridge: Cambridge Philological Society, 1987.

Robertson, Ritchie, ed. *The German-Jewish Dialogue: An Anthology of Literary Texts, 1749 –1993.* Oxford: Oxford University Press, 1999.

Rosenbaum, M., and A. M. Silbermann, *Pentateuch, with Targum Onkelos, Haphtaroth and Rashi's Commentary,* 5 vols. New York: Hebrew Publishing Company, 1929.

Rubenstein, Jeffrey, *Rabbinic Stories.* New York: Paulist Press, 2002.

Runia, David T., "On the Creation of the World." In *Outside the Bible: Ancient Jewish Writings Related to Scripture,* eds. Louis H. Feldman, James L. Kugel, and Lawrence H. Schiffman. Philadelphia: Jewish Publication Society, 2013, pp. 882–901.

Shäfer, Peter, *Jesus in the Talmud.* Princeton: Princeton University Press, 2007.

Scheindlin, Raymond P., *Wine, Women, and Death: Medieval Hebrew Poems on the Good Life.* New York: Oxford University Press, 1986.

Scheindlin, Raymond P., *A Short History of the Jewish People: From Legendary Times to Modern Statehood.* New York: Oxford University Press, 1998. (雷蒙德·P. 谢德林:《犹太人三千年简史》,张鋆良译、宋立宏校译,杭州:浙江人民出版社,2020 年。)

Scheindlin, Raymond P., *The Song of the Distant Dove: Judah Halevi's Pilgrimage,* New York: Oxford University Press, 2008.

Scheindlin, Raymond P., trans. *Vulture in a Cage: Poems by Solomon Ibn Gabirol.* Brooklyn NY: Archipelago Books, 2016.

Scholem, Gershom, *On the Kabbalah and Its Symbolism.* New York: Schocken Books, 1965.

Scholem, Gershom, "Revelation and Tradition as Religious Categories in Judaism," in idem, *The Messianic Idea in Judaism and Other Essays on Jewish Spirituality.* New York: Schocken Books, 1971, pp. 282–303.

Scholem, Gershom, *Sabbatai Sevi: The Mystical Messiah, 1626-1676.* Princetion: Princetion University Press, 1973.

Scholem, Gershom, *Major Trends in Jewish Mysticism.* New York: Schocken Books, 1974. (G. G. 索伦:《犹太教神秘主义主流》,涂笑非译,成都:四川人民出版社,2000年。)

Scholem, Gershom, "Isaac Luria: A Central Figure in Jewish Mysticism." *Bulletin of the American Academy of Arts and Sciences,* Vol. 29, No. 8 (1976): 8-13.

Schwabe, Moshe, and Baruch Lifshitz, *Beth She'arim, Vol. II: The Greek Inscriptions.* Jerusalem: Massada Press, 1974.

Skolnik, Fred, ed. *Encyclopaedia Judaica,* 22 vols., second edn. Detroit: Thomson Gale, 2007.

Spiegel, Shalom, *The Last Trial: On the Legends and Lore of the Command to Abraham to Offer Isaac as a Sacrifice: The Akedah.* New York: Schocken Books, 1969.

Suggs, M. Jack, Katharine Doob Sakenfeld, and James R. Mueller, eds. *The Oxford Study Bible.* New York: Oxford University Press, 1992.

Steinberg, Paul, *Celebrating the Jewish Year: The Fall Holidays.* Philadelphia: The Jewish Publication Society, 2007.

Stern, David, and Mark J. Mirsky, eds. *Rabbinic Fantasies: Imaginative Narratives from Classical Hebrew Literature.* New Haven: Yale University Press, 1990.

Stern, David, ed. *The Anthology in Jewish Literature.* New York: Oxford University Press, 2004.

Stern, David, "The Idea of Humanity in Jewish Tradition: from 'the Image of God' to the Jews of China." *Social Sciences in China*, 31:1 (2010): 162-183.

Stern, David, "The Brutality of Repentance." *Kerem* 13(2012): 1-6.

Strack, H. L., and Günter Stemberger, *Introduction to the Talmud and Midrash,* second ed., trans. and ed. Markus Bockmuehl. Minneapolis: Fortress Press, 1996.

Tabory, Joseph, *JPS Commentary on the Haggadah: Historical Introduction,*

Translation, and Commentary. Philadelphia: The Jewish Publication Society, 2008.

Twersky, Isadore, ed. *A Maimonides Reader.* West Orange, NJ: Behrman House, 1972.

Umansky, Ellen M., "Re-Visioning Sarah: A Midrash on Genesis 22." In *Four Centuries of Jewish Women's Spirituality: A Sourcebook,* eds. Ellen M. Umansky and Dianne Ashton. Boston: Beacon Press, 1992, p. 235.

Urbach, Ephraim E., *The Sages: Their Concepts and Beliefs,* trans. Israel Abrahms. Cambridge Mass.: Harvard University Press, 1979.

Vermes, Geza, trans. *The Complete Dead Sea Scrolls in English,* revised edn. London: Penguin, 2004.

Walzer, Michael, Menachem Lorberbaum, and Noam J. Zohar, eds. *The Jewish Political Tradition, Vol. 1: Authority.* New Haven: Yale University Press, 2000.（迈克尔·沃尔泽等编:《犹太政治传统(卷一)》,刘平等译,上海:华东师范大学出版社,2011年。）

Walzer, Michael, Menachem Lorberbaum, and Noam J. Zohar, eds. *The Jewish Political Tradition, Vol. 2: Membership.* New Haven: Yale University Press, 2003.（迈克尔·沃尔泽等编:《犹太政治传统(卷二)》,冯洁音译,上海:华东师范大学出版社,2011年。）

Weinberger, Leon J., *Jewish Prince in Moslem Spain: Selected Poems of Samuel Ibn Nagrela.* University, Alabama: University of Alabama Press, 1973.

Weiss, Raymond L., and Charles E. Butterworth, eds. *Ethical Writings of Maimonides.* New York: New York University Press, 1975.

Werblowsky, R. J. Zwi, and Geoffrey Wigoder, eds. *The Oxford Dictionary of the Jewish Religion.* New York: Oxford University Press, 1997.

Williams, Margaret, ed. *The Jews among the Greeks and Romans: A Diasporan Sourcebook.* Baltimore: Johns Hopkins University Press, 1998.

Allen, Woody, "The Scrolls." *The New Republic.* September 1, 1974. https://newrepublic.com/article/113899/scrolls-woody-allen.（伍迪·艾伦:《无羽无毛》,李伯宏译,上海:上海译文出版社,2014年,第22—23页。）

Pirkei de-Rabbi Eliezer, trans. Gerald Friedlander (London, 1916): https://www.sefaria.org/Pirkei_DeRabbi_Eliezer?lang=en&p2=Pirkei_DeRabbi_Eliezer.14.5&lang2=en.

Vatican Library: Digitized Ink Rubbings of the Stele Inscription Recording the Reconstruction of the Pure and True Temple (1489 CE): https://digi.vatlib.it/view/MSS_Borg.cin.497.